Persian Historiography

This book is dedicated to the memories of
Marilyn Robinson Waldman (1943–96)
and Kenneth Allin Luther (1934–97),
two pioneers in the study of
medieval Persian historical writing.

Persian Historiography

To the End of the Twelfth Century

Julie Scott Meisami

EDINBURGH UNIVERSITY PRESS

Edinburgh University Press
22 George Square, Edinburgh

Typeset in Linotron Trump Mediaeval
by Koinonia, Bury, and
printed and bound in Great Britain
by the University Press, Cambridge

A CIP record for this book is available
from the British Library

ISBN 0 7486 0743 9 (hardback)
ISBN 0 7486 1276 9 (paperback)

Contents

Acknowledgements

The maps are taken from G. LeStrange, *Lands of the Eastern Caliphate* (London: Frank Cass, 1966) and are reproduced with the permission of the publisher.

Maps

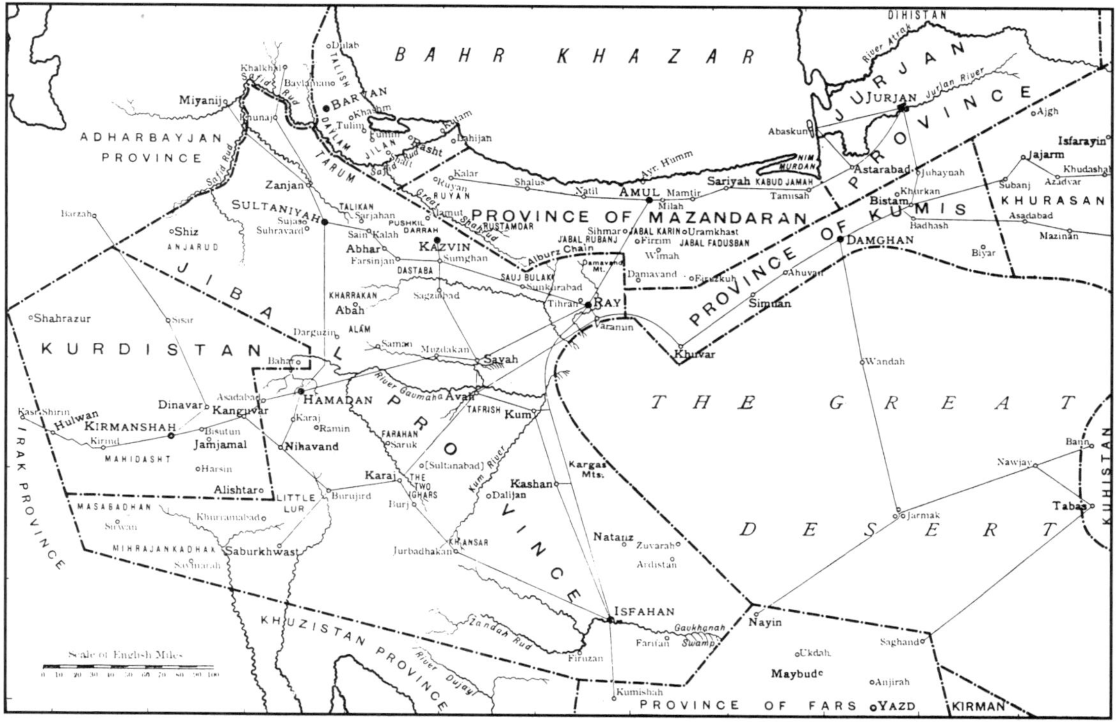

Map 1 Provinces of Jibal and Jilan, with Mazandaran, Kumis and Jurjan.

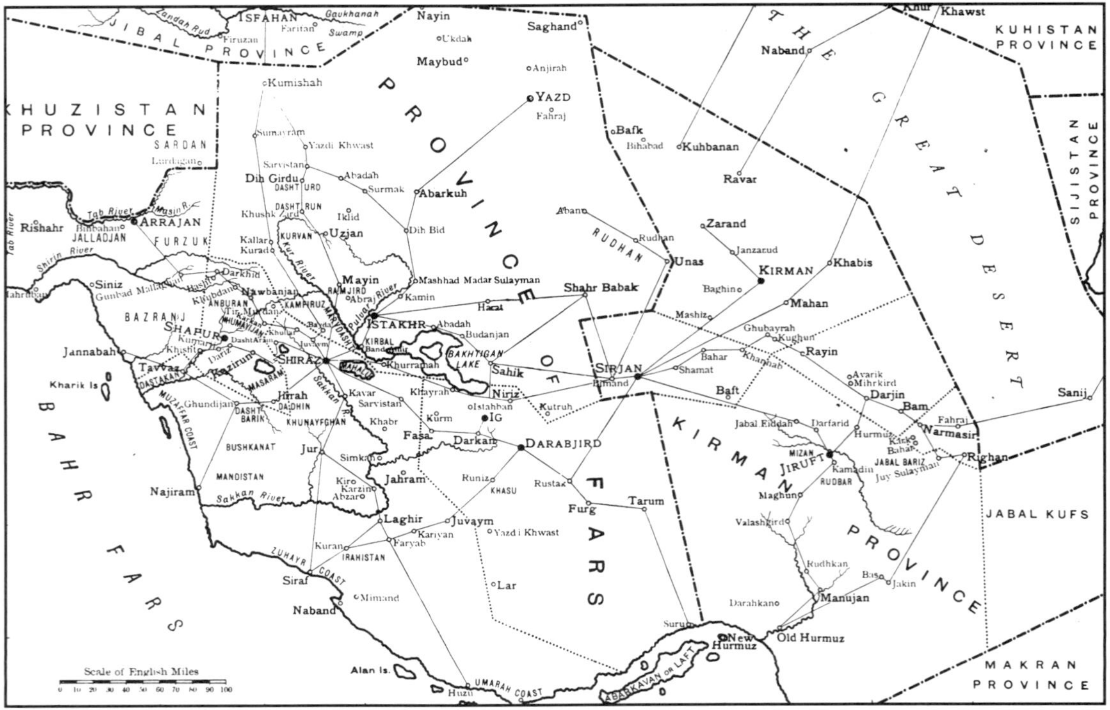

Map 2 Provinces of Fars and Kirman.

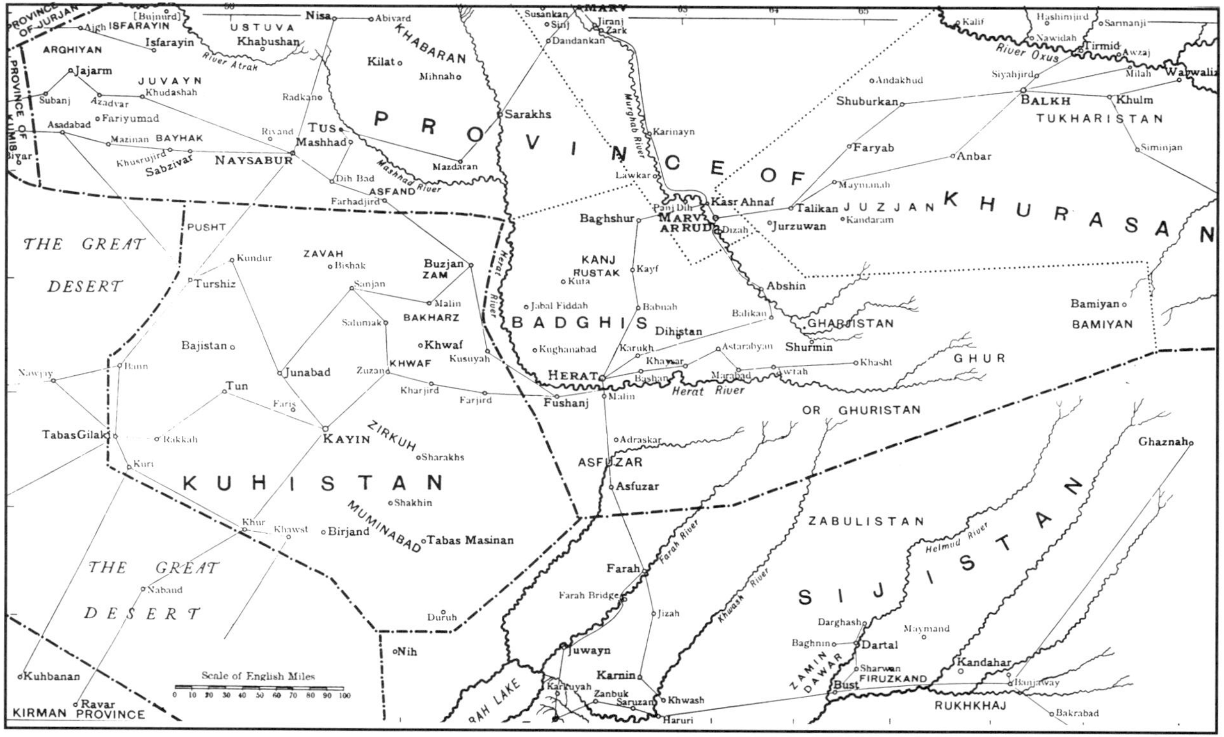

Map 3 Provinces of Kuhistan, Khurasan and part of Sijistan.

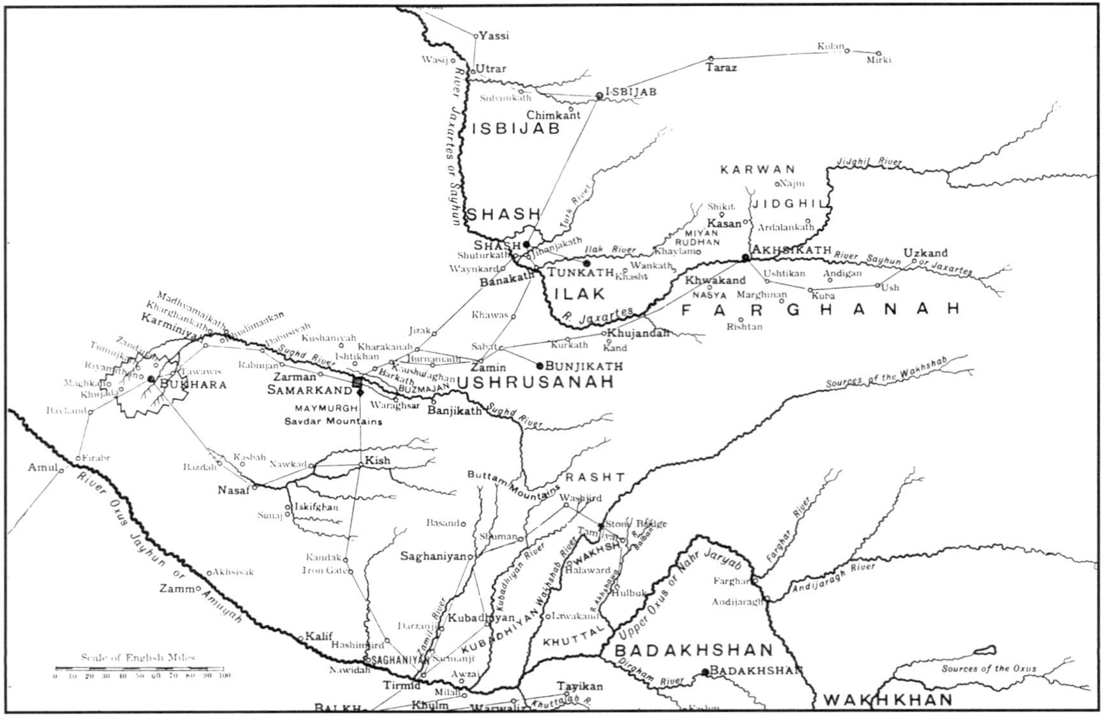

Map 4 Provinces of the Oxus and Jaxartes.

Introduction

PERSIAN HISTORIOGRAPHY AND ISLAMIC HISTORIOGRAPHY

This study aims at putting early Persian historical writing back on the map of Islamic historiography. Scholarship in this field has traditionally privileged works written in Arabic; one has only to look, for example, at Franz Rosenthal's *A History of Muslim Historiography* (1952; revised edition 1968) to see how few Persian historians figure therein. In a 1962 essay entitled 'The Evolution of Persian Historiography' Bertold Spuler wrote that 'historiography seems to have been of no great importance to pre-Islamic Iranians' and that therefore the only prototypes that Persian historians of Islamic times had to draw upon were Arabic; this despite the fact that it had long been known that the Sasanians, in particular, possessed a variety of historical traditions (ranging from 'official' royal or priestly histories to more popular works on the heroic deeds of great Iranians), and that these traditions had not disappeared with the coming of Islam, but influenced both Arabic and subsequent Persian historical writing.[1] Spuler wrote further that 'it is a well-known fact' to specialists in the field 'that hardly any work written in Persian exists which deals with the history of Persia until the beginning of the Mongol period', that is, between about 20/642 and 653/1255 (1962: 126–7). Most of the texts to be considered in this study had been published by the time Spuler wrote; all of them treat history, whether pre- or post-Islamic, from a 'Persian' perspective, that is, they focus chiefly on events in the East. Yet such assumptions as these have undoubtedly contributed to the general neglect of early Persian historiography; and it is only relatively recently that historical writing of the pre-Mongol period (4th/10th to 6th/12th centuries) has begun to arouse serious interest.

Another cause of this neglect has been the view that Persian historiography is somehow inferior to its more serious, scholarly, and religiously motivated early Arabic counterpart. In 1938, in an article originally published in the *Supplement* to the *Encyclopaedia of Islam*, H. A. R. Gibb lamented both the deleterious influence on Arabic historiography of pre-Islamic Persian historical traditions, as translated or adapted into Arabic, and the 'secularisation' of history in both languages. Noting the rise of 'connected historical narrative' (based largely on Sasanian models) in the works of such 3rd/9th century Arabic historians as Balādhurī, Dīnawarī and Ya'qūbī, he observed that, the 'mainstream of Arabic historiography' having already been contaminated, as it were, by the incorporation of materials 'derived from Jewish and Christian legend',

> the influence of the Persian tradition was equally unfavorable ... As soon as history passed outside the Islamic field the old difficulty of distinguishing between legendary, semi-legendary and historical elements reappeared, and with it the tendency to take on trust whatever materials were available. It was this tendency which was now reinforced by the character of the sources from which the Arabic compilers drew their materials for the ancient history of Persia and other lands. (1982: 116–7)

Gibb tended to see the course of historical writing as one of decline, as its pristine Islamic origins were influenced by 'foreign' elements and as historians turned, around the middle of the 4th/10th century, to the writing of 'contemporary annalistic' (that is, dynastic) history. 'It was at this unfavorable juncture', he commented, 'that historical works began to be written again in Persian' (1982: 124). This 'unfavorable juncture' was, in reality, a particularly dynamic moment in the political and cultural life of the Islamic world; and it is no accident that this moment witnessed both new departures in Arabic historiography and the first histories written in Persian.[2]

Earlier scholars who addressed themselves to early Persian historical texts generally confined themselves to philological issues rather than historiographical ones, studied the texts in the broader context of the rise of Persian prose writing, or mined them for historical data.[3] Few considered the broader hows, whys and wherefores: the motives for writing history in Persian, along with questions of style, audience, patronage, and reception. As Marilyn Waldman justly complained,

> However suggestive previous studies of the rhetoric of formal historical writing may have been, they have not forced today's historians to view or to use historical narratives from the past in new and different ways. Professional historians, however much they may try to weigh the importance of the styles, pre-commitments, and world views of the authors on whose narratives they depend, still look upon formal historical compositions essentially as a filter through which to view past 'reality', their true focus.
>
> In the field of Islamicate history, where scholars have tended to use historical narratives almost exclusively as unstructured,

> uninterpretive mines of factual information, the handling of sources has been particularly problematic. The criteria of validity for the facts obtained from historical narratives are largely external; rarely are they related to the internal dynamics of the work from which the facts have been taken or to the interaction of the author's mind with the material he has presented, matters that have long been important in European and American historiography. Systematic methods and categories of analysis through which such questions could be approached are virtually nonexistent. The usefulness of facts mined from historical writings is thus reduced and the relevance of the whole source to the history of ideas entirely neglected. Instead of asking what a premodern Muslim author was trying to do as a historian and how he accomplished his goals, the scholar of Islamicate history has usually been content to ask what information the source provides that can be useful in solving *his own* problems. (1980: 3–4; author's emphasis)

Waldman broke new ground in her study of the 5th/11th century Persian historian Abū al-Faḍl Bayhaqī (discussed in Chapter 2, below); and more recent scholarship has begun to address the issues she identified as crucial, and to draw upon the large body of literature on pre-modern Western historiography which has been concerned with just such issues. As yet, however, there has been no comprehensive discussion of the first two and a half centuries of Persian historical writing, and little comparative study of individual writers. The purpose of the present book is to attempt to begin to fill this gap, and to provide an overview which will, it is hoped, suggest directions that future research might take.

In the course of discussing Persian historians and their works, I will raise questions that have seldom been asked, and for which answers may not readily be found. Thus much will be speculative rather than conclusive, as much more work remains to be done before we can have a fuller picture of Persian historiography than we do at present, and we will probably never arrive at a complete one. Certain self-imposed limitations should be stated at the outset. First, it is a basic premise of this study that the medieval historian's primary interest lay less in recording the 'facts' of history than in the construction of a meaningful narrative. This principle has become widely accepted by students of pre-modern Western historiography – classical, medieval and Renaissance – but has yet to be fully accepted by those studying medieval Muslim historians. I shall examine questions relating to language and to style, to the ways in which the historian formulates and conveys his accounts – ways which serve to reveal the meaning (or meaningfulness) of his materials. I will not go down the highways and byways of source-hunting, unless this proves fruitful for more general purposes or where a comparison of different accounts can shed light on the reasons for an author's preference for one version of an event over another; nor will I search for 'influences' except insofar as relationships between writers may illuminate broader issues. Further, I will not consider Persian historiography in total isolation from Arabic; for if the two traditions ultimately diverge, the earliest Persian historians at least were by no means unmindful of the writings of their Arabic counterparts. I will also consider, albeit briefly, connections between historiography and other related genres, in particular that of 'mirrors for princes', insofar as they treat common themes and reveal common preoccupations. Finally, I will attempt to contextualise Persian historical writing in its immediate political and social milieux, and to draw comparisons between medieval Islamic historical writing and pre-modern Western historiography. Within the chronological framework of this study, extending from the latter half of the 4th/10th century, when the first historical works appear, to the turn of the 6th/12th, encompassing the decade which followed the fall of the Great Saljūqs in 590/1194, I shall concentrate principally on works written under the aegis of the major Persian and Turkic dynasties, the Sāmānids, Ghaznavids and Saljūqs.

John O. Ward's observation, that 'an age characterized by a rich variety of historical writing will be an age in which a significant number of persons endowed with literacy find themselves in problematical or challenging social or political circumstances' (1965: 103), might well be applied to those periods when Persian historical writing is most in evidence, and especially to that between the mid-3rd/9th century (the last decades of Sāmānid rule) and the last half of the 5th/11th (under the Ghaznavids), when a number of important Persian histories appeared in eastern Iran. The Saljūq period (mid-5th/11th and 6th/12th centuries), which saw a political and cultural shift to western Iran (particularly in the latter part of the 6th/12th century) is more problematic: for while literate persons certainly found themselves in circumstances which were both problematical and challenging, there seems to have been little attention paid to history until the late Saljūq period. This may suggest a perspective from which to approach two central questions: what circumstances motivated the initial appearance of historical writing at a certain time and in a certain place, and why did it flourish, or languish, in subsequent periods?

On the map of Persian historical writing (which is certainly not accurate, due both to the loss of many works and to medieval habits of incorporating often large parts of earlier histories into later ones) there appear to be a number of peaks and valleys. The first peak (Chapter 1) comes in the latter half of the 4th/10th century, in the Sāmānid domains of Khurasan and Transoxania. The second (Chapter 2) comes a decade or so after the Ghaznavid defeat by the Saljūqs in 431/1040, in what remained of the Ghaznavid empire in the East. The third (Chapter 3) begins around the time of the accession of the last Great Saljūq sultan Ṭughril ibn Arslān in 571/1176 and culminates a decade or so later. Then come the Mongols, whose impact on Persian historiography is beyond the scope of this study. There are, of course, some irregularities on this map (a few minor works written in the early 6th/12th century, which are largely peripheral to the mainstream of historical writing); what is more remarkable is the almost flat line which extends through the first century of Saljūq rule, when there seems to have been negligible historiographical activity in either Persian or Arabic: the first Arabic histories of the Saljūqs appear around the same time as do the Persian (see Cahen 1962: 68–9).

In general, the curves of historical writing do not duplicate those of dynastic florescence but follow them by a decade or so. By the time Firdawsī began his *Shāhnāma* – the culminating work of the indigenous Iranian historiographical tradition (see Chapter 1) – the Sāmānids were in crisis, and they themselves seem to have left no dynastic history. Ghaznavid history does not begin to be written in Persian (although at least one major Arabic history of the dynasty was written in Maḥmūd's reign) until after they had lost their Khurasanian territories to the Saljūqs. The history of the Saljūqs was not written at all until they had become seriously, and fatally, weakened by the endemic power struggles that marked the last century of their rule. Why this state of affairs obtained will be examined in more detail in the course of this study.

THE STATUS AND FUNCTIONS OF HISTORY

Franz Rosenthal has argued that in medieval Islamic societies history was not a recognised 'science' (*ʿilm*) with a specific object and methodology (as for example was the 'science' of Ḥadīth), and that it held no special place in classifications of the sciences (see 1968: 30–53). We may reserve judgement on this for now; but there is no doubt as to the importance of history in the eyes of both its authors and its audiences. If history did not form part of the higher educational curriculum of the mosque or, later, of the *madrasa* (Rosenthal 1968: 42–3; see also Ahmad 1962, especially 96), it was widely taught in other contexts, and was, as Rosenthal himself has shown, a major component of elementary education. It was, moreover, considered essential to the education of princes as well as of military leaders, viziers, secretaries and royal boon companions (see 1968: 45–53).

It is however true that, as Nancy Partner observes of classical historians, 'there were no historians who were not something else first and more importantly' (1985: 11). Those who wrote history came from many different walks of life; they included religious scholars (*ʿulamā*), court secretaries and boon companions, judges, physicians and the occasional amateur (see further Rosenthal 1968: 54–65). Each brought to his task his own professional concerns and methods; thus in considering the work of any individual historian, his professional background must be taken into consideration. For the period under discussion, most of those who wrote history were court officials: scribes, secretaries, the occasional vizier. They were members of a class who shared a common educational background, certain stylistic approaches to literary composition and specific political concerns; their writings therefore exhibit many common assumptions as to the purposes and the proper content of history, as well as to how it should be written.

The late 3rd/9th and the 4th/10th centuries have been described by some scholars as those of the 'Renaissance of Islam' (see especially Kraemer 1986a). There are obvious difficulties involved in attempting to draw parallels between the Italian Renaissance and the 'Islamic'; what is not in doubt is that the 4th/10th century in particular was a dynamic one in the history of Islamic political and intellectual life. Not surprisingly, this century witnessed important developments in Arabic historiography and equally important discussions about the nature and uses of history, which clearly affected Persian writers when they turned to the writing of history. One topic of discussion involved, precisely, the attempt to classify history among the sciences, as writers stressed the point that history was not a mere collection of discrete accounts but served other, more far-reaching ends pertaining not merely to information about the past but to wisdom and to ethical philosophy (see Arkoun 1967). Masʿūdī (d. 345/956) in his *Murūj al-dhahab* declared his intent 'to bequeathe to the world ... a well-ordered science' (Khalidi 1994: 132). He viewed history as 'the fountainhead of all the sciences' and as the repository and conservator of the learning of the past.

> For any science to exist, it must be derived from history. From it all wisdom is deduced, all jurisprudence is elicited, all eloquence is learnt. Those who reason by analogy build upon it. Those who have opinions to expound use it for argument. Popular knowledge is derived from it and the precepts of the

> wise are found in it. Noble and lofty morality is acquired from it and the rules of royal government and war are sought in it. All manner of strange events are found in it; in it too all kinds of entertaining stories may be enjoyed. It is a science ... which can be appreciated by both the educated and the ignorant, savoured by both fool and sage, a much desired comfort to elites and commoners and practised by Arab and non-Arab alike ... The superiority of history over all other sciences is obvious. The loftiness of its status is recognized by any person of intelligence. None can master it nor gain certainty as to what it includes nor receive and transmit it except one who has devoted his life to knowledge, grasped its true meaning, tasted its fruits, felt its true dignity and experienced the pleasure it bestows. (Quoted in Khalidi 1994: 133; Khalidi's translation)

The interest in the rules of government is not solely pragmatic: good government is linked with the ruler's virtue, and the lessons of history are moral ones. Muslim writers shared this attitude with classical historians (see for example de Romilly 1991); the belief 'that all politics was the work of individuals and understandable in the light of their personal qualities and experiences' (Rosenthal 1968: 101) was not limited to Islamicate societies. What Gibb saw as another indication of decline ('if history were only a branch of ethics, not a science, they [the historians] need not scruple to adapt their historical examples to their own ends' [1982: 121]) was in fact a fundamental and indispensable function of history: the past furnishes examples which may be drawn upon as guides to conduct in the present and the future. The Arabic historian Miskawayh (d. 421/1030) wrote in the preface to his *Tajārib al-umam* ('The Experiences of the Nations'):

> When I perused the accounts of peoples and the lives of kings, and read the histories of (diverse) lands and books of history, I found therein material which furnished an experience of matters whose like continues to be repeated, and whose similitudes and likenesses may be expected to recur: such as mention of the origins of states and the growth of kingdoms; of the intrusion of some flaw thereafter; of the efforts of those who repaired and put (this flaw) to rights ... and of the negligence of those who ignored and rejected (such flaws) until they led to destruction and ruin ... For the world's affairs are similar, and its conditions resemble one another; and all that a man observes of this sort of (events) becomes as if it were his own experience. (1909: 1–2; on Miskawayh see Arkoun 1967; Rosenthal 1968: 141–2; Kraemer 1986b: 222–3)

Iranian contemporaries of Masʿūdī and Miskawayh were equally concerned with the classification of history among the sciences and with its moral, as well as its practical, ends. Muḥammad ibn Aḥmad Khwārazmī (d. 387/997), whose *Mafātīḥ al-ʿulūm* (a collection of technical terms grouped with the disciplines to which they relate, intended as a manual for secretaries and dedicated to the Sāmānid vizier Abū al-Ḥusayn ʿUtbī) employs the traditional division into 'Arab' and 'Greek' sciences, numbers historical information among the former (see Rosenthal 1968: 33–4). Before him a certain Ibn Farīghūn, who was a student of the great scholar Abū Zayd Balkhī (d. 332/934) and who may have been a member of the Farīghūnid family who ruled the region of Juzjanan under the Sāmānids (Minorsky 1962: 191, and see 193–4 n. 3), dedicated his short encyclopedia the *Jawāmīʿ al-ʿulūm* (also a manual for secretaries) to the Muḥtājid ruler of Chaghaniyan and Sāmānid governor of Khurasan Abū ʿAlī Aḥmad ibn Muḥammad ibn al-Muẓaffar (whom we will meet again in Chapter 1). Abū ʿAlī and his father Abū Bakr Muḥammad were also patrons of Abū ʿAlī Ḥusayn ibn Aḥmad Sallāmī (d. c. 350/961), who wrote for them, in Arabic, his now lost *Ta'rīkh wulāt Khurāsān* ('History of the Governors of Khurasan'); there thus appears to have been considerable interest in history at the Muḥtājid court.

Knowledge of history, says Ibn Farīghūn, is indispensable for court secretaries, who must 'know the histories of the three nations' (that is, those of the Persians and 'the caliphs', presumably both Umayyad and Abbasid [f. 18b]). History itself is classified under the general rubric of 'the science of wisdom' (*ʿilm al-ḥikma*) and the specific category (*jins*) of 'knowledge of causes' (*ʿilm al-ʿilla*); a separate chapter is devoted to the 'science of histories' (*ʿilm al-ta'rīkhāt*) as a 'species' (*nawʿ*) of such knowledge (f. 68a). History comprises

> the mention of famous events which occurred in past times or over extensive periods, such as a ruinous deluge, a destructive earthquake, epidemics, or famines which annihilate nations; the names of famous rulers in the (various) regions, their number, days, and the length of their reigns, and the transfer (of rule) from one (house) to another; knowledge of the beginning of creation and its return [to its origins; that is, the events surrounding the End of Days]; and the physical and intellectual conditions of previous ages. But this (knowledge) may be contaminated by falsification because of remoteness in time ... Only that should be accepted which is spoken of in books or in reliable accounts.

History also includes

> accounts of the Prophet's birth, his mission, his battles and his circumstances up to the time of his death, which are useful for

> political matters and warfare against enemies; knowledge of the lives of the caliphs of Quraysh, their conquests, administration, the civil strife that took place between those contending for leadership from among the Khārijīs [or: rebels] and from the time of the transfer of rule from the Umayyads to the Hāshimites, so that these may provide object lessons concerning the vicissitudes of time.

Knowledge of the battle days of the Arabs and of tribal matters, 'in which eloquent language and poetry may be found', and of 'the Persian books and histories', is also of use in matters of politics and government and in dealing with the grievances of the populace. Accounts of famous rulers and their wise sayings, of 'persons of noble birth, scholars, secretaries, poets, eloquent men', and in general of those who possess outstanding virtues, are also instructive (Biesterfeldt n.d., 2: 43–4; Rosenthal's slightly different summary of this passage [1968: 34–6] reflects his use of different manuscripts). Ibn Farīghūn's statements reflect concern for both the practical and the ethical functions of history; his reference to the 'transition', or transfer, of rule has further implications for historical writing.

TYPES OF HISTORICAL WRITING

By the 4th/10th century a variety of models of historical writing were available to Persian writers. One was the universal, or more properly general, history, represented most famously by Ṭabarī, whose great *Ta'rīkh al-rusul wa-al-mulūk* ('History of Prophets and Kings') would be 'translated' into Persian by the Sāmānid vizier Abū 'Alī Bal'amī. Despite their incorporation of pre-Islamic history (that is, of the nations conquered and 'abrogated' by Islam), the chief focus of such works is Islamic history, and especially that of the caliphate, to which the accounts of past nations serve as prelude.[4] The annalistic structure elaborated by Ṭabarī and employed by some later Arabic historians was by no means uniformly used even by other Arabic writers of the 3rd/9th and 4th/10th centuries, and was rarely adopted by Persian historians. The ordering of history by reigns of rulers seems to have been a pre-Islamic Persian historiographical tradition, imported into Arabic via translations of Sasanian historical works (see Gibb 1982: 117).

Another model was local or regional history (see Rosenthal 1968: 160–6; Humphreys 1991: 131–2; Lambton 1991). The term is slightly misleading; many such works, both in Arabic and later in Persian, while devoting much space to description of their respective regions, are chiefly concerned with the history of the rulers of those regions. Moreover, Persian seems to lack early representatives of the Arabic type of local history whose chief focus is on biography, primarily (but not exclusively) of scholars. Such works as Sallāmī's *Ta'rīkh wulāt Khurāsān*, or the city histories of Bukhara, Nishapur, Jurjan, Isfahan and so on, were written in Arabic. Ibn Funduq's Persian history of Bayhaq (mid-6th/12th century; see Chapter 3) combines local history with topography and biography. Lambton has argued that local history both represents a 'reaction to centralisation' and, at the same time, expresses the belief 'that the contribution of the regions is worthy of record and that their histories, rather than [those] of larger political units, represent or reflect the vigour and strength of the community as a whole' (1991: 228–9). Local histories vary considerably however, and for their authors the history of the region often has little to do with that of 'the community as a whole'.

The pre-Islamic (Sasanian) Iranian historical tradition, which deals with the history of Iranian monarchy from its legendary beginnings until the Islamic conquest, was briefly revived during the Sāmānid period (see Chapter 1). For our purposes, however, perhaps the most important model, and one which was to have a lasting influence on Persian historiography, was contemporary dynastic history, represented by Miskawayh's account in his *Tajārib al-umam* of Būyid history up to 369/980 and by Abū Isḥāq Ṣābī's (d. 384/994) *Kitāb al-Tājī* on the same house. (On Arabic dynastic history, and possible Persian influences upon it, see Rosenthal 1968: 87–93.) General histories which focus on the caliphate or on the rise of independent dynasties may also be considered dynastic history insofar as the history of the past is seen as leading to the present ruling house.

As noted above, some scholars have seen the rise of dynastic history as evidence of the decline of what was once a noble and religiously inspired discipline. Thus Gibb lamented that with the rise of 'contemporary annalistic' history (a description that should be used with caution), 'the old theological conception which had given breadth and dignity to history was discarded, and annalistic [history] tended to concentrate more and more upon the activities of the ruler and the court' (1982: 120). The change was intimately linked to the fact that dynastic history was written by court officials and secretaries, who brought to its writing the rhetorically sophisticated chancery style (*kitābat al-inshā'*) which characterised their professional compositions, and who also elaborated an important, if not exactly new, conceptual model for history. For the very term which ultimately came to mean 'dynasty', *dawla*, was from an early period 'connected ... with a theory of recurrent cycles of political power' (Rosenthal 1968: 89); and the narrative of the rise and fall of states (or, rather, of rulers and/or houses) was to become, in the words of Aziz

Al-Azmeh, the 'essential paradigm of human history' (see 1990: 11–46; on the concept of *dawla* see also *EI*², s.v.; and see further the Conclusion).[5]

The term 'recurrent cycles' should also be used with caution. With the exception of Ismā'īlī hierohistory (and that chiefly in its later manifestations), Muslim historians do not conceive of history as cyclical: history has a beginning – the Creation – and a terminus – the End of Days. While this terminus constantly recedes into the future, its finality is unquestioned. And while the linear progression of history may be divided into ages in which certain event-types recur – the most prominent being the rise and fall of states – it is more accurate to speak of successive cycles of power, as one group replaces another. It is also perhaps misleading to speak of 'states', as the 'state' was identified as, and identical with, its ruler(s), and the causes of a state's rise and fall were intimately linked and viewed in moral terms. Greek historians

> considered the rise and fall of a state just as they would consider the rise and fall of an individual person. The pattern of rise and fall has nothing to do with states as such, nor did the Greeks conceive any difference in nature between states and individuals ... This, of course, is bound to leave out all the explanations founded on political facts as such – namely, economy, demography, social conditions or the like. The reasons for the rise and fall of states, according to Greek authors, will be mainly moral and psychological ... What [these authors] search for is the reason why the rise of a state turns to its downfall. Therefore, their interest is focused on this turning point: not on the rise, but on its dangers. (de Romilly 1991: 19)

This view is characteristic, by and large, of the Persian writers to be discussed in this study; and I shall return to this point in the Conclusion.

Dynastic history constitutes the foremost representative, in the Islamic world, of what Western scholars have termed ethical-rhetorical historiography, which has been widely studied with respect to the pre-modern West but has received little serious attention from writers on Islamic history. In such historiography the link between ethical concerns and rhetorical style is an essential one: rhetorical strategies pertaining to structure and embellishment play an important role in conveying the historian's message. Traditional scholarship has generally seen in the application of rhetoric to history yet another symptom of decline and decadence. Thus G. E. von Grunebaum observed that the 'upsurge of the educational ideal of the *kātib*, the civil official or the clerk' resulted in 'a gossipy and clever historiography' in which 'style came to be cultivated for its own sake ... and the substance of what the author had set out to convey almost evaporated in a fireworks of rhetoric' (1962: 227); while Spuler wrote that the appreciation of the style of later historians such as Vaṣṣāf (8th/14th century) by a limited class of highly educated individuals 'obscured the true purpose of historiography for many centuries and turned this literature ... into a surrogate of modern European historical fiction: the style, the arrangement of facts, was often more important than the historical truth' (1962: 132; see also Rosenthal 1968: 173, 176–85. Khalidi [1994: 129–30] raises the question of style but does not develop it). But while the figured chancery style employed by the secretary-historians may sometimes appear overdone, its use is not gratuitous; there is a method, and a rationale, behind it. In rhetorical histories, message and style are inseparable: as Allin Luther pointed out,

> The modern researcher cannot use these histories simply by 'extracting the facts'. The nature of the whole work is important if we are to understand the entirety of the author's message. We must be aware of the writer's purpose and of the way in which he arranged and ornamented his work to serve that purpose. (1990: 96–7)

The pre-modern historian's primary concern is not with facts, but with the meaning of those facts; and to convey that meaning he must shape and place his raw materials within some sort of narrative framework. Ward proposes three 'tiers of historical reality' for medieval historians: '(1) raw, unformed historical facts or events, which cannot be written about; (2) partially shaped, selected, formed facts, which can be written about (papal, royal, monastic history, etc.); and (3) the finished narrative presentation of the historian' (1985: 108). While many scholars still seek to recover a reliable picture of the past, for the student of historiographical thought, and of intellectual and cultural history in general, the historians' representation of the past in terms of its meaningfulness for the present – their present – is of far greater interest.

If history is not simply a record of the past, a collection of facts, what is it? It is, as I will argue in what follows, the presentation of a 'usable' past, in what is first and foremost a construct of language. Arabic historiography had already constructed a variety of 'usable pasts' – Prophetic, tribal, caliphal, pre-Islamic, recent dynastic, and so on – and had developed a variety of styles and structures with which to represent those pasts. The first generations of Persian historians had to wrestle with the question of what constituted their 'usable past' (or pasts; I shall discuss the issue of competing pasts in Chapter

1), and of how to represent it in appropriate language. Their answers were different; the differences have much to do with the reasons for which they wrote history, insofar as these can be recovered. One task of the present study is, therefore, to attempt to understand these reasons, to the extent possible, both by examining the writers' own statements, when available (although such statements must be read with caution), and by attempting to contextualise the histories themselves in terms of the political and cultural circumstances under which they were written, the (often tentative) identification of patrons and of intended audiences, and the issue (where this can be addressed) of contemporary and later reception. This will inevitably involve reference to historical events (as presented both by our authors and by modern scholarship), as well as digressions on topics of particular importance to our historians; and I apologise in advance for any resultant tedium. In the Conclusion, I shall review the major themes of Persian historiography, as well as a number of issues arising from the works surveyed, from both a local and a comparative perspective.

It remains for me to express my thanks to those who have, in one way or another, been involved in this project: to Carole Hillenbrand for encouraging me to write (and to stick with) this book; to Jane Feore of Edinburgh University Press, who has been congenial and sympathetic throughout; to the many individuals with whom I have discussed various aspects of this study, among them in particular the late Kenneth Allin Luther, Elton Daniel, Wilferd Madelung, Luke Treadwell, Chase Robinson, and others too numerous to mention. Steven Uran was kind enough to read drafts of the Introduction and Conclusion and to provide constructive comments. The generous assistance of Ms Gillies Tetley in tracking down references is most appreciated, as is the endless patience of my daughters Mona and Ayda, who have been a constant source of support.

A final technical note. All translations from the texts, unless otherwise indicated, are my own, and any errors my responsibility. Transcription follows the system recommended by the *International Journal of Middle East Studies* (in some instances allowances have been made for Persian pronunciation). Dates are given according to both Hijra and Common Era (Julian) calendars.

NOTES

1. For a summary of earlier scholarship on pre-Islamic Iranian historical traditions see Nöldeke 1979: 9–31 (first published 1930); for more recent overviews see Yarshater 1991: 359–70; Shahbazi 1990). See also Czeglédy 1958 for a discussion of heroic/romantic and apocalyptic traditions which continued to be developed in post-Sasanian times; and see further Chapter 1, below.

2. For a concise overview see Humphreys 1991: 128–36. Humphreys identifies several salient features of this 'new historiography': (1) It was 'written in two languages (Arabic and Persian)', each of which 'to a great extent ... enshrines a specific cultural tradition almost from the beginning'. (2) 'The better Persian writers seem more interested in contriving a fully integrated narrative than do their Arabic counterparts' (the suggestion that this 'dramatic coherence' was due to an effort 'to apply the plotlines and characterizations which they found in the epic poetry of Firdawsī ... and his successors' to their own writings must be rejected, first because the earliest Persian histories predate Firdawsī's *Shāhnāma*, and second because such 'dramatic coherence' is already seen in, for example, the Arabic histories of Dīnawarī and Miskawayh). (3) There is a 'redirection of subject matter', as historians were no longer interested in writing salvific history or in legitimating the Abbasid caliphate; 'henceforth, history would become chiefly a source of political prudence and moral admonition'. (4) These 'altered concerns' led Muslim historians 'to focus on recent and contemporary events rather than the remote past' (1991: 129–30). These issues will be addressed in the course of this study. It is important to note, however, that no simple 'evolutionary' course of development can be posited for either Arabic or Persian historiography (see Robinson 1997: 223–4).
3. This is part and parcel of a general conservatism in a field which has typically been far more interested in attempting to reconstruct the past – in particular, the early Islamic past – than in questions relating to historiographical thought and method, including the question of what materials the writers themselves considered 'history'. Wansbrough (1978) has criticised the 'distinctly positivist method' which has marked scholarship on early Arabic history, where the 'concern to discover and to describe the state of affairs at and after the appearance of Islam among the Arabs' is accompanied by 'a severely fluctuating willingness to acknowledge the presence there of notions and practices familiar from the study of earlier and contemporary cultures outside the Arabian peninsula, and ... a nearly complete absence of linguistic and literary analysis' (1978: 2; for an overview of these issues see Robinson 1997).
4. The original impulse behind universal or general history, as of chronology, was to synchronise past history from Creation to the present, and to reconcile 'salvific' history (that of the Israelite prophets) with 'secular' or 'imperial' history (that of the Sasanians and the Arabian kingdoms). The result was the integration of Islamic history into the broader framework of world history, the narrative of which was seen from the perspective of the new dispensation.
5. J. Lassner's argument, made in connection with the 'Abbasid revolution', that 'Arabic *dawlah* ... is the semantic equivalent of the English word 'revolution' which, since the time of the Renaissance, has come to denote political upheaval as well as rotation' (1986: xii), is difficult to accept. In early usage *dawla* signified a 'time of power and success', and as such could be applied to individuals (Abū Muslim, the leader of the Abbasid movement in Khurasan, was called *ṣāḥib al-dawla*, 'possessor of fortune'), and only later 'acquired the meaning of dynasty and ultimately of state' (Lewis 1973: 254).

1

Persian Historiography in the Sāmānid Period

THE BACKGROUND

The breakdown of Abbasid authority which began in the mid-3rd/9th century encouraged the rise of local dynasties in regions still nominally ruled by the caliphate. In the East, the Ṭāhirids had controlled Khurasan, Transoxania and Sistan since 198/813–4, when the caliph al-Ma'mūn appointed his general Ṭāhir ibn ʿAbd Allāh governor after the latter had effected al-Ma'mūn's victory over his half-brother and rival for the caliphate, al-Amīn. (On the civil war between al-Amīn and al-Ma'mūn see Ṭabarī 1992b.) The Ṭāhirids' fortunes were always closely linked with those of the caliphate, whose rights they were careful to respect, and they cannot be considered a truly independent dynasty. Moreover, although the Ṭāhirids came from Persian stock (they claimed descent from both the Persian hero Rustam and the Arab tribe of Khuzāʿa, of which the family's ancestor had been a client), and although their native tongue was Persian, their cultural habits were highly Arabised; they patronised Arabic letters and were themselves notable scholars, poets and littérateurs.[1]

In the latter half of the 3rd/9th century Ṭāhirid authority was challenged, first by the Ṣaffārids of Sistan (see Chapter 2) and then by the Sāmānids. While the Ṣaffārids made Persian their language of administration and supported Persian poets, they seem to have sponsored no works of Persian prose. The Sāmānids traced their descent to Sāmānkhudā of Balkh, a scion of the aristocratic *dihqān* class that had governed Persia before the Islamic conquest, who was said to have been converted to Islam by an Umayyad governor of Khurasan (see Treadwell 1991: 64–5; Gardīzī's account [1968: 145–6] that it was the caliph al-Ma'mūn who converted Sāmānkhudā and promoted his son Asad and the latter's four sons, while clearly apocryphal, reflects al-Ma'mūn's importance as a legitimating figure with respect to the rule of Khurasan).

It was the Sāmānids who became the patrons of what has been called the 'Persian literary renaissance'. When Ismāʿīl (I) ibn Aḥmad (279–95/892–907) became Amīr in 260/874 and added Bukhara to the Sāmānids' already extensive domains in Transoxania and Khurasan, that city became both the capital and the centre of a flourishing cultural and literary life. Initially this was conducted in Arabic; but the reign of Ismāʿīl's grandson Naṣr (II) ibn Aḥmad (301–31/914–33) saw a sudden florescence of both poetry and prose in Persian. It is thus to Naṣr's reign that we must look when investigating the reasons for the rise of Persian letters in general, and of Persian historiography in particular.

Naṣr came to the throne at the age of eight following the murder of his father Aḥmad (II) ibn Ismāʿīl (295–301/907–14). It is said that one of Aḥmad's secretaries, fearing punishment for having extorted bribes from important visitors to court after having sworn a solemn oath to desist, suborned several of the Amīr's *ghulāms*, promising them rewards and promotions and swearing to support Aḥmad's uncle, Isḥāq ibn Aḥmad (I), as his successor. One night in mid-Jumādā II 310/January 914, two *mamlūks* from the Amīr's household, aided by the master of the wardrobe and the royal treasurer, murdered him as he slept. But the plan to proclaim Isḥāq in Bukhara was frustrated, and the young prince Naṣr was elected Aḥmad's successor (see Treadwell 1991: 138–41). Other reasons have been given for Aḥmad's murder: that he was ill-informed about conditions in the capital and manipulated by his courtiers; that he had poor relations with his *ghulāms*; that the latter 'turned against him because he spent all his time with members of the scholarly class'. Treadwell suggests that the fact that Aḥmad ordered official documents to be written in Arabic rather than 'court' Persian (*Darī*) testifies to scholarly influence at court, but 'precisely how this worked to the disadvantage of the *mamlūks* is not ... clear' (1991: 141, and see the references cited).

What is clear is that Naṣr ibn Aḥmad's reign witnessed a transformation of 'the cultural and religious orientations of the state elite' which was to have far-reaching effects, and which was linked with 'the rise to power of members of the secretarial class who supervised the accession of the young amir Naṣr and enjoyed a measure of authority which their predecessors had lacked' (Treadwell 1991: 170). Gardīzī states that Naṣr's first vizier, Abū ʿAbd Allāh Jayhānī (301–10/914–22; d. 330/942), 'recorded the customs of all the regions of the world, considered them, adopted those that were praiseworthy, and ordered all the court officials to practise them' (1968: 150). In so doing, says Treadwell, 'he was establishing an innovatory principle – namely, that Sāmānid administrative practice was no longer to be bound by the limitations of local and ʿAbbāsid precedent.' Under Jayhānī and his successor, Abū al-Faḍl Balʿamī, the intellectual horizons of the Sāmānid court expanded; 'Bukhārā became a centre of secular Arabic learning and literature, while the court, led by Naṣr's example, began to exploit the local Iranian cultural environment through its patronage of Persian literature, particularly poetry' (1991: 171–2). Among the poets patronised by Naṣr was Rūdakī, who rendered into Persian verse the *Kalīla wa-Dimna* from the prose translation made by Balʿamī at Naṣr's request. It is tempting to speculate that Masʿūdī Marvazī, author of a verse *Shāhnāma* fragments of which are quoted in the *Kitāb al-bad' wa-al-ta'rīkh* of Muṭahhir ibn Ṭāhir al-Maqdīsī (c. 355/966), might also have been among the poets patronised by Naṣr, although he has been dated to an earlier period (see de Blois 1992: 191–2). But even if Naṣr's reign produced no history, it was marked by a hitherto unprecedented interest in the Iranian past and in the Persian language.

Persian had long been the *lingua franca* of the East; and although many local dialects were spoken in the Sāmānid domains, and the language of the region of Bukhara itself was Soghdian, Persian served as a language of verbal communication between different linguistic groups. If suggestive passages in Ṭabarī and other historians are any indication, it appears to have been used by speakers of both Arabic and Persian to communicate with Turkish *mamlūk*s as early as the 3rd/9th century (see for example Ṭabarī 1992b: 192–4 [the murder of al-Amīn]). Frye suggests that from a relatively early period, when conversion to Islam provided local governors with native auxiliary troops who became attached to the Arabs as clients, 'the Arabs probably used Persian as the *lingua franca* with their Iranian subjects in Central Asia, as well as in Iran' (1965: 17). While Arabic retained its position as the language of scholarship, Persian was used increasingly in official contexts; and the dispute over whether Arabic or Persian should be the official administrative language continued during the 5th/11th century.

Treadwell's argument that 'the use of Persian as a language of poetry, albeit in a secular courtly setting, represented a conscious decision to ignore the scholarly censure of the previous reign, and perhaps even to reverse Aḥmad's ruling' with regard to the administrative language, and further that 'the history of Persian prose literature under the later Sāmānids shows that the scholarly class was soon compelled to accept the use of Persian in the discipline … of religious scholarship' (1991: 179–80) requires qualification, as does Richter-Bernburg's view (1974) of the rise of Persian prose as 'linguistic *Shuʿūbiyya*'.[2] Richter-Bernburg posited an 'attack' on the status of Arabic 'by the emergence of an Islamic literature in Persian that was to embrace the whole scope of contemporary writing in "Arabic"' (1974: 55–6). This challenge, if it was one, was far less grandiose: none of the Persian prose works written or translated during the

Sāmānid period was truly scholarly. Persian prose literature was primarily utilitarian: 'if an author wrote in prose, it was solely for purposes of instruction or propaganda' (Lazard 1975: 630). Prose works included technical writings (for example, on medicine); 'wisdom literature' such as the *Kalīla wa-Dimna*; doctrinal works like the translation of the Ḥanafī creed, the *Sawād al-aʿẓam*, in the reign of Nūḥ II ibn Manṣūr; propagandistic works by Ismāʿīlīs and other sectarians; geography; and history. Serious scholarly works continued to be written in Arabic even by those who supported the use of *Darī* as the language of the court, and were patronised by notables 'known to have harboured an "anti-Arab" animus' like Abū ʿAbd Allāh Jayhānī. If, indeed, 'the orthodox scholarly community had to some extent become estranged from the court by the end of Naṣr's reign', the reasons for this extend beyond the issue of language, and are clearly related to the conversion of Naṣr ibn Aḥmad, as well as many important officials of his court, to Ismāʿīlism (see Treadwell 1991: 184–5).

Ismāʿīlī (or, more generally, 'Bāṭinī' or heterodox Shīʿī) missionaries had been active in the Sāmānid domains since early in the 3rd/9th century. The characteristic philo-ʿAlidism of the East, which further distanced the Sāmānids from the Abbasids, may have made them particularly receptive to Shīʿī (even heterodox Shīʿī) teachings. Early converts to Ismāʿīlism included important Sāmānid officials, among them the governor of Rayy, Aḥmad ibn ʿAlī Marvazī (d. 311/923), brother of the future head of the Khurasani mission Ḥusayn ibn ʿAlī Marvazī. According to Niẓām al-Mulk, the Ismāʿīlī *dāʿī* Muḥammad ibn Aḥmad Nasafī had converted Naṣr ibn Aḥmad's *nadīm* and private secretary Ashʿath (also related to Naṣr by marriage), the *ʿāriḍ* (chief of the military administration) Abū Manṣūr Chaghānī, and the court chamberlain Aytāsh (1978: 213), before converting Naṣr himself (who had, it seems, earlier inclined towards Twelver Shīʿism, at a time when the reappearance of the twelfth Imām from concealment [*ghayba*] was believed to be imminent [see Halm 1996: 291–3, 1997: 35–8]).

Throughout the 4th/10th century (as, indeed, during much of the previous one) apocalyptic prophecies of the approaching End of Days and of the appearance of the Mahdī (often accompanied by predictions of the end of Arab rule) were widespread; they gave impetus to the movements of the Qarmaṭīs and the Ismāʿīlī Faṭimids, and were even seen to be fulfilled in the rise to power of the Būyids (see Halm 1996; Madelung 1969: 93–7). Treadwell argues that Nasafī's predictions of the imminent 'coming of the *mahdī* and the end of the physical world was likely to strike a chord among his audience, particularly at a time when the ruling institutions were in crisis'. A series of natural disasters in the East, and especially in Bukhara, during the latter part of Naṣr's reign 'may have been taken as a portent ... that the present order was coming to an end', and might have motivated individuals in the court 'to seek refuge in a doctrine of personal salvation. Yet such ideas were surely easier to convey to uneducated peasants than to educated men.' Treadwell suggests that the converted members of the state elite 'had more worldly, political motives for adopting Ismā'īlism' (1991: 207–8).

Ismā'īlī activities in Iran were aimed less at winning popular support than at the ruling class (Stern 1983: 222). We do not know precisely what Nasafī's preaching to Naṣr, or to his courtiers, comprised. But the predictions of the end of Arab rule in circulation at this time stated also that this would be accomplished by a ruler from the East (see Madelung 1969: 95–6 and n. 51); and Naṣr might well have seen himself in this role.[3] But there was strong opposition to the spread of 'heresy' in Naṣr's court from the *'ulamā* and the Turkish soldiery, who joined forces in a plot to kill Naṣr; the plot was foiled by Naṣr's son Nūḥ, who persuaded his father to abdicate, and conducted a ruthless purge of Ismā'īlīs (real or suspected) throughout the Sāmānid domains (Treadwell 1991: 194).

Both Naṣr's conversion and his patronage of Persian culture may have been related to a wish to distance himself from the Abbasids. The fact that the rise to prominence of Persian as a literary medium went hand in hand with the revival of Iranian customs and traditions suggests that it may be more useful to view the various manifestations of 'Persianising' movements – religious, cultural, literary and linguistic – as less anti-Arab(ic) than anti-Abbasid, and the official patronage of Persian works of instruction and propaganda as linked to the legitimation of Sāmānid rule in the East. This would seem to be true for the two major prose works produced in the reign of Nūḥ ibn Naṣr's successor Manṣūr ibn Nūḥ: the translation into Persian of Ṭabarī's History and his Koranic *Tafsīr*. For as the *'ulamā* who authorised the translation of the *Tafsīr* declared: 'Here, in this region, the language is Persian, and the kings of this realm are Persian kings' (1988, 1: 5).

But before the Ṭabarī translations were commissioned other historical works appeared, works based on the indigenous Iranian historical traditions represented by the *Shāhnāma* ('Book of Kings'), which retold the history of pre-Islamic Iranian monarchy up to the Arab conquest. It is to an early example of such works, of particular importance because it was commissioned, not by a Sāmānid ruler but by a member of the Khurasanian nobility, that we turn next.

THE PROSE *SHĀHNĀMA* OF ABŪ MANṢŪR ṬŪSĪ

The reign of Nūḥ ibn Naṣr (331–43/943–54) was dominated by the revolt of the Muḥtājid prince Abū ʿAlī Aḥmad ibn Muḥammad ibn al-Muẓaffar Chaghānī, who succeeded his father Abū Bakr Muḥammad as Sāmānid governor (*sipahsālār*) of Khurasan in 329/940, and who was perhaps related to the Abū Manṣūr Chaghānī who was converted to Ismāʿīlism in Naṣr II's reign. (We may recall that it was to Abū ʿAlī Chaghānī that Ibn Farīghūn dedicated his *Jawāmiʿ al-ʿulūm*, and that Abū Bakr and Abū ʿAlī were Sallāmī's patrons.) Relations between Nūḥ and Abū ʿAlī seem to have been less than cordial; and when the latter was absent from Khurasan campaigning against the Būyids in Rayy, Nūḥ replaced him with the Turkish commander Abū Isḥāq Sīmjūrī. Abū ʿAlī launched a rebellion which lasted some four years; he finally defected to the Būyids and died in Rayy of the plague in 344/955 (see Treadwell 1991: 190, 212–20; on the Muḥtājids see Bosworth 1981).

Abū ʿAlī was joined in his rebellion by Abū Manṣūr Muḥammad ibn ʿAbd al-Razzāq Ṭūsī, who was Abū ʿAlī's governor of Nishapur around 334/945, served on and off in that position and (briefly) as *sipahsālār* of Khurasan, and also cultivated relations with the Būyids in Rayy. In 349/961 Nūḥ's successor, ʿAbd al-Malik ibn Nūḥ (343–50/954–61), replaced Abū Manṣūr Ṭūsī as *sipahsālār* with the Turkish chief *ḥājib* Alptigīn (founder of the Ghaznavid dynasty); Abū Manṣūr defected to the Būyids (for a second time) and met a sticky end in 350/962. In 346/957 Abū Manṣūr Ṭūsī commissioned his vizier Abū Manṣūr Maʿmarī to supervise the compilation of a prose *Shāhnāma*, of which only the preface has survived.[4] The eastern tradition of Iranian history represented by the *Shāhnāma* is centered on Khurasan; events in the west are, in general, of little importance. Īrānshahr, or Īrānzamīn, is, as the author of the prose *Shāhnāma* reminds us, the seventh and central of the seven *kishvar*s ('regions') of the old Iranian world-division, and is of all those regions 'the grandest from the point of view of every art' (Minorsky 1956: 171–2; see *EI*², art. 'Ki<u>sh</u>var'). It is perhaps not surprising that it was a Persian governor of Khurasan's most important Islamic city, Nishapur, descended from the aristocratic lords of one of its most important pre-Islamic cities, Ṭūs, who commissioned a work recording the pre-Islamic history of Iranian sovereignty.

Abū Manṣūr Ṭūsī's motives were at least in part pragmatic: to legitimate his position as lord of Ṭūs, and perhaps also as ruler of Khurasan. The preface contains a lengthy genealogy which is clearly linked to his claim to rule, and follows immediately Maʿmarī's adversion to the theme of the transfer of power: 'Four times kingship disappeared from Iran [and] strangers would come and seize the kingdom with humiliations ... Thus it was in the time of Ǧamshīd, at that of Naudhar, at that of Iskandar and so on' (Minorsky 1956: 174–5). The genealogy traces Abū Manṣūr's descent (and Maʿmarī's own) to the Kanārang ('Lord of the [eastern] March'), a commander of the Sasanian ruler Khusraw II Parvīz, who was rewarded for his services with the gift of the cities of Ṭūs and, later, Nishapur. In Islamic times, a descendant of his was reconfirmed by the caliph ʿUmar ibn al-Khaṭṭāb's [read: ʿUthmān's] governor of Khurasan. 'And Ṭūs always belonged to the Kanārang family until the time of Ḥumayd (ibn Qaḥṭaba) aṭ-Ṭā'ī [the Abbasid governor of Khurasan, 152–9/769–75] who took it from their hands ... (but) at the time of Abū Manṣūr, son of ʿAbd al-Razzāq, they (re-)captured Ṭūs' (Minorsky 1956: 178–9; the Kanārang is also said to have been an ancestor of Ḥasan [read: Ḥusayn] ibn ʿAlī Marvazī, the Ismāʿīlī *dāʿī*). Abū Manṣūr's descent is further traced back through a series of important commanders to a son of Jamshīd. Bīrūnī, commenting scathingly on the widespread tendency 'to invent laudatory stories, and to forge genealogies which go back to glorious ancestors', cites among others the examples of Abū Manṣūr Ṭūsī, who 'got made for himself a genealogy out of the Sháhnáma', and of the Būyids (see 1879: 44–51).

Abū Manṣūr Ṭūsī is elsewhere linked with a series of famous rulers, as Maʿmarī expounds upon the themes of the transfer of learning and the memorialising role of discourse. 'As long as the world has existed,' he states, 'people have sought knowledge, held Speech great, and considered it the greatest memorial.' The commissioning of the compilation and translation of books of wisdom is one way of preserving the memory of kings, as in the case of the 'Indian king' who 'brought forth "Kalīla and Dimna"' and other such books. The caliph al-Ma'mūn observed, 'So long as a man is in this world and possesses power, he must strive for his memory (to survive) and for his name to be alive after his death'; whereupon his secretary Ibn al-Muqaffaʿ [*sic*] reminded him how Khusraw Anūshīrvān had left a lasting memorial by having the book of *Kalīla wa-Dimna* translated from 'Indian' into Pahlavī. Inspired by this example, al-Ma'mūn ordered his secretary to translate that same work into Arabic. Upon hearing this story, the Sāmānid Naṣr ibn Aḥmad requested his vizier Abū al-Faḍl Balʿamī to translate the work into Persian, 'and thus the book fell into men's hands and every man turned its pages'. He then had Rūdakī turn the prose version into verse; and '"Kalīla and Dimna" was on the tongues of the great and the lowly, and thus Rūdakī's name has lived on and this book became a memory of him.'

The final link in this chain is Abū Manṣūr Ṭūsī, described as 'a blissful [*ba-farr*; read 'royally favoured'], successful, clever man; he was high-minded in his felicity, and possessed a fully royal establishment; his way of life was princely and his thoughts elevated. By birth he was of a great race and belonged to the seed of the ispahbads of Iran.' When he heard this story, 'and the example set by the shāh of Khorasan', Abū Manṣūr determined to ensure his own memorial, and ordered the compilation of the prose *Shāhnāma*,

> so that men of knowledge may look into it and find ... all about the wisdom of the kings, noblemen and sages, the royal arrangements, nature and behaviour, good institutions, justice and judicial norms, decisions and administration, the military organisation (in) battles, storming of cities, punitive expeditions and night attacks, as well as about marriages and respecting honour. (Minorsky 1956: 167–9)

Of the style and content of Maʿmarī's *Shāhnāma* itself we know nothing. But the date of its completion, Muḥarram 346/April 957, may be significant. In 337/948, during Abū ʿAlī Chaghānī's rebellion, Abū Manṣūr Ṭūsī, who had gone over to the Būyids, was appointed by the Būyid ruler of Rayy, Rukn al-Dawla, as governor of Azerbaijan.

> Soon, however, his secretary, who had accompanied him from Khorasan, deserted to the enemy and Ibn ʿAbd al-Razzāq, growing weary of the unfamiliar surroundings, returned to Rayy in 338/949 and began negotiations with his former suzerain Nūḥ. In the following year he returned to Ṭūs. When in 342/953 Nūḥ sent troops against Rayy, Ibn ʿAbd al-Razzāq is mentioned among the negotiators with Rukn ad-Dawla. (Minorsky 1956: 165)

Abū Manṣūr was appointed *sipahsālār* of Khurasan in Jumādā II 349/August 960, but was replaced by Alptigīn six months later, presumably because of his still friendly relations with Rukn al-Dawla. The work was thus commissioned when his star was rising once more under the Sāmānids.

Did Abū Manṣūr Ṭūsī see himself as a challenger to Sāmānid rule? Was he attempting to carve out for himself a fief in Ṭūs, independent of Sāmānid control, as the Būyid Rukn al-Dawla had succeeded in doing in Rayy? In commissioning the prose *Shāhnāma* shortly after his return to Ṭūs, was he laying the ground for his claim to rule of that city? The tone and content of the preface seem geared towards supporting such a claim on several grounds: Abū Manṣūr's descent from the rulers of Ṭūs (and, before them, from Iranian princes going back to Jamshīd), plus an authoritative Islamic validation; his recapture of his patrimony; his princely conduct and estate. Perhaps it was the dangerous nature of this claim which motivated ʿAbd al-

Malik ibn Nūḥ (who had originally favoured Abū Manṣūr) to replace him with his own Turkish *mamlūk* Alptigīn.

MANṢŪR IBN NŪḤ AND THE PERSIAN ṬABARĪ

ʿAbd al-Malik died suddenly in a riding accident; he was succeeded, after a brief struggle over the succession, by his brother Manṣūr ibn Nūḥ (350–65/961–76). Manṣūr's reign witnessed the rise to prominence of the *mamlūk*s, who dominated both the court and the strategic region of Khurasan. The seeds of this rise 'had been planted by Nūḥ ibn Naṣr when he consigned his three sons to the care of *mamlūk* guardians', presumably so that they might act as guarantors of his succession arrangements (see Treadwell 1991: 235–7; Muqaddasī 1906: 337). It may have been these *mamlūk* guardians who secured ʿAbd al-Malik's accession in 343/954; it was certainly Manṣūr's guardian, Fā'iq al-Khāṣṣa, who was responsible for deposing Manṣūr's nephew Naṣr ibn ʿAbd al-Malik (who ruled for a single day) and brought Manṣūr to the throne (Treadwell 1991: 337–8). During ʿAbd al-Malik's reign the chief *ḥājib* Alptigīn had controlled affairs in the capital; in Manṣūr's, it was the kingmaker Fā'iq. Competition between the *mamlūk*s was fierce, however, and none of them succeeded in gaining absolute dominance.

By the late Sāmānid period relations with the steppe Turks had improved, and as there were no longer regular campaigns launched against the Turks, the *ghāzī* elements in their army were obliged to look elsewhere, chiefly towards the Byzantine and Indian frontiers. Frye suggests that this situation 'led to an "exodus" of *ghāzī*s which left the Sāmānid military establishment free to impose its will on the state' (1965: 150; Treadwell [1991: 234] considers this something of an overstatement). Mass conversions of steppe Turks had also taken place, largely, it seems, at the hands of Ḥanafī preachers (Madelung 1971: 117–23; Treadwell 1991: 233–4 and the sources cited); and there were extensive efforts to convert members of other religious minorities, and not only by 'mainstream' Sunnīs. The Karrāmī Abū Yaʿqūb Isḥāq ibn Maḥmashād (d. 383/993) is 'said to have converted more than 5,000 Christians, Jews, and Zoroastrians' in the region of Bukhara (Bosworth 1960: 7). Some of these conversions may have been responses to apocalyptic expectations and to Bāṭinī and other sectarian preaching. Moreover, Sāmānid relations with the caliphate had seriously deteriorated following the fall of Baghdad to the Būyids in 333/945. At the behest of the Būyids, the caliph al-Muṭīʿ (334–63/946–74) had supported Abū ʿAlī Chaghānī's claim as governor of Khurasan; clearly the Sāmānids could no longer continue to rely on caliphal recognition, and they, in turn, refused to recognise the

Būyid-appointed caliph al-Qādir (381–422/991–1031) and gave shelter to the pretender Muḥammad ibn al-Mustakfī. They also ceased to supply the Abbasids with slave soldiers (see Daniel 1995: 6). Although several truces were concluded between Sāmānid and Būyid rulers, this did not put an end to Sāmānid–Būyid conflicts (see Treadwell 1991: 223–4; Gardīzī 1968: 164; Muqaddasī 1906: 442). All these conditions, plus the increasing influence of the Turkish *mamlūks*, contributed to what was to be a period of crisis for Sāmānid sovereignty.

It was during this period of crisis that in 352/963 Manṣūr ibn Nūḥ commissioned his vizier Abū ʿAlī Balʿamī to translate Muḥammad ibn Jarīr Ṭabarī's general history, the *Ta'rīkh al-rusul wa-al-mulūk*, into Persian. At the same time, the order was also given to translate Ṭabarī's other great work, his Koranic *Tafsīr*.

> The chronological information provided by the prefaces about the timing of the translations is quite precise. Both attribute the initiative for the translation to Manṣūr ibn Nūḥ ... and indicate that the order was conveyed by his closest mentor, the Turkish chamberlain al-Fā'iq ... Similarities in the wording of the two prefaces further suggests that they were prepared more or less simultaneously and perhaps in conjunction with each other ... In any case, the prefaces to the translations clearly imply that their production was a major innovation, which was introduced very carefully and deliberately, and at a very discrete moment in time. (Daniel 1995: 5)

Elton Daniel has argued that this translation project was linked both with the Sāmānids' efforts to legitimate their rule in the East and with their desire to present an ideologically 'correct' version of Islamic history and doctrine intended to counter the teachings of various heterodox and sectarian groups, including the Bāṭinīs and the populist Karrāmiyya sect, active in both Khurasan and Transoxania (Daniel 1990, 1995; see also Meisami 1993).[5] The project 'almost certainly constituted an effort to propagate a state-sanctioned, "official" ideology of Islamic history and dogma, presumably in defence of the Sāmānid regime' (Daniel 1990: 286). There were however other aspects to this legitimating enterprise. One was genealogical. Claims to descent from ancient Persian rulers or commanders were widespread amongst the emergent independent dynasties of the 3rd/9th and 4th/10th centuries; they included those of the Ṭāhirids (from both Rustam and Khuzāʿa), the Ṣaffārids (through the Sasanian Khusraw II Parvīz to Farīdūn, Jamshīd and the first man, Kayūmars), the Būyids (from the Sasanian Bahrām V Gūr), the Sāmānids (from Khusraw II's general Bahrām Chūbīn; see further below) and, later, the Ghaznavids (to a daughter of Yazdigird III, last of the Sasanians) (for a discussion see Bosworth 1973a). While it is unclear to what extent these claims were actually believed, they constituted a powerful propaganda weapon in attracting the allegiance of various groups.

The Sāmānids had, as it were, several major political constituencies: the aristocratic *dihqān* class of Transoxania and Khurasan, from which they themselves had sprung; a mixed group which included individuals of Arab lineage (descended from the military conquerors and from emigrants to the towns of Khurasan and Transoxania) as well as Iranian converts to Islam associated with the Arabs as clients, whose culture was highly Arabised; and a third group made up of the large numbers of Turks brought into the Sāmānid realm as slaves (*mamlūks*), many of whom rose to prominence and power in the Sāmānid court and military. All these groups were potential targets for various versions of history – and, indeed, for different versions of history. One version was represented by works in the *Shāhnāma* tradition; another was the Islamic narrative seen in Balʿamī's version of Ṭabarī.

Religiously, the Sāmānids 'generally supported the de facto position of Ḥanafī, and to a lesser degree Shāfiʿī, Islam as official state orthodoxy', perhaps in reaction both to the increasing success of the Karrāmiyya and to the 'spread of a Khurāsānī variety of Ismāʿīlī Shīʿism' among the court élites. The Sāmānid ruler, Daniel argues, would have felt 'anxiety over the spread of heterodoxy, concern to maintain ties with the ulema, fears of sectarian coups among the bureaucracy or army, and concern over the form of Islam to be adopted as the result of the conversion of Central Asian Turks' (1995: 6). Daniel also sees a connection between the succession struggle following the death of ʿAbd al-Malik ibn Nūḥ and Manṣūr ibn Nūḥ's authorisation, two years after his accession, of the Ṭabarī translations. ʿAbd al-Malik's two brothers, Naṣr and Manṣūr, were supported by different factions at court: Naṣr (the 'king for a day') by the *ḥājib* Alptigīn and Abū ʿAlī Balʿamī, Manṣūr by his mentor Fāʾiq. On his accession, Manṣūr sent Abū Manṣūr Ṭūsī in pursuit of Alptigīn, who withdrew, ultimately, to Ghazna; Abū Manṣūr, 'fearing a plot against his life', rebelled, with the consequences seen earlier.

> There is much that still seems mysterious about this account of events. Why was the Sāmānid offensive against the rebellious Alptigīn not pressed more vigorously? If, as sources such as Miskawayh suggest, Alptigīn had in fact routed the army sent against him, why would he and Balʿamī not make another effort to bring Naṣr to power? Why did Ibn ʿAbd al-Razzāq suspect treachery, and why did the Amīr Manṣūr suddenly reverse course and decide to turn against him rather than pursue

> Alptigīn? If Balʿamī was involved in the move to put Naṣr ibn Nūḥ on the throne and was known to be ... Alptigīn's right-hand man who did not make a move without consulting him, how did he manage to hold on to the office of vizier? [And] why would he then be entrusted, with the apparent blessing and support of his erstwhile rival al-Fā'iq, with the translation of Ṭabarī's history? (1995: 7)

Daniel links these questions to an account in the Saljūq vizier Niẓām al-Mulk's *Siyar al-mulūk* which asserts that, fifteen years after Manṣūr succeeded Nūḥ (no mention is made of ʿAbd al-Malik), Ismāʿīlī missionaries converted a number of important members of the court, including Manṣūr's chief *ḥājib* Manṣūr ibn Bayqārā (or Bā'iqrā), Abū ʿAbd Allāh Jayhānī (the son of Naṣr ibn Aḥmad's vizier) and Abū Manṣūr Ṭūsī. These powerful courtiers persuaded Manṣūr to imprison Abū ʿAlī Balʿamī and the Turkish general Biktūzūn (Begtuzun), chief of the palace *ghulāms*, and tried to convince him that Alptigīn had rebelled. Alptigīn's warning against the Ismāʿīlī threat went unheeded; but the chief *qāḍī* of Bukhara succeeded in alerting Manṣūr to the danger. After dealing with revolts by the Safīdjāmagān (Sipīdjāmagān, on whom see below) in Farghana and the Qarmaṭīs in Khurasan, who had joined forces to overthrow the Sāmānids, Manṣūr released his prisoners. A public debate was held at court, attended by the chief *qāḍī* and the *ʿulamā*; the Ismāʿīlīs were defeated and discredited, military measures were taken to suppress the heretics, and (Niẓām al-Mulk adds) religious scholars were sent to outlying areas 'to teach the rebels the religious law' (Niẓām al-Mulk 1978: 221–6; see also Treadwell 1991: 200–5).

Noting the clearly erroneous chronology of this account, Daniel suggests that Niẓām al-Mulk mistook Manṣūr for Nūḥ I's immediate successor, and that the 'fifteen years' should be counted from ʿAbd al-Malik's accession; thus the events in question would have occurred around the time of ʿAbd al-Malik's death and Manṣūr's accession. This is supported by somewhat obscure references in other sources to disturbances towards the end of ʿAbd al-Malik's reign and to 'policy shifts such as his cultivation of Ibn ʿAbd al-Razzāq, his apparent removal of Alptigīn as commander-in-chief, and his alienation from predominately Turkish elements in the army'. It might have been suspected that he was 'reverting back to policies reminiscent of those of his grandfather Naṣr ibn Aḥmad – including allowing the Ismāʿīlīs to resume their activities and aligning himself with the old Persian aristocracy and culture', and that initially Manṣūr too might 'have been seen as associated with these interests', until he 'realized that his position was in greater jeopardy from Ibn ʿAbd al-Razzāq and the

Ismāʿīlis', and came to a rapprochement with Alptigīn and Balʿamī. 'If so, Niẓām al-Mulk's account actually offers a great deal to flesh out what might be the other half of the Alptigīn episode ... and ... would throw an entirely different light on the commissioning of the Ṭabarī translations and the problems connected with them insofar as they suggest that Balʿamī was the ideological point-man in the assault on religious heterodoxy' (1995: 7–8). Balʿamī was in all probability the motivating force behind the translations; that the commission for both was delivered via Fāʾiq lends strength to the argument that they were designed to unite heterogeneous elements under the banner of Persian Islam.

Balʿamī presents a unified narrative of Islamic (and pre-Islamic) history which leads directly (if only implicitly) to the Sāmānids. He restructured Ṭabarī's discrete accounts into a continuous narrative, omitting some, correcting others and adding yet others – all in a style which is simple, straightforward and entertaining, and accessible to a broad and relatively unsophisticated audience.[6] While the manuscript tradition of the History presents many problems – the central one being whether any of the various traditions represents Balʿamī's original, 'authentic' text (see Daniel 1990) – my feeling is that, even if no recension can be considered totally reliable, certain topics stand out which address issues of concern in the latter half of the 4th/10th century.[7]

Two problematic passages (both usually considered spurious; see Daniel 1990) appear at the beginning of the work, following the preface (of which two, one in Arabic and one in Persian, exist, the Arabic one generally considered as being the older, 'original' preface, although there is no particular reason why they should not be viewed as 'alternatives' intended for different audiences: the Arabic for the patron, the Persian for a more general audience). The first passage, on the 'duration of the world' (*rūzgār-i ʿālam*), explicitly designated as not in Ṭabarī, begins with the views of the Greek astronomers on the position of the planets at the moment of Creation, gives various Persian traditions ('preserved by the *dihqāns*') on the age of the world at the time of the Prophet's appearance, cites sundry Jewish, Christian and Muslim traditions to the same effect, and concludes with another (going back to David) that no one but God knows the date of the Day of Judgement.

As similar passages occur in other works (for example in Maqdisī's near-contemporary *Kitāb al-badʾ wa-al-taʾrīkh*) there seems no good reason why Balʿamī should not have treated a subject which was a matter of obvious concern. The preface to Maʿmarī's prose *Shāhnāma* contains a similar passage, but there the authorities cited are entirely

Persian, being, in the first instance, 'the book(s) of Ibn Muqaffa', Ḥamza Iṣfahānī, and their like' (confirmed by earlier Middle Persian sources), who stated that when they began writing (which was around two centuries apart) 5,700 years had elapsed since the creation of Adam to their own time. 'And from their collapse' (it is unclear whether this refers to the Sasanians, who have just been mentioned, or to Ibn al-Muqaffa''s contemporaries the Umayyads [132/749], which seems more likely) 'let (another) 200 years pass and we shall say how many years have passed from Adam's time' (Minorsky 1956: 173). Counting the '200 years' from the collapse of the Umayyads [132/749], we arrive at the (approximate) date when the prose *Shāhnāma* was compiled: 346/957; this date (5,900+ years) also signals the approach of the seventh millennium following Adam's creation, which according to the Ismā'īlīs would be the last of the seven thousand-year cycles of prophecy and would witness the appearance of the Mahdī who would usher in the End of Days.

While several passages in the *Tafsīr* also deal with the 'duration of the world', these do not refer to Greek traditions. We may recall that Bal'amī's commission to translate the History was transmitted by the *ḥājib* Fā'iq, who is sometimes referred to as 'Rūmī', that is, of Greek, rather than Turkish, origin (see Treadwell 1991: 58 and n. 81, 316). This suggests a heterogeneous, probably courtly, audience for the work. The view that the world has a finite, divinely determined beginning and ending and that the date of its end is unknowable to humankind, even to the Prophet himself, does indeed seem intended to counter the Ismā'īlī concept of cyclical history; there are however some ambiguities in the passages in the *Tafsīr* (see further below.)

The second passage also has parallels (with some variation) in the *Tafsīr* (see the commentary on Sūra 2, 'al-Baqara' [1988, 1: 24–44]). While there are precedents for this account in earlier Arabic sources (albeit rather brief and sketchy), there is nothing comparable to its elaboration here. The pagans of Mecca go to the Jews of Khaybar, Fadak and Wadī al-Qurā and ask them to set questions for the Prophet, drawn from the Torah, which he must answer to prove the truth of his mission. 'The Jews examined the entire Torah and drew from it the most difficult questions, twenty-eight in number, and told them, "Ask him these questions; if his answers accord with what is found in the Torah, you will know that he is a true prophet and must be believed in"' (Bal'amī 1984: 28). The twenty-eight questions (we may note the importance of the number seven and multiples thereof for the Ismā'īlis, twenty-eight having a special significance as, among other things, the number of speech) essentially encompass knowledge of all that is in creation, beyond which no other knowledge –

specifically, of astronomy and cosmology – is necessary. (The *Tafsīr* notes the Prophet's prohibition of the search for such knowledge beyond what is practically necessary [see 1988, 1: 16–18].) In replying to the question, 'What is the date of the Hour?' the Prophet denies that he, or any human, has been granted knowledge of what only God can know. Aside from the structural function of this passage, which reorganises Ṭabarī's disjointed and rambling accounts of cosmology (and other materials) into the more coordinated, not to say dramatic, format of the Prophet's responses to the questions, it serves to demonstrate both the extent of prophetic and the limitations of human knowledge. The Koran revealed to the Prophet contains all necessary knowledge; thus there is no need for any other teacher to explain what Revelation left unsaid, or for esoteric interpretation (*ta'wīl*) of a 'inner meaning' (*bāṭin*) that does not exist.

Underlying both of the Ṭabarī translations is another theme of significance: that of the transfer of learning as indicative of the transfer of power (we may recall Maʿmarī's treatment of this theme in the prose *Shāhnāma*). While this theme is not stated explicitly, it is of central importance to the translation project. Following the Arab conquests, when temporal power passed from the Persians to the Arabs, so did Persian learning, translated into Arabic, as well as Persian cultural, administrative and imperial traditions. Now that learning was, as it were, coming home, as it was retranslated into Persian at the behest of Persian-speaking rulers. What better way for the Sāmānids to symbolise their appropriation of temporal power in the East than by the appropriation of Ṭabarī's authoritative History, 'Persianised' with respect to both its perspective and its form?

The Persianisation of form is represented by the transformation of Ṭabarī's discrete accounts into continuous narrative. As to that of perspective, while Balʿamī follows the broad outlines of Ṭabarī's History, he is much more concerned to coordinate the components of pre-Islamic history – the history of the prophets of Israel, from Adam onwards, and that of the kings of Persia – from the standpoint of the chronology of the latter, which many historians considered the only reliable pre-Islamic chronology. If, as Tarif Khalidi suggests, Ṭabarī's History presented the Islamic *umma* as 'the prophetic heir of the Biblical tradition and the imperial heir of Persian dominion' (1994: 79), for Balʿamī, Persian history is central; and Islamic history is presented from a Persian – largely Khurasanian – perspective, focusing on the conquests during the early caliphate, on the governors of Khurasan under the Umayyads, and on events in Khurasan during the Abbasid caliphate. (Conspicuously, Balʿamī omits any references to the early Sāmānids, whom Ṭabarī treats as governors of Transoxania and thus as vassals of the Abbasids, and to their victories over the Turks.)

Balʿamī's lengthy account of the rise of the Abbasids (which, he states, he collected and organised from Ṭabarī's 'scattered' accounts, adding to them much that was not in Ṭabarī [1994, 2: 1,006]) illustrates this Khurasanian perspective. It focuses almost exclusively on the rise of the *daʿwa* in the East, attributing to the Prophet a prediction, made to his uncle ʿAbbās, that the caliphate would pass to his descendants, whose rule would last until the End of Days, and that the support for their *daʿwa* would come from the East [1994, 2: 1,031]), stressing that the Abbasids' success was due to the Persians (1994, 2: 1,035), and presenting the outcome – the assumption of the caliphate by the Hāshimites (who had become 'greedy for the caliphate' [1994, 2: 1,024]) rather than the ʿAlids as a betrayal of the revolution and of the expectations of many who had supported it (1994, 2: 1,042). He treats at some length events in the career of the charismatic Abū Muslim, leader of the *daʿwa* in Khurasan, and his account of Abū Muslim's murder by the second Abbasid caliph, Abū Jaʿfar al-Manṣūr (which is something of a set piece for most historians), is both detailed and dramatic. (On Abū Muslim see Lassner 1986: 99–133; Mélikoff 1962.)

Al-Manṣūr had long harboured an animus against Abū Muslim, and had urged his brother Abū al-ʿAbbās al-Saffāḥ, the first Abbasid caliph, to kill him. Al-Saffāḥ refused, saying that the caliphate had need of Abū Muslim, that if he were killed the provinces would rise up against the Abbasids, and that such a deed would earn him (the caliph) lasting blame (see 1994, 2: 1,081). When al-Manṣūr became caliph he began to plot Abū Muslim's downfall. First, he summoned him from his camp on the river Zab near Harran (the base for his successful campaign against an ʿAlid rebel), ostensibly to reward his services. Abū Muslim declined, and wrote back,

> 'Today you have no need of me. In the Persian books they say that viziers must be in greatest fear of kings at that time when the world is at peace and the kings have no more foes; for as long as the kingdom has enemies, and kingship is unsettled, the king requires a vizier to protect him, but when all is at peace, he will soon destroy him.' (1994, 2: 1,082)

After some time Abū Muslim was prevailed upon to obey the caliph's summons. His comrades warned him that, should the caliph forget his obligations towards his servant, break his bond of loyalty and make an attempt upon his life, Abū Muslim should himself turn upon the caliph; this he approved (1994, 2: 1,084). When he appeared in the caliph's presence, still wearing his travelling clothes, al-Manṣūr was so angry he could not speak politely, and told him to go away and rest for the night. Then he regretted his action, fearing that Abū Muslim might leave and he would lose his chance. His secretary-vizier Abū Ayyūb (al-Mūriyānī) advised him to be patient overnight, and on the morrow he would deliver Abū Muslim to him. He then went to Abū Muslim, who had been frightened by the caliph's manner, and reassured him that all was well.

None of the parties slept that night; on the morrow, Abū Ayyūb devised a scheme to kill Abū Muslim. Armed guards were stationed behind the curtains of the caliph's tent, while he himself placed his sword on the ground beside him, so as to appear harmless. When Abū Muslim entered al-Manṣūr enquired if he had slept well, and Abū Muslim was somewhat calmed. The caliph managed to divest Abū Muslim of his sword on the pretense of examining it, set it aside and began to rebuke Abū Muslim for his past actions. Abū Muslim responded to his charges one by one. The caliph exclaimed, 'Woe to you, Abū Mujrim [criminal]! Whatever I say, you bring an argument against it, hoping to save yourself!' He clapped his hands; the guards appeared, swords drawn.

> Abū Muslim said, 'O Commander of the Faithful, do not kill me! Retain me, so that whenever an enemy appears against you I may sacrifice my life for you!' Manṣūr replied, 'Woe to you! I have no worse enemy on the face of the earth than you!' Then he said: 'Strike!' (1994, 2: 1,090–1)

The guards fell upon Abū Muslim and killed him. They rolled him in the blood-drenched carpet on which he had stood, hid it in a corner of the tent, and spread a new carpet. No one outside knew what had happened; al-Manṣūr's nephew ʿĪsā ibn Mūsā (the governor of Kufa) entered and, thinking Abū Muslim had not yet arrived, offered to bring him, reminding the caliph of his services and urging that he be treated well. Al-Manṣūr replied, 'I have done so; there he is, in that carpet!' ʿĪsā reproached him, saying, 'He was my friend'; the caliph told him, 'By God, you had no worse enemy on the face of the earth; for as long as he lived, neither would my caliphate be strong, nor would you succeed me' (1994, 2: 1,092). Thus was the Abbasid caliphate made firm by the death of the man who had brought it to power and served it well. (Compare Ṭabarī's account of these events, 1995: 18–44.)

It was maintained by its Persian administrators, without whom the Arabs would have been incapable of governing the lands they had conquered or running the affairs of the caliphate. This is the conclusion arrived at in Balʿamī's account of the destruction of the Barmakid family of viziers by the Abbasid caliph Hārūn al-Rashīd –

an event which provided generations of historians with an occasion for constructing exemplary narratives (see Meisami 1989, and the references cited). The Barmakids' influence, high position and great wealth excited jealousy, and they were accused of treachery, embezzlement and heresy. The reasons adduced for their fall from favour (including the involvement of Jaʿfar the Barmakid with Hārūn's sister ʿAbbāsa) need not concern us here; what is important is Balʿamī's comment that after his destruction of the Barmakids Hārūn al-Rashīd lost all respect and was, without those able (Persian) administrators, unable to govern his domains. In this we sense a foreshadowing of the decline of Abbasid power.

Of interest in connection with the argument that the History was designed to counter heretical teachings is Balʿamī's account of the heresy of Muqannaʿ, the 'Veiled Prophet'.[8] Muqannaʿ appeared during the disturbances which preceded the fall of the Umayyads; he took control of the region of Soghdia and collected taxes there. He attracted many converts and assembled a large army (among them many Turks); his followers were called the Sipīd-Jāmagān, 'Wearers of White', because of the colour of their robes. The Abbasid caliphs al-Manṣūr, al-Mahdī and al-Hādī sent their commanders against them, and a number of battles took place, in which victory went first to one side and then to the other. Finally Muqannaʿ, besieged in one of his fortresses, poisoned all of his (one hundred) wives, then slew all of his fighting men. One woman, named Bānūqa, escaped.

> Bānūqa relates: 'I saw him, like a frenzied camel, sword in hand. He had a servant; he hacked that servant limb from limb. There was a fiery oven; he threw himself into that oven, and said, "I have destroyed so many people; in the end, I myself must be burned!"'
>
> When Bānūqa saw that he was dead, she went to the roof of the fortress and shouted [to the troops below], 'Do you want me to open the gates of the fortress?' Saʿīd [Ḥarashī, the Muslim commander] replied, 'Yes, I do.' She said, 'I'll do so on condition that you don't touch my gowns and robes, and give me ten thousand dirhams from the treasury.' Saʿīd agreed; he thought, however, that Muqannaʿ was still alive. Bānūqa came and opened the gates of the fortress; the troops entered, and fulfilled their promise (to her), and removed the treasuries. ʿAbd Allāh ibn ʿĀmir ibn ʿAmr al-Qurashī was there; they brought him to Saʿīd. Saʿīd spat in his face and said, 'Your forefathers were enemies of the Family of Muḥammad, and you – cursed one! – became an unbeliever at a stroke!' He (then) commanded that his head be cut off. Saʿīd (and his troops) returned, conquering and

> victorious, sent a *fatḥnāma* to the Caliph Mahdī [read: Hādī] and the Muslims, and the Muslims rejoiced without limit. (1984, 3: 1,598–9)

Remarkably, this account contains no reference to Muqanna''s teachings, nor does it accuse him (as for example does Gardīzī) of claiming to be a prophet or of deceiving his followers by charlatanry. He is treated primarily as having claimed rule over Soghdia. The Sipīd-Jāmagān were still active in Transoxania (and if Niẓām al-Mulk is to be believed, had recently joined the Bāṭinīs in a revolt against the Sāmānids). If they were viewed as a threat, why are their beliefs not censured? The one person singled out for censure is the (unidentified) 'Abd Allāh al-Qurashī, said both to have first opposed the 'Alids (that is, the Abbasid *da'wa*) and then to have converted to Muqanna''s heresy.

Nor does Bal'amī mention other heresies that sprang up around the same time, such as that of Bihāfarīd, which was put down by Abū Muslim. He does mention Sunbādh's revolt, but not his teaching: that Abū Muslim had not died but was in concealment (along with the Mahdī and Mazdak) and would return to usher in the End of Days. Sunbādh is presented as a wealthy Magian whom Abū Muslim had treated well, who felt obliged to seek revenge for his murder, and who was defeated by an Abbasid general who appropriated his treasuries for himself (see 1994, 2: 1,093–4; for a contrasting view see *EI*², s.v.). If the purpose of the history was indeed to counter heretical beliefs prevalent in Transoxania and Khurasan, one would have expected a more determined effort to refute them.[9] But opportunities seized upon by later historians (largely pro-Abbasid), including the tendency to trace all heresies back to that of Mazdak and to see them as attempts to re-establish not only Persian rule but Persian religion, are ignored by Bal'amī.

Lastly, in the context of the Sāmānid legitimatory project, we may examine Bal'amī's treatment of the revolt of the commander Bahrām Chūbīn against the Sasanian rulers Hurmuz and his son Khusraw II Parvīz, which is far more detailed than Ṭabarī's brief account. The Sāmānid claim to descent from Bahrām Chūbīn may well have been genuine, or based on local traditions. (It is mentioned by Narshakhī in his history of Bukhara and by the geographer Iṣṭakhrī, and was accepted without question by Bīrūnī.) It has however seemed somewhat puzzling, since from the point of view of official Sasanian historiography Bahrām Chūbīn was a rebel against the legitimate sovereign. Treadwell suggests that the reason behind this claim was Bahrām Chūbīn's fame as a scourge of the Turks (1991: 30; see also Iṣṭakhrī 1870: 143); but by Manṣūr ibn Nūḥ's reign campaigns against the steppe Turks had ceased, and Turkish *mamlūk*s were an important and influential element at court. Moreover, Balʿamī omits any references to Sāmānid victories against the Turks. Might there have been other reasons to promote this claim at this particular time?

Bahrām Chūbīn was descended from the Sasanian princely house of Mihrān, who ruled the city of Rayy, and ultimately from the Arsacids (see Czeglédy 1958: 25; *EIr*, art. 'Bahrām Čōbīn'). The Sāmānids claimed Rayy as part of their domains, and it was a major bone of contention in their conflicts with the Būyids; descent from Bahrām Chūbīn would have reinforced their claim to it. Moreover, especially in popular traditions, in part due to the influence of the popular *Romance of Bahrām Chūbīn* which appeared in late Sasanian times and was preserved by various Arabic historians (see Czeglédy 1958; Altheim 1958), the official Sasanian view of Bahrām as villainous usurper had given way to his portrayal as eschatological hero, often conflated with other such figures both Zoroastrian and Islamic, and identified with the 'King from the East' whose appearance would restore justice to the earth, as well as Persian religion and Persian rule, and would herald the approach of the End of Days.

The Arabic historian Dīnawarī presented Bahrām Chūbīn as a man of honour compelled by his troops to rebel against his sovereign (see Altheim 1958). A similar treatment is seen in Balʿamī's Ṭabarī, as well as in Thaʿālibī's *Ghurar akhbār mulūk al-Furs* and in Gardīzī. Bahrām, summoned by Hurmuz to combat external foes (Arabs, Byzantines, Turks) who have joined forces and threaten the very existence of Īrānshahr, defeats them; after which Hurmuz doubly insults him, first by accusing him of treacherously appropriating part of the spoils due the ruler, and second by sending him women's garments and a spindle in place of robes of honour. This last insult outrages Bahrām's troops, who threaten to desert him if he does not rebel against Hurmuz. He does so, and briefly (in 589 Common Era) occupies the throne; but he is ultimately defeated by Hurmuz's son Khusraw Parvīz, and forced to flee to Tūrān (Transoxania), where he is murdered. (Firdawsī's treatment of this story in the *Shāhnāma* is, despite the view of some scholars to the contrary, less sympathetic, if more complex: Bahrām is presented from the outset as arrogant, hot-tempered, and quick to take rash and irrevocable decisions, and his stated aim is no less than the overthrow of the Sasanians and the extermination of their line.)

Balʿamī's detailed treatment of the story of Bahrām Chūbīn seems designed to validate the Sāmānid claim to rule of the East (and in particular of Khurasan, of which Rayy was considered a part). The Būyid ruler of Rayy, Rukn al-Dawla, had assumed the Persian title of *shāhanshāh* ('king of kings') (it appears on coinage of 351/962; according to another source, it was used even earlier, in 325/936–7, by his elder brother 'Īmād al-Dawla 'Alī [see Madelung 1971: 85, 89]). The Sāmānids may well have been launching a counter-claim by virtue of which they presented themselves as truly authentic Persian rulers of the East – a claim both prior chronologically to that of the Būyids (in view of Bahrām's ultimate descent from the Arsacids) and broader territorially (by virtue of his descent from the rulers of Rayy), as well as authentically Persian. Moreover, in view of the extent to which the Sāmānids' own vassals (Abū 'Alī Chaghānī, Abū Manṣūr Ṭūsī) were wont to shift allegiance to and from the Būyids, the claim might also have been intended to align the latter with the unjust (Sasanian/Abbasid) usurpers. All of this requires more detailed study; but Bal'amī's generally sympathetic portrayal of Bahrām Chūbīn can scarcely have been fortuitous.

Daniel argues that the Ṭabarī translations were designed 'to reshape [Ṭabarī's] texts and in effect to discourage the reading of the Arabic originals. In that sense, [they] constituted a virtual declaration of political and cultural autonomy conceived as part of a futile effort to save the Sāmānid polity' (1995: 5, 11). They were also intended to discredit Ismā'īlī cyclical history 'and ... to reassure readers that the end of the world, and thus the collapse of Sāmānid authority, was not imminent' (1995: 11). They 'could be used to instruct unsophisticated believers in a uniform way and avoid the dangers of ad hoc responses to heterodoxy by local religious leaders', while serving to promote 'the further Persianization of frontier areas and the acculturation of the new Turkish military elite' (1995: 12).

There are a number of passages, especially in the *Tafsīr*, which seem to express anti-Ismā'īlī themes. But I believe that the situation is more complex. The inclusion (especially in the History) of many Jewish, Christian and Zoroastrian traditions not found in Ṭabarī suggests a potential audience for the translations which has not, to my knowledge, been explored: that they were aimed at convincing members of those non-Muslim communities of the truth of Islam as mediated by the Sāmānids, legitimate Persian-Islamic rulers of the East. This can be argued both from the alignment of non-Muslim traditions with Islamic universal history and from the frequent invocation of Jewish authority as proof of Islam. We may also recall the efforts during this period to convert members of non-Muslim communities, in which 'orthodox' Sunnī (largely Ḥanafī) preachers competed with the Karrāmīs and with heterodox Shī'ī movements.

There are interesting differences, in terms of tone and of emphasis, between the translations of the History and of the *Tafsīr*. The *Tafsīr*'s commentary on the opening Sūra of the Koran, 'al-Fātiḥa', dwells at length on the theme of gratitude, which includes 'thanking God for creating you and giving you health and making you a member of the community of Muḥammad, the Seal of the Prophets, for whose sake God created both this world and the next; and for having brought you forth at the End of Time, that is close to Resurrection'. Here, as elsewhere, there is a strong suggestion that, despite the disclaimer that no one (not even the Prophet) knows the exact date of the Hour, that the End of Days is imminent. (Elsewhere, enumerating the signs that will precede the End of Days, the *Tafsīr* quotes a Prophetic tradition in circulation at this time to the effect that these will appear as the year 400 (1009–10) approaches [1988, 3: 1,615–16].)

Gratitude, states the *Tafsīr*, is incumbent upon all; ingratitude towards one's benefactor, as manifested by disloyalty, treachery or rebellion, is among the greatest of sins. Other comments address points of doctrine (although with little complexity); while a gloss on the verse, 'Guide us in the straight path, the path of those on whom You have bestowed [favour], not of those who have incurred [Your] wrath, nor of those who are astray', identifies the latter as the 'unjust' ('tyrants', 'oppressors') against whom God is angry, 'like the Jews, the Christians, the heretics and those who go astray' (perhaps the Karrāmīs?) (1988, 1: 19). This focus upon the objects of God's wrath, which is appropriate to the *Tafsīr*, finds few parallels in the History, where the issue of loyalty (or gratitude) is approached from a different perspective: that of the obligations of loyalty between rulers and those who serve them. (This issue will be discussed further in Chapter 2.) This suggests that, despite their similarities and frequent overlap in content, the two works were intended to perform different, if complementary, functions. Further evidence for this is the fact that Arabic quotations in the History (Koranic verses, Prophetic traditions, poetry, letters, speeches) are not ordinarily translated, whereas the *Tafsīr* renders the Koranic verses into Persian paraphrase. Thus it appears that the two works were designed to be read in two different contexts. The History would have addressed, first and foremost, a courtly audience, including educated officials, Turkish *mamlūk*s, and other members of a heterogeneous court. The Arabic quotations would have been understood by the royal patron and others cognisant of Arabic. The work's straightforward, often dramatic, style would have appealed to other members of the court and military with less erudition, among whom one can imagine were, in particular, Turkish *ghulām*s being trained up to hold positions of importance. The *Tafsīr* translation seems more suited to teaching, in the mosque or elsewhere, and aimed at a wider audience which might have included members of the court, but which would certainly have incorporated recent or potential converts to Islam of various ethnic origins or communal persuasions. Its apocalyptic references would have addressed contemporary anxieties and underscored the necessity for correct belief.

FIRDAWSĪ'S *SHĀHNĀMA*

In contrast to his father, Manṣūr ibn Nūḥ's son and successor Nūḥ II (365–87/976–97) seems to have reverted to favouring the Iranian historical narrative. By this time, under ʿAḍud al-Dawla (who was recognised as supreme head of the Būyid clan in Jumādā I 365/January 976, but who subsequently had to contend with various rivals), the Būyid effort to appropriate Iranian imperial traditions was in full swing. In 368/979 ʿAḍud al-Dawla ordered Abū Isḥāq al-Ṣabī' to compose his encomiastic history of the Daylamid reign, the *Kitāb al-Tājī*.[10] Although the Sāmānids did not adopt (as did the Būyids) Iranian imperial titulature, they may have seen in the patronising of works in the *Shāhnāma* tradition an effective way of legitimating their rule in the East and their claim to territories contested by the Būyids.

By the latter half of the 4th/10th century the writing of *Shāhnāma*s had become a growth industry. Maʿmarī's prose work was followed by others, in both prose and verse, most of which were composed or begun during the reign of Nūḥ II ibn Manṣūr. Shortly after his accession, Nūḥ commissioned the poet Daqīqī to write a *Shāhnāma* in verse; it was left unfinished when Daqīqī was murdered around 367/977. It was probably shortly after this that Firdawsī, apparently independently of royal patronage, began his own *Shāhnāma*; it was completed in 400/1010, by which time the Sāmānids were themselves history.[11] It is often argued that Firdawsī must have been displeased by the Sāmānids' replacement by the Turkish Ghaznavids. We do not know Firdawsī's views on the Sāmānids, as he does not mention them, although he does refer to, and praise, a number of the notables of his native city of Ṭūs. But when Maḥmūd of Ghazna became established as supreme Ghaznavid sultan in 389/999 Firdawsī began sending that ruler portions of his poem, accompanied by panegyrics (see Rypka 1968: 155–7, and the references cited). The panegyrics present Maḥmūd as ruler of a unified Īrānzamīn whose history proceeds from its earliest rulers to the Muslim conquest. This 'dream or fiction' – which, states Frye, was possible of realisation only in Islamic times, 'with the expansion of Persian ... and other local traditions into a general, synthetic all-Iranian, but Islamic, tradition' (1965: 98) – finds its fullest expression in Firdawsī's poem.

The *Shāhnāma* details the history of three successive Iranian dynasties, the Pīshdādīs, Kayānids and Sasanians. Consistent with its eastern orientation, the Seleucids are ignored, the Achaemenids omitted except for the last few rulers, and the Parthians/Arsacids of Western Iran (the petty kings) dismissed in a few lines. Each dynasty begins auspiciously, then falls into moral and political decline, and ends with the assumption of rule by an outsider. Kayūmars, the first king, establishes the institution of kingship; his grandson Hūshang inaugurates the Pīshdādīs dynasty, whose fourth ruler, Jamshīd, begins as a just king who brings all the accomplishments and amenities of civilisation to his subjects. Later however he becomes prideful and turns away from God. His nobles rebel and replace him with the evil Arab king Ẕaḥḥāk, who kills Jamshīd and begins a thousand-year rule of cruelty. This is finally ended when the blacksmith Kāva, with the help of a legitimate prince of the line, Farīdūn, captures Ẕaḥḥāk and imprisons him forever in Mount Damāvand.

Farīdūn, who restores the Pīshdādī line, divides the world between his three sons: the west to Salm, Tūrān (Transoxania) to Tūr, and Iran to Īraj. Salm and Tūr, jealous of Īraj, murder him; his death is avenged by his son and successor Manūchihr. These events inaugurate a lengthy cycle of wars of revenge between Iran and Tūrān which dominates the Kayānid period, whose line is founded by a descendant of Farīdūn, Kayqubād. This portion of the work incorporates the saga of the heroes of Sistan – Sām, his son Zāl, and his grandson Rustam – who support and maintain the monarchy, and whose fortunes are interwoven with those of its rulers. The conflicts engendered by the heroes' moral obligation to support the legitimate ruler are exemplified by the career of Rustam, whose life spans nearly the whole of this period, and who serves sovereigns who are often weak, arrogant and foolish. We may suspect, perhaps, an allusion to contemporary conditions under the later Sāmānids, when weak rulers were manipulated by their *mamlūk*s, and embarked upon disastrous military adventures such as that in Sistan in the late 360s/970s (see Chapter 2).

The prophet Zoroaster appears in the Kayānid period, and the current ruler Gushtāsb adopts Zoroastrianism as the state religion. Here Firdawsī incorporates some 1,000 lines by Daqīqī on the rise of Zoroastrianism. Scholarly opinion has seen this as an attempt on the poet's part to distance himself from this account in order not to offend the ultra-orthodox Maḥmūd; since for the most part we cannot know which parts of the poem were written when, this must remain speculation. Rustam's death at the hands of his half-brother Shaghād anticipates the decline of the Kayānids, whose rule is ended by

Alexander's defeat of his half-brother Dārā (Darius). Dārā, like Jamshīd, has become proud: addressing his nobles, he claims complete supremacy and demands tribute from Alexander. Defeated, he refuses to make peace and is murdered by his generals; dying, he entrusts his kingdom to Alexander, who promises to marry his daughter and to uphold the Zoroastrian faith. Unlike Ẕaḥḥāk, Alexander's claim to the throne is legimate, both by descent and by virtue, as he rules justly and supports the true faith. Firdawsī's attribution to him of an Iranian lineage (in which he follows pseudo-Callisthenes) was the subject of some scepticism; Bīrūnī commented on 'the vague opinions which the Persians have devised in a hostile spirit' (see 1879: 22–36). His portrait of Alexander as a just ruler contrasts with the 'mainstream' historiographical tradition (seen for example in Gardīzī) which depicts him as pillaging the Persian cultural heritage: he ordered the Persian books translated into Greek, the originals destroyed and the translations carried back to Greece.

On the advice of Aristotle, Alexander divides Iran into a series of petty kingdoms ruled by the Ashkāniyān (Arsacids/Parthians), to whom Firdawsī devotes a scant twenty-odd lines. Legitimate Iranian rule is finally restored by Ardashīr Bābakān, who reunites the fragmented empire and founds the Sasanian dynasty. Ardashīr, whose testament and counsels establish the principles of royal justice and sound government, is followed by a succession of kings of varying ability, among them Khusraw I Anūshīrvān, guided by his wise minister Buzurgmihr and famed for his justice and support of the true faith. Anūshīrvān's son Hurmuz, who provokes a revolt by his formerly loyal general Bahrām Chūbīn, is deposed by his nobles in the civil war which follows. (As noted earlier, Firdawsī is clearly unsympathetic towards Bahrām Chūbīn, although neither Hurmuz nor Khusraw Parvīz is presented in the best of lights.) Hurmuz's son, Khusraw II Parvīz, seeks military assistance from Rūm (Byzantium), defeats Bahrām and reigns, at first, wisely and justly, bringing Iran to new heights of glory. But towards the end of his long and prosperous reign he inexplicably 'turns from justice to injustice'; his nobles revolt in favour of his son Shīrūya, who imprisons his father and has him murdered. This rebellion and parricide set in motion the rapid decline of the Sasanians; Shīrūya, poisoned after a brief reign, is succeeded by a series of rulers (including several women), most of whom are either killed or die after a short reign. Under the last Sasanian monarch, Yazdigird III, the Iranians are defeated by the Muslim Arabs; Yazdigird, in flight, is betrayed by his Khurasanian governor, who covets the throne, and is murdered at his command. The Sasanian line, and with it Iranian monarchy, is at an end.

The destruction of Iranian sovereignty has been described as the tragic final scene of Iranian history. G. E. von Grunebaum wrote that, 'as a Persian, Firdausī was irremediably humiliated by the Sassanian defeat; as a Muslim he should have felt elated at a development that had brought the true faith to his people and to himself. So the national tradition ended in a melancholy key' (1955: 175). In support of the argument that Firdawsī must have been disillusioned by the replacement of the Persian Sāmānids by the Turkish Ghaznavids, the wars between Iran and Tūrān, and the Sasanian commander Rustam Farrukhzād's warning prophecy, on the eve of the Persian defeat, that 'a worthless slave shall become king, and lineage and nobility shall count for nought' (Yd 104), have been taken as implying disapproval of the Ghaznavids.

Much, indeed, hinges on this prophecy, which states further that 'from Iranians, Turks and Arabs shall appear a race neither high born [*dihqān*], nor Turk, nor Arab' (Yd 105–6). This is a role for which the Daylamid Būyids (neither high born, nor Turk, nor Arab, and enemies both of the high-born Sāmānids and the Ghaznavids) seem better suited. Firdawsī's sources for this prophecy, which he follows closely, have been identified as two Zoroastrian apocalyptic texts: the Middle Persian *Jāmāspnāma* (or more probably a later version thereof) and the *Zarātushtnāma*, written in New Persian verse by one Kay-Kā'ūs (ibn) Kay-Khusraw of Rayy in 347/978, around the time Firdawsī began writing his *Shāhnāma* (see Krasnawolska 1978; de Blois 1992: 171–6). Both works predict the cataclysmic events which will conclude the millennium of Zoroaster: the Arab invasion and the fall of the Sasanians, followed by the domination of the world by evil, the appearance of several 'false rulers' who will, however, be unable to rule Iran for long, and the final appearance from the East of 'a true heir of the [Sasanian] dynasty' (Krasnawolska 1978: 174–5). (These works were moreover considered as sources for predictions of the end of Arab rule and the restoration of Persian; see for example Baghdādī 1935: 119–20.) Krasnawolska argues that 'for Ferdousi – a moslem author who commented the events from the perspective of four hundred years – the Arab invasion was deprived of a manifest eschatological meaning' (1978: 175); but Rustam's prophecy that this disastrous period will last 400 years (Yd 46) ties in both with the eschatological expectations of the Sāmānid period and with Firdawsī's panegyrics to Maḥmūd.

The *Zarātushtnāma* also mentions a 'group dressed in black', of whom Firdawsī states, 'They shall turn away from covenants, and uprightness, and lies and baseness shall be honoured' (Yd 97); this precedes the references to the 'worthless slave' who will become king and the 'race neither high-born, nor Turk, nor Arab' who will 'seek the ruin of others for their own gain, and give religion as the pretext' (Yd 92). Krasnawolska (following Mohl) identifies the 'group dressed in black' as the Abbasids (1978: 178). Black was also the colour of the Sāmānids, emblematic of their loyalty to the caliphate. The impression grows that Firdawsī's feelings towards the Sāmānids, whose rule was by his time clearly in crisis, were ambivalent – not least because those he singles out for praise are not the Sāmānids themselves, but various of their rebellious Ṭūsī vassals. One of these was Abū Manṣūr Ṭūsī, whose prose *Shāhnāma* was a major source for Firdawsī's poem. Another was Amīrak Ṭūsī, an associate of Abū ʿAlī (II) Sīmjūrī, governor of Khurasan under Nūḥ ibn Manṣūr, whose claim to independent rule of Khurasan will be discussed in Chapter 2. (According to the heresiographer Baghdādī, both Abū ʿAlī Sīmjūrī and Amīrak Ṭūsī had Ismāʿīlī sympathies, and both were executed by Maḥmūd [1935: 129–30].)

Implicit in the *Shāhnāma*'s cyclical structure, which embodies the basic historical paradigm of the rise and fall of states and the transfer of rule from one group to another, is the hope for the appearance of a ruler of the East combining Iranian and Islamic ideals of sovereignty. Each Iranian dynasty is founded by a ruler who establishes order and justice; each ends with the moral decline of the current ruler, the political decay of the state, and the assumption of rule by an outsider. The cruel reign of Ẓaḥḥāk and the just rule of Alexander (followed by the petty kings) end with the restoration of Iranian sovereignty; the Islamic conquest concludes both the cycle of Iranian monarchy and the poem. But inscribed in this cycle is the eschatological paradigm: the rule of foreigners will, in the end, give way to that of the legitimate 'King from the East' who will restore Iranian sovereignty and right religion.

That this hope was embodied in Maḥmūd of Ghazna is evident from Firdawsī's panegyrics to that ruler, which punctuate the poem at strategic points (see further Meisami 1993). The first, which concludes the Exordium (A 178–225), refers to Maḥmūd as a 'march lord' (*marzbān*) whose like 'has not appeared since the Creator made this world' (A 178), and whose accession to power is described in traditional Persian imagery: the world enjoys a new spring; Maḥmūd's brilliance outshines the sun. Then, says the poet, 'my sleeping fortune woke, and I knew that it was time to speak, and that now the days of old would be renewed' (A 183–4). In a dream-vision he sees a blazing candle rise from the water to illuminate the world and bring it spring; amidst the brocade-like verdure, the ruler sits upon a turquoise throne, 'like the moon, with a diadem [*tāj*] on his head, in place of the tiara [*kulāh*]' (A 190). (Both diadem and tiara were elements of Sasanian ceremonial headgear; the *tāj*, moreover, had been adapted by the Abbasids; the reference suggests Maḥmūd's assumption of both Iranian and Islamic kingship.) Waking, the poet takes his dream as an auspicious portent, and praises the 'ruler of the age' and his family.

A second lengthy encomium appears at the beginning of the long section on the most heated phase of the war between Iran and Tūrān, which ends with the defeat of Tūrān and the death of its ruler Afrāsiyāb (Jb 3–93). It depicts Maḥmūd as defender of the true faith, whose deeds have 'illuminated the works of history' (Jb 48), and incorporates praise of his vizier, whom the poet thanks for having 'brought to fruition my scattered efforts' (JB 35). (The vizier was Abū al-ʿAbbās Faḍl ibn Aḥmad Isfarā'īnī, former Sāmānid *ṣāḥib-barīd* (chief of intelligence) of Marv, who served Maḥmūd from 385/995 until his fall from favour in 403/1013, and who changed the language of the chancery from Arabic to Persian (see Nāẓim 1971: 135).Then, addressing Maḥmūd, he states:

> O prince, I have performed a service which will remain my memorial in this world. Prosperous buildings become ruined by rain and the heat of the sun; but I have laid in verse the foundation of a lofty palace which will not be harmed by wind and rain. Years will pass over this book, and it will be read continually by all who possess wisdom, and who will praise the world-ruling monarch. (Jb 63–7)

(The motif of the memorialising function of discourse is repeated in a brief panegyric which precedes the account of Rustam's death; see RŠ 21–6.)

Of particular interest are two short passages which introduce the reign of Gushtāsp. In the second of these (GoD 25–33) Firdawsī apologises for incorporating Daqīqī's weak verses, in comparison with which his will be seen to be all the more praiseworthy. In the first (GoD 4–13), Daqīqī appears to Firdawsī in a dream to announce the appearance of a ruler for whom he predicts great achievements, and entreats Firdawsī to include his own verses in the poem, that he may thereby achieve immortality. Daqīqī's prediction is as follows: 'From today till the year 400 his troubles will diminish, but his treasury will not; then he will take his armies to Chīn, and all those great ones will open the way' (GoD 6–7). The date, 400/1009–10, coincides with that of the completion of the *Shāhnāma*; and while it may refer to contemporary events, the resonances of this reference to the end of the fourth Islamic century suggest that Maḥmūd is envisioned as the triumphal ruler whose reign will mark the commencement of the final age.[12]

A longer passage which introduces the brief account of the Ashkāniyān (As 1–45) contrasts the Ghaznavids' far-reaching empire with the divided Iran of the petty kings: Maḥmūd is 'Emperor of Iran and Zabul, from Qannawj [India] to the borders of Kabul; praised be he and his armies, himself, his house and his realm' (As 5–6; Zabul, in Sistan, was Maḥmūd's birthplace). Maḥmūd's brother and commander-in-chief, Abū al-Muẓaffar Naṣr, and his family are also praised, and the poet expresses his gratitude for the remission of the land-tax (*kharāj*) due from him (As 18), an act by which 'the age of Anūshīrvān is renewed' (AS 21; see also Yd 851–3). Firdawsī invokes Anūshīrvān's authority to warn against tyranny on the part of kings, followed by a reminder of the transience of worldly power: 'Where have Farīdūn, Ẕaḥḥāk and Jam gone? the Arab nobles, the Persian kings? Where are those great Sasanians, (those rulers) from the Bahrāmīs to the Sāmānids? ... [All, good and evil, have departed;] only discourse survives in this world as a memorial' (As 34–8).

Two brief passages following Anūshīrvān's counsels celebrate Maḥmūd's defence of the faith and his Indian campaigns (Kn 3,817–21, 3,882–4). In the final panegyric, which concludes the poem (Yd 856–60), the poet complains of old age and poverty and of going unrewarded for his efforts. He praises Maḥmūd – 'the lamp of the Persians, the crown of the Arabs' (Yd 860) – and announces the completion of his work, which will remain his own memorial: 'Henceforth I shall never die; for, having scattered wide the seeds of discourse, I shall live on, and he who possesses wisdom, judgement and faith will praise me after my death' (Yd 864–5).

The panegyrics support the argument that 'in Sultan Maḥmūd the poet evidently thought to find the ardently longed-for man of the "unification of Iran"' (Rypka 1968: 156). They associate Maḥmūd with the defeat of Iran's enemies, with defence of the true faith, with royal justice and the bringing of renewed prosperity to a reunited, Islamic Iran. Both the panegyrics and the poem's major themes reflect the disorder which accompanied the Sāmānids' decline and the hope for a strong ruler who would restore order and justice. Among these themes is one which has received much comment: that of conflict between ruler and vassal, treated at length in the section on the Kayānids and in the account of the revolt of Bahrām Chūbīn. Firdawsī stresses the necessity for loyalty on the part of vassals to their legitimate ruler, even though that ruler may be morally unworthy. Rebellion may lead to evil consequences, among them the imposition of rule by foreigners (Ẕaḥḥāk, the Muslim Arabs). It was disloyal vassals – and particularly Turkish *mamlūk*s – who brought about the fall of the Sāmānids. These rebels were ultimately destroyed by

Maḥmūd, who (like Alexander, who though technically an outsider is not a 'foreigner' because of his Iranian descent) restored order and justice to a realm in moral and political crisis.

It is recorded that Maḥmūd was not pleased by the poet's dedication to him of the *Shāhnāma*, and that his niggardly reward inspired Firdawsī to compose a bitter satire against him.[13] We will address this issue in Chapter 2. Von Grunebaum argued that 'Firdausī is alone among the major contemporary students of history in that he seems to be utterly unable to extract any general ideas from the developments which he presents in such masterly fashion' (1955: 175). Elsewhere in the same essay, however, von Grunebaum himself seems to disagree with this argument (see 1955: 173–4); and, indeed, it is untenable. Firdawsī shares with other historians, and with writers such as Ibn Farīghūn, the notion that the patterns of history constitute a valid paradigm to which the cycle of the rise and fall of states and the transfer of power from one group to another testifies. It is this view of history which infuses an optimistic note into the otherwise gloomy tale of the destruction of Iranian monarchy, by providing hope for a new cycle of prosperity.

Firdawsī's *Shāhnāma* marks the culmination of the tradition it represents. Various spin-offs from this tradition, dealing with figures not treated in detail by Firdawsī and reflecting various local traditions, and often highly Islamicised, were used as historical sources by other writers; but they themselves are beyond the scope of this study (see Hanaway 1978). The intended audience for the poem was presumably, at least in the first instance, those noble Iranian *dihqān*s whom it praises, and who are known to have spent the long winter nights listening to recitations of the Iranian historical-epical traditions. As for the *Shāhnāma*s commissioned by Sāmānid princes, they were most likely intended to reinforce their claim to be authentic Persian rulers of the East, carrying on the traditions of Persian sovereignty, in order to attract the support of local princes and provincial governors who might have been attempted to transfer their allegiance to the Sāmānids' Būyid rivals.

Because the composition of Firdawsī's *Shāhnāma* spans the last two decades of Sāmānid rule and the first of Ghaznavid hegemony, it presents problems with respect to its reception, to which we will return in Chapter 2. The Sāmānids fell; their fall was chronicled in the histories of their Ghaznavid successors. Although they left behind no contemporary history (so far as we know), they did leave two major historical monuments: Firdawsī's *Shāhnāma*, the last, monumental treatment of the Iranian historical narrative, and Balʿamī's Ṭabarī, the first Persian treatment of the Islamic historical narrative. For a brief moment in time, the two narratives coexisted; but it was, ultimately, the all-encompassing Islamic narrative that was to dominate subsequent historical writing in Persian.

NOTES

1. See Bosworth 1969a: 47–9, especially on Ṭāhir's conflicting genealogical claims; Bosworth 1969b; Bosworth 1973b: 53–4, 56; on Ṭāhir's (Arabic) treatise on kingship and government, Bosworth 1970b.
2. The *Shu'ūbiyya* movement was manifested in a challenge by non-Arab Muslims to Arab superiority on the basis of descent, and was expressed largely in literary terms by poets and writers who boasted of the cultural superiority of the Persians and of their own literary abilities in Arabic. For a discussion of the basic issues involved see Mottahedeh 1976, and the references cited.
3. In 316/928 Naṣr's Daylamid commander Asfār ibn Shīrūya, also an apparent convert to Ismā'īlism, took control of Rayy and other regions and rebelled against Naṣr, intending, it appears, to revive Persian kingship; he was later obliged to seek peace with Naṣr. Asfār was challenged by the Gīlid Mardāvīj ibn Ziyār, founder of the Ziyārid dynasty, who occupied Isfahan in 322/934, and is said to have asserted that he would put an end to the rule of the Arabs and restore that of the Persians. See Madelung 1969: 86–8.
4. On this work see Minorsky 1956 (on Abū Manṣūr Ṭūsī, 164–6, and see Treadwell 1991: 225–6). On the *Shāhnāma* tradition see Hanaway 1978; Rosenthal 1968: 179–80.
5. The Karrāmiyya sect was founded by Abū 'Abd Allāh Muḥammad ibn Karrām, an ascetic and preacher who began his preaching in Sistan, later extended his activities to other regions, and finally took up residence in Nishapur, from which base he and his successors sent missionaries far and wide, especially to Transoxania. He denounced both Sunnīs and Shī'īs and preached an ostentatious asceticism. Heresiographers generally brand the sect as heretical. See further *EI*², s.v.; Bosworth 1960; Madelung 1971; Chabbi 1977, especially 38–72.
6. Bal'amī often contradicts Ṭabarī's accounts, or adds to or substitutes for them materials he has found elsewhere, both in oral traditions and in books; he sometimes cites specific sources and at others refers to 'accounts current among the people' or 'in the Persian books'. On materials in the History that amplify accounts found in Ṭabarī, correct or refute others, or are not found in Ṭabarī at all see Daniel 1990: 284–5.
7. For the complexities of the manuscript tradition and the publication history of Bal'amī's work see Daniel 1990, 1995: 3–5. I have had recourse to Zotenberg's translation of the first sections (1984); the edition of the pre-Islamic sections by M. T. Bahār, revised by Gunābādī (1974); and Rawshan's edition of the Islamic sections (1994).
8. This account does not occur in the manuscript used as the basis for Rawshan's edition; it is however found in others, and Rawshan includes it in his notes. Its source was presumably a Persian work,

the *Akhbār-i Muqanna'*, which Bīrūnī mentions as having been translated into Arabic. See Rawshan's discussion, Bal'amī 1994, 3: 1,592–3. The account is considerably longer and more detailed than Ṭabarī's.

9. There is, at the beginning of the reign of al-Hādī, a lengthy section on the rise of the *zindīqs*, who are however treated as dualists and materialists; no connection is made between them and later heretical movements, as is common with the heresiographers.
10. Ṣābī' had served 'Aḍud al-Dawla in Baghdad when the latter was still in Fars, and represented his interests in the capital. When 'Aḍud al-Dawla first conquered Baghdad from his cousin and rival for power, 'Izz al-Dīn Bakhtiyār (in 364/975), Ṣābī' wished to return with him to Fars but did not, fearing for his family's safety. He was briefly imprisoned by 'Izz al-Dawla but was then restored to his service. When 'Aḍud al-Dawla re-entered Baghdad in 367/977 he confirmed Ṣābī''s position; shortly after, however, he came into possession of correspondence between 'Izz al-Dawla and the Ḥamdānid ruler Abū Taghlib, which contained letters written by Ṣābī'. He ordered the latter to be arrested; 'Aḍud al-Dawla's vizier al-Muṭahhar kept him under house arrest, and induced him, at 'Aḍud al-Dawla's command, to write the book. 'Piece after piece of his draft was brought to 'Aḍud al-Dawla, who read it, added to it, and expunged from it ... The work thus may be considered to represent his views and to reflect his political aims' (Madelung 1967: 18, and see 17–20; see also Madelung 1971: 105–6). Ṣābi''s history publicised the Būyid claim to descent from Bahrām Gūr.
11. There are numerous editions of the *Shāhnāma*, of varying reliability. I have used that of E. Bertels' (1962–71). Section and line references follow de Fouchécour 1976.
12. In 399/1008 Maḥmūd had conducted a successful campaign in India; in 401/1011 he was to launch another against Ghūr (see Nāẓim 1971: 89–91, 70–2). It is possible that Firdawsī may be referring to one or another of these events; but it is more likely that the 'year 400' should be interpreted in connection with prophecies of the appearance of the victorious 'King from the East' who will usher in the final age.
13. See Niẓāmī 'Arūẓī 1899: 81–3; Nöldeke 1979: 45–8; for the satire see Mohl 1966: *alif-sīn*; the text, which consists largely of interpolations from elsewhere in the poem, is generally considered spurious.

2

Historiography in the Ghaznavid Period

THE GHAZNAVID ASCENDANCY

The Ghaznavid house was founded by the Sāmānid *ḥājib* Alptigīn, who, after the abortive attempt to install Naṣr ibn Nūḥ on the Sāmānid throne following the death of ʿAbd al-Malik, had withdrawn to Ghazna (Ghaznīn) (in present-day Afghanistan), expelled the local Sāmānid governor, and had his own governorate regularised by Manṣūr ibn Nūḥ. He died shortly after. In 366/977 the governorate devolved upon Alptigīn's former *mamlūk* Sabuktigīn (see Gardīzī 1968: 162; Treadwell 1991: 227; Bosworth 1973a: 36–9). The Ghaznavids considered themselves, and were considered by the historians, as loyal vassals of the Sāmānids; thus it was that Nūḥ II Manṣūr, faced with a revolt by the combined forces of his governor of Khurasan Abū ʿAlī Sīmjūrī and Abū ʿAlī's former rival Fā'iq, called upon Sabuktigīn for assistance (see Treadwell 1991: 248–55).

Under Nūḥ II the power of the *mamlūks* had reached its height. Fā'iq continued to dominate affairs in the capital; and in 371/982 the new vizier Abū al-Ḥusayn ʿUtbī replaced Abū al-Ḥasan Sīmjūrī, *sipahsālār* of Khurasan, with his own protégé, the *ḥājib* Abū al-ʿAbbās Tāsh (see Gardīzī 1968: 165–6). When Tāsh was defeated by the Būyids in Jurjan, ʿUtbī took charge of military affairs; but soon after, Abū al-Ḥasan Sīmjūrī and Fā'iq arranged to have him murdered 'in broad daylight in the streets of the capital' by some of Manṣūr ibn Nūḥ's former *mamlūks* (in 372/983; see Treadwell 1991: 245; ʿUtbī 1869, I: 121–2). The next vizier, appointed by Tāsh, was dismissed and replaced by ʿAbd Allāh ibn Muḥammad ibn ʿUzayr (an enemy of both the ʿUtbī family and their protégé Tāsh), who in 376/986–7 reinstated Abū al-Ḥasan Sīmjūrī. Tāsh rebelled, but was defeated and fled to Jurjan, where he died of the plague (ʿUtbī 1869, I: 149); Abū al-Ḥasan died in the following year (377/988; see Gardīzī 1968: 168; Treadwell 1991: 246–7).

Fā'iq, whom Nūḥ now made *sipahsālār* of Khurasan, was driven out by Abū al-Ḥasan Sīmjūrī's son Abū ʿAlī, whom Nūḥ was forced to appoint in his place. Fā'iq rebelled openly, and sought support from the Qarakhānid Īlak Khān; the *dihqāns* of Transoxania had meanwhile been corresponding with the leader of the Qarakhānid confederation, Bughrākhān Hārūn ibn Īlak. (On the Qarakhānids see

EI[2], art. 'Ilek-Khāns'.) The Ghaznavid historian Abū Naṣr 'Utbī remarks 'that they had had enough of the Sāmānids and wanted a new *dawla*'. Treadwell finds this explanation 'not very illuminating', and suggests that they were probably 'alarmed by the breakdown of law and order in Transoxania', or may have 'really believed that the Sāmānids' time had come after the breakdown of relations with Sīmjūrid Khurāsān' (1991: 247). Nūḥ II was forced to flee Bukhara when Bughrākhān briefly occupied the city in 382/992. On his departure, the Qarakhānid installed Nūḥ's uncle 'Abd al-'Azīz ibn Nūḥ ibn Naṣr as ruler (Gardīzī 1968: 169); when Nūḥ returned to Bukhara later in the year he promptly arrested and blinded his uncle.

This state of affairs continued 'until God set right Nūḥ's affairs' by means of Sabuktigīn, who, summoned by Nūḥ, was joined by other local princes. Fā'iq and Abū 'Alī Sīmjūrī were no match for the Sāmānid–Ghaznavid coalition. Following the rebels' defeat in 383/993, Nūḥ granted the titles of Nāṣir al-Dawla ('support of the state') to Sabuktigīn and Sayf al-Dawla ('sword of the state') to his son Maḥmūd, whom he appointed *sipahsālār* of Khurasan and governor of Nishapur (Treadwell 1991: 256–7; Gardīzī 1968: 169–70). Successive engagements between the Sāmānid-Ghaznavid forces and their opponents led in 386/996 to a second defeat outside Ṭūs; Fā'iq fled to Transoxania, and Abū 'Alī Sīmjūrī was eventually captured and imprisoned in the citadel of Gardīz, where he either died, or was executed (probably the latter), in the following year (see 'Utbī 1869, 1: 252–3; Baghdādī 1935: 130; Treadwell 1991: 258; Baghdādī's view that it was Abū 'Alī's Ismā'īlī sympathies which provoked his revolt against Nūḥ [1935: 129–30] is supported by Jūzjānī [1970, 1: 47]).

In that year (387/997) Sabuktigīn removed Ibn 'Uzayr and appointed his own candidate, a move which, says Treadwell, 'amounted to no less than a *de facto* takeover of the Sāmānid administration by the Ghaznavids' (1991: 259). Ibn 'Uzayr went into hiding; a few months later the new vizier was murdered by his *ghulām*s, at which point Nūḥ consulted Sabuktigīn as to a suitable replacement, and the latter appointed Abū al-Muẓaffar al-Barghūthī (see 'Utbī 1869, 1: 235–40, 250). Sabuktigīn also concluded a treaty with the Īlak Khān, which did not, however, survive the deaths of both Sabuktigīn and Nūḥ ibn Manṣūr in the same year. Urged to march on Bukhara by the reinstated Ibn 'Uzayr, now vizier of Nūḥ's successor Abū al-Ḥārith Manṣūr III (387–9/997–9), the Īlak's attempt was foiled by Fā'iq's intervention; and while the Ghaznavids were preoccupied with the disputed succession to Sabuktigīn, Manṣūr extended his authority once more into Khurasan. But it was not long before Fā'iq and his Turkish *ḥājib* and *sipahsālār* of Khurasan, Biktuzūn, betrayed Manṣūr.

Suspecting that he inclined towards Maḥmūd – who had secured his succession in Ghazna, been reappointed over Khurasan by Manṣūr, and was now marching towards Nishapur – in Ṣafar 389/February 999 they deposed and blinded Manṣūr and placed his younger brother Abū al-Fawāris ʿAbd al-Malik II on the throne (Gardīzī 1968: 173; Treadwell 1991: 260–2).

Maḥmūd – who sought, say the historians, to avenge Manṣūr – at first agreed to a truce with ʿAbd al-Malik II; but when his baggage train was attacked by some Sāmānid *mamlūks*, he defeated Biktuzūn and Fā'iq, who retreated with ʿAbd al-Malik to Bukhara, where Fā'iq died soon after. In recognition of Maḥmūd's assumption of rule in Khurasan the caliph al-Qādir (whom the Sāmānids had refused to recognise) bestowed on him the titles Yamīn al-Dawla wa-Amīn al-Milla, 'right hand of the state and trusty (guardian) of the faith'. Fā'iq's death facilitated a second occupation of Bukhara in 389/999 by the Īlak, who seized Nūḥ's sons and sent them to Uzgand; the occupation was unopposed, as the city's *faqīh*s advised its inhabitants 'that they should not take up arms against Muslims' (Treadwell 1991: 263).

Treadwell comments that when they occupied Bukhara a second time 'the Qarākhānids displayed the same unwillingness to unseat the old order as had former Muslim rebels against the Sāmānids.' Both Bughrākhān and, before him, Abū ʿAlī Chaghānī, had turned the city over to a Sāmānid pretender. Thus the Qarakhānids 'did not come as conquerors, but chose instead to masquerade as allies of ʿAbdalmalik against his Ghaznavid enemies' (1991: 249–50; cf. ʿUtbī 1869, 1: 319). 'In short, they behaved in the same way as participants within the Sāmānid state. This must have had something to do with their status as Muslims' (1991: 307–8).

This raises several issues with respect to the historiography of the period. If the basic paradigm of history is that of the rise and fall of states, what constitutes a 'state'? Treadwell comments on the Sāmānid state's lack of 'formal organization' and the importance of personal relations of patronage between the ruler and his civil and military officials (1991: 279–80, 302–3). 'To betray a patron was regarded as morally reprehensible and a transgression of the tenets of Islam; such a betrayal was a highly public event which, in theory, would disqualify the perpetrator from enjoying the confidence of his peers.' But despite repeated acts of betrayal and rebellion by Sāmānid commanders and military governors, the sources reveal 'no sense that observers were shocked by rebellion, nor do they seem to have had any expectation that loyalty to the ruler was inviolable', so long as the rebels did not attempt 'the ultimate crime of unseating the dynasty' (1991: 280–1). He argues that the emphasis on personal loyalty denied the ruler the freedom to dismiss a rebellious governor and the governor any guarantee that he would be retained: 'If the governor had been a servant of the state, rather than of the ruler, he could have been removed by order of the bureaucracy, but he was not' (1991: 303).

As Al-Azmeh has pointed out, the ruler *is* the state; or rather, the identification of 'state' with ruler or ruling house is total (1990: 14).[1] The 'state' was identified, not by 'constitutional limitations' or 'national' boundaries (see Treadwell 1991: 305–6), but with the ruler and his apparatus of government, bound to him by personal loyalty.[2] It is at this level that issues of loyalty and betrayal do indeed form a major theme in the histories, and historians are not hesitant to blame rebels for their treachery. While bureaucrats or military chiefs could and did move from the service of one ruler to that of another if relations between them and their sovereigns broke down, or if there was no ruler to perpetuate the ruling house (or, often as not, for reasons of self-interest), they could also be (and often were) reinstated after sufficient protestations of renewed allegiance (and, usually, the payment of a large fine or indemnity).

The status of rebellion in Islamic law is a complex one. In theory, rebellion against authority (unlike apostasy) is 'not regarded as a criminal act' and 'does not carry a fixed legal penalty'; in practice, 'Muslim authorities tended to treat secession, disobedience and disloyalty to the State as tantamount to apostasy' (Kraemer 1983: 35–6). The first priority is, however, the unity of the community (or the 'state'), and every effort will be made to bring the rebel back into the fold.[3] Rebels against individual rulers might be considered legitimate if they produced an acceptable counter-claimant; rebels like Abū ʿAlī Sīmjūrī, who collected taxes on their own or withheld them from their rightful recipient, were another matter.

While rulers of one house might have no compunctions about unseating those of a rival one (usually on the pretext of restoring order in situations of civil strife, or of suppressing heresy or apostasy), rebellious vassals were generally careful to produce a legitimate claimant from the ruling house. From the historians' point of view, the Ghaznavids did not unseat the Sāmānids, but inherited their mantle of rule when that dynasty could no longer produce strong rulers capable of maintaining civil order. The last three Sāmānid rulers came to the throne as minors, lacked powerful viziers, and were at the mercy of intriguing bureaucrats and *mamlūk*s. The Ghaznavids, faced with a situation where there was no viable Sāmānid candidate for rule, assumed it for themselves. Treadwell's argument that the

Qarakhānids were unopposed because they were Muslims (which, indeed, was the *faqīhs*' view) perhaps misses the point: lack of opposition to them reflects the ruler's inability to defend the city and its inhabitants; and the occupiers did, eventually, appoint a Sāmānid pretender. By contrast, when Sabuktigīn was sent against the Īlak, and the latter wrote to him arguing that, since they were brothers in God who had fought together against the pagans and, as Muslim brothers-in-arms, should not fight each other, Sabuktigīn responded that he would not break the bonds of loyalty to his Sāmānid lord ('Utbī 1869, 1: 232–5). And after the Ghaznavids and Qarakhānids had carved up the Sāmānid domains between them, this did not end their rivalry over various territories, the adherence of both sides to Sunnī Islam notwithstanding.

In general, the Ghaznavids continued the cultural and linguistic policies of their predecessors, though with some vacillation and with one important exception: their relative lack of interest in Iranian cultural traditions. (This was truer of Maḥmūd than of his successor Mas'ūd I.) It has been said that Maḥmūd was no lover of Arabic, although he knew it well; it is also said that he wrote a book in Arabic on *fiqh* (jurisprudence; see Bosworth 1973a: 129; 'Utbī 1869, 2: 238–40.) Bosworth quotes Minorsky to the effect that 'the feelings of the renaissance of New Persian passed by Ghazna' (1973a: 33; no reference given); this, however, requires qualification. Maḥmūd's language policy shifted and his viziers promoted now Persian, now Arabic, as the language of the court. 'Utbī scornfully refers to the vizier Isfarā'īnī (whom Firdawsī praised), who changed the language of the chancery to Persian, as ignorant and unlettered (1869, 2: 170–1); it was changed back to Arabic by his successor Maymandī. But Maḥmūd patronised Persian court poets to an extent unprecedented even under the Sāmānids (1869, 1: 52), and Persian poets far outnumbered Arabic at his court.

Shortly after Maḥmūd came to power in 389/999 Badī' al-Zamān Hamadhānī declared, in an Arabic panegyric addressed to him,

> Is this a Farīdūn who wears the crown, or the second Alexander?
> The sun of Maḥmūd has darkened the stars of the Sāmānids;
> The house of Bahrām have become slaves of the son of the Khāqān.
>
> ['Utbī 1869, 1: 384–5]

The Ghaznavids' Turkish ethnicity has been seen as one reason for Maḥmūd's unenthusiastic reception of Firdawsī's *Shāhnāma*. (The satire attributed to that poet accuses Maḥmūd of base origins but makes no mention of his Turkish descent.) Hamadhānī's references to him as 'son of the Khāqān' and 'the second Alexander' date from early in

Maḥmūd's reign; they find no parallels in later poems, especially those addressed to him by his Persian court poets, who do not refer to his Turkish ethnicity and rarely employ the more or less standard comparisons of the ruler to great Iranian kings or heroes of the past.

Various reasons have been adduced for Maḥmūd's indifference, if not hostility, to the *Shāhnāma*: that Firdawsī was suspected of heresy; that he was intrigued against by rivals; that Maḥmūd was displeased by the poem's Zoroastrian elements; that the Turkish Ghaznavids had no interest in the Iranian past. The Ghaznavids had been brought up in the Sāmānid Perso-Islamic cultural milieu; but the extent to which there may have been an interest in Iranian traditions in the milieu of Ghazna itself is uncertain. However, Maḥmūd's brother and *sipahsālār* of Khurasan, Abū al-Muẓaffar Naṣr (whom Firdawsī suggested might be sympathetic to his poem; see Xp 3,373–8), commissioned Abū Manṣūr Tha'ālibi (d. 449/1057–8) to write a universal history in Arabic, the *Ghurar siyar mulūk al-Furs wa-akhbārihim*, which included a lengthy account of the Persian kings, and which must have been completed prior to Naṣr's death in 412/1021. Naṣr's commissioning of this work suggests that Iranian traditions were still valued in Khurasan and that he himself was not averse to using them to legitimate his own governorate there.

Turkish ethnicity was perhaps less of an issue than was Maḥmūd's self-image as the *sulṭān-i ghāzī* dedicated to extirpating heresy and unbelief, and as supreme and unequalled ruler of the East. An anecdote in the *Tārīkh-i Sīstān* reports him as commenting, on hearing the stories of the exploits of Rustam, 'One soldier in my army is worth a thousand Rustams' (1935: 7), a remark probably meant to mollify his own Turkish commanders. More to the point are Maḥmūd's shifting cultural and linguistic policies, which appear to have been tied to his shifting relations with the caliphate. Rypka points out that the replacement of the disgraced Isfarā'īnī with Aḥmad ibn Ḥasan Maymandī (in 404/1013–14), who promoted Arabic as the language of the chancery, coincided with Maḥmūd's attempts at closer relations with the caliphate (1968: 165–7). The decline in status of the *dihqān*s had also altered the political makeup of the Ghaznavid state, which relied heavily on a largely Turkish military machine, a highly Arabised, conservative religious establishment in the towns, and a similarly Arabised court bureaucracy.

Literary tastes were also changing; and such changes are relevant both to the reception of the *Shāhnāma* and to the subsequent development of Persian prose and poetry. For although the *Shāhnāma* is a polished literary work, its language, Darī, is deliberately archaic, and far from the more polished Fārsī of the court poets. Moreover, its content was seen as definitely outmoded; and the court poets – like the historians – preferred to celebrate the achievements of the present rather than the legendary glories of a remote past. The panegyrist Farrukhī Sīstānī began his *qaṣīda* on Maḥmūd's campaign against the Indian city of Somnat (416/1025–6; see Nāẓim 1971: 115–21) by contrasting the 'ancient tale of Alexander' – now 'an antiquated legend', a 'history full of lies' – with the newer, more pleasing tale of 'the world-ruler' Maḥmūd (1932: 67). And indeed, after this campaign 'Sulṭān Maḥmūd became transformed into an almost mythical figure and generations of enthusiastic authors surrounded his name with a huge literature of fanciful stories which were intended to glorify him as a king and a warrior' (Nāẓim 1971: 120, and see 219–24).[4]

By the time of its completion the *Shāhnāma* was something of an anomaly: not quite literature and not quite history. The Islamic narrative, leading ultimately to the ruling monarch or house, was becoming firmly established. But if scholars like Bīrūnī thought that the Persian language was 'fit for nothing but the histories of [Persian] kings and night-time storytelling' (1973: 12 [Arabic text]), over and above Bīrūnī's apparently pro-Arabic bias (see 'al-Bīrūnī' entry in *EI*[2]) this statement, in a work dedicated to the Ghaznavid Mawdūd (432–40/1041–48?), is accompanied by animadversions on the appointment of officials unlettered in Arabic, 'the language of religion and of rule'. J. T. P. de Bruijn has moreover argued for an increasing influence of Arabic at the later Ghaznavid court (1983: 151). And if historians like Bayhaqī evince a negative attitude towards Iranian historical traditions, this is of a piece with his insistence that true history has little to do with legendary rulers and their deeds. For Bayhaqī, as for his predecessor Miskawayh, the reliability of historical accounts was uppermost, especially with respect to contemporary or near-contemporary events; and the appeal to reason was invoked as a further criterion of credibility, if not of veracity. Thus if ʿUtbī lauded Maḥmūd as having 'made naught of Ardashīr in his age, and of [the caliph] al-Manṣūr in his rule', he also wrote, 'The earth trembled in terror of him, (for deeds) the like of which no ruler had ever been heard to achieve except in the legends of the ancients, which aim at prolixity, the inspiration of terror, and the impression of amazement and familiarity, exceeding the truth of what is witnessed by the eyes and expressed by proof' (1869, 1: 41, 40).

GHAZNAVID DYNASTIC HISTORY: ʿUTBĪ'S *TA'RĪKH AL-YAMĪNĪ*

The Sāmānids produced no dynastic history, either contemporary or retrospective. Sallāmī's *Ta'rīkh wulāt Khurāsān* might merit such a designation; but nothing is known about either the organisation or the scope of that work (see Treadwell 1991: 7–9). But the Ghaznavids produced several contemporary histories, of which one, Abū Naṣr ʿUtbī's *Ta'rīkh al-Yamīnī*, extending from the rise of Sabuktigīn to the year 412/1021, survives.[5] Before turning to the Persian historians of the Ghaznavid period, we may look first at this influential work.[6]

Abū Naṣr Muḥammad ibn ʿAbd al-Jabbār al-ʿUtbī (350–427 or 31/961–1036 or 40), a descendant of the Sāmānid vizier Abū al-Ḥusayn ʿUtbī, wrote his history of the Ghaznavids so that 'the people of Iraq might benefit from a book on this subject in the Arabic language' (1869, 1: 53). In Treadwell's view, 'his target audience was undoubtedly the caliphal court at Baghdad, where Maḥmūd was celebrated as the caliph's principal ally in his struggle against the Būyid rulers of Iraq' (1991: 10). ʿUtbī, who chose to write his history in the ornate Arabic chancery style, with a heavy use of rhyming prose (*sajʿ*), compares his work with Abū Isḥāq Ṣābī's history of the Būyids the *Kitāb al-Tājī*, one of his acknowledged sources.[7] ʿUtbī's work became a model of Arabic prose style; it was used by later writers, formed the subject of numerous commentaries, and was translated into Persian by Jarbādhqānī at the beginning of the 7th/13th century (see further Chapter 3).

Treadwell comments that ʿUtbī 'naturally takes pains to stress that the Ghaznavids came to power through a legal transfer of dynastic authority from the Sāmānids', providing the justification that Maḥmūd 'felt compelled to avenge the unlawful deposition' of Manṣūr [II] ibn Nūḥ by Fā'iq and Biktūzūn, and making no mention of Maḥmūd's 'strategic imperatives', namely, 'preventing the emergence of an independent Sīmjūrīd state which would have threatened [the Ghaznavids'] western flank'. ʿUtbī's 'version of events was ... designed to present the Ghaznavids in the best possible light and to cast their enemies as the architects of the Sāmānids' downfall' (1991: 11–12).

There is little doubt that ʿUtbī meant to present the Ghaznavids in a good light; this assessment, however, does scant justice to his project, of which he states:

> Generations of writers and secretaries have written books and compositions on their own times, and on the changing ways of Time which affected them, according to their powers of expression and their share of eloquence of mind and fingers, up to the time that Abū Isḥāq Ibrāhīm ibn Hilāl al-Ṣābī' wrote his famous book the *Tājī* on the history of the Daylamids ... But if there was ever a house [*dawla*] whose proven virtues demanded eternal preservation, and whose great deeds immortalization, it is this one, which requires writers to make their words immortal by writing down its sublimities, and to adorn their pens by recording its achievements. (1869, 1: 47–8)

ʿUtbī's treatment of the Ghaznavids Sabuktigīn and, especially, Maḥmūd is, indeed, highly encomiastic; that is, after all, his duty as Ghaznavid propagandist. But his affirmation of the necessity for kingship and of the principle of the transfer of rule goes beyond mere propagandistic motives to reaffirm this universal truth. Quoting the dictum traditionally attributed to Ardashīr-i Bābakān, 'Religion and kingship are (twin) brothers', he amplifies it at some length:

> Religion is the foundation, and kingship is its guardian. That which has no guardian is lost; and that which has no foundation will be destroyed. The sultan is God's shadow on His earth, His vice-gerent over His creation, and His guarantor of the observance of the rights due Him. With him governance is perfected, and by him both élite and populace are kept in order. His awesome grandeur removes calamities and civil strife; by his regency fears and trials are ended. Without him order would be violated, elite and populace would become equal, chaos would prevail, and disorder and dissension become general. (1869, 1: 20–2)

While the sentiments are conventional, they were probably genuinely felt: for when Maḥmūd assumed rule of Khurasan, he brought order to a region that had suffered at the hands of weak rulers and rebellious vassals for several decades.

Having begun his history with the account of Alptigīn's arrival in Ghazna, the election of Sabuktigīn as his successor, and the latter's early achievements, ʿUtbī turns to 'the causes which made the Turks covet the realm' of Nūḥ II ibn Manṣūr, 'their intervention [or: interference] in his rule, and his dislodgement from his capital and his territories' (1869, 1: 89; Jarbādhqānī, unlike ʿUtbī, stresses Nūḥ's youth and inexperience [1966: 34]). Nūḥ's vizier Abū al-Ḥusayn ʿUtbī appointed Fa'iq as *ḥājib* and Abū al-Ḥusayn (read: al-Ḥasan) Sīmjūrī as *sipahsālār* of Khurasan; through their efforts the affairs of the kingdom flourished 'until its sleeves began to unravel and its collar to tear. And one (cause) of this was the matter of Sistan' (1869, 1: 96b).[8]

The Sāmānid military involvement in Sīstān began in the 360s/970s, when Manṣūr ibn Nūḥ intervened to support its ruler Khalaf ibn Aḥmad against his co-ruler and deputy Ṭāhir ibn Ḥusayn and Ṭāhir's son and successor Ḥusayn ibn Ṭāhir. Reinstated, after some years of quiet Khalaf broke off relations with Bukhara and withheld the annual tribute to the Sāmānids; some seven years of battles, sieges and general turmoil followed (see 1869, 1: 96–101; and see further the section on the *Tārīkh-i Sīstān*). 'This was the beginning of the enfeeblement of the *dawla*; from then on its knots weakened, frenzy burst forth, ruptures increased, and rents (in its fabric) widened. For every affair has its terminus, and every people its appointed end, and every rule its final point. "God effaces and establishes what He wills" [Koran 13: 41]' (1869, I: 102; Jarbādhqānī [1966: 44] has *intiqāl*, 'transfer', for *nihāya*, 'final point').

People began to criticise Abū al-Ḥasan Sīmjūrī for his slowness to support the Sāmānid ruler and called for his dismissal. Informed that Tāsh had been appointed in his place, he thought first of rebelling, but reconsidered, summoned the messenger and professed loyalty to Nūḥ, saying: 'I am a sapling which the Sultan planted with his own hand and gave to drink from the water of his generosity; it is his will whether it be left to bear fruit or cast into the fire' (1869, I: 102). Abū al-Ḥasan left for his own province of Qūhistān, and Tāsh and his army entered Nishapur, in 371/981 (1869, I: 104).

Further troubles had erupted after the death of the Būyid Rukn al-Dawla, whose sons 'Aḍud al-Dawla, Mu'ayyid al-Dawla and Fakhr al-Dawla disputed his division of his territories amongst them. Fakhr al-Dawla took refuge with the Ziyārid Qābūs ibn Vushmgīr in Jurjan; 'Aḍud al-Dawla marched on Jurjan, destroying everything in his path and appropriating the revenues, and ultimately defeated the Gilanis. Qābūs and Fakhr al-Dawla fled to Nishapur, where Nūḥ ibn Manṣūr ordered Tāsh to secure their return to their kingdoms. After a difficult, and ultimately unsuccessful, campaign they retreated back to Nishapur. The vizier 'Utbī then determined to take command of the armies himself. Nūḥ bestowed robes of honour upon him which 'added to the garments of secretaries the apparel of the commanders of armies; and that was a robe of honour [*khil'at*] which stripped [*khāli'a*] him of his breath, cut off his life, and ended his affair' (1869, I: 121); he was murdered soon after. Jarbādhqānī observes:

> With him the vizierate came to an end; and the realm of Khurasan never again saw a vizier like him, nor did any noble official like him ever occupy the seat of the vizierate. And there is no mention in the histories of any vizier who possessed such great accomplishments and noble qualities. (1966: 60. There is no parallel to the first sentence in 'Utbī [1869, I: 123], who simply praises the vizier's qualities and virtues)

With 'Utbī's death any remnants of order in the Sāmānid domains soon disappeared, as viziers were appointed and dismissed and Turkish *mamlūks* grew openly rebellious. After Tāsh's death the most prominent among the latter were the Sīmjūrīds, Abū al-Ḥasan and his son Abū 'Alī, who had designs on Khurasan. When Abū 'Alī became *sipahsālār* of Khurasan following his father's sudden death in the arms of one of his favourites, he learned that Fā'iq had been appointed over Herat. He wrote reproaching Fā'iq for forgetting his obligations, and they agreed that Fā'iq would govern Herat while Abū 'Alī retained Nishapur and command of the army.

> Robes of honour were sent from Bukhara according to the custom for military governors. Abū 'Alī thought that he was their intended goal and the recipient of this honour, until, when the envoy reached the middle of his journey, he and his companions turned away in the direction of Fā'iq, and he knew that this was a despicable plot ... and that he was the goal of evil. (1869, 1: 154)

Hearing that Fā'iq had marched from Herat, Abū 'Alī moved swiftly and intercepted him between Herat and Pushang. He forced Fā'iq to flee towards Marvarrud, where they engaged again. In this battle Fā'iq took some prisoners, whom he sent to Bukhara; Abū 'Alī, meanwhile, went to Marv to demand reinstatement in his father's position, which he was granted.

His prestige and power greatly increased, Abū 'Alī now controlled Khurasan and its revenues, which he withheld from his Sāmānid suzerain while extracting even greater sums from the populace. It was at this time that he adopted the title of 'Supreme Commander, Supported by Heaven' (Amīr al-Umarā' al-Mu'ayyad min al-Samā') (1869, 1: 155). Meanwhile, though he retained Nūḥ's name in the *khuṭba* 'in order (as he averred) to dissimulate his true position, or perhaps to earn the populace's praise (rather than their blame)' (1869, 1: 163), he was secretly corresponding with Hārūn, the son of Bughrākhān, and plotting with him to divide the Sāmānid lands between them when Hārūn took Bukhara from Nūḥ.

In 382/992 Bughrākhān occupied Bukhara, where he was welcomed by Fā'iq, and Nūḥ was forced to flee across the Oxus. For some time Nūḥ had been writing to Abū 'Alī Sīmjūrī seeking his help; Abū 'Alī deceived him with false promises and bided his time, while secretly plotting to divide up his kingdom between himself and Bughrākhān. 'A group who had attached themselves to his service extolled this decision ... in order to curry favour with him, and put it to him that the days of this house were over' (1869, 1: 172; Jarbādhqānī adds, 'and that helping Nūḥ's rule would cause (him) humiliation and result in tribulation' [1966: 96]). Following Bughrākhān's withdrawal Fā'iq fled to Abū 'Alī in Marv. They decided to join forces against Nūḥ and went to Nishapur; the beleaguered Nūḥ called on Sabuktigīn and Maḥmūd for help.

Sabuktigīn managed to secure a pardon for Abū 'Alī; but when a group of the latter's hotheaded supporters raided his camp he decided to do battle, and defeated Abū 'Alī. Abū 'Alī and Fā'iq eventually succeeded in ousting Maḥmūd from Nishapur (in 385/995); but 'God destined (his return) to be the cause of his downfall and his ruin'. Ignoring advice to pursue Maḥmūd and throw the Sāmānids out of Khurasan, Abū ʿAlī stayed in Nishapur, 'where he behaved like one whose sight has grown dim and his strength enfeebled, blinded as to his goal, his seriousness departed from him'. He set about emptying the treasuries, ignored his troops' treachery, and began writing both to Nūḥ and to Sabuktigīn, begging for pardon, protesting his innocence and putting the blame on Fā'iq and others among his army (1869, I: 207–8; Jarbādhqānī adds, 'His lying excuses and repugnant words revealed his weak spirit and base nature' [1966: 118]). Sabuktigīn prepared to march on Abū ʿAlī; meanwhile, Fā'iq had gone to Ṭūs, where he too opened negotiations with Sabuktigīn, 'who wrote him an answer befitting his hypocrisy and conceit, and paid him back in good measure' (Jarbādhqānī 1966: 118, expanding upon ʿUtbī's 'he replied to him in kind' [1869, I: 209]).

Defeated outside Ṭūs, Abū ʿAlī and Fā'iq fled once more. Fā'iq determined to cross the Oxus and enter the Īlak's service, and advised Abū ʿAlī to do the same. He, however, ignored this advice, and thus brought about his own downfall: 'Abū ʿAlī ... took the wrong road, and deprived (himself of) success; he became weighed down by the disobedience he had committed, and filled with shame at the wasted opportunities for piety and benevolence' (1869, I: 220). He was captured, en route to Jurjaniyya, by some troops of the Khwārazmshāh, and after some delay was sent to Nūḥ in Bukhara.

> He departed for Bukhara, travelling towards his own death. For the passage of time had caused him to forget that his actions and his slips would meet their destined end, and that verily God requites all deeds. When he drew near Bukhara the vizier ʿAbd Allāh ibn ʿUzayr came out to meet him, with the commanders, ranged in their ranks, voicing greetings and congratulations. He passed through them till (he reached) the *sahla* [the plain before the entrance to the palace], where he dismounted, and began to kiss the ground until he reached the royal seat, where the veil was lifted for him, and the *ḥājib*s proceeded before him, until he reached al-Riḍā [Nūḥ]. There he fulfilled the rites of obeisance, and disguised the baseness of ingratitude.

When he and his supporters were preparing to depart, they were tricked into turning into another room, where they were seized and put in chains. 'On that day Abū ʿAlī's affair ended, that day when his deviations were put to rest and he fell from his pride, and he reaped the fruit (of his actions) ... Even so is ingratitude not requited save by (bringing) wrath upon the ingrate' (1869, I: 230–1).

Abū ʿAlī died in the prison of Gardīz. His son Abū al-Ḥasan (II), on learning of his father's defeat outside Ṭūs, had fled to Rayy, where he remained until, returning to Nishapur 'because of some passion' (see 1869, 1: 251–2; other historians often say, 'because of a woman'), he too was seized and imprisoned. But the disappearance of the Sīmjūrīds from the scene (including Abū ʿAlī's brother Abū al-Qāsim, who, defeated by Biktuzūn, retired to Qūhistān) did not put an end to the Sāmānids' troubles, which increased after Sabuktigīn's death. ʿUtbī credits the *ḥājib* Biktuzūn with contributing to the Sāmānids' decline as, installed as governor of Khurasan, he collected the taxes (and made free with them) and controlled that province without opposition,

> until arrogance assailed his mind, and he advanced from that which his ruler and benefactor desired to that which exposed the kingdom to destruction and the *dawla* to lamentation; and Time recorded a fault from which, and from the damage of which, it will never be purified, and the dust of which will never be cleansed from its face. (1869, 1: 271–2)

With Maḥmūd temporarily absent securing his succession things rapidly deteriorated. On his return he realised that the kingdom was on the brink of ruin and made for Nishapur. Biktuzūn fled; the youthful Abū al-Ḥārith Manṣūr (II) marched on Khurasan; Maḥmūd, knowing that he could easily defeat him but preferring to maintain respect for the ruler and honour his obligations to him, withdrew towards Marv. Shortly after, Fā'iq and Biktuzūn seized and blinded the young ruler, and placed his brother ʿAbd al-Malik on the throne. Maḥmūd wrote to them rebuking them for their crime against their benefactor and the violation of their obligation to him, 'without respect for (the principles of) religion, or of avoiding (a sin against) Islam and the Muslims, nor fearing that this shameful event (would be) on the tongues of all till the end of time'. He determined to take revenge 'for the (sake of the) faith and Islam'.

> And God willed that vengeance would be wreaked upon them by means of Sayf al-Dawla [Maḥmūd] in requital for their violent deed, their shameful wrongdoing, and their blameworthy action, (which would be) despised by all ... 'Such is the chastisement of thy Lord which He inflicts upon corrupt cities. Surely, His chastisement is grievously painful' [Koran 11: 103]. (1869, 1: 299–300).

By defeating ʿAbd al-Malik, Fā'iq and Biktuzūn, Maḥmūd inherited the rule of Khurasan; and this was God's vengeance for their having violated the bonds of loyalty (1869, 1: 310). When ʿAbd al-Malik died, a prisoner, in Uzgand, 'The last remaining flame of the Sāmānid *dawla* in Transoxania and Khurasan was extinguished; and it was as if they had never been, as is the way with the past kingdoms of other ages. "And in that is a marvel for those who will consider" [Koran 16: 12]' (1869, 1: 320).

While ʿUtbī may not be 'shocked' at the disloyalty of those Sāmānid viziers, officials and military leaders who betrayed their rulers and benefactors in the service of their own interests, he nonetheless expresses outrage at the state of affairs which brought about the final collapse of the Sāmānids, with its climactic scene of the ultimate disloyalty – the blinding of the young Manṣūr II – whose perpetrators will be remembered till the end of time for their perfidy. Loyalty is a predominant theme throughout ʿUtbī's history. Lapses may be mended through renewed attestations of loyalty; local power struggles may be resolved; but when betrayal becomes the norm, it leads to chaos, civil strife and the fall of states.

The decline and collapse of the Sāmānids provides a foil for Maḥmūd's assumption of rule. In contrast to the weak, ineffectual and misguided Sāmānid rulers, Maḥmūd is bold, decisive, sound in judgement and forbearing. He restored order, justice and prosperity to Khurasan, suppressed heretics, campaigned against the pagans, and supported the caliphate. His struggle with his brother Ismāʿīl over the succession is presented as a conflict between a weak and inexperienced prince whose inability to govern soon became apparent, and a strong, capable ruler. When attempts at reconciling the brothers failed, Maḥmūd realised that 'the affair could be decided only by the sword' and, reluctantly, marched on Ghazna. When he reached its outskirts, Ismāʿīl's commanders wrote secretly proclaiming their allegiance to him; 'And God willed that which was destined, made known what was right and gave victory to the rightful (party)' (1869, 1: 278). Ismāʿīl was defeated; Maḥmūd treated him well thereafter.

When Maḥmūd had defeated Fā'iq and Biktuzūn and was awarded the titles of Yamīn al-Dawla and Amīn al-Milla by the caliph al-Qādir, he made a solemn vow to campaign in India each year 'for the sake of the faith' (1869, 1: 316–18). During his reign he was obliged to deal with treacherous vassals, with provincial rebels, and with the Būyids, all of whom are presented as deceitful and treacherous. (The accounts of the squabbles between the Būyid princes are undoubtedly meant to discredit them, and reinforce Maḥmūd's reputation, at the caliphal court.) He enjoyed good relations with the reinstated Ziyārid Qābūs ibn Vushmgīr; such was not the case with the Īlak Khān, who, when Maḥmūd took possession of Khurasan, had 'acted with perfidy towards the Sāmānids, and seized the opportunity to cleanse Transoxania of everyone related to that ancient family' (1869, 2: 26). A marriage was arranged between Maḥmūd and a daughter of the Īlak, and relations remined outwardly cordial 'until Satan created strife between them, and they began to harbour resentment ... and the sword took over the policy of that union' (1869, 2: 32; Jarbādhqānī states that their good relations were 'destroyed by Time's evil eye' [1966: 250]). 'Utbī indicates that the Īlak's apparent amity was fabricated, and that he was awaiting his opportunity, which came when, while Maḥmūd was absent campaigning against the Ismā'īlīs in Multan, the Īlak sent a force into Khurasan. Maḥmūd returned to deal with them, and the Turks were soundly defeated.

Maḥmūd's annexation of the territories of various local rulers is seen, by and large, as resulting from the need to suppress rebellious vassals or rulers who tolerated or encouraged heresy. This is exemplified by the account of Maḥmūd's conquest of Khwarazm in 408/1017 (see Nāẓim 1971: 56–60). The Ma'mūnid Khwārazmshāh Abū al-Ḥasan 'Alī ibn Ma'mūn had married the sultan's sister, Ḥurra-i Khuttalī; when he died, his successor Abū al-'Abbās Ma'mūn ibn Ma'mūn asked permission to marry his brother's widow. This was granted; but when the sultan demanded his rights of *khuṭba* and *sikka*, Ma'mūn's commanders told him, 'If you place your cheek (on the ground) in obedience, we will place swords on necks and depose you, remove you, and fight against you' (1869, 2: 253). Maḥmūd's envoy reported this flagrant breach of the obligations of loyalty and obedience to the Sultan; meanwhile Ma'mūn was murdered under mysterious circumstances. The army, knowing that Maḥmūd would seek revenge for his sister's husband, determined to resist him should he attack (1869, 2: 364–5; Jarbādhqānī [1966: 375] adds that this enabled him to acquire Khwarazm). Maḥmūd marched on the capital Jurjaniyya (Gurganj); many perished in the ensuing carnage, or were taken prisoner, and many others were executed because of suspect beliefs. Maḥmūd had the following lines inscribed on Ma'mūn's tomb:

> This is the grave of so-and-so son of so-and-so, whose army rebelled against him, and whose servants had the temerity to shed his blood. God sent him Yamīn al-Dawla Amīn al-Milla, who triumphed over them for his sake, and who crucified them on tree-trunks as an object lesson to observers and a marvel to the wise. (1869, 2: 258)

He sent the prisoners back to Ghazna, and installed his *ḥājib* Āltuntāsh as Khwārazmshāh.

Such accounts were undoubtedly designed to impress the caliphal court, especially by contrasting Maḥmūd's expansion of his territories, his suppression of rebellious vassals, heretics and pagans, and the firm hand he kept on his domains, with the constant squabbles of the Būyids. Much is made of the capability of Maḥmūd's administrators (with the exception of the disgraced Isfarā'īnī, who, appointed vizier on Sabuktigīn's advice, abused his position to acquire wealth, failed to ensure justice and prosperity, ruined Khurasan and impoverished its populace and, moreover, being unskilled in the secretarial art, changed the language of official correspondence to Persian; this was quickly rectified by his replacement, Maymandī, who proved an able vizier and a good advisor to the sultan [1869, 2: 170–1]). It must be said however that ʿUtbī's attitude towards heresy seems, at times at least, ambivalent; for while he makes much of Maḥmūd's successful campaigns against the pagan Indians, as well as of his early conquest of the Ismāʿīlī state of Multan, he has – with one major exception – little to say about heresy. The exception is his account of the fate of the Fāṭimid envoy Tāhartī and its aftermath.

This account is preceded by a passage on Maḥmūd's assiduous study of religious learning, the methods of religious debate, and knowledge of previous heresies, as he 'reflected on (the principles of) religion and sought assistance in the suppression of heretics'. To this end he read many books, heard teaching on exegesis, dialectical method, and the sciences of Ḥadīth; he 'learned concerning the principles of religion what innovations were not permissible therein, and considered whatever conflicted with its external meaning [*ẓāhir*] as repugnant and abominated it' (1869, 2: 239–40; Jarbādhqānī's language [1966: 370] is somewhat stronger, and he embellishes ʿUtbī's account considerably).

> It was reported to him that there were groups among the gullible populace of Khurasan associated with the [Fāṭimid] Egyptian ruler who professed the Bāṭinī doctrine, whose outward (appearance) was Shīʿism but whose inner (purport) was pure unbelief, (based on) forged interpretations (of Scripture) which lead to the removal of the principles of the faith. (1869, 2: 241)

Maḥmūd appointed spies to infiltrate these groups; they happened on a man who served as an envoy between the Fāṭimid and his propagandists, and who knew their names and descriptions. He delivered up a number of them, who were brought to court, crucified and stoned: Maḥmūd continued to pursue their followers. The Ustādh Abū Bakr Muḥammad ibn Isḥāq ibn Maḥmashād, leader of the Karrāmiyya (whom Jarbādhqānī terms simply the 'shaykh of the Sunnīs' [1966: 370]), who was 'noted for his vigilence in pursuing extremist (Shīʿī) sects and vile innovations (in religion)' (1869, 2: 242), supported Maḥmūd's decision that all who followed divergent beliefs deserved destruction, and informed on a number of people who were falsely accused of heresy, who also perished.

> From doing that which brought him close to the Sultan in his apparent defense of God's religion, (making) his accusations in

> the name of the rights due to God, and cleansing the egg of Islam from every doubtful person, respect paid to him increased; people became desirous (of his favour) and put their hopes in him. And that magnificence on which God had placed the stamp of religion (rises to) proximity with the stars; its place is elevated and it station exalted. (1869, 2: 243–4)[9]

Shortly after, a man from Iraq (Tāhartī), who boasted of his ʿAlid lineage and claimed to be an envoy bearing a letter and gifts from the Fāṭimid ruler to the sultan, appeared in Nishapur. He was seized and the Sultan was informed; then he went on to Herat, making for the court at Ghazna. Maḥmūd ordered him to be sent back to Nishapur to present his letter publicly (lest it be thought the Sultan and the Fāṭimid were in secret correspondence) and make good his claim. There he was searched, and several works on Bāṭinī and 'extremist Ḥanafī' teachings were found in his possessions. Abū Bakr Maḥmashād debated with him and found him wanting; Tāhartī was sent to the Sultan's court, where he was further examined by an assembly of notables, judges, jurists and trustworthy persons. The ʿAlid Ḥasan ibn Ṭāhir ibn Muslim was present, having come from Medina to Khurasan to seek refuge at the Sultan's court. (The account of his descent, and various episodes concerning his father and grandfather, do not concern us here; suffice to say that he was not directly descended from ʿAlī ibn Abī Ṭālib.) When Tāhartī appeared Ḥasan denounced him, claiming that he was lying and deserved death. The Sultan absolved himself of shedding his blood and delegated the task to Ḥasan, who performed it with dispatch (1869, 2: 250).

This account must be read in conjunction with one which follows and which relates how the Karrāmīs, and Abū Bakr Maḥmashād, were themselves discredited. The two accounts frame three others, which deal with several successful Indian campaigns, Maḥmūd's conquest of Khwarazm, and his building of the Friday mosque in Ghazna. Abū Bakr continued to be well regarded because of his father's reputation for piety and asceticism, a path which he too followed, 'or so he claimed' (1869, 2: 310; Manīnī explains that by this he means that Abū Bakr followed the teachings of the Karrāmiyya). Sabuktigīn, impressed by this outward piety, had favoured the Karrāmīs, and for a while Maḥmūd followed in his footsteps in his respect for and preferment of them. When the Bāṭinī heretics appeared and fell victim to the Sultan's zealous measures to suppress them, 'this Abū Bakr was one of the Sultan's supporters, who rounded them up and executed them, and thus sanctioned his decision'. Innocent and guilty alike feared for their lives, and 'people saw that his saliva was deadly poison and his delation meant ruin' (1869, 2: 311; translation by

Bosworth, 1960: 10). They humbled themselves before him and appointed him *ra'is* of Nishapur, 'under the woollen cloak (of piety), placing their hopes and fears in him'. His followers treated the Nishapuris with contempt and greed, exploited them and extorted money from them, and accused those who protested of heresy.

These trials lasted some years, with no hope of change or betterment. 'For no one knew that Time is the the guarantor of change and the pledge to (the appearance of) difference in the customary form (of things); he who is patient as time passes will see the elevated brought low and the powerful humbled' (1869, 2: 312). The agent of change was the *qāḍī* of Nishapur, Abū al-ʿAlā' Ṣāʿid Ṣābūnī, who in 402/1012 went on pilgrimage, and was received en route by the caliph al-Qādir in Baghdad. On his return, he brought letters from the caliph to the Sultan. In the Sultan's assembly the talk turned to the subject of the Karrāmīs and their anthropomorphic beliefs. (It is not so stated, but it would appear that concern for this matter was expressed in the caliph's letters, and that it was the *qāḍī* Ṣāʿid who introduced the subject.) The Sultan rejected these 'vile doctrines', summoned Abū Bakr Maḥmashād and questioned him about his beliefs; Abū Bakr denied that he shared these beliefs and dissociated himself from the Karrāmiyya, 'thus saving himself from harsh rebuke'. The Sultan ordered an investigation; those who repudiated the beliefs of the Karrāmiyya were left alone, while those who persisted in them were placed under house arrest (1869, 2: 314). The *qāḍī* was given robes of honour, and things went on much as before.

Abū Bakr harboured resentment against the *qāḍī*. An opportunity for revenge came when the *qāḍī* was accused of Muʿtazilī leanings. Abū Bakr and his supporters enthusiastically filed accusations against him; another investigation was launched, and the two were summoned to provide reliable testimony concerning their accusations before an assembly of notables. Abū Bakr, fearing exposure, stated that it was rancour that had caused each to accuse the other of beliefs he did not hold; as for the other parties, they were motivated by personal animus. This incensed the Ḥanafī jurists, and a riot nearly broke out; but awe of the Sultan made them hold their tongues. The *qāḍī* was exonerated, and retired (at the Sultan's suggestion) to a life of study and pious observance; but Abū Bakr's power and status increased, as did his excesses and those of his supporters. The Sultan's tolerance reached its limit, and he removed Maḥmashād from the *riyāsa* and appointed Abū ʿAlī Ḥasan ibn Muḥammad Mīkālī (the future vizier Ḥasanak). Maḥmūd's goal in this, says ʿUtbī, was to suppress 'him who was (formerly) appointed' (Abū Bakr) on the basis of his reputation for piety and asceticism, to falsify the claim of

Abū Bakr and his followers that the station they had attained was so closely bound to religion that it could not be loosed without damage to the faith and thought that 'their crescent moon would never wane', and to restore 'that which was required by (true) piety, (namely) the renunciation of high positions and worldly desires'. When Abū ʿAlī (ʿUtbī does not use his Persian sobriquet Ḥasanak) entered Nishapur,

> he directed its people [firmly] ... He quieted even the chirping of the grasshoppers and stilled even the creeping of scorpions, suppressed the discord over position and silenced the sectarians. It was as though every poisonous snake and baneful viper had taken refuge in its hole and concealed itself in its cave. (1869, 2: 322–3)[10]

The Sultan takes the credit; but it is clear, from the manner in which the two episodes are treated, that there is some doubt as to whether he deserves it. This is not stated openly, but is rather suggested by ʿUtbī's language (as Manīnī notes in his commentary), and by his positioning of the two accounts of the Karrāmī's anti-Bāṭinī activities, which frame three campaigns in India, the annexation of Khwarazm, and Maḥmūd's building of the Friday mosque in Ghazna – all of which could be said to demonstrate that ruler's piety. That he could be so deceived by the appearance of piety as to appoint Abū Bakr to a position of power – a *ra'is* in a woollen cloak (*libsa*, 'garment', has also the sense of 'dissimulation'), a wolf in sheep's clothing – does not redound to his good judgement. Nor, in the end, does his violent religious prejudice, which was fanned by those seeking to advance their own status and achieve their own, distinctly worldly, ambitions. ʿUtbī depicts an atmosphere poisoned by suspicion, intrigue and false accusation, as well as a disjunction between the ideal of the Islamic sovereign and the reality. Perhaps he was not so single-mindedly encomiastic after all.

The remaining portion of ʿUtbī's history describes how Nishapur prospered under the *riyāsa* of Abū ʿAlī (Ḥasanak) and his deputy Abū Naṣr Manṣūr ibn Rāmish, and the good works of Maḥmūd's brother the Amīr Naṣr during his governorate of Khurasan. He laments the latter's untimely death, and includes elegies on that prince and a lengthy *risāla* he composed on Naṣr's qualities and achievements. (The appended account of what happened to him after he had reached this point in his history does not concern us here.) I have discussed ʿUtbī's work at some length, first because it illustrates how the transfer of rule from the Sāmānids to the Ghaznavids was generally perceived; second, because it was extremely influential on later Persian historians; and third, because it illustrates concerns shared by other historians to be dealt with. Moreover, it provides a basis for comparison with later works (including the Persian translation by Jarbādhqānī) which will help to illustrate changing perceptions, particularly with regard to the transfer of power and the rise and fall of states.

GARDĪZĪ'S *ZAYN AL-AKHBĀR*

ʿAbd al-Ḥayy Gardīzī's general history, the *Zayn al-akhbār*, was written in the mid-5th/11th century at the court of ʿAbd al-Rashīd (440?–3?/1049?–52?) in Ghazna.[11] A few words by way of preface are necessary to situate Gardīzī's work (as well as that of Bayhaqī, discussed in the next section) in historical context. In 420/1029 Maḥmūd of Ghazna launched a campaign against the Būyids in Rayy. Taking the city without effort, he sent its ruler Majd al-Dawla (who had, it seems, not learned the lessons of history) as a prisoner to Ghazna, killed or took captive all the heretics (Bāṭinīs and philosophers) in the city and burnt their heretical books.[12] Suffering from the illness which afflicted him during the last years of his life, he left his son Masʿūd in charge of Rayy, entrusting him also with the conquest of Hamadan and Isfahan, and returned to Khurasan, where he spent the summer of 420/1029, moving to Balkh for the winter. Balkh's climate did not agree with him, and he returned to Ghazna in the spring of 421/1030, but his condition worsened, and he died on 23 Rabīʿ II 421/30 April 1030 (see Nāẓim 1971: 123–4). 'With his death, the world turned towards ruin, base men became ennobled and the noble abased' (Gardīzī 1968: 193–4).

Shortly before his death Maḥmūd had replaced his designated successor Masʿūd with the latter's half-brother Muḥammad. When Maḥmūd died Masʿūd was camped outside Isfahan, which he had taken successfully; Muḥammad's supporters quickly brought him from his own province of Juzjanan to Ghazna and put him on the throne, while Masʿūd's supporters wrote to him secretly urging him to return, and some openly defected to him. Muḥammad's six-month rule ended when, preparing to march against Masʿūd (who was now in Nishapur, where the Khurasani army had declared for him), he was arrested by his own courtiers, and Masʿūd's accession was assured (see Gardīzī 1968: 194–6). One of Masʿūd's first acts was to seize and imprison or execute a number of his father's former officials, in particular those who had supported Muḥammad's succession out of loyalty to Maḥmūd: 'All who had opposed Masʿūd, or had agreed with his opponents, he seized and punished in some way, so that all were ruined' (Gardīzī 1968: 197).

Masʿūd's policies and ill-conceived military adventures led to increasing disaffection among his troops, his courtiers and the populace at large, as we shall see when we turn to Bayhaqī's history of his reign. But perhaps the greatest threat to him, and one whose gravity he failed to appreciate until it was too late, came from the Turkmen Saljūqs, nomadic steppe Turks whom Maḥmūd had allowed to settle in limited numbers on the Khurasani side of the Oxus in return for military service to him (see Bosworth 1973a: 223–6). In 426/1035, expelled from Khwarazm, more Turkmens migrated across the Oxus in large numbers; their depredations aroused vehement complaints, and Mas'ūd and his generals were ultimately unable to deal with them. In 428/1038, when Mas'ūd was campaigning in India, they occupied Nishapur, which Mas'ūd retook the following year. A temporary truce was short-lived; Mas'ūd determined to march against the Saljūqs, and on 8 Ramaḍān 431/23 May 1040 they met on the plain of Dandānqān. Mas'ūd, surrounded, 'fought that day as no king has ever fought in person' (Gardīzī 1968: 203); but many of his troops went over to the Turks, the rest were put to flight, and Mas'ūd was obliged to retreat in disarray, first to Marv and from there to Ghazna (see Bosworth 1973a: 240–68).

Amid deteriorating conditions, Mas'ūd determined to retreat to India to gather an army with which to confront the Saljūqs. He ordered all of Maḥmūd's treasuries brought to Ghazna, had them loaded onto camels, and, with the women of his household and the baggage train, proceeded towards India. En route (or perhaps while still in Ghazna; Bayhaqī's version of events differs somewhat from Gardīzī's) he had his half-brother Muḥammad, along with the latter's sons, brought to his camp, where he treated them with great honour. Near the fort of Marigala, Mas'ūd's troops raided the treasure train. 'Since they had committed an offence, they knew it would not be set aside unless there were a new ruler.' They chose Muḥammad (who agreed, unwillingly), and swore allegiance to him. Mas'ūd retreated to the fort, and fought against the rebels on the next day; 'but the divine decree had come, and he could do nothing'. The troops seized Mas'ūd and sent him to the fortress of Gīrī, where he remained till 11 Jumādā II 432/13 February 1041; then they had him killed by the *kutvāl* of the fort, sending him an order in Muḥammad's name (though he, says Gardīzī, knew nothing about it [1968: 204–5]).

Mas'ūd's son and designated heir Mawdūd determined to avenge his father and make good his own claim to the throne. After securing Ghazna, the following spring he marched against Muḥammad. Obtaining a guarantee of neutrality from his uncle 'Abd al-Rashīd (Maḥmūd's sole surviving son, Mawdūd's eventual successor and Gardīzī's patron), he engaged Muḥammad in battle; in the ensuing slaughter Muḥammad, his sons, and a number of other Ghaznavid princes and officials from the previous regime were killed. Breaking his promise to ʿAbd al-Rashīd, he had that prince arrested and imprisoned in the fortress of Mandīsh (Gardīzī 1968: 205–6; Bosworth 1977: 20–5). Although Mawdūd 'still dreamed of regaining the lost territories' from the Saljūqs (Bosworth 1977: 26), he was unable either to accomplish that aim or to retain control of Sistan; but he succeeded in asserting his authority in India against the claim of its commander-in-chief, Masʿūd's son Majdūd (see Bosworth 1977: 30–3). He died in December of either 440/1048 or 441/1049 (on the discrepancies in dating see Bosworth 1977: 36–7); the ensuing struggle for the succession ended with the release of ʿAbd al-Rashīd (probably due to the action of Mawdūd's capable vizier, ʿAbd al-Razzāq ibn Aḥmad Maymandī), who was placed on the throne. It was during his reign that Gardīzī wrote his *Zayn al-akhbār*, named for one of the ruler's honorifics, Zayn al-Milla ('ornament of the faith'); it was in his reign also that Abū al-Faḍl Bayhaqī was made head of the chancery, a position he subsequently lost. Along with other of ʿAbd al-Rashīd's officials, Bayhaqī was imprisoned during the usurpation of the Turkish slave general Ṭughril which put an end to ʿAbd al-Rashīd's reign and which lasted for some two and a half years (see Bosworth 1977: 39–47).

Little is known about Gardīzī. He may have been a scribe or a minor official at Maḥmūd's court, since he states that he witnessed many of the events he describes in his account of Maḥmūd's reign; he was perhaps related to the Gardīzī who brought the standard of office from the caliph al-Qādir to Masʿūd in Nishapur (Gardīzī 1968: 196). His history lacks a preface and breaks off at the point of Mawdūd's defeat of Muḥammad, and there is little personal information to be gleaned from what remains.

Gardīzī's general history is almost exclusively oriented towards Persian history, especially that of Khurasan. It treats in succession the ancient Persian kings, divided into five classes: (I) Tahmurāsb to Tahmāsb; (II) the Kayānids, beginning with Kay Qubād; (III) the Petty Kings; (IV) the Sasanians; (V) the Akāsira (plural of Arabic *kisrā* = Persian *khusraw*), beginning with Khusraw Anūshīrvān (a periodisation somewhat different from those of his predecessors); the Prophet and the succeeding caliphates; the governors of Khurasan; the Ṣaffārids, the Sāmānids and, most important, the Ghaznavids. It includes tables of each class of rulers and, at the end of the historical section, an attempt at synchronising various chronologies, followed by chapters on Muslim, Iranian, Jewish, Christian, Zoroastrian and Hindu holidays (with explanations for the reasons for them), and materials on various ethnic groups (Turks, Byzantines, Hindus, and so on). The

Zayn al-akhbār has been termed 'a brief and colourless chronicle of dry facts' (Nāẓim 1971: 6), and that is, in general, a fair description. Gardīzī's accounts of the pre-Islamic Persian monarchs and of caliphal history are generally brief and cursory, concentrating on such events as major battles, the founding of cities, and so on. He has a clear aversion to the sort of fantastic and legendary elements for which the *Shāhnāma* was criticised; for example, he omits mention of Rustam's famous 'seven trials', and although he includes the parallel and more 'realistic' set of exploits by Isfandiyār, there is no mention of the mythical bird, the Sīmurgh, who helped Rustam to kill that prince in battle. He does however show a marked interest in accounts of dreams and prophecies, in horoscopes and in astrological predictions.

Several major concerns run through the work and link its otherwise often disjointed accounts. A principal theme is the transfer of power, the Ghaznavids being the final link in the chain of such transfers which begins (in Islamic times) with the defeat of the Sasanians by the Arab Muslims. A further (if implicit) link lies in the fact that the Prophet was born in the reign of Khusraw I Anūshīrvān, last of the great just rulers of Iran. Anūshīrvān's successor Hurmuz, an arrogant ruler who faced both conflicts within his domains and threats from outside, alienated his loyal general Bahrām Chūbīn by insulting him; Bahrām's armies rebelled, deposed and blinded Hurmuz, and placed Khusraw II Parvīz on the throne. Gardīzī blames Bahrām Chūbīn's rebellion on his troops more than on the general himself; Khusraw Parvīz is presented in a negative light, as he both plots the murder of the defeated Bahrām Chībīn and rejects the Prophet's summons to Islam (1968: 34–5). The seeds are being planted for the ultimate collapse of the Sasanians, finalised by the defeat of Yazdigird III. 'The rule of the Persians ended with him. Then the Muslims took Īrānshahr, and continue to hold it, and will hold it until Resurrection' (1968: 40).

A second link is the overthrow of the Umayyads (who are clearly seen as illegitimate, and who are of interest chiefly with reference to affairs in the East) by the Abbasids. Thus Gardīzī notes that ʿUmar I's general Khālid ibn al-Walīd 'removed the treasures of the kings of Persia that they had amassed for four thousand years', and that ʿUthmān sent the first Muslim army to Rayy and conquered it (1968: 54), but omits any mention of ʿUthmān's murder, normally a controversial issue for Muslim historians. Events leading to the Umayyad defeat, and the role played by the Khurasani leader Abū Muslim, are treated briefly in the section relating to the caliphate, but are taken up at greater length at the beginning of that dealing with the Muslim governors of Khurasan, in which accounts of the rivalries between various Umayyad personalities over the appointment of governors are clearly meant to show that the region was an important player in Umayyad politics, and that it was the Umayyads' misrule that precipitated their fall.

Now Gardīzī provides a more detailed account of the Abbasid *da'wa* in Khurasan. The appearance of Abū Muslim, he states, confirmed an apocalyptic *ḥadīth* related by 'Alī ibn 'Abd Allāh ibn 'Abbās: that one of the signs of the Hour is that 'from the East 70,000 swords will come to the support of the Prophet's family' (1968: 119). Abū Muslim's activities in Khurasan following the Abbasid victory (including his killing of the false prophet Bihāfarīd; see below), and his murder by al-Manṣūr, are related at greater length and with suitable prophetic overtones. When Abū Muslim went on pilgrimage to Mecca, he was warned in Rayy by his officials, 'Don't go, for you will not return!' (1968: 121). When he criticised the newly enthroned al-Manṣūr, the latter sought an opportunity to kill him. On his return from the pilgrimage, an aged Christian monk delivered the following prophecy:

> 'You have achieved enough; you have brought your efforts to perfection; and you have reached the termination. You have burnt yourself, and dispersed your labours, and have seen your own murder!' Abū Muslim became melancholy. Then the old man said to him, 'Defects do not arise from perfect resolve, nor from correct judgement, nor from fruitful planning, nor from the cutting sword; but no one achieves all his desires, for Time catches up with him, when (only) some of his goals have been achieved.'
>
> Abū Muslim asked, 'What do you think? Where will this affair end?' The old man replied, 'When two caliphs agree on a matter, it will take place. The decree rests with Him before Whom all plans are in vain. If you go to Khurasan, you will be safe.' Abū Muslim wished to return (to Khurasan); but Manṣūr had sent messengers (to him, instructing him), 'Come quickly!' The divine decree had come; and Abū Muslim had lost his powers of perception. He asked someone, 'What do you think they will do with me?' That person replied, '(They will treat you) well, and the reward for what you have done for them can be only good.'
>
> Abū Muslim said, 'I suspect otherwise.' (1968: 121)

Abū Muslim's murder, and the confrontation with the caliph which preceded it, are related in a similarly vivid and dramatic style which departs from Gardīzī's generally unlively prose.

> They say that when Abū Muslim ... was going to Abū Ja'far (al-Manṣūr) he asked for a horse which was the finest in the stable.

> He mounted that horse intending to go to Manṣūr; the horse bolted beneath Abū Muslim three times. One of his followers said to Abū Muslim, 'Go back!' Abū Muslim replied, 'Let what God wills, be.' When he came into Manṣūr's presence (the caliph) seated him and asked after him politely. Then he said, 'With what sword did you achieve all those conquests and victories?' Abū Muslim replied, 'With this one,' and pointed to the sword he had girded on. Manṣūr said, 'Give it to me,' and he did so. Then Manṣūr said, 'Do you know what you have done against me?' and enumerated (his charges) one by one. Abū Muslim replied to each, until Manṣūr grew angry, and shouted at him.
>
> Abū Muslim said, 'O Commander of the Believers! This is no (just) reward for all the good things that I have accomplished!' Manṣūr replied, 'O Abū Mujrim! Remember when you came before Abū al-ʿAbbās (al-Saffāḥ), and did obeisance to him, and I was seated there, and you paid no attention to me?!'

The caliph enumerated a number of other charges (mostly involving slights to his person), all of which Abū Muslim answered. Then he said,

> 'It was not out of friendship for us that you did these things! It was (due to) a heavenly affair and divine favour, for it was the rise of our *dawlat*.' Then Manṣūr signalled to that person who was standing over Abū Muslim. He struck (him) with his sword, and Abū Muslim fell, crying, 'Oh! Oh!' Manṣūr said, 'You, who accomplished the deeds of the mighty: now you are crying like a baby.'

Several others struck Abū Muslim, until he perished. Outside, his soldiers were in an uproar. Al-Manṣūr's *ḥājib* went out and delivered the caliph's message to the Khurasani troops: 'Abū Muslim was our slave, and we have punished him for his disobedience' (1968: 122).

Another link in the chain of transfer of power is the caliph al-Ma'mūn. The caliphal section contains an account of the civil war which resulted from Hārūn al-Rashīd's divided succession; its cause is said to have been treachery on the part of Hārūn's vizier Faḍl ibn Rabīʿ and Ṣāliḥ ibn al-Rashīd, who after the caliph's death at Ṭūs disobeyed his orders to take the wealth he had brought with him to al-Ma'mūn in Khurasan, and took it instead, along with an army, to al-Amīn in Baghdad. Al-Ma'mūn is portrayed as an ideal ruler who spread justice throughout Khurasan, while al-Amīn pursued pleasure in Baghdad and the real ruler was Faḍl. There is a lengthy account of the siege of Baghdad, in which al-Ma'mūn's general Ṭāhir ibn Ḥusayn is credited with having prevented the sack of that city (1968: 73).[13]

These events are recounted once more at the beginning of the section on the Ṭāhirids, where the reason is given for Ṭāhir ibn Ḥusayn's sobriquet Dhū al-Yamīnayn ('he of two right hands'). When Ṭāhir was sent by al-Ma'mūn against al-Amīn's general 'Alī ibn 'Īsā, the vizier Faḍl ibn Sahl cast the horoscope for the time of his departure. He saw the two Yemeni stars, Suhayl (Canopus) and Sha'rī (Sirius) in the middle of the heavens, and for this reason called Ṭāhir Dhū al-Yamīnayn ('he of the two Yemeni stars'). As he tied the caliph's banner for Ṭāhir, Faḍl told him, 'O Ṭāhir! I have tied a banner for you which no one will loose for sixty-five years'; and from then to the end of the *dawlat* (with Ya'qūb ibn Layth's seizure of Muḥammad ibn Ṭāhir (II); see the section on the *Tārīkh-i Sīstān*) was sixty-five years (1968: 135).[14]

The Ṭāhirids, appointed by al-Ma'mūn, are a further channel for the transfer of power in Khurasan. The final link in the chain is, of course, the Sāmānids. At the beginning of his section on this dynasty Gardīzī gives their genealogy and recounts the (apocryphal) story of Sāmānkhudā's conversion to Islam by al-Ma'mūn. Al-Ma'mūn's links with Khurasan are, again, crucial: as his presence in Khurasan served to legitimate its Ṭāhirid governors, his conversion of Sāmānkhudā legitimates the Sāmānids. In both cases, power passes through the caliph to his favoured governors. Al-Ma'mūn favoured (Asad ibn) Sāmānkhudā's sons because (unlike the Ṣaffārids) they were of noble birth, and commended them to his then governor Ghassān ibn 'Abbād; the latter assigned Samarqand to Nūḥ, Farghana to Aḥmad, Chach and Usrushana to Yaḥyā, and Herat to Ilyās, 'and Ṭāhir [who replaced Ghassān] let them be' (1968: 146).

This rather neat line of succession is slightly complicated by the decline of the Ṭāhirids and what might be called the 'Ṣaffārid interlude'. Muḥammad ibn Ṭāhir – described as 'negligent and heedless of consequences' and devoted to wine and pleasure – was unable to put down the rebellion of the 'Alid Ḥasan ibn Zayd in 251/865, and the latter occupied Khurasan. Muḥammad's paternal cousins, envious of him, encouraged the Ṣaffārid Ya'qūb ibn Layth to attack Khurasan; and thus began 'the *fitna* of Ya'qūb ibn al-Layth, a nobody [*mard-i majhūl*] from the villages of Sistan' (1968: 138). The former coppersmith, now brigand chief, Ya'qūb, depicted as clever and ruthless, took Sistan and Zabulistan, occupied Nishapur and defeated Ḥasan ibn Zayd, then made for Baghdad in an attempt to remove al-Mu'tamid from the caliphate and install his brother al-Muwaffaq, but was defeated by al-Muwaffaq's stratagem and forced to retreat (1968: 140–1; compare the account in the *Tārīkh-i Sīstān*). Ya'qūb's successor, his brother 'Amr, was given caliphal patents for Khurasan,

Sistan and Fars, put down a rebellion in Nishapur (having been asked for help by that city's scholars, *muṭawwiʿa* [volunteers] and *fuqahā*, who 'inclined towards ʿAmr, who was the caliph's representative'), and restored order in Khurasan (1968: 143). ʿAmr's attempt to annex Transoxania is seen as the cause of the fall of the Ṣaffārids; defeated by the Sāmānid Ismāʿīl ibn Aḥmad in 287/900, ʿAmr was sent to the caliph al-Muʿtaḍid in Baghdad, where he died in prison (1968: 144–5).

A foreshadowing of Abbasid decline is seen in al-Muʿtaḍid's explanation of why he never killed an ʿAlid.

> He said: 'One night I saw ʿAlī ibn Abī Ṭālib in a dream. He said to me, "Respect my descendants," and gave me a pickaxe. I struck the ground three times. ʿAlī said: "To the number of these blows your offspring will be caliphs." I vowed never to harm an ʿAlid.' (1968: 80)

Earlier accounts of the Abbasids also anticipate their collapse; predictably, one concerns the fall of the Barmakids, depicted as wise and just counselors. 'In the end (Hārūn al-Rashīd) broke faith (with them), and turned against them because of what their enemies said, and committed a crime against them, who were guiltless.' 'The cause of this change of heart', Gardīzī asserts (following Balʿamī's version of Ṭabarī's account), was the affair between Jaʿfar the Barmakid and the caliph's sister ʿAbbāsa. Fond of both, the caliph married ʿAbbāsa to Jaʿfar on condition that no marital relations take place between them. But since ʿAbbāsa was beautiful and Jaʿfar handsome, they could not resist temptation.

> Secretly they employed ruses, and came together (as man and wife), and ʿAbbāsa bore Jaʿfar a child ... So (in the end) Hārūn suddenly turned against them and killed them all, annihilating them, so that not a trace of them remained in the world.
>
> And when they had all been annihilated, defects crept into the affairs of rule, and there was no one to put them right or to devise strategies. Revenues began to decrease, and Hārūn repented his deed, but to no avail, for he had lost control of affairs. (1968: 70; Gardīzī abbreviates and paraphrases Balʿamī's version.)

Following al-Muʿtaḍid's reign, civil disorder in Baghdad increased. Things were put right only when, under al-Muṭīʿ, Baghdad came under Būyid control, and justice and order were restored. The Būyids are generally viewed positively: the conflict between the Būyid Bakhtiyār and the Turkish general Sabuktigīn (no relation to the Ghaznavid), for example, is presented as one between good Daylamids and bad Turks (1968: 88–9), and the good relations between Sāmānids and Būyids (described as 'vassals' of the Sāmānids) are noted. The sections on the Sāmānids contain little that is new. The accounts of the last Sāmānids emphasise the chaotic conditions during their reigns and the efforts of Sabuktigīn and Maḥmūd to restore order to Khurasan, ending with their assumption of rule. Elsewhere, under the entry for the caliph al-Qādir, Gardīzī states that the caliph 'heard so much about Maḥmūd ibn Sabuktigīn' and his accomplishments that at the end of Dhū al-Qa'da 389/November 999 he transferred rule of Khurasan to Maḥmūd and, when he died, to Mas'ūd (1968: 91), providing further legitimation for Maḥmūd's succession in the chain of Sāmānid-Ghaznavid rule. Now, he turns to the history of the Ghaznavids; for 'their [the Sāmānids'] time had come to its end, and their age and fortune was reversed' (1968: 173).

Before turning to this account, let me comment on another theme which looms large in Gardīzī (as in many other historians) and which is particularly relevant to Maḥmūd's presentation as the warrior sultan: that of the ruler's duty to support and propagate the true faith, suppress heretics, and prevent the spread of heterodox beliefs. The Sasanian Shāpūr I is praised (in a few brief lines) for destroying Mānī and his followers (1968: 21–2). A slightly more detailed account is given of the appearance of Mazdak (1968: 31); after Anūshīrvān had discredited him and seized and killed Mazdak and his followers, he exhorted his subjects: 'Learn (true) religion, so that when a Mazdakī appears he cannot impose his lies on you' (1968: 31). In his treatment of Islamic history Gardīzī has more to say about heretics and 'false prophets'. In his second account of Abū Muslim he tells of the appearance of Bihāfarīd in the villages of Khvāf (1968: 119–20). Bihāfarīd enjoined his followers to perform seven daily prayers in the direction of the sun, forbade the eating of carrion flesh and marriage with mothers, sisters, nephews and nieces, as well as the payment of large dowries, and established a tithe of one-seventh on wealth and produce. This drew many converts away from Zoroastrianism; the *mawbad*s complained to Abū Muslim, saying, 'He has destroyed both your religion and ours', and Abū Muslim seized and crucified Bihāfarīd and killed many of his followers. After Abū Muslim's murder more false prophets led popular revolts against the Abbasids. Barāz-banda, who claimed to be Ibrāhīm ibn 'Abd Allāh al-Hāshimī and bore a white ('Alid) banner, was invested by the then governor of Khurasan; his revolt was ended when al-Manṣūr gave his son al-Mahdī control of Khurasan and the latter put down the rebels (1968: 124). Later, Ustādsīs appeared in Badghis; he 'followed the way of Bihāfarīd', and 'some say Ustādsīs's daughter Marājīl was al-Ma'mūn's mother, and his son Ghālib al-Ma'mūn's maternal uncle, who was killed in a bath at Sarakhs by Faḍl ibn Sahl on al-Ma'mūn's order' (1968: 124–5).

The governorate of Ḥumayd ibn Qaḥṭaba saw the appearance of the veiled prophet Muqannaʿ, who also bore a white banner and at first claimed prophecy, then divinity, asserting that 'when God created Adam He entered into his form', then into those of Noah, Abraham, Moses, Jesus, Muḥammad, Abū Mūslim, and Hāshim' (that is, himself) (1968: 125). Muqannaʿ was supported by the 'Wearers of White', who now appeared in Bukhara and Sughd. In 161/777–8 the governor Musayyab ibn Zuhayr defeated Muqannaʿ's supporters; Muqannaʿ, besieged, gathered his womenfolk, promised them Paradise, had them take poison and then did so himself. One of his followers beheaded him and ordered his body burned so that it would not be found. Thus some thought that he had ascended to heaven, and were thus attracted to belief in him, 'so that there still exist Muqannaʿīs today' (1968: 127–8).

Gardīzī twice notes the appearance of a false prophet in Khurasan in the reign of Nūḥ (I) ibn Naṣr, in the caliphate of al-Muṭīʿ, whose followers called him the Mahdī. He performed 'tricks' of charlatanry, such as pulling coins out of a pool of water; he was killed on Nūḥ's order by Abū ʿAlī Chaghānī (1968: 87). This account recurs, with some variation, in the section on the Sāmānids: a false prophet appeared in Chaghaniyan during the reign of Nūḥ ibn Naṣr.[15] This prophet, who called himself the Mahdī, carried a sword and fought all who disagreed with him; he knew magic and spells, and performed 'miraculous' feats (1968: 158).

In general these accounts are somewhat perfunctory, and reveal none of the near-hysteria seen in, for example, Niẓām al-Mulk or Ibn al-Balkhī (see Chapter 3). They point, however, to one of the qualifications of the virtuous ruler: support for true belief and opposition to heresy. Maḥmūd combined this with justice, the maintenance of order, and conquest. He was the sort of ruler the Sāmānids could not produce, and whose appearance the chaos of the last period of their rule necessitated. This is the moment Gardīzī's entire history has been leading to, as he sets out to glorify Maḥmūd's reign as the shining pinnacle of all previous history. Now, he states, he will begin 'the history of Yamīn al-Dawla ... for of all the historical accounts that we have read, none has the rank of his. We have heard these accounts or read them in books ... but our own accounts are chiefly (of) those (events) that we have witnessed with our own eyes.' These are, in general, accounts of Maḥmūd's various conquests and campaigns, in which 'he traversed fearful deserts, mountains and roads' and defeated mighty kings: deeds the likes of which 'no one had ever seen or heard of before'. 'And I shall also tell,' he states, 'of how it happened that [the current ruler] ʿAbd al-Rashīd ... became king without effort ... and achieved his goal without opposition or delay' (1968: 173–4).

Gardīzī describes Maḥmūd's campaigns, his holy wars against pagans and heretics, and his courtly ceremonials at length, recording also such points of interest as his ordering the execution of Tāhartī, his conquest of the Indian valleys of Qirat and Nur and the conversion to Islam of their pagan kings (1968: 185; but see Bosworth 1973a: 118), and his campaign against the Indian prince Nanda (Ganda) and the sieges of Gwalior and Kalinjar in 413/1022–3, both of which were concluded with a truce and gifts of elephants. Nanda, we are told, composed a poem for Maḥmūd in 'Indian', which Maḥmūd had read out before all his poets (Indian, Persian and Arabic), and rewarded Nanda lavishly. The great military review in the Dasht-i Shāhbahār which followed these events, in the spring of 414/1024, provided the occasion for a a *qaṣīda* by Farrukhī celebrating Maḥmūd's achievements. Gardīzī also provides a detailed description of Maḥmūd's meeting with the Qarakhānid ruler Qādir Khān Yūsuf in 416/1025, at which he himself was present (1968: 187–9). Following the conclusion of a truce between the two rulers, there was lavish feasting and drinking (except on the part of Qādir Khān; Turks, Gardīzī observes, don't drink), music, and the distribution of costly gifts; the celebrations lasted several days, and the Turks were duly impressed.

Troubles with the Saljūqs began when Maḥmūd allowed a group of them to cross the Oxus. The Amīr of Ṭūs, Arslān Jādhib, objected, urged that they be killed, and warned Maḥmūd he would repent his act: 'and so it was, and (the matter) has still not been properly resolved' (1968: 189–90). Gardīzī also tells of the famous Somnat campaign and the difficulties of the return journey, on which many perished (1968: 190–1; these hardships go unmentioned in Farrukhī's *qaṣīda* celebrating this campaign). Maḥmūd subsequently received new titles from the caliph al-Qādir, who encouraged him to appoint an heir. Gardīzī also recounts (without much detail) Maḥmūd's successful campaign against Rayy (based on the account of a 'reliable informant', who was presumably present) and the events which preceded his death. He is particularly informative concerning the intrigues surrounding Muḥammad's accession and subsequent deposition, and presents that prince as both benign and just: under him, 'prices dropped, the people were at ease, and merchants from all parts headed towards Ghazna' (1968: 194). Despite this, however, both court and populace inclined towards Mas'ūd, and Muḥammad ultimately proved an ineffectual ruler. Faced with the desertion of the palace *ghulāms*, led by Maḥmūd's former favourite the Turkish Amīr Ayāz, Muḥammad devoted himself to pleasure, drank heavily, and ignored the warnings of those close to him. After four months of rule he proceeded towards Bust, intending to march against Masʿūd in Nishapur; but before reaching Bust he was arrested by his nobles and military leaders, who declared for Masʿūd (1968: 195).

Masʿūd's vindictiveness against his father's former officials and Muḥammad's erstwhile supporters is duly noted. The arrest and execution of the former vizier Ḥasan al-Mīkālī (Ḥasanak), given detailed and dramatic treatment by Bayhaqī (see below), is dealt with briefly and without comment. Describing Masʿūd's campaign in Jurjan against his vassal Bākālījār in 426/1035, Gardīzī mentions the sack of Sārī by 'some ruthless soldiers', whom Masʿūd restrained when its inhabitants protested; but he is silent on the subsequent extortion of monies from the citizens of Āmul and the sack and burning of that town (described, and deplored, by Bayhaqī), and merely notes that Masʿūd concluded a truce with Bākālījār and returned towards Ghazna (1968: 199). There follow accounts of the depradations of the Turks, unsuccessful attempts to deal with them, disturbances in India, and a detailed description of the newly completed Kushk-i Naw in Ghazna, with its golden, jewel-studded throne and seventy-*man* crown suspended from golden chains (1968: 200). Masʿūd's disastrous campaign against the Turkish chief Buritigīn in 430/1038–9 is presented in a relatively good light, with no mention of the hardships endured by the army (1968: 201; compare Bayhaqī's version, below); the account of the battle of Dandānqān includes a description of the Turks' military tactics, which ensured their victory against Masʿūd's less mobile army. Gardīzī recounts in some detail Masʿūd's betrayal by his rebellious troops and his subsequent arrest and murder, supposedly on the order of his half-brother Muḥammad. One senses, both here and in the earlier account of Muḥammad's first sultanate, that Gardīzī perhaps felt more sympathetic towards that prince than towards Masʿūd.

The historical section ends with the account of the slaughter of the Ghaznavid princes and officials by Mawdūd, the avenger of his father's murder. The sections which follow are beyond the scope of this study. It is certain that Gardīzī intended to include an account of the accession of ʿAbd al-Rashīd, as indicated in his introductory remarks to the reign of Maḥmūd. It is generally agreed that this chapter is missing; one may conjecture, however, that the writing of the book may have been interrupted during the disturbances leading to the usurpation of Ṭughril, and never resumed (indeed, Gardīzī himself may have been among the officials imprisoned by Ṭughril, and may even have perished). Gardīzī's reference to ʿAbd al-Rashīd's effortless accession takes certain liberties with the facts, as that ruler came to the throne as the result of a *putsch* which deposed his nephew (see Bosworth 1977: 41–7). ʿAbd al-Rashīd was Maḥmūd's sole surviving son; Gardīzī clearly wished both to legitimate his rule and to encourage his emulation of Maḥmūd's military achievements. This is implicit in his linking of father and son at the beginning of his account, and would seem to express the hope that this mature and potentially able ruler would succeed in putting down the insurrection that threatened his rule and the stability of the realm. One also suspects that there is an additional hope that a strong ruler would be able to regain the Ghaznavids' lost western territories, especially Khurasan, which is the main focus of the historical sections preceding that on the Ghaznavids, presented as legitimate heirs to its rule via the chain that leads from the ancient Iranian kings through al-Ma'mūn, the governors of Khurasan, and the Sāmānids to Maḥmūd. And while there are extensive accounts of Maḥmūd's campaigns in India and elsewhere, Khurasan is not neglected; moreover, while there is a wealth of information on India, its peoples and their customs in the appended ethnographical sections, there is also much on the populations of the western lands and the customs of their peoples.

Gardīzī may be dry and perfunctory at times; but at other times he rises above this, particularly when treating topics of obvious interest to him. These include prophecies (always fulfilled); the dangers presented by heretics and false prophets (a leitmotif which links Sasanian times with Islamic); accounts of such important Iranian or Khurasani figures as Abū Muslim, the Barmakids and the caliph al-Ma'mūn, and those involving the unfortunate Amīr Muḥammad. The theme of loyalty also concerns him, and he is critical of those who violate the bonds of loyalty and of vassals who betray their rulers (with the notable exception, for the most part, of Bahrām Chūbīn, presumably because, as the ancestor of the Sāmānids, it would not do to introduce such a suspect link in the chain leading to Maḥmūd's inheritance of rule): Faḍl ibn Rabīʿ, who betrayed Hārūn's instructions to him, and so was also disloyal to al-Ma'mūn; and Hārūn himself, who broke the bonds of loyalty with the Barmakids.

At times Gardīzī explicitly links past events to contemporary issues. In the account of the murder of Siyāvash (son of the Kayānid Kaykāvūs) by the Turanian prince Garsīvaz (son of Afrāsiyāb), he observes: 'When the news [of Siyāvash's death] reached Iran the world was filled with turmoil, and the lords of Iran made a great uproar, and between Iran and Tūrān there arose enmity and strife which exist even to this time' (1968: 11). The Turks, as ever, present a serious threat. Royal justice is also a recurrent theme: thus he criticises

Bahman (equated with 'Ardashīr darāz-bāzū', Artaxerxes Longimanus), who was 'the best of the Persian kings' save for his unjust conduct in seeking vengeance for Isfandiyār (killed in battle by Rustam when the latter refused his order to convert to Zoroastrianism) and the resulting devastation of Sistan. Bahman's actions in avenging the death of his son perhaps provide an analogue for Mawdūd's wholesale slaughter of Muḥammad and the other Ghaznavid princes (all his blood relatives) in vengeance for his father's murder.

Gardīzī, like Bal'amī, also connects the transfer of learning with that of power. This is most clearly exemplified in his account of Alexander's conquest: Alexander devastated Iran and burnt the Zoroastrian books; he had the Persian books of learning translated into Greek, sent the translations to Rūm and then destroyed the library of Iṣṭakhr; he buried whatever treasures he could not carry off. Yet Alexander's example also serves to illustrate the necessity for kings in order to prevent disorder and chaos: 'When he died the world was left without a king; each person seized a region or town for his own purposes. The base dominated the noble; no security remained in the world, and kingship became weakened' (1968: 17). At last, Ardashīr appeared, 'called himself Shāhinshāh', and commanded that the dispersed books be collected, so that the Persians' learning was restored to them.

Gardīzī's structuring of his work in terms of the transfer of power from one series of rulers to another, with the Ghaznavids at the pinnacle of this pyramid of rule, provides a clear and deliberately designed framework for his project, which is at once encomiastic, legitimatory and hortatory. For whom was it designed? Its relatively straightforward and simple style, devoid of self-conscious rhetorical flourishes, with occasional high points of dramatic immediacy and vividness, suggests a work of pedagogical intent. Was it intended for the edification of the court (including perhaps those ignorant officials, unlettered in Arabic, castigated by Bīrūnī)? Was it meant to inspire 'Abd al-Rashīd to emulation of his famous father, or to inculcate young princes in the principles of rule – a rule that had devolved upon the Ghaznavids as last in the chain of rulers of the East? Was it meant to legitimate 'Abd al-Rashīd's own claim to the throne? Perhaps these various motives were interlaced in what is the earliest surviving Persian work to combine general and dynastic history.

BAYHAQĪ'S HISTORY OF MAS'ŪD OF GHAZNA

Abū al-Faḍl Muḥammad ibn Ḥusayn Bayhaqī (385–470/995–1077) was born in the the district of Bayhaq. After studying in Nishapur, he entered the Ghaznavid chancery around 412/1021–2, where he served as assistant to its head, Abū Naṣr Mishkān (or Mushkān; d. 431/1039). He continued to serve under Mas'ūd I and his successors, and was head of the chancery under 'Abd al-Rashīd until he fell into disgrace and was imprisoned. According to Ibn Funduq, after Farrukhzād's death (451/1059) Bayhaqī retired from court service to devote himself to writing his history; but from his own statements it is clear that he was working on it long before this time, and had been collecting materials from the time that Mawdūd ascended the throne in 440/1048 (1971: 423; see also 130, 220, 252, 332). Ğ.-Ḥ. Yūsofī argues that he did not in fact work at Farrukhzād's court (*EIr*, s.v.); but he shows clear familiarity with its goings-on, and it was he who was called upon to draft the peace treaty between the Ghaznavids and the Saljūq Chaghrī Beg.[16] His *Zīnat al-kuttāb*, a manual on the secretarial art, is lost; of his major work, his compendious history of the Ghaznavids (called collectively the *Mujalladāt*), said to have comprised thirty volumes, only six survive (vols 5–10), which deal with the reign of Mas'ūd I.[17]

'Bayhaqī is a courtier and a historian, but not a court historian. The two faces of his activity, literary and administrative, are integrated and mutually illuminating, and an analysis of the work presupposes a consideration of the social conditions under which the author operated' (Bertotti 1991: 43–4). Much of the dramatic immediacy which marks Bayhaqī's work stems from the fact that he was witness to, and participant in, many of the events he recounts, and includes materials from his own diaries and his copies of chancery documents (many of which were however destroyed during his period of disgrace). Such resources make possible the inclusion of a wealth of circumstantial detail; as he himself states, 'No other history is so detailed', and in it 'there is no story that does not contain a valuable point' (1971: 11). But his project, in this part of his history at least, goes beyond the mere recording of historical events.

> My purpose is not to recount to the men of this age the deeds of prince Mas'ūd; for they have seen him, and have recognized his greatness, courage, and peerlessness with respect to all the instruments of governance and leadership. My purpose is rather to compose a foundation for history [*tārīkh-pāya*], and to erect a noble edifice (thereon), such that it will continue to be spoken of till the end of time. (1971: 112)

Bayhaqī's views on historical authority are expressed in the opening section of volume 10.

> The history of the past is of two sorts, without a third: one must either hear it from someone or read it in a book. The reporter of history must be reliable and truthful, and reason

> must also testify that his account is correct … And the same (is true) for books; for whatever is read in histories which is not rejected by reason the hearer will believe, and wise men will read and accept. Most of the common people … prefer false and impossible things, such as stories of demons, peris, ghouls of the desert, mountains and seas, which some fool invents, and others like him gather round, and he says, 'In such and such a sea I saw an island; five hundred of us landed there and cooked bread and set up our pots. When the fire was hot and its heat reached the ground it moved; we looked, and (saw) it was a great fish …' and similar fantastic tales which bring sleep to the ignorant when they are told to them at night. But those who desire true discourse which may be believed are considered wise; and their number is very few. (1971: 905)

These remarks echo Miskawayh's criticism of histories 'filled with anecdotes that follow the mode of stories to be told at night, and of fanciful tales with no use but to bring on sleep and to entertain' (1909: 4). Throughout his history Bayhaqī stresses his reliance on what is seen and observed: 'I … have placed upon myself the obligation that whatever I write should be from my own experience, or from the true account of a reliable person' (1971: 905). One may imagine that Bayhaqī shared Bīrūnī's aversion to fantastic tales; but he did not share Bīrūnī's scorn for the Persian language, and his own project seems a deliberate effort to provide a model for dynastic history in Persian.

Bayhaqī's project is far different from Gardīzī's, and closer to that of his older contemporary Miskawayh, by whom he was profoundly influenced (an influence which, to my knowledge, has gone unnoticed). An important aspect of this project is its ethical dimension, announced explicitly in the *khuṭba* (exordium) to his account of Mas'ūd's reign.[18] Concluding volume 5 (which must have dealt with Muḥammad's reign, his deposition, and Mas'ūd's consolidation of power), he observes:

> I have recounted the history of this king [Mas'ūd] up to this point. I ought to have said that from the day that he learned that his brother had been arrested … he ascended the throne of rule. But I did not; for that rule was still on the rise, and he was on the way to Balkh. Now that today [that is, in the account] he has reached Balkh, and things have become settled, the telling of the history must take on a different hue. First I will write a *khuṭba*, and join to it a few sections of discourse, and then recount the history of his royal days; for this will constitute a separate book. (1971: 110)

The *khuṭba* proper (to which I will return) deals primarily with the transfer of power. Of greater significance is the section which follows, and which is clearly distinguished from the *khuṭba* itself: 'Now that I have completed the *khuṭba*, I have found it necessary to compose another chapter which will be of use both to kings and to others.' He begins with a discussion of 'the qualities of the wise and just man, which permit that he be called virtuous', contrasted with the qualities of the tyrant.

> The greatest sages who lived in ancient times said thus: that part of the ancient revelation sent by God to the prophet of that age was that he told men, 'Know yourselves; for when you know yourself you will understand other things.' Our Prophet also said, 'He who knows himself knows his Lord'; and this is a phrase which is brief but full of meaning. For how can one who does not know himself know other things? (1971: 118)

This statement shows the clear influence of Miskawayh, and especially of his treatise on ethics, the *Tahdhīb al-akhlāq* ('Refinement of Character'). In combining the 'wisdom of the ancients' (that is, the Greek philosophers – here, Socrates) and the Prophetic saying, Bayhaqī, like Miskawayh, demonstrates the harmony between philosophical and Islamic principles: 'the precepts given by the Prophet and by philosophy are identical' (Walzer 1956: 619). Self-knowledge is the key to human perfection; when man acquires knowledge of his place in creation, he will understand the necessity for self-governance through reason, and will be able to acquire virtue. There are two aspects to self-knowledge, which might similarly be termed religious and philosophical. Man must know that he is living, that he will die, that he will be resurrected by the power of God, and that the Creator is not like the created; then he will have acquired true faith and correct belief. Then he must understand that he is composed of four elements, which must be maintained in equilibrium, and must further be acquainted with the faculties of the tripartite soul (which are themselves also termed 'souls'): reason and speech, anger, and desire.

After a brief discussion of these faculties, of the three divisions of reason and speech (imagination, distinction, and memory), and of the role of reason in maintaining the whole in equilibrium, Bayhaqī clarifies his argument by means of an analogy – an analogy which, contrary to the views of most commentators (see Bosworth (1973a: 50; Waldman 1980: 84–5; Bertotti 1991: 68–70) does not represent his conception of the organisation of the state, but draws on that organisation to describe the functions of the soul's three faculties.

> The Speaking Soul is the king, dominant, victorious, prevailing; he must possess strong and perfect justice and sovereignty, yet

> not so (strong) as to be destructive, as well as kindness, but not so (much) as to resemble weakness. The Irascible Soul is this ruler's army, by means of which he discovers flaws and strengthens his borders, repels his enemies and protects the populace. The army must be always at the ready, but must be obedient as well. The Concupiscent Soul is the king's subjects, who must fear the king and his army utterly and obey them. Every man whose state is as I have described, and who maintains these three faculties perfectly so that they are in correct balance and equilibrium, may truly be called virtuous, perfect, and the possessor of complete wisdom. (1971: 120)

History plays an important part in the acquisition of virtue: the man who, aided by reason, 'reads the histories of past men and considers them, and observes the affairs of his own age as well, will be able to know good actions from bad, whether the consequences of each (action) will be good or bad, what men will say about them and what approve, and what remains the best memorial of men' (1971: 123). But since not everyone is possessed of perfect wisdom, it is necessary to seek wise advisors who will point out one's faults so that they may be corrected. This is particularly important for rulers, who are (as Galen observed) 'in greater need of what I have mentioned [that is, wise counsel] than anyone else, for their commands are like a cutting sword, and their mistakes can be redressed (only) with difficulty' (1971: 125). Just as physicians are employed to cure ailments of the body, so it is fitting to choose physicians and healers of the soul. The remedies used by these physicians are 'wisdom and praiseworthy experiences, whether observed or read in books' (1971: 126–7). This section concludes with a lengthy story about the Sāmānid Naṣr ibn Aḥmad, whose character, when he came to the throne as a youth of eight, was marred by quickness to anger and to punish. Disciplined by well-chosen advisors, Naṣr became an exemplary ruler, known for his justice and clemency. Bayhaqī ends by observing that 'men of other ages will return to this and understand it' (1971: 127–9).

Before considering the significance of this section in terms of the history as a whole, let us consider its relationship to those which precede and follow it. The *khuṭba* proper, which precedes, deals with issues relating to the transfer of power and to the legitimation of the Ghaznavid house. Bayhaqī begins by recalling two rulers who have been called the greatest kings of the past, 'Alexander the Greek, and Ardashīr the Persian'. He does so, however, only to dismiss them: 'Since our lords and kings have surpassed both in all things, it must be recognized ... that our kings were the greatest on the face of the earth. For Alexander was a man whose rule gained strength like fire, blazed high for a few brief days, and then became ashes.' Bayhaqī criticises Alexander for conquering territories too vast to be administered and for needlessly exposing his person to danger: 'Alexander was a man of deceit and artfulness, full of great sound and lightning and thunder like the clouds of spring and summer, who passed over the kings of this earth, rained upon them, and disappeared, like a summer's cloud which disperses quickly' (1971: 112–14). Following Alexander's division of the Persian empire into petty kingdoms, Greek rule over Īrānshahr persisted for five hundred years, until the divided territories were reunited by Ardashīr. 'The greatest thing said of him was that he restored the vanished rule [*dawlat*] of the Persians and established the custom [*sunnat*] of justice among kings, which some of them followed after his death. He was indeed great; but God had brought the period of the petty kings to an end, so that this task became easy for Ardashīr' (1971: 114).

To these two examples – cut down to size, as it were – Bayhaqī now contrasts the Ghaznavids.

> The members of this great house possess deeds and qualities the like of which no one had possessed before, as has been recounted in this history and is yet to come. Thus, should a slanderer or envious person say that the origin of the nobles of this great house came from a (lowly) youth, that fool should be answered thus: Since God created man, the divine decree has been that sovereignty has been transferred from one people to another and from one group to another. The greatest proof of this ... is the words of the Creator: 'Say, O God, Lord of sovereignty, You bestow sovereignty on whom You please, and take sovereignty from whom You please; You exalt whom You will, and humble whom You will; in Your hand is good, and You have power over all things' [Koran 3: 26]. Thus one must know that when God's decree removes the robe of kingship from one group and places it upon another, in this there is a divine wisdom and a general benefit for men on this earth, which men are helpless to comprehend. (1971: 114)

It was in accordance with the divine decree that the Ghaznavids came to power: because 'God wished such a noble house to appear', he inspired the 'just prince Sabuktigīn to become a Muslim', and 'elevated him so that from the root of that blessed tree branches sprung forth much stronger than the root. With those branches He adorned Islam, and bound to them the power of the caliphs of the Prophet of Islam' (1971: 116).

If divine providence is instrumental in the transfer of rule, the retention of rule depends upon human agency, and specifically upon the virtue, and the political skills, of the just ruler. This point is forcefully brought home by the account of the reign of Mas'ūd, whose shortcomings are anticipated in the section which follows the *khuṭba* and the discussion of the acquisition of virtue, in an episode which is part of a long account of Mas'ūd's youth. Bayhaqī states that, when he was in Nishapur and before he had entered Ghaznavid service, he had heard stories of Mas'ūd's youthful achievements, but had always wished to hear such accounts from a reliable authority who had witnessed them himself. When he began writing his history his desire for such information increased. By happy chance, in 450/1058 he encountered Īhvāja Bū Sa'd 'Abd al-Ghaffār ibn Fakhīr ibn Sharīf (whom he had met once, years before), who had served Mas'ūd since the age of fourteen and was still in Ghaznavid service during Farrukhzād's reign. Khvāja Bū Sa'd related a number of accounts, and wrote them down for Bayhaqī in his own hand. These include information on how he himself entered the service of the young princes Mas'ūd, Muḥammad and Yūsuf (Maḥmūd's younger brother); how Bū Sa'd's grandmother ('a pious woman who read the Koran, knew how to write, and knew Koranic *tafsīr*, the interpretation of dreams, and the life of the Prophet' [1971: 133]) interpreted a dream of Mas'ūd's as predicting his succession to Maḥmūd and his future greatness; on Mas'ūd's successful campaigns in Ghur while he was governor of Herat, his hunting prowess, his generosity towards his subordinates, and so on.

Midway through this relation there occurs an episode of a somewhat different nature, which is introduced as an example of Mas'ūd's 'vigilance, resolve and circumspection' (1971: 145) – all qualities desirable in rulers. At the time that he was governor of Herat, Mas'ūd had built for himself in the garden of the palace complex a pleasure house, decorated inside and out with erotic texts and paintings. There, accompanied by poets, singers and musicians, he would withdraw in the heat of the afternoon to take his siesta. Due to the complex spy system which obtained at the Ghaznavid court, Maḥmūd, who used constantly to rebuke his son for his devotion to pleasure, was informed, and sent a cavalry officer to investigate. Forewarned by his own spy at Maḥmūd's court, Mas'ūd had the building whitewashed so that no trace of the offending pictures remained, and the officer found nothing. He was given a tour of the palaces and grounds, and richly rewarded by Mas'ūd; on his return to Ghazna, Maḥmūd exclaimed, after hearing his report, 'Now let people cease telling lies about my son!' (1971: 149).

The story is not without humour, and the episode is treated by Khvāja Bū Sa'd as a youthful peccadillo ('young men do such things, and their like' [1971: 145]); but coming as it does in an account in which Mas'ūd otherwise displays all the virtues and qualities of an ideal prince, that he is shown demonstrating such princely virtues in order to escape Maḥmūd's censure strikes a jarring note. We should also note the positioning of this story in relation to the entire section which introduces the account of Mas'ūd's reign proper. First comes the *khuṭba*, with its emphasis on the transfer of power and on the nobility of the Ghaznavid house, singled out for rule by divine election. Next is the section on self-knowledge and the path to virtue, which concludes with the exemplary anecdote concerning Naṣr ibn Aḥmad. Finally, there is Khvāja Bū Sa'd's long narration, which is meant to be encomiastic even in its inclusion, as its central item, of the story of the pleasure house. There is a clear relationship between these three sections; the implication is that divine election must be reinforced by the individual pursuit of virtue, and that in this respect Mas'ūd falls short of the ideal of the virtuous man, and hence of that of the virtuous ruler. The history of his reign will bear this out.

A marked feature of Bayhaqī's style is his use of digressions. One form of digression is the excursuses seen in the *khuṭba*s to volumes 6 and 10. Another, which modifies the chronological framework of the historical narrative, is the use both of flashbacks to earlier events which establish the background for present ones, and of inserted anecdotes, drawn almost exclusively from Islamic history. A good example of the latter is seen in volume 5. On his return from the West to claim his throne from Muḥammad Mas'ūd camped in Damghan. There he was joined by Bū Sahl Zawzanī, his former vizier in Herat, who had escaped from the prison where he had been confined by Maḥmūd on a charge of heresy. Arriving in markedly (not to say ostentatiously) reduced circumstances, he was welcomed by Mas'ūd and showered with gifts; and despite his bad nature and their own dislike and envy of him, Mas'ūd's courtiers treated him with respect, 'since they had known him when he was powerful, and such respect becomes habitual' (1971: 27–8). Moving on, Mas'ūd camped in a village with an irrigation canal. A messenger arrived bearing a bag of letters which had been written by various officials proclaiming their loyalty to Muḥammad. Bū Sahl advised Mas'ūd, 'Keep them, so that men will read them and know what the father [Maḥmūd] had planned, and what God willed, and the loyalties and beliefs of their authors.' Mas'ūd rejected this advice, observing that officials have little choice but to obey their masters, and ordered the letters torn up and thrown into the canal (1971: 29–30).

These events remind Bayhaqī of two stories, one relating to Bū Sahl's importance and the respect shown him, the other to the letters.

The first concerns Hārūn al-Rashīd's vizier Faḍl ibn Rabīʿ, who loyally supported Hārūn's designation of al-Amīn as caliph, went into hiding following al-Amīn's defeat by his half-brother al-Ma'mūn, and was eventually captured, put under house arrest, and forbidden to appear at court. (Compare Gardīzī's account discussed earlier.) In the end, due both to his former importance and to the intercession of his powerful friend Ṭāhir ibn Ḥusayn, he was restored to favour. The second story tells how the victorious al-Ma'mūn was presented with sacks of letters written by officials in the camp of each brother declaring their support of the other. He consulted his vizier, Ḥasan ibn Sahl, on what to do with them.

> [Ḥasan replied] 'The traitors on both sides should be exiled.' Ma'mūn laughed and said, 'Ḥasan, in that case no one will remain from either party; they will go and join our enemies, and deliver us up to them ... Now that God has given us the caliphate, we will overlook this, and not cause anyone anguish.' Then he ordered the letters to be burnt. (1971: 37–9)

Both stories contrast two viziers, one upright (Faḍl) and one devious (Ḥasan ibn Sahl, who here parallels Bū Sahl Zawzanī), and demonstrate the magnanimity of the two rulers (al-Ma'mūn, Masʿūd). The common ground is the struggle between brothers for the succession (and, implicitly, the evils of a divided succession); but whereas the conflict between al-Amīn and al-Ma'mūn led to a bloody civil war, that between Masʿūd and Muḥammad was resolved peacefully. But the portrayal of Masʿūd as forbearing and merciful is not without irony, as we will soon hear of his vendetta against Maḥmūd's former officials, in particular those who had supported Muḥammad.

Bayhaqī explains that his purpose in introducing such anecdotes, 'the deep meaning of which wise men will understand', is so that 'this history may be adorned and ornamented thereby', and further, so that men who attain kingship may be inspired to high aspiration and achievement. 'Such is the value of books, stories, and histories of the past: that men may read them, bit by bit, and take from them that which is fitting and useful' (1971: 39). Elsewhere he observes that 'although these stories may be far from "history", for in history one reads that this king sent that general to such-and-such a battle, and peace was made on a certain day, or this one defeated the other ... I bring in what is necessary, in its proper place' (1971: 451) – a statement which might be construed as a dig at his contemporary Gardīzī, whose history consists in the main of just such accounts.

Marilyn Waldman has argued that Bayhaqī's use of digressions, historical anecdotes and so on is a form of *taqiyya* (a largely Shīʿī practice relating to the concealment of heterodox beliefs under the outward guise of orthodoxy) which serves to dissimulate views which might be unpopular or offensive, and that, while wanting 'the ordinary person to look no further than he wishes or than is safe', he provides clues 'for those who are more intelligent ... to look and think much further' – for example, by placing 'radical statements in harmless mouths, [by] explicit statements contradicted in practice, juxtaposition of contradictory ideas, and especially the raising of possibilities and ideas in interpolated material not raised in the narrative.' Although most of those he was writing about were dead, and he was no longer in the ruler's service, 'he definitely intended the work to be read in his lifetime and could not say anything offensive about the royal family. He also seems to have been flirting with ideas that could have been offensive to a variety of readers unconnected with the court' (this is not explained) (1980: 72–3). While it is true that Bayhaqī 'requires the reader to read analogically' (Waldman 1980: 73), this would have been second nature for the sophisticated reader. But Bayhaqī is no dissembler (although he gives good manners their due), and he is not slow to criticise either Mas'ūd or his courtiers. This may be seen in his lengthy account of the arrest and execution of Maḥmūd's former vizier Ḥasanak, an event which Gardīzī reported without comment but which becomes with Bayhaqī a rhetorical set piece which brings home profound ethical lessons.

Formerly *ra'īs* of Nishapur, Ḥasanak (the sobriquet was given to him by Maḥmūd) was appointed vizier in 416/1025. (On Ḥasanak see Shafi' 1933: 124–31; Nāẓim 1971: 136–7; Bosworth 1973a: 182–4 and passim.) A powerful and influential official, he was also arrogant; but though Bayhaqī stresses that Ḥasanak brought disaster upon himself, his description of the events leading up to his execution, and of the indignities he was forced to suffer, present him in the role of a martyred victim of personal revenge. He begins his account with the background to Ḥasanak's execution. After begging to be excused of prejudice, he paints a vivid portrait of both the vindictive Bū Sahl and the arrogant Ḥasanak, who is compared to the equally arrogant 'Ja'far the Barmakid and that group who were viziers in the days of Hārūn al-Rashīd, and who met the same end as this vizier' (1971: 222), a comparison which will be repeated later. 'Servants and bondsmen should watch their tongues when speaking to their masters, for jackals cannot quarrel with lions', he observes; but Ḥasanak did not do so. A supporter of Muḥammad, he had offended Mas'ūd by telling his confidant 'Abdūs, '"Tell your master Mas'ūd that whatever I do is in accordance with my master Maḥmūd's orders. Should he one day become sultan, let Mas'ūd execute me." Thus when Mas'ūd ascended the throne, Ḥasanak mounted the scaffold. What did Bū Sahl or anyone else have to do with this? Ḥasanak suffered for his own temerity' (1971: 223). Ḥasanak had also offended Bū Sahl Zawzanī when, during his vizierate, the latter came to his palace 'barefoot and wearing a coarse cloak', and was mocked and thrown out by Ḥasanak's chamberlain (1971: 225).

Neither of these incidents figured in Ḥasanak's trial; instead, he was hauled up on an old charge of heresy incurred during Maḥmūd's reign when, as leader of the pilgrimage in 414/1023, he had brought the pilgrims back through Fāṭimid-held Palestine and Syria rather than by the more dangerous route through Arabia and Iraq, had bypassed Baghdad (and the caliphal court), and had accepted a robe of honour from the Fāṭimid caliph al-Ẓāhir. The Abbasid caliph al-Qādir demanded that he be tried for heresy; Maḥmūd declined, in his customary forthright manner, saying, 'If Ḥasanak is a heretic, then so am I!' (1971: 227). Although at first he vacillated, Mas'ūd was ultimately prevailed upon by Bū Sahl to revive this charge; Ḥasanak was tried, his property confiscated, and he himself condemned to death.

Bayhaqī's description of Ḥasanak's public execution at Balkh, which forms the central portion of this lengthy section, is characterised by a powerful dramatic style (see further Meisami 1995a). He describes the preparations: two men were dressed up as if they were messengers from the caliph who had brought his letter ordering that Ḥasanak be crucified and stoned. Mas'ūd, 'with his boon companions, familiars, and minstrels', rode off to hunt and make merry for three days. A scaffold was erected at the bottom of the city, and everyone headed there, including Bū Sahl Zawzanī, who watched on horseback from a high place near the scaffold. When Ḥasanak was brought out from the Bāzār-i 'Āshiqān by mounted troops and footsoldiers, a certain Mīkā'īl, an old enemy of his, 'who had halted his horse there, came to meet him, called him a traitor, and cursed him foully. Ḥasanak paid no attention to him, and did not reply. The common people cursed him [Mīkā'īl]; and what the elite said about this Mīkā'īl cannot be told' (1971: 232).

Ḥasanak was taken to the foot of the scaffold, 'where they had placed the two messengers, (got up) as if they had come from Baghdad', and ordered to remove his clothing.

> He put his hand beneath his garments, tightened the belt of his trousers [*izār*] and closed their ankle-strings; then he took off his cloak and shirt and cast them aside, along with his turban. He stood there naked, in his trousers, his hands folded; his body was like white silver, his face like a hundred thousand beautiful idols. The people all wept in anguish. They had brought an iron-banded helmet – deliberately, one that was too small, so that it did not cover his head and face – and cried out, 'Cover his face,

> that it may not be ruined by the stones, for we are going to send his head to the Caliph in Baghdad.'

They kept him there – 'his lips moving, reciting something under his breath' – until a larger helmet was fetched; meanwhile, Mas'ūd's Master of the Robes approached Ḥasanak on horseback and delivered this message:

> 'Our lord the sultan says: This is what you wished for when you said, "When you become sultan, then execute me." We wished to be merciful to you; but the Caliph has written that you have become a Qarmaṭī; it is by his order that we execute you.' Ḥasanak made no reply at all.

The helmet was brought and Ḥasanak's head and face covered. Ordered to run to the scaffold, he paid no attention and did not move. 'Some people cried out, "Aren't you ashamed to make a man you're going to kill run to the scaffold?"' and an imminent riot was quelled by mounted troops. 'They brought Ḥasanak to the scaffold and placed him there; they set him on a mount he had never ridden.' The executioner bound him and tightened the noose round his neck. The order was given to stone him, but the assembled populace refused to do so, 'and all wept bitterly, especially the Nishapuris. Then they paid a bunch of ruffians to stone him; but he himself was dead, since the executioner had put a cord around his neck and strangled him.'

> Such was Ḥasanak and his fate … And if he had wrongly seized the land and water of Muslims, neither land nor water remained (to him); all those slaves, properties, possessions, gold and silver and luxuries were of no profit to him. He departed, and those who plotted (against him) have departed, and this story is a great admonition: for they left behind them all those causes of conflict and strife for the sake of worldly rubbish. How stupid is the man who fixes his heart on this world! For it gives blessings, but takes (them) back in an evil way … And when they were finished with all this, Bū Sahl and his people left the foot of the scaffold, and Ḥasanak remained alone, just as he had emerged alone from his mother's womb. (1971: 232–4)

Bayhaqī describes the gruesome aftermath of the execution, when the gloating Bū Sahl, drinking and feasting with his friends, served them Ḥasanak's head (not sent to Baghdad after all) on a covered tray said to contain first fruits. All were shocked and repelled by this act. Ḥasanak's body was left to rot on the cross for nearly seven years; then Mas'ūd commanded it be taken down and buried, 'so that no one knew where his head was and where his body'.

> Ḥasanak's mother was a strong-minded woman. I heard that this affair was concealed from her for two or three months;

> when she heard of it, she did not grieve as women do, but wept so in anguish that those present wept blood at her pain; then she said, 'What a great man was this son of mine, to whom a king like Maḥmūd gave this world, and a king like Mas'ūd the next.' She held a fine mourning ceremony for her son; and all wise men who hear of this will approve, and so they should. (1971: 236)

Ḥasanak goes to the scaffold abused and humiliated, but disdains to react, preserving a calm demeanour, muttering private prayers (or perhaps curses) under his breath. Though his enemies torment him – even the absent sultan Mas'ūd cannot resist a Parthian shot at his victim – he remains silent. The onlookers will not raise a hand to stone him, and weep at his distress. Disrobed, stripped of all worldly possessions even to his clothing, Ḥasanak becomes an icon: skin like beaten silver, features more beautiful than a thousand idols. The humiliating helmet becomes a martyr's crown.

Whether this description of events is accurate or 'realistic' is irrelevant; Bayhaqī's ultimate purpose is not to record the facts, or even to arouse sympathy for the man, but to present Ḥasanak as an emblematic victim of royal injustice. This becomes clear from the lengthy digression which follows. 'Such a thing has happened (before) in the world', Bayhaqī states, and launches into a long story about the anti-caliph 'Abd Allāh ibn Zubayr. Besieged in Mecca by the army of the Umayyad caliph 'Abd al-Malik ibn Marwān, commanded by the ruthless Ḥajjāj, 'Abd Allāh and his supporters took refuge in the mosque. The Umayyad siege engines cast stones upon the shrine, causing considerable damage. Ḥajjāj attempted a ruse, promising to send 'Abd Allāh to 'Abd al-Malik in Syria, unbound, if he would surrender, in order to save the shrine and prevent further bloodshed. Most of his supporters urged him to accept; but 'Abd Allāh's mother, Asmā' bint Abī Bakr (daughter of the first Rightly Guided caliph, and sister of the Prophet's wife 'Ā'isha), advised him to 'stand fast in the face of death, execution and mutilation', as had his brother Muṣ'ab (killed by Ḥajjāj) and Ḥusayn ibn 'Alī ibn Abī Ṭālib, martyred at Karbalā' (60/680). 'Abd Allāh is, like them, a scion of the nobility of Quraysh, Zubayr ibn 'Awwām and the family of Abū Bakr.

'Abd Allāh agreed, but told his mother he feared he would be mutilated after his death; she replied, 'When a sheep is slaughtered it feels no pain when it is mutilated and skinned.' 'Abd Allāh stood fast, and exhorted his followers to do the same (Bayhaqī includes the Arabic text of the oration); all were killed in the ensuing battle. Ḥajjāj had 'Abd Allāh's head sent to 'Abd al-Malik and his body exposed on a cross. On hearing this, his mother did not grieve, but said, 'We are

God's, and to Him we return; if my son had not done as he did he would be neither the son of Zubayr nor the grandson of Abū Bakr.' After some time Ḥajjāj asked, 'What is that old woman doing?' Told of her words and her endurance, he said, 'Praise be to God Almighty! If 'Ā'isha and this sister of hers had been men, this caliphate would never have passed to the Umayyads! Such indeed is courage and endurance! We must find a scheme to make her pass by her son, and see what she says.' A group of women were persuaded to take Asmā' in that direction; when she saw the cross and recognised her son, 'she turned to one of the noblest of those women and said, "Isn't it time this rider was brought down from this horse?" She said no more, but went away; they reported this to Ḥajjāj, who marvelled, and ordered that 'Abd Allāh be taken down and buried' (1971: 241).

Ḥasanak and his mother are in illustrious company: the martyred Ibn Zubayr and the pious and noble Asmā'. But there is more, as Bayhaqī continues:

> Although this story is somewhat long, yet there is benefit in it. I have produced two other cases as well, so that it may be seen that Ḥasanak had companions in this world greater than he; if what happened to him happened to them, it should not be marvelled at. Further, if his mother did not grieve, but uttered such words, let no slanderer say that this could not be so; for there are many differences between men and women. (1971: 241–2)

The first case is that of Ja'far ibn Yaḥyā the Barmakid, executed by Hārūn al-Rashīd, who ordered his body quartered and exhibited on four gibbets and commanded his spies to report anyone who might pass by them and express pity for Ja'far, so that they might be punished. Later Hārūn regretted his actions; and when a man was brought before him who had been caught reciting sympathetic verses beneath one of the gibbets, and who explained that he was thus discharging his obligation to the Barmakids and was ready to accept punishment, the caliph wept and pardoned him (1971: 242–3). Hārūn's repentance and clemency are surely meant to contrast with the lack of same on the part of Mas'ūd. The second story concerns the Būyid vizier Ibn Baqiyya, who was crucified when 'Aḍud al-Dawla took Baghdad after his rebellious nephew 'Izz al-Dawla Bakhtiyār was killed in battle. Ibn Baqiyya too was unable to guard his tongue, was insolent towards 'Aḍud al-Dawla, and failed to foresee the consequences of his actions. Bayhaqī quotes in full Ibn al-Anbārī's famous elegy on the vizier which begins, 'Elevated both in life and in death – indeed you are a miracle!' as well as another line by the same poet – 'You rode a mount which Zayd beforehand [mounted in years long past]' – which refers to Zayd ibn 'Alī ibn Ḥusayn ibn 'Alī ibn Abī

Ṭālib, who rebelled against the Umayyads during the caliphate of Hishām and was killed, crucified, and left on the cross for three or four years (1971: 245–6). He concludes with a brief comment on the poet Sudayf, who urged the Abbasids to destroy the Umayyads by citing the examples of Ḥusayn and Zayd.

This lengthy and self-contained section (some thirty-five pages in the Fayyāẕ edition) is carefully structured; Ḥasanak's execution occupies the precise midpoint between the events leading up to it and the digression which follows. It is clearly meant to be taken as a whole; but commentators often fail to do so, ignoring the stylistic clues and concentrating on the account of Ḥasanak's trial and execution. Thus for example R. S. Humphreys finds Bayhaqī's 'moral evaluation of politics' to be a 'dark and tragic' one, in which

> normal religious and ethical standards seem only a bitter irony ... What judgment should be levied against Mas'ūd for having put to death a devoted servant of his father and one of the most capable men in his empire? In this regard Bayhaqī follows the newly emerging Perso-Islamic tradition: Mas'ūd had the right to do whatever he wished with his servants, and Ḥasanak had in fact merited punishment by his own arrogance ...
>
> What is striking ... however, is the sultan's punctilious concern for form and due process. We see a complex charade: caliphal envoys from Baghdad presenting complaints to Mas'ūd about Ḥasanak's supposed conduct on the pilgrimage, the sultan reluctantly submitting to caliphal commands to rid his kingdom of heretics, and demanding formal charges and proofs of guilt, a solemn assembly in which Ḥasanak legally transfers all his property to the sultan, etc. What is all this about? Bayhaqī's answer is only implicit, but it is unmistakable. In order for the state to maintain itself, there must appear to be law even when there is no law. Without a careful observance of this fiction, chaos would ensue ... Bayhaqī is a realist; he knows that no king really fulfills the criteria demanded by his role ... But the maintenance of form in a kind of theatrical performance permits the illusion to be sustained, and this illusion – so long as reality does not too grossly violate the ideal – lends at least a degree of credibility to the system. (1991: 141–2)

Bayhaqī is indeed a realist; but Ḥasanak's trial and ritualistic execution are described in terms which unmask the 'system', which is here (as often elsewhere) revealed as manipulative play-acting. Ceremony and ritual were important features of the medieval display of power; but Bayhaqī shows what happens when these are used to further injustice and self-interest. Moreover, Humphreys ignores the importance of Bayhaqī's method of juxtaposing narrative with digression. If Ḥasanak was arrogant, so were Jaʿfar the Barmakid and Ibn Baqiyya; but what of ʿAbd Allāh ibn Zubayr, a martyr to Umayyad tyranny? There is no simple answer; Bayhaqī raises moral issues, but does not, here, resolve them. If Ḥasanak was punished for his insolence, how many others were not? What of Bū Sahl's conduct, and Hārūn's repentance? The reader must judge; and he must do so on Bayhaqī's terms. These terms do not include abstractions such as 'the state', 'law' or 'the system': all these, insofar as they exist, are embodied in the ruler, whose conduct is here held up for moral judgement.

The anecdotes generated by the account of Ḥasanak's execution serve didactic and moral ends which are part and parcel of the writing of history, as they point to the folly of worldly ambition; this is, however, perhaps their least important purpose, as it is also the most predictable. More important, they provide political and moral commentary on Ḥasanak's death: by placing him in the company of such figures as Ibn Zubayr and Zayd ibn ʿAlī, on the one hand, and the insolent and short-sighted viziers Jaʿfar and Ibn Baqiyya, they suggest that not only must officials govern their own conduct wisely but that rulers as well must practise justice and clemency. Finally, as Miskawayh announced in the preface to his *Tajārib al-umam*, history, writ large, reveals recurrent patterns of events: Ḥasanak's story, and those which follow, remind us that both the righteous and noble and the arrogant and proud are subject both to Time's vicissitudes and to human malevolence, and that a spectacular rise to greatness may be followed by an equally spectacular fall. By observing such patterns, men can learn from history.

> Every man to whom God has given illumined reason, and who displays events before that reason, which is his true friend; whose reason is assisted by knowledge; who reads and contemplates accounts of the past, and who also considers the events of his own age, will be able to understand what is good conduct and what bad, whether the consequences of either will be good or no, what men will say and what approve, and what it is that will remain as the best memorial of men. (1971: 123)

Ḥasanak's memorial has been provided by Bayhaqī; both he and the lessons he exemplifies will live on in history when the facts of the matter have faded into oblivion.

Bayhaqī's history of Masʿūd's reign paints a picture of the affairs and intrigues of his court which is both detailed and intimate. Gossipy his work is (and Bayhaqī is without doubt the most readable of historians); but it is far more. His history is both too extensive and too detailed for us to attempt to follow Masʿūd's steps along the path to moral and political decline. These are marked, at the beginning of his reign, by his vendetta against Maḥmūd's former officials, his unprecedented attempt to recoup the *māl-i bay'at* distributed by Muḥammad,[19] and the abortive murder plot (in which he was enmeshed by Bū Sahl Zawzanī) against the Khwārazmshāh Āltuntāsh, one of Maḥmūd's most esteemed vassals and valued advisors.[20] Later, we observe his propensity for accepting bad counsel rather than good, and finally his unwillingness to listen to any counsel at all, leading to his embroilment in disastrous military adventures, the increasing disaffection of army and officials, and his ultimate downfall.

One episode that cannot go unnoted is the disastrous campaign in Jurjan in 426/1035 (treated only briefly by Gardīzī), which was provoked both by Mas'ūd's greed and by the self-interest of his courtiers. Jurjan was ruled by the Ziyārid Bākālījār (Abū Kālījār), who had succeeded to its rule (under somewhat suspicious circumstances) in 422 or 3/1031 or 2. In the following year a marriage was celebrated between Mas'ūd and Bākālījār's daughter. Mas'ūd's government was by this time showing severe signs of strain: his provincial governors (in particular the tyrannical Sūrī in Khurasan) were the source of many complaints, and the Turkmens were making themselves unpopular in Khurasan.

In Ṣafar 426/December 1034 Mas'ūd, in Sarakhs, declared his intention to go to Marv, where the army could take on much-needed fodder; two days later however he announced that he would go to Nishapur instead, to be nearer to Rayy (which was afflicted by civil strife), 'and no one had the courage to say anything against this'. Mas'ūd's vizier, Aḥmad ibn 'Abd al-Ṣamad, saw in this the machinations of Mas'ūd's secretary 'Irāqī, but observed to the head of the chancery, Bū Naṣr Mishkān, that

> 'Today is not the time to say anything. We'll go to Nishapur; if 'Irāqī puts it into Mas'ūd's head that he should go to Gurgan and Sari, for his own purposes, to show off his standing with the prince, we will point out the error of this. For 'Irāqī is mad, and says whatever he likes to the prince, who listens; and he pretends to be the wisest of advisors. Khurasan and Iraq will be lost because of him.' (1971: 573)

Mas'ūd arrived in Nishapur, which was afflicted by drought and famine, and met with his advisors. He announced his intention to send envoys to collect overdue revenues from Rayy and the long-overdue tribute from Bākālījār in Gurgan, and to summon the latter to the court to pay homage. If necessary, he himself would march against Bākālījār. The vizier's advice that it was unwise to leave Khurasan in disorder and danger was ignored, and Mas'ūd set out for Gurgan on 12 Rabī' I 426/25 January 1035. Bayhaqī was among the officials who accompanied him; he writes,

> On the way there was great cold and a strong wind, especially at the head of the Dinar Sari valley (this was in the month of Isfandurmad [February–March]); although I was wearing ... a robe of red fox fur and a rain-cloak and other suitable things I felt so cold, as I rode, as if I had nothing on, and by the time we reached the valley ... my garments were soaked. I came out of the valley into a world filled with narcissus and violets, and thickly packed trees upon the plain which seemed to have no end or limit. It might be said that there is no lovelier place than Gurgan; but it is full of plague ... (1971: 580)

Mas'ūd arrived in Gurgan two weeks later and camped at Muḥammadābād, beside a large river. There he executed a soldier who had stolen a sheep, and warned against mistreating the populace. Meanwhile, Bākālījār and the Gurganis 'had left their houses full of wealth and gone to Sari' (1971: 582); their houses were searched and looted. A envoy arrived from Bākālījār with a message in which he excused himself (he was unable to entertain Mas'ūd properly and felt ashamed) and stated that he awaited his command at Sari; Mas'ūd replied that he intended to proceed to Astarabad, and would issue his commands from there. After ten days (during which he drank continually) Mas'ūd left Gurgan for Astarabad, two stages away, via a road full of forests and streams.

> Had it rained, he would have been forced to return, for the road is narrow and the ground soft, with many streams; had it rained even once in a week, several days would be needed before even a small army could pass, to say nothing of a great army like this ruler's. But since Fate had decreed that there should be great trouble in Khurasan, the divine decree was such that in a region where it rains constantly no rain should fall, so that the king traversed this route easily and came to Amul, as I shall recount. (1971: 585)

Despite a letter from Bākālījār maintaining that the road was too narrow, Mas'ūd proceeded to Sari, and seized and pillaged a nearby fortress. Then he made for Amul.

> The roads were narrow ... and surrounded by forests, stretching to the mountains, with streams so broad elephants could not cross them. We came to a wooden bridge over a great, winding river, which the army crossed with great difficulty, for although the water was not deep the ground was such that every beast that stepped there sank up to its neck. They camped on the road to the city, where there was abundant forage, and space enough for a large army to camp. (1971: 589–90)

Messengers came from Amul to say that Bākālījār had fled. Mas'ūd responded by remitting the taxes of Amul, and ordered its inhabitants to remain in the city, which he entered on 6 Jumādā I/19 March, and was greeted by a large multitude. He camped outside the city and ordered the troops not to mistreat the populace. Then, leaving his officials behind, Mas'ūd continued to pursue the Gurganis, whom he finally bested in a battle near Nātil; he then returned to Amul, where he held court, and ordered Bayhaqī to write down all the wealth which was to be collected from Amul and Tabaristan. Bayhaqī showed the letter to the vizier, who laughed and said,

> 'You'll see; they'll destroy and burn these regions and gain a bad name and not find 3,000 dirhams! What a great crime! If they turned all Khurasan upside down they would not obtain this much! But the sultan is drinking, and has said this on the basis of his own luxuries, wealth and treasuries.'

The vizier then addressed the Amuli representatives, reminding them that the Sultan had secured the region and must be recompensed for his expenses. They replied that the region was poor and that their tribute had always been set at a certain amount; the vizier showed them the list, and said he would try to see that as much as possible was taken from elsewhere. The Amulis were stunned, said they could never produce such wealth, and asked leave to speak to all the people about this. Bayhaqī reported this to Mas'ūd, who said, 'Good! They'll go away and come back ripe tomorrow. This wealth must be collected quickly, so that we need not remain here long' (1971: 598–9).

The next day, when the Amulis still protested their inability to pay up, Mas'ūd ordered the city taken by force. A *dīvān* was set up to collect the money and pay the troops' wages with it, and many people were seized. Then the army was let loose. They went riot in the city, set fire to it and seized its citizens indiscriminately. 'The sultan was unaware of this, and no one dared tell him.' In four days they acquired 160,000 dinars towards their maintenance (though they had seized more than twice that), 'and gained both their maintenance and a very bad name' since some months later the victims went and complained to the caliph in Baghdad, 'and it is said they even went to Mecca'.

> For the people of Amul are weak, but vocal and stubborn; and they had good reason to speak out. All that sin and ruin rebounded upon Bū al-Ḥasan 'Irāqī and the others; but the Amīr too should have stood firm in these matters. It is difficult to write these words, but I have no choice; there is no favouritism in history. If those who were with us in Amul read these sections and seek justice, let them speak (with) justice; for what I have written is true. (1971: 600–1)

Meanwhile conditions in both Khurasan and Rayy had worsened. Masʿūd decided to turn his attention to Rayy (although the situation in Khurasan was more pressing); he left Amul on 22 Jumādā II/4 April and reached Gurgan on 8 Rajab/19 May. There it was very hot and still, and the animals were greatly weakened. Bayhaqī states that he heard from Bū Naṣr Mishkān that the prince repented what had happened in Amul, and said to the chief *dabīr*, 'What have we done? May God curse ʿIrāqī! We achieved nothing, the army gained nothing, and I have heard that the populace there were abused.' Bū Naṣr replied, 'I and others said as much, but there was no way to protest further against the royal judgement, as it might have been misinterpreted.' Pressed to speak out, Bū Naṣr told the prince that Bākālījār had gained a great advantage through this affair. This was indeed so; for though Bākālījār was soon won back, 'no one knew that when [Masʿūd left], the people would go over to him, and all honour would be lost' (1971: 608–9). Shortly after this interview, news reached Bū Naṣr that the Saljūqs had brought many men across the Oxus and gone to Nasa. He told Bayhaqī that they had persuaded Sūrī to leave Nasa to them; in return, one of their leaders would come to court, serve Masʿūd and provide him with troops. He exclaimed, 'O Bū l-Faḍl! Khurasan is lost! Go and tell the vizier.' The vizier had just risen from sleep and was reading. When he heard the news he said, 'Here is the result of going to Amul and of the secretary ʿIrāqī's plans!' (1971: 610).

There are several levels to this lengthy account. On the one hand there is the ethical level – Masʿūd's propensity for heeding bad advice (so long as it catered to his own motives), his greed, his pursuit of his own pleasure while Amul burned. This is scarcely mitigated by his later regrets: the wise ruler must restrain his troops from abusing the populace. The topos of the prince who ignores affairs of state while pursuing pleasure conventionally signals the impending fall of the ruler, or the dynasty; here, however, it is integrated with a series of other factors. A causal link is made between Masʿūd's Gurgan campaign and his loss of Khurasan, as his absence from that province enabled the Saljūqs to increase their strength there. Above all, we see the prince becoming increasingly alienated from his more competent advisors (the vizier Aḥmad ibn ʿAbd al-Ṣamad, Abū Naṣr Mishkān), which bodes ill for the future.

The events leading to Masʿūd's defeat at Dandānqān are treated with similar complexity. Returning to Nishapur in Rajab 426/May 1035, Masʿūd determined to send a force against the Saljūqs, even though he was advised that, since the Turks had been quiet so far, they should not be stirred up. This force, led by the general Bigtughdī

(Begtoghdī), was defeated, largely because a number of younger officers refused to follow Bigtughdī's orders. 'This was the first great weakening that happened to the Amīr. After this came more and more weakenings, until the end, when he was martyred, and departed this deceitful world in pain and regret' (1971: 636). The Turks themselves were amazed at the rich spoils they obtained and surprised at their victory, which they attributed not to their own ability but to the disorder of Mas'ūd's army. They sent an apologetic letter to Mas'ūd, and an envoy to seek the vizier's intercession on their behalf; the upshot was that Dihistan, Nasa and Farava were made over to the three Saljūq leaders Dā'ūd, Ṭughril and Yabghū, who were received and honoured at court.

The Turks did not remain quiet. Early in 427/1035, news reached Mas'ūd, in Balkh, that the Saljūq and Iraqi Turks had joined forces and were harrying the populace and seizing whatever they could find. Mas'ūd sent a force to Khurasan, led by the chief *ḥājib* Sūbāshī. In Muḥarram 428/November 1036 the Saljūqs sent envoys to Mas'ūd stating that other Turkmens, not they themselves, were responsible for the disturbances in Khurasan, that they were loyal allies of the prince, but that if Sūbāshī attacked them they would be forced to defend themselves. At the end of the year Mas'ūd left to campaign against the Indian fortress of Hansi (fulfilling a vow made earlier that year, when he had been struck by a fever) – despite advice to the contrary, and despite increasing raids by the Turks in Khurasan – returning to Ghazna in Ṣafar 429/November 1037. There, he received reports that Sūbāshī, rather than moving against the Saljūqs, was enjoying life in Nishapur: 'The *ḥājib* never used to drink [ran the report]; but now, a year since his appointment, he continually drinks and sports in private with moon-faced Turkish slave-girls' (1971: 706).

> Of course the prince was upset over this. And it was not as they said; for Sūbāshī took careful precautions, so that the Turks called him 'Sūbāshī the sorcerer'. But when the prince's accusations of delay and reproaches passed all limits, the *ḥājib* was obliged to make war, as I shall tell (later). May God Almighty give no one knowledge of the unseen! Since Khurasan was destined to be lost to us, and this group's [the Saljūqs'] affairs to reach the station that they reached, consequently all plans fell into error. One cannot fight against fate. (1971: 707)

Sūbāshī was ordered to proceed against the Turks at Sarakhs. Mas'ūd, in Ghazna, was celebrating the completion of his new palace and royal throne, despite his anxiety over Sūbāshī. A few days later, news arrived of Sūbāshī's defeat by the Turks and his retreat, with the remnants of his troops, to Herat. Mas'ūd then learned that, on hearing of Sūbāshī's defeat, Sūrī, the tax-governor of Khurasan, had abandoned Nishapur, taking much wealth with him. Shortly after, the Saljūqs occupied Nishapur, where they met with no opposition, and the *khuṭba* was pronounced in Ṭughril's name.

Mas'ūd wrote secretly to the notables of Nishapur assuring them that he would march to retake the city after the feast of Mihragān 429/September 1038. (Bayhaqī informs us that his information is reliable, as he was in charge of copying the correspondence during this period, and that, moreover, he still possesses his diaries, which bear witness to these events [1971: 734]). He left Ghazna early in Muḥarram 430/October 1038. En route to Nishapur he was informed that the Turkish chief Būritigīn (Böritegin) had been raiding in the area of Khuttalan, and decided to deal with him first. Advised against pursuing Būritigīn across the Oxus in winter and with only a small troop, but rather to wait until he could muster more soldiers, Mas'ūd nevertheless held fast to his decision. The vizier told Bū Naṣr Mishkān, 'Do you see all these obstinacies and bad policies on the part of the prince? I fear we will lose Khurasan; for I see no signs of success.' Bū Naṣr replied,

> 'The vizier has been away a long time; this prince is not the one he knew (before), and will not listen. In these affairs God decrees that which men cannot understand; we can only be silent and patient. But our duty to our patron requires that we tell what we know, whether it is heeded or not' (1971: 740–1).
>
> Many things had been done without thought during these nine years whose consequences now appeared. Most amazing was that he [Mas'ūd] did not desist from his obstinacy – and how could he? for the Creator's decree lay in wait for him. The vizier said to my master several times, 'Do you see what he will do? He will cross the water for the sake of attacking Būritigīn … God knows how this affair will end; it is unimaginable.' Bū Naṣr replied, 'There is nothing to do but to be silent; for advice which is turned to accusation cannot be offered.' The troops all knew about this, and spoke of it to one another, and said all sorts of things outside his presence, and obliged Bū Sa'īd the *mushrif* to write them down, but it did no good. And in Mas'ūd's presence they would say whatever he agreed with, for (otherwise) he became angry. (1971: 746–7)

As Mas'ūd was preparing to cross the Oxus news arrived from Ghazna announcing the death of his favourite son and heir-apparent, Amīr Sa'īd. Mas'ūd was drinking, and no one dared tell him; the next day, as he was about to hold court, a servant gave him the letter. 'When the prince read the letter he came down from his throne, sighed a great sigh which was heard to the very bottom of the palace' and announced that there would be no court. The officials waited to see if he would sit in mourning, until the message came that he would not, and telling them to go home. 'This unexpected death was yet another bad occurrence which (meant that) no one dared tell him he should not cross the water, for he would receive no one; he mounted up still stunned by this calamity, and went to Tirmidh' (1971: 747–8). They crossed the Oxus in pursuit of Būritigīn, and passed through the valley of Shuman, 'where the cold was of a different sort, and snow fell continuously. The army had never suffered so much as on this journey' (1971: 749). In the end the campaign was abandoned when Mas'ūd received news that the Saljūqs were approaching the bridge over which he had crossed, and withdrew across the Oxus before they could cut him off. The army's sufferings during this harsh winter expedition further contributed to the disaffection which was to influence the outcome of the battle of Dandānqān.

Following another engagement a truce was concluded with the Saljūqs. Bayhaqī relates Bū Naṣr Mishkān's account of his conversation with Mas'ūd on this matter. Bū Naṣr told the ruler that the Saljūqs' actions in Khurasan were without precedent, nor did history record their like.

> 'Yet despite this, when they make war victory is always theirs. How wretched are we that God has made such people dominate us and given them victory! The world's affairs depend on kings and on the Law; rule and religion are brothers, who go together and are inseparable. When God removes His favour from a king so that he can be beaten by such people it is a sign that God is angry with him. Let the king reflect on how he stands with that heavenly Lord.' [Mas'ūd] replied: 'I know of nothing that has happened to anyone or has been done that was displeasing to God.'

Bū Naṣr urged Mas'ūd to consider more carefully his standing with God, to seek forgiveness if necessary, and to humble himself before his Maker with prayers and solemn vows and show repentance for any past lapses, in the hope that on the morrow he might begin to see the effects. '(Mas'ūd) replied, "I accept, and excuse you, for you spoke on my order, and fulfilled your obligation to myself and my father"' (1971: 772–3).

Mas'ūd returned to Herat, where he busied himself with pleasure while his troops collected taxes (often by force). The Turks continued their raids in Khurasan, and many common people crossed the Oxus in the hope of plunder. Early in 431/1039 Bū Naṣr Mishkān died; he was replaced as head of the chancery by Bū Sahl Zawzanī, since even though Bū Naṣr had recommended Bayhaqī for the post Masʿūd objected that the latter was too young (he was then about forty-six). In Ṣafar Masʿūd decided to move against the Turks, who still occupied Nishapur. On learning of his approach, Ṭughril and his troops fled; Masʿūd entered Nishapur on 27 Rabīʿ II 431/17 December 1039.

> This time Nishapur was not as we had known it. All was in ruins, with only a few signs of habitation; bread was three dirhams per *man*, and the quartermasters had broken up the roofs of houses and sold them. Many men, along with their wives and children, had perished of hunger; the price of property had dropped (dramatically). (1971: 809)

All Khurasan was afflicted by drought and famine, and provisions for the army and their animals were scarce.

In Nishapur a letter arrived from the caliph ordering Masʿūd not to leave Khurasan until the disturbances of the Turkmens had been quelled, after which he should come to Rayy and the Jibal, where there were also troubles. On 28 Jumādā II 431/15 February 1040 Masʿūd marched forth from Nishapur. The Turks were also on the move, and there were frequent skirmishes between the two groups. Fodder was scarce and was obtained from the villages by force, after which Sūrī (who had reappeared when Masʿūd reoccupied Nishapur) put the villages to the torch. 'Many men and beasts died from lack of provisions; for it was clear how long they could (expect to) live on grass (alone). Things reached the point where it was feared that the army would rebel, and all order would collapse.' Masʿūd moved on towards Sarakhs; countless animals died along the way, and the troops were desperate and exhausted from hunger. Sarakhs 'was dry and barren; there was not a blade of fodder. The people had all fled, and had burned the plain and the hills; there was no grass at all' (1971: 817). Masʿūd's advisors suggested he go to Herat, where fodder was abundant, and attack the enemy when the animals had been provisioned and rested. But Masʿūd, determined to make for Marv, would brook no opposition, and reviled those who advised otherwise.

They set out on 2 Ramaḍān/10 May. 'It was extremely hot; provisions were scarce, fodder nonexistant, the beasts emaciated and the men fasting. On the way the prince passed several men who were leading their horses and weeping.' He took pity on them and gave them some money; 'everyone began to hope that he would go back; but fate was more powerful, and ... he himself put down these rumours and said, "This suffering and hardship is only till (we reach) Marv."' There was no water; all the streams had dried up, and the troops were obliged to dig wells. 'The reedbeds had been set afire; the wind blew and carried the smoke and brought it to the men's breastplates, blackening them' (1971: 824). Marauding bands of Turks, strengthened by defectors from the Ghaznavid army, constantly harried them. Each day their numbers increased, and the army's progress was greatly impeded.

> We camped by a stream, in disorder, like those who have lost heart. All the men had lost hope, and it was certain that a great disaster was about to happen. In secret they began to prepare the baggage animals, to ready strong animals as extra mounts, to make arrangements for the cash and goods and to bid one another farewell, as if the Day of Judgement were about to take place. (1971: 830)

The next day (9 Ramaḍān/24 May) they advanced again, still harried by Turks. By broad daylight they had reached the fort of Dandānqān, where Mas'ūd halted and called for water. 'Many people had come to the fortress walls; they lowered pitchers of water from the walls, and men stood and drank, for they were very thirsty and distressed. The great streams were dry, and there was not a drop of water' (1971: 834). Mas'ūd decided to make for a nearby pool to water the animals. When he rode off, 'all order dissolved'; the palace *ghulāms* dismounted from their camels and began to seize the horses of the Persians, 'on the pretext that they were going to fight,' but as soon as they mounted up they joined the Turkmens. The Ghaznavid troops were routed. Mas'ūd and a small group stood fast and fought bravely; but in the end they were obliged to retreat over a dry stream, 'and all who crossed to the other side of the stream escaped catastrophe' (1971: 835–6). Bayhaqī, exhausted, fell behind, and did not see Mas'ūd until a week later.

> I rode till night, and came upon two female elephants without litters, ambling along. I knew their driver, and asked, 'Why have you fallen behind?' He said, 'The prince left hurriedly; he gave me directions, and I am following.' ... I went along with those elephants, while scattered men caught up. All along the road we passed breastplates, mail-coats, shields and other possessions that had been discarded.
>
> At dawn the elephants went faster, and I was left alone, and dismounted.

The next day he learned from some acquaintances he had met up with that the prince had gone towards Marv. On foot, with a few companions, he reached the fortress of Gharchistan, where the prince had stopped to wait for those who could to catch up with him. 'In the whole camp I saw only three tents: those of the sultan, Amīr Mawdūd, and [the vizier]; the rest had only canvas shades, and we ourselves were in a wretched state' (1971: 838–40).

From an acquaintance Bayhaqī learned of the fate of the former *nadīm* Abū al-Ḥasan Karajī.

> 'The day that the sultan left (the field) ... I saw Abū al-Ḥasan Karajī, fallen beneath a tree, wounded and groaning. I went up to him; he recognized me, and wept. I said, "What sort of state is this?" He replied, "The Turkmens arrived and saw my equipment and animals; they shouted, 'Dismount!' I started to do so, but was slow getting off my horse, because of my age; they thought I was being stubborn, speared me in the back and stomach, and took the horse. With effort I reached this tree, and am now near death. This is my state; tell it to any of my acquaintances and friends who ask." He asked for water; with difficulty I brought him a bit of water in a pitcher. He drank, then fainted; I left the rest of the water near him, and withdrew, (waiting) to see what would happen to him. I know that he survived the night. [In the morning] I saw banners [signalling the approach of the Turks]; I left, and don't know what else happened.' (1971: 841)

As the prince continued his retreat, news arrived that Ṭughril had been proclaimed Amīr of Khurasan. On 8 Shawwāl/22 June Mas'ūd and his army reached Ghazna. A force was sent to Balkh, which had been attacked by the Saljūqs but was resisting, under the leadership of the *ṣāḥib-barīd* of Khurasan, Amīrak Bayhaqī. The generals Sūbāshī and Bigtughdī, whom Mas'ūd blamed for his defeat, were seized and their properties and possessions confiscated. Amīr Muḥammad and his sons were brought out from their confinement and treated with great honour (this was in Muḥarram 432/September 1040). But Mas'ūd had abandoned hope of Ghazna, and preparations were secretly being made to collect all the gold, cash and other valuables in the treasuries and prepare them to be moved. A message was sent to the royal women ordering them to make ready to go to India.

> Whether they wished to or no, all began to make preparations. The sultan asked [his aunt] Ḥurra-i Khuttalī and [his] mother to give their opinions on the matter; they did so, and were told in reply, 'Let those who wish to fall into the enemies' hands remain in Ghazna.' After that, no one dared say anything. (1971: 895)

Volume 9 ends with Mas'ūd's departure for India. What happened subsequently we know from Gardīzī: Mas'ūd's troops attacked the treasure caravan, murdered Mas'ūd and proclaimed Muḥammad his successor.

Bayhaqī's concern with both the ethics and the practice of rule is seen clearly throughout his history. The section following the *khuṭba* to volume 6 stressed the necessity to choose wise advisors and to heed their counsel; Mas'ūd provides a negative example of both principles, as he becomes increasingly alienated from such competent officials as Bū Naṣr Mishkān and his viziers Maymandī and Aḥmad ibn 'Abd al-Ṣamad and favours self-interested opportunists like Bū Sahl Zawzanī and the secretary 'Irāqī. The issue of loyalty figures prominently, as Mas'ūd repeatedly violates his obligations towards his subordinates and even towards his own kin. Such was the case with his treatment of his uncle the Amīr Yūsuf (which Bayhaqī quite openly condemns as scandalous) having sent Yūsuf to govern Quṣdār, in India, Mas'ūd set Yūsuf's former *ghulām* Ṭughril (whom Yūsuf had loved, and had treated as his own son) to spy on him. Ṭughril's betrayal of his master is not exonerated by the fact that he was suborned to do so; for if, as Mas'ūd once observed, servants are bound to obedience, Ṭughril's first loyalty was to his original master and benefactor.

For Bayhaqī, moral qualities are not abstractions, but arise from and are illustrated by the events of the narrative and are linked to the character of its actors. As Miskawayh wrote, 'Virtues are not non-existences; they are actions and deeds which are manifested when one participates and lives with other people, and has dealings and various kinds of association with them' (1968: 26). Virtues and vices are possessed by individuals and made manifest by their actions. It is the working out of this principle which informs Bayhaqī's project to create a 'foundation for history', and which links history with ethics. It is this too which lifts it above *adab* literature and 'mirrors for princes', with which it is sometimes associated (see Waldman 1980: 60–1; Bertotti 1991: 62–74).

But Bayhaqī's history does not lack a pragmatic, political dimension, as is to be expected from a writer who was for so long closely associated with the Ghaznavid court. Following Mas'ūd's death, the Ghaznavids had undergone a period of serious political instability – threatened both externally, by the Saljūqs, and by internal dissension – which culminated in the usurpation of Ṭughril. In the bloodbath which followed, 'Abd al-Rashīd and the remaining sons of Mas'ūd were slaughtered; only Farrukhzād and Ibrāhīm survived (see Bosworth 1977: 44–7). Only under Ibrāhīm (451–92/1059–99) was stability restored; and there must have been doubts as to the viability of the house. Part of Bayhaqī's overall project was undoubtedly to demonstrate the legitimacy of the house's origins with Sabuktigīn, its peak under Maḥmūd, its (temporary) slide into decline beginning with Mas'ūd, and its restoration under Farrukhzād and Ibrāhīm, presented as the ultimate heirs of the divinely elected Sabuktigīn. Announcing Farrukhzād's untimely death and Ibrāhīm's accession, he states:

> When he [Farrukhzād] passed away, God brought that (even) more excellent memorial of (past) rulers, the Great Sultan ... Abū al-Muẓaffar Ibrāhīm ... to the capital, which he adorned by ascending the throne of his forefathers. (Then) the elders of the former (administration) saw (restored) the effaced traces of Maḥmūd's and Mas'ūd's (rule). (1971: 483)

Ibrāhīm (like Farrukhzād before him; see for example 1971: 116) is linked directly with Sabuktigīn. The principle of divine sanction is invoked, here as elsewhere, in order to legitimate both rulers as legitimate heirs to Ghaznavid rule.

As regards Bayhaqī's reference to the 'elders of the former administration' (*pīrān-i qadīm*), a prominent feature of his work is the tribute paid therein to former members of the Ghaznavid bureaucracy and military, which involves noting both their devoted service in the past and their present circumstances – this usually in conjunction with praise of the current ruler. Thus for example Bayhaqī recalls how Mas'ūd rewarded the chief of the elephant-keepers, one Bū al-Naḍr (who had suffered much abuse under Maḥmūd, but who served Mas'ūd with loyalty and devotion), by elevating him to his personal service. Bū al-Naḍr rose in status, until he finally became chief *ḥājib* (presumably under a later ruler). 'And today, in 451 [1059], he is still alive – and may the Great Sultan Abū Shujā' Farrukhzād ... live (long), who honoured him and recognized the rights (due him) for his former service – and musters armies and gives commands ... and advises on affairs of state when he is in Ghaznin', as well as performing many other important duties (1971: 377). Elsewhere he notes the fates of Amīr Yūsuf's former servants, dispersed after the latter's seizure, after first remarking on that of the slave Ṭughril who had betrayed his master, and who then became despised by Mas'ūd and most others, was ruined, and died young and disappointed: 'And such are the consequences of ingratitude.' His steward first had his properties confiscated, but was later appointed tax official of Bust, in which position he died. His vizier, Khvāja Ismā'īl, suffered many ups and downs, but looked after Yūsuf's children and maintained their rights; under Mawdūd his position improved, and he was now entrusted with important duties. A certain Āmūy renounced court service after Yūsuf's seizure to devote himself to a life of piety, and resisted all efforts to persuade him to return. Amīr Yūsuf's *nadīm*, Bū al-Qāsim Ḥakīmak, similarly retired from service; 'and today both are alive, here in Ghaznīn, and are (my) friends. What other course have I than to acknowledge the friendship of all; for this is not remote from the custom of history' (1971: 331–3).

We should not think of such references as a mere paying of debts in recognition of the obligations of friendship. They point to a more important issue: the vicissitudes of court service, the possibility of being in favour at one moment and out of favour and destituted (or worse) at the next (as Bayhaqī himself well knew). They point further to the issue of loyalty, and not only of a servant's duty of loyalty to his master (flagrantly violated by Yūsuf's slave Ṭughril) but of the ruler's obligation to reward faithful servants. Finally, they suggest that it is the veterans of former administrations, who have proven their devotion to the house, who should be retained in its employment, in preference to younger and more ambitious aspirants, who perhaps cannot be trusted, as they serve their own ambitions rather than their rulers' interests. (This theme resonates throughout the history of Masʿūd's reign, in which the intrigues and machinations of 'arrivistes' [*naw-khāstagān*, literally 'newly risen'] like the secretary ʿIrāqī contributed to his ultimate downfall.)

One final aspect of Bayhaqī's history deserves mention. His indifference to, if not disdain for, the Iranian historical tradition has generally gone unremarked, as scholars assume that, as an Iranian, he will have recourse to the indigenous traditions. Humphreys states that 'Bayhaqī uses a number of devices to draw attention to critical passages in his narrative,' including 'exemplary tales ... from the Sassanian tradition, a sprinkling of wise saws and proverbs at appropriate points, or passing references to the stock embodiments of wisdom, piety, or tyranny'. All these provide 'signals to the alert reader to reread and ponder the passage before him' (1991: 143). While this is true in principle, the facts are wrong. Bayhaqī's interest in the 'Sassanian tradition' is virtually nil, his sources are (as far as can be ascertained) exclusively Arabic-Islamic, and he takes a dim view of 'Persian' versions of history.[21] His historical digressions are drawn almost entirely from Islamic history; and while he sometimes employs the standard hyperbolic comparisons of present rulers to those of the past – for example, the newly enthroned Ibrāhīm is lauded as a 'second Anūshīrvān' (1971: 484) – his use of such clichés is limited to encomiastic contexts.

The single lengthy anecdote in which Bayhaqī reverts to the Sasanian past follows his account of Masʿūd's imprisonment of Bū Sahl Zawzanī for his part in the plot to murder Āltuntāsh. It tells how Anūshīrvān imprisoned his vizier Buzurgmihr when the latter converted to Christianity, and contrasts the vizier's piety and nobility with the injustice of the king, who finally has him executed: 'Thus he went to heaven, and Kisrā went to hell' (1971: 428; and see 425–8). Waldman calls this 'a potentially explosive story, placed so as not to call attention to it, labeled mere decoration' (1980: 104), and notes F.

R. C. Bagley's argument that the figure of Buzurgmihr 'was actually the creation of the Islamic writers of *adab*' (1980: 70; see Ghazzālī 1964: lxvi–lxx). But it is precisely the placing of this story which reveals its purpose: to point the contrast between the pious Buzurgmihr and the devious Bū Sahl, the tyrannical Kisrā and the clement Mas'ūd (who later released his official).[22] This is, above all, an Islamic story: Buzurgmihr's conversion was brought about by a dream which foretold the coming of the Prophet. The proto-Muslim Buzurgmihr was the first Muslim martyr.

For Bayhaqī, history begins with Islam; and by virtue of his analogical method his own history becomes a near-seamless interweaving of Islamic present and Islamic past. Unlike Gardīzī, he does not present Mas'ūd as heir to unified Iranian-Islamic rule (and what survives in other sources of his accounts of Maḥmūd do not suggest that he saw that ruler in such a role). He does, however, show a great esteem for the Persian language, and a clear interest in moulding that language to become a vehicle for sophisticated expression. His 'foundation for history' demonstrates a conscious development of the stylistic and rhetorical means provided by that language not seen, in prose, since Bal'amī, whose own purposes were arguably different. For Bayhaqī's history is clearly not aimed primarily at a Turkish audience requiring education via the Persian language, but at an audience of courtiers and officials (and presumably also scholars) who would be aware of, and appreciate, his rhetorical subtleties and his use of the analogical method. He found no imitators (although passages in Ibn Funduq's history of Bayhaq, discussed in Chapter 3, are strongly reminiscent of his style); it was, first, the somewhat dry, straightforward style of a Gardīzī, and later the quite different rhetorical sophistication of a Rāvandī, which were more commonly employed by later Persian historians. Perhaps because of the uniqueness of his work, whose complexity distinguishes it from the customary historiographical styles (see Bertotti 1991: 43), it was considered both too vast and too innovatory a project to be emulated.

THE *TĀRĪKH-I SĪSTĀN*

This anonymous history of Sistan is clearly the work of more than one hand. The first and major part, the 'core text', which deals with the early history of Sistan and with the Ṣaffārids, breaks off around 448/1062; a continuation, in a different style and by a different author (or authors), briefly covers events from 465/1073 to 726/1326. The authors are unidentified and the work's original title unknown (the editor, M. T. Bahār, supplied the descriptive title 'History of Sistan'); the text lacks prefatory material and contains a number of lacunae.

The first author cites a variety of sources, both Arabic and Persian, most of which are relatively early. Bahār argued that the absence of references to such writers as Ṭabarī, Miskawayh, ʿUtbī, Bayhaqī, or Gardīzī (the latter two too late for this author) indicated that the work was composed before their histories had become well known (1935: *z*); but the real reason may be that most historians treat the Ṣaffārids unsympathetically or as peripheral to mainstream events. Bahār described the style of the core text as simple and straightforward, reminiscent of Balʿamī's Ṭabarī and other 4th/10th century prose works (1935: *yd*).[23]

Milton Gold, the English translator of the *Tārīkh-i Sīstān*, termed it '*Islamic* history', since its author treats the birth of Muḥammad as 'the most significant event in Sistān's entire history' (1976: xxvi; Gold's emphasis). This points to one of the author's main themes: the special status of Sistan in Islamic times. This special status is foreshadowed in the foundation myth of its chief city, Zarang, by the Kayānid Garshāsb, four thousand solar years before the Prophet's appearance. Assembling the sages of the world, Garshāsb declared his intention to found a city which, 'when Ẓaḥḥāk lays waste the whole world' (*sic*), would provide refuge for its inhabitants, for it would not be ruled by him. He instructed the sages to make astrological calculations so that the city's foundations might be laid at an auspicious time, to ensure that it might 'endure as long as possible, even though the world and all in it is transitory, and in the end will turn to nothing'. It was determined that the city would endure for four thousand solar years, and that when the Prophet appeared, revealed the faith of Islam and summoned the Persians to it, the Sistanis would be the first to respond, willingly or no. 'In the time of his religion there would be four hundred and forty-four years of battles', after which 'the city would once more flourish at the hands of' a scion of the Kayānids (1935: 4).

Sistan's prehistory is treated briefly, as are its local heroes, the family of Narīmān: Sām, Zāl, and Rustam.[24] The author enumerates some of Sistan's superiorities, mostly of a miraculous or legendary nature and involving such figures as Adam, Noah, Solomon and Alexander the Great, whose fortress, the Arg, still stands. Mention of the fortress leads to a discussion of the city and region of Sistan, its climate, its economic prosperity and self-sufficiency, its marvels and so on. Among the marvels are several springs and mines, now inactive, that will become active again when the millennium (of Zoroaster) comes to a close.

A discussion of Sistan's various names, its revenues, its cities and regions is followed by a section on its religion prior to Islam.

Garshāsb and his descendants up to the time of Farāmarz ibn Rustam maintained 'the faith of Adam', that is, monotheism, and were virtuous and pious. Rustam did not accept the Zoroastrian faith, and rebelled against Gushtāsb, who sent his son Isfandiyār against him, knowing that the latter (whom he feared) would be killed. After an account of the building of the fire temple of Karkūy by Kaykhusraw, the author moves to the Prophet's birth and, more specifically, to the miraculous events which led up to it – the passing of the 'light of the Prophet' from Adam through subsequent prophets to Muḥammad, and predictions of his appearance. He concludes with accounts of Muḥammad's birth and the miracles worked in his childhood, praises the Sistanis for having known and accepted the truth of his mission, of which they had read in their prophetic books – this is their 'greatest superiority over all other lands' – and summarily notes the Prophet's commencement of his mission in his fortieth year, his victories and his death.

Gold is puzzled as to why the author, whose account of the Prophet's childhood is so detailed, treats his adult years and his mission so briefly. Does he perhaps (as he himself states) not wish to be prolix? Does he depend on his readers' familiarity with the events of the Prophet's career? Or does he consider such matters irrelevant to his purpose? 'The suspicion persists that our author, whose pages so clearly reflect a weariness with the centuries of religious strife disintegrating the unity of Islam, may have sought refreshment in contemplating the innocence of Mohammad, the child' (1976: xxvi–xxvii). Perhaps; but the author's sole focus is on Sistan, and events in Arabia do not concern him. The history of the Prophet's mission is irrelevant to that of Sistan. What is important is the truth of that mission (demonstrated in the prophecies and miracles recounted by our author), the manifest nature of which caused the Sistanis to accept at once the summons to Islam, even though they had never seen its Prophet. They had however heard of his coming, and already believed in his mission; moreover, the Prophet did not merely bring a new faith to Sistan; in a sense, he restored the original, monotheistic faith of Adam and Garshāsb. The Sistanis were, so to speak, Muslims before the fact.

Islamic history is seen almost wholly from a Sistani perspective. Thus while the Persian defeat at Qādisiyya (14/636) is dealt with briefly, the conquest of Sistan by Rabīʿ ibn Ziyād (30/650) receives more detailed treatment. After several furious battles, with heavy casualties on both sides (but more among the Muslims), the Sistanis were forced to retreat into the city. There the Shāh of Sistan summoned the chief *mawbad* and the nobles and told them,

> 'This is not a matter which will pass in a day, a year, or a thousand years, as our books make clear. This religion and this age will last until the end of time, and (things) cannot be made right by killing and warfare, for no one can change Heaven's decree. It is wisest to make peace'.

The Sistanis sent an envoy to tell Rabīʿ that their books had predicted the coming of the Arabs and Islam and that 'that *dawlat* would long endure'; Rabīʿ responded that he preferred peace to war. He then ordered the bodies of the slain piled up and covered with cloth, with a place to sit atop also made of bodies. When the Shāh and the chief Mawbad arrived and saw him seated there ('and Rabīʿ was tall, dark, with large teeth and thick lips'), the Shāh said to his companions, 'They say that Ahriman cannot be seen by day; yet here is Ahriman, visible!' Rabīʿ laughed; and peace terms were concluded (1935: 81–2).

Elswhere in Sistan Rabīʿ met with resistance; many Sistanis were killed; others were taken prisoner and sent to the caliphal court, where 'they became important men', and 'through the blessings of Islam and of learning became princes, found freedom after slavery, and themselves gained many slaves' (1935: 82–3). But the Sistanis did not remain docile; and in 33/654–5 ʿAbd al-Raḥmān ibn Samura, accompanied by Ḥasan al-Baṣrī and a number of important *fuqahā'*, was sent to subdue the region. During the struggle for the caliphate between ʿAlī ibn Abī Ṭālib and Muʿāwiya, Ibn Samura, at first uncertain as to which to accept, defected to Muʿāwiya after the Battle of the Camel (24/656); the latter sent him back to Sistan after the Battle of Ṣiffīn (25/657). There, he built the Friday mosque of Zarang, in which Ḥasan al-Baṣrī taught, while Ibn Samura led the prayers. When he decided to settle in Sistan, the people assembled and told him that they required 'a true Imām, in accordance with the Prophet's *sunnat*'; for although ʿAlī still lived, Ibn Samura had been sent by Muʿāwiya, and in the dispute between the two eighty thousand believers had been killed. 'Our *khuṭba* and prayer must be sound', they insisted; 'we are not satisfied with the present situation.' ʿAbd al-Raḥmān went to Kufa to get a decision from the governor of Iraq, Ziyād ibn Abīhi, but died on his arrival (1935: 89). Subsequent governors appointed by Muʿāwiya after the murder of ʿAlī ibn Abī Ṭālib are praised for their pious actions, which inspired many Zoroastrians to accept Islam.

These early sections of the *Tārīkh-i Sīstān* reveal its author's concern with piety and justice. His pietism, however, betrays no specific orientation, and his focus is ever on Sistan. His accounts of the murder of ʿAlī ibn Abī Ṭālib (40/661; he omits to mention that the assassin was a Khārijī) and of the martyrdom of his son Ḥusayn at

Karbalā' (60/680) are fairly brief; but the latter event's aftermath is of interest to him, as it has a Sistani connection.

Ḥusayn's head was taken to Syria by the victorious Umayyad troops, along with the captive 'Alid women and children, walking barefoot and unveiled. At every stopping place the head was taken from its box, set atop a spear, and closely guarded until it was time to depart. At one stopping place they encountered a Christian hermit.

> They set the head up in the same way, atop the spear. When night came the hermit, who was busy with worship in his oratory, saw a light which rose from the earth to the heavens, so that no darkness remained, only brilliant light from heaven to earth. He cried out from the roof, 'Who are you?' 'We are Syrians,' they said. 'Whose head is this?' 'The head of Ḥusayn ibn 'Alī.' 'You are an evil group; for had Jesus left a son, we would have honoured him.'

The hermit paid them ten thousand dinars for the loan of the head overnight. He washed it, anointed it with rosewater, musk and camphor, kissed it and set it aside, and spent the night gazing at it. 'At daybreak he said, "O noble head, I am my own master. I bear witness that there is no god but God, and that your grandfather Muḥammad is God's Prophet."' He then returned the head. When the Syrian troops drew near Damascus, they saw that the hermit's gold 'had all turned to clay; on it, instead of a seal, there had appeared on one side, "Think not that God is unaware of the deeds of wrong-doers" [Koran 14: 43], and on the other ... "Those who do wrong will know to what place they will be transferred" [Koran 26: 228].' They threw it into a stream. Many people wept, repented and scattered through the countryside; others insisted that the captives be set on camels and taken to Damascus. When they arrived, Ḥusayn's head, in a basin, was placed before the caliph Yazīd ibn Mu'āwiya, 'and he continually struck its mouth and lips with a staff' (1935: 99–100). When this news reached Sistan, the Sistanis censured Yazīd for his treatment of the Prophet's kin and began to riot; the Umayyad governor made off for Basra, taking with him a large amount of money from the public treasury.

That piety and justice are the supreme virtues is reflected in our author's attitude towards legitimacy of rule, which depends on both but particularly on the former. Thus he condemns Abbasid support for the Mu'tazila as exemplifying heresy and unbelief. Respect for piety also influences his treatment of the Khārijīs, who play a large part in Sistan's early history. Gold argues that the Sistanis viewed the Khārijīs as 'interlopers' because of their violent depradations, and that it was only the first Ṣaffārid, Ya'qūb ibn Layth, who brought about a *rapprochement* between the Khārijīs and the Sistanis in opposition to the Abbasids and their local representatives (1976: xxvii–xxviii). Our author presents precisely the opposite picture (and, in fact, Ya'qūb made no serious *rapprochement* with the Khārijīs), as seen in the sympathetic account he gives of them.

> The Khārijīs had rebelled everywhere, and people, élite and commoners alike, continued to join them. Their commanders were Arab princes and notables from among the Prophet's Companions. When battles took place between Muslims, and things were done for which they found no justification in the Koran and *sunnat*, they despaired. Yet such things increased daily.

A long list of outrages follows: the murder of 'Uthmān, the Battle of the Camel, Mu'āwiya's rebellion, the battle of Ṣiffīn and the arbitrations, the murder of 'Alī ibn Abī Ṭālib and Mu'āwiya's ultimate triumph, the deposition of Ḥasan ibn 'Alī from the caliphate and the massacre of the Prophet's kin at Karbalā', the taking of Ḥusayn's head and the Prophet's womenfolk to Syria, the killing of Muṣ'ab ibn Zubayr, Ḥajjāj's siege of Mecca, in which the shrine was damaged and 'Abd Allah ibn Zubayr and his supporters killed, 'and other such things which, if all of them were mentioned, would make a long story'. Such outrages caused a group of the Prophet's Companions to wash their hands of the Umayyads and absolve themselves of allegiance to them. Among them was Qaṭarī ibn Fujā'a, described as a 'noble-natured' Arab aristocrat who had come to Sistan with Ibn Samura and was on friendly terms with the Sistanis. When he rebelled in Iraq, and was pursued and forced to fight many battles, 'he sent agents to Sistan who told the tale of the (evil) things that had been introduced into Islam; and the Sistanis, élite and commoners alike, joined them [the Khārijīs]' (1935: 109–10).

This period of Sistan's history is dominated by the conflict between the Khārijīs and the Umayyad, and later Abbasid, armies sent against them. The Khārijīs are generally presented as pious warriors fighting corrupt and ruthless officials who exploited the Sistanis through heavy taxation and extortion of money and property. The chaos in Sistan – governors appointed and dismissed, ongoing rebellions – reflects the chaotic state of the waning Marwānid caliphate, as does the factionalism between the Arab tribes of Tamīm and Bakr ibn Wā'il, whose dispute 'over the (comparative) superiority of the Companions of the Prophet' led to disturbances which continued even after the Abbasid victory (1935: 131).

The most important Khārijī rebel from the Sistani perspective was Ḥamza ibn 'Abd Allāh (or Atrak, Āzarak), who appeared in 181/797–8 in the caliphate of Hārūn al-Rashīd (see 1935: 156, n. 1 for versions in other historians; see also Baghdādī 1920: 98–102). Claiming descent from the Pīshdādī Zaw-Tahmāsb, and described as 'a great and courageous man and a scholar ['*ālim*]', Ḥamza had reprimanded a local revenue agent for corruption and commanded him to proper pious conduct. 'The official wanted to destroy him; in the end, he (himself) was killed.' Ḥamza went on pilgrimage; when he returned he was accompanied by some of Qaṭarī's (former) supporters. The Khārijīs of Sistan, who had fallen out with their own leader, swore allegiance to Ḥamza, who now rebelled openly. In 182/798 he appeared before the gates of Zarang just before daybreak. He heard many calls to prayer coming from the city; amazed, he told his army, 'Go back! The sword should not be drawn against a city which so praises God.' Camping near Zarang, he sent an envoy to the city saying that he would not fight the populace but only the caliph's representative; the latter, however, had gone into hiding. Then Ḥamza summoned all the people of the region and said,

> 'Do not give another dirham in tax or property to the (caliphal) authority, because he cannot protect you. I want nothing from you, and will take nothing, because I will not stay in one place.' From that day till now no more taxes or tribute reached Baghdad from Sistan. However, they agreed to continue to proclaim al-Rashīd in the *khuṭba*; and the *khuṭba* is still (said) in the name of the Abbasids; but the money stopped. (1935: 158–9)

The *Tārīkh-i Sīstān* contains much information about Ḥamza's career not found in other sources, including the texts of a letter allegedly written to him by Hārūn al-Rashīd in 193/808 offering him a pardon if he would come and profess allegiance to the caliph, and of Ḥamza's reply.[25] Ḥamza laments the decline of Islam: in the latter part of 'Uthmān's reign the Muslims have fallen into error, and since then have become divided by disagreement after having been united. God guided rightly the true believers and led astray those who neglected His Book and violated His Prophet's *sunnat*; the true believers steadfastly followed the right path,

> until the falsity of this community overcame its righteous men, and it became clothed in factions and some were made to taste the power of others. They are still divided, except for him to whom your Lord shows mercy; and Islam and its people will continue to decline until the Hour arrives. That is the promised end of this community, because of its agreement upon error, as He sayeth: 'Yea, the Hour is their appointed time, and the Hour will be most grievous and most bitter' [Koran 54: 47]. (1935: 165)

Hārūn died in Ṭūs shortly after receiving Ḥamza's letter; Ḥamza, meanwhile, was preparing for war. Most of those who joined him were Arabs. They 'gave marriage portions to their wives, and made their testaments; (then) they donned shrouds, over which they wore their weapons. Thirty thousand horsemen, all ascetics and Koran reciters, rode out', reciting verses attacking Hārūn and praising Ḥamza, acclaimed as 'the divinely-sanctioned Imām' (1935: 168–9). When they reached the outskirts of Nishapur they heard that Hārūn had died and his army had returned to Baghdad. Ḥamza exhorted his followers to go forth and wage holy war against idolators; in groups of five hundred, five thousand horsemen dispersed to Khurasan, Sistan, Fars and Kirman. Ḥamza instructed them,

> 'Do not allow these tyrants to oppress the weak. The affairs of these armies will reach the point where they will fight against one another. Let us not interfere, so that they may kill many of one another; for Hārūn divided rule into three parts, for his sons, and [as the proverb says], "Kings are jealous."' (1935: 169–70)

Following al-Ma'mūn's victory over al-Amīn and the appointment of Ṭāhir ibn Ḥusayn as governor of Khurasan (including control of Sistan) Ḥamza reappeared. The Ṭāhirid governor Layth ibn Faḍl made peace with him and gained his support in suppressing a local rebellion. Layth treated the *'ayyār*s of Sistan well, and was accessible to the Khārijīs, who could come and go freely in the city.[26] Ḥamza died in 213/828; and though there were to be more Khārijī rebellions in Sistan, no leader was to reach the stature of, and earn as much admiration as, Ḥamza.

The heart of the *Tārīkh-i Sīstān* deals with the rise and fall of the Ṣaffārids, beginning with Ya'qūb ibn Layth and his brothers, 'Amr and 'Alī. In 238/852 the leader of the *'ayyār*s of Bust, Ṣāliḥ ibn Naḍr (or Naṣr), rebelled against Abbasid authority and was declared Amīr; his chief military commander was Ya'qūb ibn Layth, a former coppersmith (*ṣaffār*) turned brigand. (On Ṣāliḥ ibn Naḍr, his revolt, and Ya'qūb's elimination of other rivals, see Bosworth 1994: 71–5.) 'This was the beginning of Ya'qūb's rise' (1935: 193), a meteoric rise which was to culminate in his becoming master not only of Sistan but of other Abbasid provinces in eastern and south-western Persia. His success was undoubtedly aided by the disarray of the Samarran caliphate and its provincial representatives and by the massive drain on money and manpower required by the struggle against the Zanj rebellion in southern Iraq; but it was also due to Ya'qūb's ruthlessness and military expertise and to his policy of alternately conciliating or disposing of his foes and rivals.[27]

Our author makes no mention of Ya'qūb's humble origins; instead, he is provided with a genealogy passing through many Sasanian, Kayānid and Pishdādī rulers back to Kayūmars. Ya'qūb's claim to descent from the ancient Persian kings appears in an Arabic panegyric composed for him by Ibrāhīm ibn Mamshādh.[28] In it, Yaʿqūb proclaims:

> I am the son of the noble descendants of Jam, and the inheritance of the kings of Persia has fallen to my lot.
> I am reviving their glory which has been lost and effaced by the length of time.
> Before the eyes of the world, I am seeking revenge for them …
> Say then to all sons of Hāshim [the Abbasids]: 'Abdicate quickly, before you will have reason to be sorry …
> Our fathers gave you your kingdom, but you showed no gratitude for our benefactions.
> Return to your country in the Ḥijāz, to eat lizards and to graze your sheep;
> For I shall mount on the throne of the kings, by the help of the edge of my sword and the point of my pen!'
> (Stern 1971: 541–2; Stern's translation)

S. M. Stern observed that to ask 'how far the ideas expressed in the poem are really those of the ruler and how far those of the poet' would be to miss the point.

> We have here a piece of political propaganda, and … it is more important to ask what effect it was meant and expected to achieve among the public than to try to assess how seriously it was taken by the ruler whose interests it promoted or by the poet who actually wrote it. (1971: 543)

Yaʿqūb's 'political manifesto' expresses the pro-Shuʿūbī and anti-Abbasid sentiments that were strong in Sistan. Whereas the Khārijīs provided a focus for such sentiments among the Arabs of Sistan (although Khārijī leaders and supporters often came from the indigenous Persian population), Yaʿqūb's claim was presumably meant to raise his stock among those who still valued Persian traditions (particularly the *dihqāns*), and perhaps to muster support for his break with the caliphate.

Established as master of Sistan, Yaʿqūb treated the people well, released prisoners and gave them robes of honour, took oaths of allegiance and paid the army. He then sent a messenger to the Khārijī leader ʿAmmār ibn Yāsir, telling him that the Khārijīs had been able to pursue their activities because Ḥamza had never attacked Sistan nor harmed a Sistani, but had only rebelled against the unjust caliphal authorities. Then foreigners ruled Sistan, and Ḥamza's rebellion made its people secure.

> 'But now things are different. If you wish to escape harm, put this (claim to be) Commander of the Believers out of your head;

> rise, with your army, and join us, for we rebelled in the firm conviction that we will never again deliver Sistan to anyone. (1935: 202–3; see Bosworth 1994: 79, on how Yaʿqūb dealt with ʿAmmār)

Many Khārijīs went over to Yaʿqūb, who soon gained the reputation of being undefeatible. As the vanquished Ṭāhirid military commander of Khurasan told its governor Muḥammad ibn Ṭāhir,

> 'One cannot fight this man; he has a terrible army, who think nothing of killing, and who fight recklessly and without restraint. They have no other occupation but fighting; you'd think they had been born to fight. The Khārijīs have joined him and obey him; the best thing is to conciliate him, so that his evil and that of the Khārijīs may be averted.' (1935: 208–9)

Muḥammad ibn Ṭāhir sent gifts to Yaʿqūb, together with the patents for various provinces, and Yaʿqūb withdrew. When the *khuṭba* was read in his name in Zarang, poets recited panegyrics to him in Arabic. He asked his secretary, Muḥammad ibn Waṣīf, 'Why should they recite something I can't understand?' Ibn Waṣīf responded with a panegyric in Persian; this, states our author, was the 'first Persian poem' (1935: 212; that is, the first composed according to the Arabic model of panegyric poetry). While this claim is not strictly accurate, it reflects our author's pride in things Sistani, and provides a further example of Sistan's superiority. Gold suggests that it was Yaʿqūb's awareness of, and sensitivity towards, his Persian heritage which led him to be the first Persian ruler 'to encourage the use of Persian, both as a literary language and for administrative purposes' (1976: xxxv); but one may question the extent to which Yaʿqūb (who knew no Arabic and relied on his secretaries to interpret for him) was aquainted with, or interested in, Persian cultural traditions.

Yaʿqūb sent gifts to the newly enthroned caliph al-Muʿtamid (256–79/870–92), and was rewarded with the patents and standards for yet more provinces. After more victories against rebels, Khārijīs and Abbasid provincial governors, in 259/873 he occupied Nishapur, where he met no resistance, and imprisoned Muḥammad ibn Ṭāhir and his nobles. Previously, in Bust, Yaʿqūb had come upon a ruined house which had belonged to his rival Ṣāliḥ ibn Naḍr; some Arabic verses were written on its wall. His secretary explained that they recalled the fall of the Barmakids and predicted that of the Ṭāhirids. Yaʿqūb replied,

> 'There can be no greater miracle for such as us than that God most High brought us to a ruin to read and understand these verses; for revelation is granted (only) to Prophets. This means that I shall be the cause of the removal from the Muslims of the

> Ṭāhirids and their oppression. Write down these verses somewhere and keep them until that day when I ask you for them.' The secretary wrote them on a piece of paper and kept it. On the day when (Ya'qūb) put Muḥammad ibn Ṭāhir in chains, he summoned the secretary and said, 'Bring those verses that I entrusted to you that day in Bust.' He brought them; (Ya'qūb) said, 'Didn't I tell you that I would be that person?' ... Then the verses were shown to Muḥammad ibn Ṭāhir, who wept, and said, 'There is no averting God's decree.' (1935: 220–1)

Ya'qūb now controlled Nishapur. Hearing that people were complaining that he did not have the caliph's patent and was, besides, a Khārijī, he summoned the notables of Nishapur to his court that he might show them the caliph's writ. He received them seated like a king, with two thousand armed slaves standing at the ready in two lines, each bearing a shield, a sword, and a mace of silver or gold, all taken from the Ṭāhirids' treasury. He commanded those assembled to sit, and told his chamberlain, 'Bring the Caliph's writ so that I may read it to them.'

> The chamberlain entered, bearing a Yemeni sword wrapped in a kerchief of Egyptian stuff. He removed the kerchief and placed the sword before Ya'qūb. Ya'qūb took the sword and brandished it; people nearly swooned, and asked, 'Does he mean to kill us?' Ya'qūb replied: 'I did not bring this sword in order to kill anyone. But you complained, saying, "Ya'qūb doesn't have the Caliph's patent." Know, then, that I have!' The people collected their wits; Ya'qūb asked, 'Didn't this sword establish the Caliph in Baghdad?' They answered, 'Yes.' Then he said, 'This same sword has set me in this place. Thus my writ and that of the Caliph are the same!' (1935: 222–3; compare the somewhat different account in Gardīzī [1968: 140], and see Bosworth 1994: 13.)

The *Tārīkh-i Sīstān* is chiefly concerned with Ya'qūb's campaigns in southern Persia, from whose rich provinces he profited greatly. While he continued to reaffirm his support of the caliphate, he expanded his control over its territories; and while the caliphate conciliated Ya'qūb, it was perhaps also trying to undermine his authority. Thus in 262/875–6, at the same time that al-Mu'tamid sent Ya'qūb the patents for Khurasan and several other regions, he also appointed the Sāmānid Naṣr I ibn Aḥmad ibn Asad as Amīr of Khurasan. In Ya'qūb's absence, Ṣaffārid power in Sistan itself became weakened by internal divisions amongst his deputies and by the ambitious commander Aḥmad Khujistānī, who was to play a major, and damaging, role in Sistani affairs for seven years. Khujistānī, whom our author includes among those who flocked to Ya'qūb after he took Nishapur, soon struck out for himself, taking control of Nishapur in 261/875. By the time of Ya'qūb's death Ṣaffārid authority in Khurasan had collapsed.

In 262/876 the caliph al-Mu'tamid and his brother and regent al-Muwaffaq managed to cut short Ya'qūb's advance into Iraq. Ya'qūb determined to march on Baghdad. Gardīzī states that he intended to depose al-Mu'tamid and replace him with al-Muwaffaq. Other historians claim that a caliphal pretender had sought Ya'qūb's help against al-Muwaffaq; later, Niẓām al-Mulk presented his action as part of an Ismā'īlī plot to kill the caliph and subvert the Abbasid caliphate (see Bosworth 1994: 154–7; Gardīzī 1968: 141). The *Tārīkh-i Sīstān*, 'in an access of local patriotism aimed at building up Ya'qūb as a world-hero', asserts that al-Muwaffaq 'was so overawed by Ya'qūb's rise to the status of "lord of the world", *malik al-dunyā*, and protector of Islam, that he had placed his name in the *khuṭba* as the worthy successor of Abū Bakr and 'Umar' and wrote to Ya'qūb 'offering him complete power and authority over the Islamic world, reserving only to himself the sacral role of caliph and the *khuṭba* (sc. in the caliphal capital) as descendent of the Prophet' (Bosworth 1994: 156; Bahār [1935: 231, n. 3] notes that no other source confirms such a letter). Al-Mu'tamid had indeed granted Ya'qūb concessions (several governorates, the *shurṭa* in Baghdad), and sent an emissary with a letter detailing them. According to Ṭabarī, Ya'qūb 'wrote back that he was dissatisfied ... and was going to come to the gate of the caliphate itself to settle matters'. Al-Mu'tamid, seeing there was no chance of compromise, 'pronounced a formal curse on the Ṣaffārid, took up his bow in order to fire the first arrow in battle, and assumed the mantle and rod of the Prophet, thereby invoking divine support for his venture' (Bosworth 1994: 157–8). The two armies finally met at Dayr al-'Āqūl, fifty miles south-east of Baghdad on the Tigris.

The *Tārīkh-i Sīstān*'s account of the battle and Ya'qūb's defeat presents Ya'qūb in a heroic light while minimising, if not actually discounting, the caliph's role. On hearing that Ya'qūb had set out for Baghdad in response to his invitation, al-Mu'tamid came out to meet him with an army. A group of the caliph's troops, led by Ibrāhīm ibn Sīmā (an officer from the caliphal guard at Samarra) and bearing al-Mu'tamid's standard as if to indicate that the caliph was present, attacked Ya'qūb. Recognising the trick, Ya'qūb counter-attacked, but was pushed back to the river, where the floodgates were opened, forcing Ya'qūb and his troops to flee (1935: 231–2; the *Tārīkh-i Sīstān* understandably omits reference to the caliph's public proclamation following the victory, denouncing Ya'qūb's ingratitude for the concessions and honours granted him; see Bosworth 1994: 161; Ṭabarī 1992b: 168–72).

Bahār noted that 'less impartial' historians have 'suggested or stated clearly' that al-Muwaffaq ordered the floodgates opened (1935: 231, n. 2; see Bosworth 1994: 159–61). Gold states that our author 'does not make it clear that neither side intended that this confrontation would be peaceful, and that Al-Movaffaq's gestures of conciliation were designed precisely to deter Ya'qub from invading Iraq' (1976: 184 n. 1, where the date is given, wrongly, as 878). One source states that, when criticised by one of his commanders for bad strategy, 'Ya'qūb replied that he had not expected the caliph actually to fight, but had assumed rather that the latter would capitulate to his demands' (Bosworth 1994: 161). Gold conjectures that Ya'qūb either 'wanted to dominate Persia' or sought 'recognition of his primacy' there, 'for ... there is no reason to suppose that Ya'qub had any aspirations to become Caliph himself' (1976: xxxv) – a possibility that is scarcely likely. He also argues that Ya'qūb's raids were undertaken 'for booty alone, and not with the intention of extending his dominion' – for despite his numerous victories, 'he never seemed able to hold, invest, and completely subordinate' the provinces he conquered, and 'soon withdrew to more profitable enterprises elsewhere' – and that the Khārijīs who joined him 'did so because of the attraction of his strong personality and the promise of booty in his service and not ... because they had discovered in Ya'qub a new Pretender'. He suggests further that, because Ya'qūb seems to have 'accepted his orthodoxy [*sic*] with simple piety', his attack on Baghdad was more of 'a punitive expedition against a regime he despised, rather than a conflict over religion or a war of conquest and annexation' (1976: xxxvi).

Ya'qūb presumably had no more far-reaching plan than to make himself rich from the revenues of Abbasid provinces. His piety, 'simple' or otherwise, is not a matter of great concern to our otherwise pious-minded author (and it is doubtful whether the early Ṣaffārids had particularly strong religious feelings); he does however attribute to him the wish to free Sistan from foreign rule (a project scarcely furthered by his absence from that province). (Bosworth argues that 'the early Saffarids seem personally to have had no strong religious feelings' [1994: 15].) He was certainly no empire-builder: the notion of a centralised administration seems to have been utterly foreign to him. His success was due to military expertise and to his ability to exploit the weaknesses of his adversaries. Until the confrontation with the caliphate, he seems to have taken pains to ensure caliphal recognition; in the end, however, he overreached himself.[29]

Our author's admiration of Ya'qūb's military achievements and his personal bravery (his ruthlessness is seldom mentioned, and was in any case not exceptional for the time), and for his good treatment of the people of Sistan, who had long suffered the effects of raids by rebels and Khārijīs and the abuses of Abbasid officials, reflects his own hostility to foreign rule of Sistan and his pride in a local, home-grown hero. Elsewhere he states that with the fall of the last Ṣaffārid ruler Khalaf ibn Aḥmad (see below) Sistan reverted to its former troubled state; the first and last Ṣaffārid rulers thus provide a frame for the two lines of the dynasty, indigenous Persian rulers who are contrasted with foreigners: the Arab Abbasids, the Turkish Ghaznavids and Saljūqs.

After Ya'qūb's death in 265/879 (our author provides a brief encomium on his victories, piety and justice), his brother and successor 'Amr was faced with the task of reestablishing Ṣaffārid authority in Sistan. He conciliated the caliph (still fighting the Zanj) by offering tribute and promising to pay the land tax for Sistan, in return for which he received various governorships and important offices which increased his power and influence in Iraq and the Hijaz and left him free to deal personally with matters in the east (see Bosworth 1994: 186–9). It was his increasing ambitions in that direction that would bring about his downfall. The main focus of the *Tārīkh-i Sīstān* now moves to 'Amr's lengthy struggle to regain control of Khurasan from Khujistānī and (after the latter's death in 268/882) from Rāfi' ibn Harthama (both of whom were encouraged by 'Amr's older brother 'Alī), and to his changing relations with the caliphate. Our author fails to mention that in Dhū al Qa'da 271/April 885 al-Mu'tamid announced to an assembly of Khurasani pilgrims in Baghdad 'that 'Amr was deposed from all his governerships, that he was to be cursed from the *minbar*s and that Muḥammad b. Ṭāhir (II) was reappointed governor of Khurasan' (Bosworth 1994: 203). A lacuna in the text may have contained the account of 'Amr's battle with the caliph's army in 272/886, in which he was defeated and put to flight (see 1935: 243–4). In 274/887–8 'Amr concluded a peace treaty with al-Mu'tamid, the terms of which are found only in the *Tārīkh-i Sīstān* (1935: 244–5; see Bosworth 1994: 206–8).

Around this time Rāfi' ibn Harthama (to whom 'Alī ibn Layth had fled after escaping from the prison in which 'Amr had confined him) launched a campaign against the Zaydīs in Gurgan and Tabaristan. The perceived dissension in the Ṣaffārid family encouraged the caliph to repudiate his recent restoration of 'Amr in 276/890. 'Amr, in Fars, defeated a caliphal army sent against him. Shortly after, 'the news reached 'Amr [in Shiraz] that his name had been removed from the standards in Baghdad; and he, too removed Muwaffaq's name from the *khuṭba*' (1935: 248; for discrepancies in this account see Bahār's notes, and Bosworth 1994: 213, n. 639). When al-Muwaffaq died in 278/891, his successor al-Muʿtaḍid made peace with ʿAmr, restored his privileges and ordered him to march against Rāfiʿ, who had allied with the Zaydī Imām Muḥammad ibn Zayd (our author does not mention that Rāfiʿ had killed ʿAmr's brother ʿAlī; see 1935: 250, n. 1). ʿAmr entered Nishapur in 280/893; three years later (283/896), during ʿAmr's absence, Rāfiʿ reoccupied the city, 'raised the white banners [of the ʿAlids] and lowered the black ones [of the Abbasids], and said the *khuṭba* in the name of Muḥammad ibn Zayd' (1935: 252). ʿAmr returned and defeated Rāfiʿ in battle; in the end he fled across the Oxus to Khwarazm, where he was killed by ʿAmr's governor. ʿAmr sent his head to Baghdad, where it was publicly displayed.

Bosworth speculates that al-Muʿtaḍid 'was content to leave ʿAmr ... as effective ruler in the East' provided he maintained the 'caliphal fiction' that his rule was the result of caliphal delegation and that he sent, periodically at least, tribute and gifts to Baghdad (1994: 223–4). But ʿAmr was growing more and more ambitious. A force sent against the Sāmānid Ismāʿīl ibn Aḥmad in 285/898 met with defeat; for Ismāʿīl 'was a seasoned warrior [*ghāzī*], as were his whole army, who day and night performed public and private prayers and read the Koran'. Disheartened ('for his former fortune was now reversed'), ʿAmr wrote to the caliph requesting the governorship of Transoxania. If his request was granted, he promised to remove the Zaydī Imām of Tabaristan; if not, he would overturn Ismāʿīl ibn Aḥmad (1935: 254; Bosworth states that this letter was written when ʿAmr sent Rāfiʿ's head to Baghdad [1994: 225]). When the letter was read to him, 'the caliph bowed his head, remained thus for a while, then raised his head and said: "Reply to ʿAmr's letter (giving him) what he has asked for; for I know that in it lies his destruction. And write to Ismāʿīl ibn Aḥmad (saying) "We have not curtailed your authority in doing this"' (1935: 255).

In our author's version of ʿAmr's downfall, his ambition is defeated by Ismāʿīl's resolve and, more important, by his piety. The Sāmānid had it proclaimed throughout Transoxania that ʿAmr intended 'to seize Transoxania, kill its inhabitants, plunder its wealth and enslave its women'. Thus every able-bodied man in the region supported him against ʿAmr, saying, 'It is better to be killed like a man than to be taken prisoner.'

> ʿAmr was in Balkh, Ismāʿīl at its gates, and many battles took place. Ismāʿīl turned round the allegiance of a group of ʿAmr's commanders, and put the fear of God into them, saying, 'We are *ghāzī*s. We possess no wealth; but this man ever seeks (the things of) this world. What then does he want from us?' In the

end a harsh battle took place one day. A wind arose like a lightning-bolt, and day turned to night. ʿAmr's army fled; ʿAmr fought until he was captured. (1935: 255–6)

ʿAmr was detained by Ismāʿīl ibn Aḥmad in Samarqand. His grandsons Ṭāhir and Yaʿqūb had withdrawn to Khurasan, where the army swore allegiance to Ṭāhir; they procrastinated over paying the ransom set for ʿAmr (to be sent to the caliph), as the new regime in Sistan was not pleased at the prospect of his return. When a letter from ʿAmr arrived saying the ransom had been reduced, the commanders told Ṭāhir and Yaʿqūb, 'It is in neither our interest nor yours that he be released; for when he is, neither you nor we will survive' (1935: 258). Ṭāhir appointed Yaʿqūb as his viceroy in Sistan, while he himself 'pursued pleasure and amusement night and day'. As the situation grew worse, Ṭāhir and Yaʿqūb finally wrote to ʿAmr apologising for withholding the ransom, told him of the unrest in Sistan, and promised to rectify matters and send the money. The letter was accompanied by a poem by Muḥammad ibn Waṣīf; when ʿAmr read his verses, on man's helplessness before God's decree, 'he despaired, and detached his heart from this world' (1935: 260).

Now al-Muʿtaḍid wrote to Ismāʿīl ibn Aḥmad ordering him to send ʿAmr to Baghdad. Ismāʿīl, having no choice but obedience, told ʿAmr, 'It should not have been I who captured you, nor, having captured you, should I send you there. I do not wish to be responsible for the decline of your fortune.' He arranged to send ʿAmr via the Sistan road with only a small force, and advised him to arrange for the Sistanis to rescue him, 'so that I will have an excuse, and no harm will result'. The rescue did not materialise, and ʿAmr was finally delivered up to al-Muʿtaḍid in Baghdad, who at first treated him well and remanded him to prison while he considered his fate. But immediately upon seeing ʿAmr the caliph had fallen ill; his commander Badr al-Kabīr reminded him of ʿAmr's ambition, and the caliph ordered ʿAmr to be killed, then regretted his action and had Badr killed as well. Al-Muʿtaḍid himself died soon after (1935: 261–3; see Bosworth 1994: 234–5; Badr was certainly not killed, as he appears later in caliphal history).

Both Bahār and Bosworth doubt the authenticity of the story of ʿAmr's fall, just at the height of his power: 'The sudden reversal of ʿAmr's fortunes, all within a single day, gave rise subsequently to a crop of folkloric stories ... attached to his capture after the battle and his later conveyance to Baghdad as a prisoner' (Bosworth 1994: 230). Bosworth also doubts that al-Muʿtaḍid set ʿAmr against Ismāʿīl ibn Aḥmad in the knowledge that this would bring about his ruin (1994: 224–5). The facts may indeed be otherwise; but they are of no intrinsic interest to the historian bent on drawing object lessons. Our author's view that al-Muʿtaḍid plotted ʿAmr's downfall was shared by the caliph's nephew Ibn al-Muʿtazz, who later wrote in an elegy on al-Muʿtaḍid:

> Then there appeared the caliph's good fortune and an adroit and subtle stratagem,
> And Ismāʿīl swooped down on him (sc. ʿAmr) from his land until he fell under his control, submissive.
> Such is the inevitable penalty of rebelliousness and of letting men's souls be in thrall to Satan.
>
> (Bosworth 1994: 224; Bosworth's translation)

ʿAmr, who had acquired even vaster territories than had Yaʿqūb, overreached himself. This is the lesson both the poet and our author draw from his sudden and precipitous downfall. The contrast between the ambitious ʿAmr and the pious *ghāzī* Ismāʿīl ibn Aḥmad points this lesson: ʿAmr was destroyed, not by the treachery of his troops (though some blame is laid at the feet of Ṭāhir and Yaʿqūb and of ʿAmr's corrupt officials), but by the piety of his opponent, who clearly had God on his side.

The account of ʿAmr's downfall is followed by a brief résumé of the qualities of Yaʿqūb and ʿAmr: Yaʿqūb's faith in God, piety, liberality, chastity and resistance to temptation; his dispensation of justice and his accessibility to all; his sagacity; his daily routine; and, pointedly, the fact that he was wont to observe of the Abbasids that their state 'is founded on treachery and deceit', citing their treatment of Abū Salama (who had helped them to victory and was subsequently murdered), Abū Muslim, the Barmakids and al-Ma'mūn's vizier Faḍl ibn Sahl, 'despite the fact that these men served them well. One should not trust this house!' (1935: 267–8). Yaʿqūb's military expeditions, his wars against infidels, his charity and other virtues are also mentioned. ʿAmr, we are told, tried to maintain Yaʿqūb's 'virtuous habits and customs', engaged in building and good works, was generous and treated the poor kindly (1935: 268).

The rule of Sistan by ʿAmr's successors Ṭāhir and Yaʿqūb was a series of disasters. Ṭāhir, when not abroad, would shut himself up in Zarang, 'and night and day would give himself up to drink and amusement. He would befriend mules and pigeons, and would spend entire days surrounded by them, observing them' (1935: 275). When Sistan was riven by a dispute between the 'Samakī' and 'Ṣadaqī' parties concerning a legal decision on which the brothers themselves took opposite sides, 'neither brother cared about this dispute which was taking place during their rule, in their city and among their subjects, and which would cause this kingdom to fall' (1935: 276; on the Samakīs and Ṣadaqīs see Bosworth 1994: 253). They were too young and inexperienced to cope with events; instead, they spent all they accumulated 'on buildings, gardens, amusements, and in satisfying mere caprices ... Wealth decreased, revenues declined, expenses increased; and (so) their rule came to an end.' But Ṭāhir refused to seize or request money from his subjects, saying, 'Why should I practise oppression and injustice?' (1935: 276–7).

We now begin to hear of the progenitor of the second Ṣaffārid line, Muḥammad ibn Khalaf ibn Layth – 'a man of great intelligence and flawless character' – whom Ṭāhir appointed commander of the army. In the brothers' absence, Muḥammad ibn Khalaf conciliated the Ṣadaqīs and Ṣamakīs, telling them, 'There must be agreement between you, so that even if all the provinces are lost, this one would remain in your hands and not fall into the hands of foreigners or the unworthy.' In 293/906 Khalaf's son Abū Ja'far Aḥmad, who would be the first ruler of this line, was born, 'with both hands outstretched; his women kinfolk exclaimed, "As long as he lives, he will destroy, consume, and give away"' (1935: 278–9).

Ṭāhir's extravagances alarmed his troops, who knew 'that rule does not last long (when accompanied) with pigeon-flying, drinking day and night, and taking from the treasury without putting anything into it'. Ayās ibn 'Abd Allāh, the chief of the Arab troops, who had served under Ya'qūb, requested and received permission to depart; before he did so he said to Ṭāhir, 'We took this kingdom by the sword; but you expect to hold it by indulging in pleasure! Rule cannot be held in jest! A king must have justice, piety, discipline, eloquence, the whip, and the sword.' But Ṭāhir did not heed him (1935: 279). The treasury empty of cash, the brothers melted down gold and silver vessels to coin money needed for their daily expenses and lavish building projects, as Ṭāhir refused to impose a *corvée*. In 295/908 Layth ibn 'Alī ibn Layth (nephew of 'Amr ibn Layth) arrived in Sistan with an army and, while professing loyalty to Ṭāhir, secretly fomented mutiny among his commanders. Although he succeeded in forcing Ṭāhir and Ya'qūb to flee Zarang, which he burned and sacked (296/909), Layth was ultimately defeated and sent to Baghdad; he was later to be succeeded by his brother Muḥammad. Three months later, in Fars, Ṭāhir and Ya'qūb were defeated, captured and sent to Baghdad.

Here our author quotes a Persian poem by Muḥammad ibn Waṣīf which laments the passing of the glorious empire acquired by Ya'qūb and 'Amr, and which clearly anticipates the impending fall of the first line of the Ṣaffārids. Soon after Muḥammad ibn 'Alī ibn Layth's accession (Muḥarram 298/September 910) the caliph al-Muqtadir gave the Sāmānid Aḥmad ibn Ismā'īl the patent for Sistan and ordered him to send his army there. Muḥammad fled to Bust, where he tyrannised the people; riots broke out, and the *khuṭba* was pronounced in the name of the Sāmānid. As the plunder continued, Aḥmad ibn Ismāʿīl arrived with troops, captured the fleeing Muḥammad, entered Bust and restored order, entrusting the city to Ḥātim ibn ʿAbd Allāh Shāshī, 'a devout Muslim [who] renewed the teachings of the Prophet among the people'. Zarang fell to the Sāmānid commander Ḥusayn ibn ʿAlī Marvazī soon after (298/911); his general Sīmjūr, who had been given the patent for Sistan two months before, occupied the Yaʿqūbī palace. 'This was the end of the glory of Sistan' (1935: 293–4).

Aḥmad ibn Ismāʿīl soon replaced Sīmjūr with his own cousin, Abū Ṣāliḥ Manṣūr ibn Isḥāq, who made himself unpopular by increasing the tax assessment for Sistan and billeting his troops in private houses. The next thirteen years saw a series of rebellions and riots, as the Abbasids attempted to contain Sāmānid expansion in the east, Sāmānid governors came and went, and local warlords rose and fell (see Bosworth 1994: 274–9). In 311/923 the Sistani populace declared for Abū Jaʿfar Aḥmad ibn Khalaf ibn Layth, who was invested as Amīr. Although still a youth, Abū Jaʿfar 'possessed the wisdom of old age, for he had acquired much knowledge, and in him were also manifest the grandeur and the majesty of kings' (1935: 278–9). The former governor of Rukhkhadh, mustering an army to come to support Abū Jaʿfar, who was faced with civil strife in the city, told them: 'We have found a ruler who is a scion of our own kings, and have been freed from serving foreigners and slaves' (1935: 311).

> Amīr Bā Jaʿfar was alert, generous, learned, and virtuous. He was versed in all branches of learning. He spent day and night (drinking) wine, bestowing gifts, and dispensing justice. During his reign everyone in the world felt tranquil. No (other) ruler of his age possessed his valor. He had divided up his time: a period for prayer and reading (the Koran), a period for pleasure and eating, a period for attending to royal affairs, a period for rest and ease in private. His fame grew great among the rulers of the world. (1935: 314–5)

Abū Jaʿfar was a major patron and promoter of scholarship and letters; his circle boasted many of the leading intellectual figures of his time (see Bosworth 1994: 291–7; Kraemer 1986b: 8–24 and passim). An episode involving the Daylamid Mākān ibn Kākī and one of Abū Jaʿfar's envoys, which, when reported to Naṣr II ibn Aḥmad in Bukhara, occasioned considerable amusement, provides our author the opportunity to cite a lengthy *qaṣīda* composed by Rūdakī at Naṣr's request and sent to Abū Jaʿfar along with many gifts.

During most of Abū Jaʿfar's reign Sistan seems to have been

relatively peaceful. In 341/952 however his claim to rule was challenged by supporters of Abū ʿAbbās ibn Ṭāhir ibn Muḥammad ibn ʿAmr ibn Layth, who preferred him because 'he was of Ṣaffārid princely descent on his father's side' (Bosworth 1994: 299). This resulted in a decade of turmoil; and while Abū ʿAbbās's supporters were finally defeated, he himself was involved in Abū Jaʿfar's murder in 352/963 (for reasons not specified by our author) by some of that ruler's personal slaves, who plundered the treasury and installed another Ṣaffārid pretender. On learning of his father's murder Abū Jaʿfar's son Khalaf, who had been absent at the time of the event, marched on Sistan and secured the succession, appointing as his co-ruler Ṭāhir ibn Muḥammad ibn Abī ʿAlī Tamīmī, the great-grandson of ʿAmr ibn Layth; both names were proclaimed in the *khuṭba*. Within a year of his accession Khalaf determined to go on the pilgrimage, and left Ṭāhir behind as his viceroy, with instructions to find and kill Abū Jaʿfar's murderers. This he quickly did. Ṭāhir is described as 'learned and able, generous, just, and of good character. Under his rule Sistan became tranquil, so great was his justice and equity towards his subjects, both élite and commoners, and (towards) the army' (1935: 328). Our author paints a heroic portrait of Ṭāhir as skilled in the manly arts of polo and warfare, generous, loyal and noble, and much admired and respected by the Sāmānid court.

The events which followed Khalaf's return were to bring about the downfall both of the Ṣaffārid line and (if we accept ʿUtbī's judgement) of the Sāmānids. He went first, not to Sistan, but to the Sāmānid Nūḥ ibn Manṣūr (read: Manṣūr ibn Nūḥ) to ask for assistance against Ṭāhir, and returned with a Sāmānid army, entering Zarang in 358/969 (on discrepancies in the dates see Bosworth 1994: 305–7). The next thirteen years saw a protracted struggle between Khalaf and his Sāmānid supporters and Ṭāhir (who died in 359/970) and his son and successor Ḥusayn. In 360/971 Khalaf defeated Ḥusayn and entered Zarang, rounded up those who had supported Ṭāhir and Ḥusayn, killed them, seized their wealth, and plundered the Fars Gate quarter, where they were especially numerous. 'In this way he saw to it that no supporter of Ḥusayn remained in Sistan; they either went to Khurasan or abroad, or were killed' (1935: 335). In the following year Ḥusayn reoccupied Zarang, and his commander ʿAbd Allāh Ṣābūnī blocked the citadel gates against a possible siege. Then a letter reached Khalaf from Manṣūr ibn Nūḥ (not, as our author has it, Nūḥ ibn Manṣūr), who instructed him to send Ḥusayn ibn Ṭāhir and Ṣābūnī to Bukhara so that he might hear their side of the story. They were allowed to do so; the upshot was that Manṣūr provided Ḥusayn with troops, and he defeated Khalaf at Juvayn in 369/979. Khalaf took refuge in the citadel, where Ḥusayn and his troops besieged him.

Now the Sāmānid sent 'all the amīrs and army commanders in Khurasan and Transoxania' with their troops to Sistan; but they were unable to defeat Khalaf, who would come out, skirmish and retreat to the citadel. Then Abū al-Ḥasan Sīmjūrī appeared on the scene, ostensibly to take stock of the situation and to deliver letters from the Amīr to Khalaf. ('Utbī also states that it was Abū al-Ḥasan [1869, I: 99–104; according to Gardīzī [1968: 166] it was his son Abū 'Alī. See further Bosworth 1994: 309–12.) Khalaf was persuaded to leave the citadel for the fortress of Ṭāq; Abū al-Ḥasan Sīmjūrī communicated with him secretly, to the effect that the Amīr was in despair at the great number of Khurasani nobles and commanders killed in the fighting, and that he, Khalaf, was to do nothing until the Sīmjūrid had concluded his task and departed. An agreement was reached dividing rule between Khalaf and Ḥusayn, and the latter entered the citadel. Abū al-Ḥasan Sīmjūrī remained in Sistan for several months; before leaving, he obtained written statements from the city elders and from Ḥusayn stating, 'The commander came here, took the city and the citadel and delivered them to me; my business is taken care of.' Then he left (1935: 337–8; compare Jarbādhqānī's version of 'Utbī's account, discussed in Chapter 3).

Immediately the fighting resumed. In 373/983 Khalaf forced Ḥusayn and his followers to retreat into the citadel, which had been emptied of provisions and furnishings; without supplies, many died of starvation. Ḥusayn requested, and received, provisions from Sabuktigīn in Bust; but Khalaf sent the latter money and a message accusing Ḥusayn of being a heretic (*zindīq*) and a supporter of (?; a word is missing here, but it seems clear that Ḥusayn was accused of Bāṭinī sympathies). Sabuktigīn (who was a Karrāmī) withdrew, and sent troops to support Khalaf. Ḥusayn was forced to sue for peace, which was concluded in 373/983. Then Khalaf escorted Ḥusayn to his paternal estate of Farāh, sent him lavish gifts, and invited him to go riding, hunting and drinking with him so as to dispel his cares. He feasted Ḥusayn at every inn along the way; and when they reached the Ṭāq, Khalaf entertained him there for twenty days with extravagant hospitality – at the end of which time, Ḥusayn died. Khalaf mourned him with proper ceremony and rewarded his slaves. Now his own position was secure.

Our author pauses for an encomium of Khalaf, who now 'spread the carpet of justice, put aside military dress and donned the clothing of scholars and jurists'. He held sessions for the discussion of (religious) learning and for hearing *ḥadīth*s, 'cultivated the *'ulamā* and despised fools'. Though he was familiar with all the sciences he preferred the religious ones, and dedicated a session to *ḥadīth* and disputation every night (1935: 342). Among the scholars who came to him from all parts was the famed Badīʿ al-Zamān Hamadhānī, who remained at his court until Khalaf's fall. (On Khalaf as a scholar and patron of learning see Bosworth 1994: 328–37; on his commissioning of a massive Koran commentary, 335–6 and notes.)

Yet Khalaf's ultimate legacy was the end of independent rule for Sistan.

> By his unbalanced savagery towards his own family and by his arbitrary and severe measures against the people of Sistan at large, Khalaf had turned what had been, at various critical periods of Sistan's history ... a vigorous legitimist feeling for the Ṣaffārid house ... in favour of a change of régime and a belief that the people would be better off under the outsider Maḥmūd of Ghazna. Of course, this was speedily to prove a delusion ... and in this wise, Khalaf, the last Ṣaffārid, bequeathed to his people a *damnosa haereditas*. (Bosworth 1994: 328)

In 383/994 Khalaf's son ʿAmr rebelled against him; the rebellion was suppressed, and Khalaf had ʿAmr seized and put in prison, where he died soon after. Two other sons died of natural causes (1935: 344); the sole surviving one, Amīr Ṭāhir, a somewhat flamboyant figure, 'rose to the heroic stature of Rustam the son of Dastān, and was admired by all' (1935: 345). He assisted Sabuktigīn against the rebellious Abū ʿAlī Sīmjūrī; but after the victory was won Sabuktigīn's commander Bughrājuq turned against him. Ṭāhir defeated Bughrājuq (this was after Sabuktigīn's death), killed him and brought back his head and a large amount of booty. This was to prove a fatal mistake. (For different versions of these events see Bosworth 1994: 321–6.)

> Amīr Khalaf was happy with him [Ṭāhir], and he with his father, until his fortune was reversed and the Evil Eye afflicted him. Amīr Khalaf went to Mount Ispahbad, with his wives and his servants, on some errand [in Jumādā 390/May 1000]. It happened that Sultan Maḥmūd ibn Sabuktigīn passed by, with a large army and many elephants, and heard that Khalaf was there with his womenfolk and Amīr Ṭāhir's army was in Sistan. Sultan Maḥmūd came to the foot of the mountain ... and there was no one with Amīr Khalaf but women and black slaves. (1935: 346)

Maḥmūd's troops surrounded the hill and menaced Khalaf with arrows and siege engines. Khalaf sued for peace and agreed to pay Maḥmūd a large indemnity and to pronounce the *khuṭba* and strike coins in his name. (Other historians have it that Maḥmūd was avenging the death of Bughrājuq; our author makes no mention of this.) Khalaf, we are told, had expected Ṭāhir and the Sistani troops to come to his aid against Maḥmūd; but they had been 'negligent', and by the time they were prepared, Maḥmūd had gone. Ṭāhir, fearing Khalaf's anger, rebelled, 'took his father's elephants and troops and went to Kirman and thence to Fars, and no one opposed him' (1935: 347). After further battles and reconciliations, Ṭāhir entered Sistan (1 Muḥarram 391/1 December 1000) and, with the support of the army, the *'ayyār*s, and the mob, attacked Khalaf in the Ṭāq. Eventually peace was concluded, and Khalaf sent his retinue to Ṭāhir to pay their respects. Ṭāhir rose to go to Khalaf, taking with him only a few retainers.

> Those who were on familiar terms with him said, 'You must not go. Amīr Khalaf is deceitful, and has been stricken by a great trial. You are his sole surviving son; no mistake must be made that (would allow) the continuity of this realm and rule to be cut off from this family because of his seeking vengeance. For when fortune abandons someone, it shows (him) crooked ways, so that his kingdom and royal fortune vanish.' (1935: 349–50)

Nevertheless, Ṭāhir went to his father, who ordered two black slaves to lie in wait for him and seize him as he entered the fortress, breaking the solemn oaths that the two had sworn mutually. 'They imprisoned him and bound him in chains; and thus he died, in chains' (in 392/1002). 'On that day the house of 'Amr and Ya'qūb came to an end and passed away; for after that none of (their house) was blessed by rule, and (only) God Most High knows who may be' (1935: 350).

The Sistanis closed the city gates and declared for Maḥmūd. They sent a letter informing him the city was his, and a messenger who told him, 'Ṭāhir is no more, and on that subject there is no dispute. But fortune abandoned that man [Khalaf], and he uprooted the tree of his own house with his own hand.' Maḥmūd marched on Sistan and camped before the Ṭāq until he had reduced it completely and Khalaf sued for peace. 'Then, at the time of the night prayer, on Saturday night 12 Ṣafar 393 [21 December 1002], Amir Khalaf came down (from the fortress), wearing a wadded garment and shawl as do scholars and ascetics, mounted on an Egyptian donkey, with lighted torches before him.' Maḥmūd sent Khalaf, with his women and baggage, to Khurasan; then he began the business of appointing a governor and administrators over Sistan (1935: 351–2).[30]

> When they delivered the *khuṭba* from the pulpits of Islam in the name of the Turks, this marked the beginning of a period of trial ... for Sistan, and the Sīstānīs had never till then experienced such a calamity. In the time of Ya'qūb and 'Amr no country in the world had enjoyed so much prosperity as Sistan.

> Nimruz had indeed been known as 'The Land of Good Fortune' (*dār al-dawla*) until that time when they deported Amīr Khalaf from Sistan because the populace had rebelled against him. As a result, the people have experienced unpleasant things and are still experiencing them; only God Most High knows what time will eventually bring round. (1935: 354; translated by Bosworth, 1994: 365–6)

This concludes the first portion of the *Tārīkh-i Sīstān*, as it does 'Sistan's brief presence on the centre stage of events in the Eastern Islamic world'. From here on the narrative 'becomes more and more parochial in its scope except when outside powers ... obtrude on local Sistan events' (Bosworth 1994: 365). We need not follow the account of Sistan's sufferings under the Ghaznavids and, later, the Saljūqs: brutal suppressions of rebellions, the sacking of Zarang by Maḥmūd's troops in 393/1003, the extortions of oppressive administrators, the famine and cholera which afflicted Sistan in 401/1013, the struggles between Ghaznavid officials and local leaders. After Maḥmūd's death the Sistanis declared for Masʿūd; our author's assertion that when Amīr Muḥammad heard of the Ghaznavid governor's defection he marched on Sistan to exact vengeance from the Sistanis but was deposed before reaching Sistan, is highly unlikely (and otherwise unsubstantiated), and is clearly meant to show both the ruthlessness of the Ghaznavids and the continued importance of Sistan. Towards the end of Masʿūd's reign the Turkmens extended their raids from Khurasan to Sistan. In 432/1040 its governor Abū al-Faḍl Naṣr, refused troops by Masʿūd, sought aid from the Turkmens themselves, and concluded an agreement with the Turkish commander Ertash, after which the *khuṭba* was read in the name of Bayghū [= Yabghū] ibn Saljūq. Further struggles between Ghaznavids and Turkmens increased Sistan's sufferings, as did attacks by Mawdūd's chamberlain Ṭughril (who later deposed ʿAbd al-Rashīd) in 434/1043 (1935: 368; Bahār, n. 2, states that this is the only known source for an attack at this early date) and again in 443/1051, when Ṭughril was in open rebellion against the Ghaznavids. He was ultimately unsuccessful and withdrew, 'went to Ghaznīn, seized it, and killed ʿAbd al-Rashīd ibn Maḥmūd and most of the princes. But God Most High destroyed him as well, as he deserved' (1935: 372). This section concludes by recording that on Friday 8 Muḥarram 445/30 April 1053 the *khuṭba* was read in Sistan in the name of the Saljūq Ṭughril, 'May God make his rule endure!' (1935: 373).

Here the text breaks off. When it resumes its style changes: sentences become shorter, the syntactical structure is different, as is the style of the rubrics. Bahār conjectured that the core text was written during Ṭughril's reign, on the basis of the prayer for continuance of his rule, and that the same author continued the work – albeit in a summary fashion – until it breaks off again in 448/1056. But it seems likely that a third hand was involved, since the stylistic changes begin with the paragraph that follows the account of the rebel Ṭughril's first attack on Sistan. The comments on his seizure of Ghazna, as well as on his ultimate fate (he was murdered in 443/1052), and the brief paragraph on events between 443/1051 and 445/1053, agree stylistically with the sections which follow; moreover, the paragraph in question contains another feature found in the later sections (up to 448/1056) but not in either the core or the post-448 accounts: it states that when the Amīr Abū al-Faḍl and his army, having learned of Ṭughril's withdrawal, returned to Sistan in Ramaḍān 443/January 1052, they did so 'under an auspicious portent' (1935: 372). The addition of astrological references and mention of auspicious and inauspicious portents is a distinguishing feature of this section not found elsewhere; not even the foundation myth provides a specific horoscope.[31] Such references suggest a Saljūq context.

A second break, covering a seventeen-year span between 448/1056 and 465/1073, occurs at this point. When the account begins again (with a brief note on the death of the Amīr Abū al-Faḍl Naṣr (I) in 465/1073) the style changes once more, becoming even more summary. Each brief account is preceded by such phrases as 'the death of', 'the arrival of', 'the seizure of' (features not reflected by Gold's translation, which retains the continuous narrative style of the core). Vocabulary items occur which are not found in the earlier sections. All this points to another author having completed the work; but the style of this section differs from that of both the preceding sections, and it contains almost nothing of interest until it reaches the account of the Mihrabānid Rukn al-Ḥaqq wa-al-Dīn Shāh Maḥmūd, 'sovereign of Nīmrūz' and son of Naṣīr al-Dīn Muḥammad (653–718/1255–1318), that is, around the end of the 7th/13th century.

Bosworth observes that from here on the author's viewpoint becomes even more parochial; he says little about Sistan's connections with the Saljūqs or Ghaznavids, or of 'the new sectarian forces on the eastern Persian fringes, Quhistānī Ismā'īlism' (1994: 387, and see 388–91, 418–19). In fact, a distinguishing feature of this section is its author's pronounced interest in heretics, to which only sparse references are found in the core text, which nowhere refers to the Khārijīs as heretics and ignores the heterodox movements in Sistan around the time of the Abbasid takeover (compare, for example, Gardīzī).[32] Moreover, neither Bāṭinī activities in Sistan during the Sāmānid period nor Khalaf ibn Aḥmad's execution of the *dā'ī* Abū

Ḥātim Sijistānī (if indeed the story is true) receive mention (see Bosworth 1994: 331 and n. 1020; Kraemer 1986b: 22–3 and notes). Such omissions may be deliberate, designed to preserve the image of the Sistanis as pious, God-fearing followers of the true faith; but their piety is never demonstrated by opposition to or rejection of heretical movements.

Our third author is however interested in such matters, as he is also in omens (as opposed to astrology). He records that a Qarmaṭī (read: Nizārī) force was defeated by the Sistanis in 489/1096 in a battle in which 400 Qarmaṭīs were sent to Hell, but only one Sistani was killed. In 495/1101 the Qarmaṭīs were in Daraq, where they killed its *qāḍī*. In Jumādā II 499/February 1106 a mysterious sign, shaped like a white pillar, appeared in the heavens at night and remained there for about a month (1935: 390; see also Ibn al-Athīr 1965, 10: 145). On 2 Jumādā II 562/26 March 1167 a total solar eclipse occurred. The year 523/1129–30 witnessed another appearance of the *malāḥida* (no details are given), as did 590–1/1194–5, when a combined force of Sistanis, Ghuris and Khurasanis chased them back into Quhistan and despatched them before the gates of Qā'in. Here another break occurs in the text which may have provided more details of this event. (Bahār states that this battle took place in 596/1199 [1935: 393, n. 2], but see Bosworth 1994: 400.)

Following the Mongol defeat of Sultan Muḥammad Khwārazmshāh (in 617/1220, not 616/1219; see Bosworth 1994: 404) accounts become more detailed, especially for events concerning the rise of the Mihrabānid rulers of Sistan from 633/1236 onwards. These sections conclude with an account of the peace agreed between the 'Sovereign of Nīmrūz', Rukn al-Ḥaqq wa-al-Dīn Shāh Maḥmūd, and his brother, the Mihrabānid ruler Nuṣrat al-Dīn Muḥammad (718–31/1318–30 or 31), which at the time of writing had lasted for eight years and had brought peace to the previously troubled region of Sistan (1935: 415; see Bosworth 1994: 438–40). These last sections were thus written during Shāh Maḥmūd's lifetime (and probably for him); earlier history was of little real interest to this author, but was a requisite part of his undertaking.

It thus appears that three separate authors, distinguished by style and by thematic interests, contributed to the composition of the *Tārīkh-i Sīstān* in its final form. The author of the core brought his work up to the late 1040s-early 1050s, after Ṭughril's first attack on Sistan but probably (if the stylistic changes are a reliable indication) before his second attack, his seizure of Ghazna and his murder. A second author continued the work, beginning with a brief mention of the latter events and the Saljūq takeover of Sistan in 445/1053; it is possible, in view of its cursory treatment of events, that this section represents notes intended to serve as the basis for a more detailed, 'finished' continuation which never materialised. Both these authors (the second may have been an apprentice to the first) were contemporaries of the Saljūq sultan Ṭughril. Much later, a third author completed the work, picking up somewhere between 448/1056 and 465/1073, briefly summarising events up to the rise of the Mihrabānids, and closing in the reign of Rukn al-Dīn Shāh Maḥmūd.

Who the authors were remains a mystery. The simple, slightly archaic style of the first author probably reflects the relative isolation of Sistan; he may well have been a scribe or secretary, as was probably his continuator, whose style seems more in tune with that of the early Saljūq period. If the core text was completed under Ghaznavid domination (whose abrupt end could scarcely have been anticipated at the time), the emphasis on Sistan's special status would justify its claim to independence on the basis of its past under the Ṣaffārids, who, despite their shortcomings, were considered by Sistanis as indigenous, legitimate rulers. And if the second author was writing under Saljūq occupation, the entire work – to which he adds little but the record of Saljūq depradations – would serve to bolster this special status with a view to legitimating Naṣrid rule. The third author (whose more Arabised style is typical of prose of the Mongol period) may in turn have seen the whole history of Sistan, whose prosperity under independent local rule contrasts with its sufferings under foreign domination, as, in turn, legitimating yet another independent dynasty, the Mihrabānids.

Gold concluded that, if the *Tārīkh-i Sīstān* 'compels no radical changes in the over-all interpretations of what is already known of the Islamic East at this time', it is valuable as local history which casts new light on the Ṣaffārids and the activities of the Khārijīs in Sistan. In this connection we may note the first author's use of documentary materials not found in other sources, such as the correspondence between Hārūn al-Rashīd and Ḥamza, or ʿAmr ibn Layth's peace treaty with the caliph al-Muʿtamid, which lends further support to the speculation that he was a scribe or secretary who had access to archival records. Bosworth voices frequent objections as to the authenticity of various accounts: those concerning the ransom set for ʿAmr (which is found in no other source; 1994: 231) and of the rescue attempt which never materialised (which conflicts with accounts in other, generally hostile, sources; 1994: 231–2); the story of ʿAmr's fall; and the connection between the story of Mākān ibn Kākī and Rūdakī's poem (see 1994: 189–91). While it is likely that such accounts have been embellished to serve the author's purposes (among them his pro-Sistani bias), it is also unlikely that they have been made up out of whole cloth. This is a broad issue, and I shall return to it in the Conclusion.

Gold stressed that the *Tārīkh-i Sīstān* should be considered not only as a source of historical data but also 'as one of the finest specimens of an early phase in the stylistic development of modern Persian', and that the (first) author, 'very self-consciously proud of the new instrument he is helping to forge, is pleased to bring to our attention many previously unknown examples of Persian poetry written by his predecessors, Rūdakī's *qasida* being only the most noteworthy' (1976: li). To whose attention? one might ask. These examples were scarcely 'unknown': Rūdakī's fame was widespread long before our first author began writing, and the inclusion of his poem redounds less to the importance of the 'new instrument' of the Persian language than to the fame of Sistan's ruler, Abū Ja'far Aḥmad, whom the poem praises. Nor was this instrument 'new': its use for the writing of history had, as we have seen, been pioneered by Bal'amī nearly a century earlier.

Gold also argues that our author manifests 'a hatred and mistrust of the Omayyad and 'Abbāsid Arabs as foreign, oppressive, and self-seeking, and the later Turks, by and large (when they were not Persianized), as uncouth and destructive barbarians', and further that, 'as a pious Muslim of the eleventh century', he 'was deeply disturbed by the schismatic developments rending the unity of Islam', which contributes to 'a tone, variously of rage or indignation, but mostly of sorrow or hopelessness in treating of religious matters' (1976: li–lii). Except for counting religious schism and disunity among the justifications for Khārijī rebellions against rulers who had corrupted Islam (his generally positive, or at least neutral, treatment of them contrasts markedly with the attitude of other historians, for example Ibn Funduq, whose *Tārīkh-i Bayhaq* describes Khārijī depradations in the region), he shows little interest in such matters. He makes almost no mention of heterodox movements in Sistan or of conflicts between the Karrāmiyya and other Sunnī *madhhab*s; even purely local squabbles, such as that between the Samakīs and the Ṣadaqīs, are important chiefly because they weakened independent Sistani rule. Moreover, there is no evidence of hostility to Arabs who were part of the Sistani milieu, or to Arab governors who ruled well; whereas the 'Persianised' Ghaznavids (with whom the 'rule of the Turks' began; our author is exceptional in calling attention to their Turkish ethnicity) are just as anathematised as the barbarian Saljūqs.

The *Tārīkh-i Sīstān* is, says Gold, 'heroic history' because 'its narrative is essentially a succession of leaps, the military exploits and other claims to celebrity, of individual men ... Our hero ... is the means and end of the state' (1976: lii). History is the record of great deeds performed by rulers who personify the state and who exemplify kingly virtues; and in this the *Tārīkh-i Sīstān* is no exception. Gold's final comment is that this 'is history as written by a Sistāni' and that, 'consciously or unconsciously', our author 'may have undertaken to write about the life and death of Sistān, in the way he wanted Sistān understood' (1976: lii–liii). This is true not only for the author of the core text, but for those who followed him and who used his work as the basis for their own and as the proof of their vision of an independent Sistan. Unlike other historians, who regard Sistan as peripheral and its rulers (with the partial exception of the Khalafids) as uncouth nobodies, our authors – and particularly the author of the core – created a uniquely Sistani vision of Sistan as playing a central role in the medieval Islamic world.

NOTES

1. Thus 'states are designated by the names of their improprietors, whether these be persons or peoples' (Al-Azmeh 1990: 14). Our historians never refer to the 'Ghaznavids' (a geographical designation), but to the 'Maḥmūdiyyān' or to the House (Āl) of Sabuktigīn or of Maḥmūd.
2. For a comprehensive study of the issue of loyalty in this period see Mottahedeh 1980. The violation of oaths of allegiance was considered among the most heinous of sins; but the oaths were taken to individuals, not to the 'state' (1980: 62). Moreover, the primary loyalty of a *mamlūk* was to his original owner (1980: 86).
3. Kraemer's detailed study of the legal issues involved shows that the jurists were primarily concerned with rebellion against the Imām (the caliph), for which ideological arguments (a differing interpretation of God's Word) or ethical justifications (revolt against an unjust ruler) may be invoked.
4. Maḥmūd's poet-laureate ʿUnṣurī is said to have written a metrical *Tāj al-futūḥ* (now lost) extolling Maḥmūd's military exploits (see Nāẓim 1971: 1 and n. 2); on later epic poems celebrating Ghaznavid achievements see Bosworth 1968b: 41–2.
5. Bayhaqī notes that a history of the Ghaznavids up to the year 409/1018–19 was written by his contemporary, Maḥmūd (ibn) Warrāq, in 450/1058–9 (1971: 342). Ibn Funduq mentions another history written in Maḥmūd's reign, as well as a *Sīra Masʿūdiyya* ('Life of Masʿūd') (1965: 20). Bertotti refers to a work by Bīrūnī, *Tāʾrīkh ayyām al-sulṭān wa-akhbār abīh* ('History of the Sultan's Reign and Accounts of His Father') (in Persian?) but does not provide the source of this attribution (1991: 36); he also states that ʿUtbī's history was commissioned by Maḥmūd's son Muḥammad. None of these works are extant.
6. There is no critical edition of ʿUtbī's history, although one is in preparation by Professor Everett Rowson of the University of Pennsylvania. On the various mss. and the problems of an edition see

Rubinacci 1982. I have used the Cairo 1869 lithograph, with the commentary of Manīnī. For other recensions see Bosworth 1973a: 9–10.

7. Treadwell (1991: 9) asserts that Ṣābī''s style was comparatively simple, as does Madelung (1967: 23; see also Rosenthal 1968: 177). Bosworth states that the *Tājī*'s 'exaggerated, eulogistic style provided a model for the *Yamīnī*' (1963: 3, and see 6–7); see also the entry 'al-Ṣābi', Abū Isḥāq' in Meisami and Starkey 1998.
8. Compare Jarbādhqānī's considerably more flowery version: 'the affairs of the kingdom reached Capella, until the eye of perfection did its work, and with the evil eye of the days and the vicissitudes of fortune it turned its face towards reversal; and so firm a foundation and so well smoothed a rule became weakened and filled with strife ... And the source of weakness and beginning of disorder in that rule was the affair of Sistan' (1966: 41).
9. Manīnī's commentary is instructive; he misses none of the nuances of this passage, whose hyperbole is intended to undermine what it appears to assert, and notes, for example, that at the beginning of this passage, 'How he excelled here, by not referring to Abū Bakr as "Ustādh".'
10. On these events see further Bosworth 1980: 8–14; Bulliet 1972: 134–6 and, on the *qāḍī*, 201–4. Manīnī comments that 'Utbī's use here of fifth-form verbal nouns – *ta'alluh*, 'devout behaviour', *ta'abbud*, 'pious conduct', and so on – makes it clear that these qualities were sham, fabricated for the purpose of gratifying worldly ambitions.
11. The standard edition is that of 'Abd al-Ḥayy Ḥabībī, who published the section on the Ghaznavids in 1928 and a full edition in 1968, based on two relatively late manuscripts, which has had several reprintings. Both manuscripts are incomplete, lacking prefatory material and part of the beginning of the work, and breaking off in the reign of Mawdūd ibn Mas'ūd (432–40/1041–9).
12. It is said that when Maḥmūd conquered Rayy he summoned Majd al-Dawla and asked him, 'Have you not read the *Shāhnāma*, which is the history of the Persians, and Ṭabarī's History, which is that of the Muslims?' When Majd al-Dawla replied that he had, Maḥmūd told him, 'Your situation is not that of one who has read them' (Ibn al-Athīr 1965, 9: 371–2). For the account of this conquest in the *Mujmal al-tavārīkh va-al-qiṣas* see Chapter 3, below.
13. Because of lacunae encompassing the latter part of al-Ma'mūn's reign and the beginning of al-Mu'taṣim's – the account of which starts with the revolt of Bābak (1968: 75; cf. nn. 16, 17) – and between the Iranian general Afshīn's pursuit of Bābak and the revolt of Rāfi' ibn Harthama in the reign of al-Mu'taḍid, we do not know what Gardīzī might have had to say on the *miḥna* instituted by al-Ma'mūn, on Afshīn's trial and execution for heresy, or on the murder of al-Mutawakkil.
14. This account is clearly apocryphal. Dhū al-Yamīnayn means 'Possessor of Two Right Hands'; Ṭāhir was, apparently, so called because, in battle against 'Alī ibn 'Īsā, he had grasped his sword in both hands to strike the blow that killed his opponent (see Ṭabarī 1992b: 54, and n. 237 on the identity of the striker).
15. The date, given as 322/933–4, is clearly wrong, although the placing

of this account in Nūḥ's reign is confirmed by the references to the death of Abū al-Muẓaffar Chaghānī and Nūḥ's appointment of Abū ʿAlī as *sipahsālār* of Khurasan.

16. On this peace, concluded either towards the end of Farrukhzād's reign or at the beginning of Ibrāhīm's, see Ḥusaynī 1933: 27–9; Bosworth 1977: 10–11, 48–9, 51–2.
17. Excerpts from other parts are cited by later writers; these have been collected and published by Saʿīd Nafīsī (*Dar pīrāmūn-i Tārīkh-i Bayhaqī*, Tehran 1963; 2nd ed. Tehran 1973). The most comprehensive, brief account of Bayhaqī's career and works is the article by Ğ.-Ḥ. Yūsofī in *EIr*, which updates and corrects that of S. Naficy in *EI*[2] and provides a list of editions and translations of Bayhaqī's history and additional bibliography. I have used the 1971 edition by ʿAlī Akbar Fayyāẓ.
18. The term *khuṭba* does not – *pace* Waldman – indicate an affinity with the sermon pronounced in the mosque on Friday (see 1980: 152). In the context of prose writing *khuṭba* is a technical term meaning 'exordium' or 'preface'; its usage in this sense is attested at least as early as the Arabic prose stylist Jāḥiẓ (d. 265/868–9). The composition of a *khuṭba* to mark the transition from one ruler to another is, Bayhaqī tells us, a self-imposed constraint (1971: 112).
19. The *māl-i bayʿat* is was money distributed to those who swore the oath of allegiance (*bayʿa*) to the ruler (or, on occasion, to his designated successor); see Mottahedeh 1980: 50–4.
20. For a discussion of this episode see Bertotti 1990: 53, who comments on the various levels of information relating to the attempt: the 'official' version provided by Masʿūd's representative (*ṣāḥib-barīd*) in Khwarazm; the secret communications sent by this representative to Ghazna; Masʿūd's own version, as he attempted to exonerate himself and place the blame on Bū Sahl and other officials; the narrative of these events by Bū Naṣr Mishkān; and a later account provided Bayhaqī some years later by Altuntāsh's former vizier, (Aḥmad ibn) ʿAbd al-Ṣamad.
21. For example, he refutes a claim made in a 'history of Persian kings' (unidentified) that a Sasanian prince had established himself in Khwarazm: 'For when the *dawlat* of the Arabs (may it endure!) abrogated the customs of the Persians ... Khwarazm was a separate entity', that is, not part of the Sasanian empire (1971: 902–3; Bīrūnī, however, accepted the claim of the Afrīghid Khwārazmshāhs to descent from 'the progeny of [the Kayānid] Siyāvush b. Kai Kā'ūs' (Bosworth 1973a: 55).
22. Bertotti suggests that this story was included solely for the value of Buzurgmihr's moral teachings, embodied in his advice to his sons (1991: 85). But as is usual with Bayhaqī, it has clear topical relevance.
23. The text was first published in 1935 by M. T. Bahār, who based his edition on what was believed to be a unique manuscript copied before 864/1460. On other mss. discovered since, see E. Yarshater's introduction to M. Gold's translation (1976); Bosworth 1994: 24. I have not been able to consult the edition published in Tehran in 1994. Bahār's edition was the basis of Milton Gold's English translation (1976), which is often unreliable and reveals unfamiliarity with the work's historical and literary context. For a

discussion of primary and secondary sources on Sistan, including those cited in the *Tārīkh-i Sīstān*, see Bosworth 1994, Chapter 1. On the problem of authorship see the conclusion to this section.

24. As Bahār noted, the sources for these accounts, which often differ considerably from those in the *Shāhnāma*, are most likely the various 'minor epics' which dealt with events from a local perspective and/or with figures not treated in Firdawsī's poem.
25. For the texts of the letter and reply see 1935: 162–8. According to Baghdādī it was al-Ma'mūn who, on acceding to the caliphate, wrote to Ḥamza (1920: 101); this may reflect al-Ma'mūn's particular importance for Khurasan.
26. On the *'ayyār*s, a prominent element in Sistani history, see Bosworth 1968a: 538–40, 1994: 68–9, 341–5. The *'ayyārūn* (also termed *muṭṭawwi'a*) were volunteer bands which had arisen to fight the Khārijīs. They played an ambivalent role in Sistani politics: 'They stood for law and order and Sunnī orthodoxy, and yet engaged in destabilizing, revolutionary activity. They were, in particular, always the vanguard of local resistance against outside power domination' (Kraemer 1986b: 6, n. 14). The term also means 'rogues, vagabonds, bandits'.
27. The Zanj were not (*pace* Gold) 'recalcitrant Negro praetorians' (1976: xxxv), but black slaves working in the salt marshes of southern Iraq. In 255/869 an 'Alid rebel recruited support from among them; their revolt lasted for nearly thirty years, to devastating effect. See Ṭabarī 1992a, the bulk of which deals with the first phase of this revolt.
28. Yāqūt identifies the poet as an envoy from the caliph Mu'tamid who decided to remain with Ya'qūb (see Bosworth 1994: 177–8). Stern argued that the poem's 'violent attack on the 'Abbāsid caliph suggests that the poem was written after Ya'qūb's final break with the caliph, probably in the course of the invasion of 'Irāq' in 262/876 (1971: 540).
29. Mas'ūdī relates, on the authority of one of Ya'qūb's 'intimates and confidants', that that ruler 'never wasted time on desultory social intercourse or nocturnal story-telling sessions ... but spent the greater part of his time by himself, formulating his plans and strategies for the future' (quoted by Bosworth 1994: 170; Bosworth's translation). Ya'qūb, in short, did precisely the opposite of what rulers are enjoined to do: seek out informed and experienced company, and listen to stories of past kings that they may learn therefrom. While his single-minded pursuit of power may have contributed to his success, from the historians' perspective his ignorance of the principles of kingship would have doomed him to ultimate failure.
30. Khalaf was first sent to Guzgan, where he could be closely supervised, and later imprisoned in Gardīz, where he died; see Bosworth 1994: 316–27.
31. For examples see 1935: 373 (the battle of Bada, Ramaḍān 445/January 1054, with 'the two ill-omened planets', Mars and Saturn, in Pisces); 378 (the battle of Zara, with the two planets again conjoined, in Aries; the arrival in Sistan of an embassy from Chaghrī Beg on 2 Rabī' I 448/19 June 1056, 'with an auspicious portent'); 380 (a detailed ascension horoscope for Chaghrī, 25 Rabī'

II 448/12 July 1056); 382 (the arrival of Būrī, Bayghū/Yabghū's son, on 14 Jumādā II 448/29 August 1056, at dawn, with the ascendant three degrees in Libra).

32. The author notes an insurrection in Bust in 150/767–8 led by 'Muḥammad ibn Shaddād of the Laghbariyyān' (read: Laghsariyyān) and two 'Magians', Āzaruya and Marzbān, but gives no indication of its nature. Stern has shown that 'Laghsariyya' was the name of the sect headed by Ustādsīs; see 1983: 42, 45–6, and the references cited; see also Bahār's conjecture to this effect, 1935: 142–3 and n. 3.

3

The Historiography of the Saljūq Period

THE RISE OF THE SALJŪQS

The Saljūqs' swift rise to power following their victory at Dandānqān in 431/1040 surprised the eastern Islamic world (and, indeed, as Bayhaqī observed, their successes seem to have surprised the Saljūqs themselves). Ṭughril, leaving his brother Chaghrī in control of Khurasan, moved westwards; making Rayy his base, he expanded further into Iraq and the Jibal. In Ramaḍān 447/December 1055 he entered Baghdad and deposed the last Būyid amīr, al-Malik al-Raḥīm Khusraw Fīrūz; the *khuṭba* was pronounced in his name, and he was confirmed as sultan by the caliph al-Qā'im. He was then obliged to leave Baghdad to deal with dissent among the Turkmen amīrs; during his absence the Turkish general Arslān Basāsīrī occupied Baghdad in the name of the Fāṭimids, pronounced the *khuṭba* in the name of al-Mustanṣir (427–87/1036–94), and captured the caliphal insignia, which he sent to Cairo. His occupation lasted approximately a year (Dhū al-Qa'da 450/December 1058–Dhū al-Qa'da 451/December 1059); the Fāṭimids withdrew their support, and Basāsīrī was forced to leave Baghdad and was eventually killed in battle (see Daftary 1992: 205–6; Makdisi 1963, especially 90–102).[1]

By the time of his second entry into Baghdad a few days after Basāsīrī's departure, when he received further titles and robes of honour from the caliph, Ṭughril's power was firmly established. Yet despite further expansion under his successors Alp Arslān and Malikshāh (who boasted that his domains stretched from Antioch in the west to Khwarazm in the East; see Rāvandī 1921: 128–9), the Saljūq sultans never ruled, or conceived of themselves as ruling, the type of centralised empire developed by the Sāmānids or the Ghaznavids. While their centres of power were mainly in Hamadan and Isfahan, they themselves were peripatetic, energetic campaigners; and the influence of their tribal past resulting in their allocating rule of various provinces to male relatives on the basis of seniority or experience contributed to the decentralisation and, sooner rather than later, the fragmentation of their domains.[2]

No contemporary historian chronicled their achievements. The Būyids and the Ghaznavids had their chroniclers; the Saljūqs did not. It was almost a century after the death of Malikshāh (485/1092) that works on Saljūq history were written in either Arabic or Persian. The two earliest extant Persian histories of the Saljūq period, the *Fārsnāma* and the *Mujmal al-tavārīkh va-al-qiṣaṣ*, both of which date from the early 6th/12th century, have relatively little to say about the Saljūqs. Moreover, information on the early Saljūq rulers – Ṭughril, Alp Arslān, and Malikshāh – is decidely sparse. As Cahen observes, 'As is the case for every house come from nothing, the first steps of the Saljūqs are lost to us in a night broken only by rare, fragmentary indications, often of a semi-legendary nature' (1949: 31).

What explains this absence? Was it that the Persian secretaries and officials who passed from the Ghaznavid into the Saljūq administration were less than eager to memorialise their conquests? The transfer of rule to the Saljūqs came about by force of arms; and while this was hardly unusual (the same was true of both the Būyids and the Ghaznavids), they could claim neither putative links with the ancient Iranian kings and with Iranian traditions of kingship, as did the Būyids, nor the moral high ground as successors of a collapsed and incapable dynasty, as did the Ghaznavids.[3] Moreover, due to the fragmentation of their rule and to the endless competing claims to the sultanate which began with Malikshāh's death, it seems that it was only retrospectively that it was possible to present the Saljūqs as a *dawla* embodied in a succession of sultans rather than in individual rulers.

Wansbrough writes that

> in common with other literary forms historiography presupposes and expresses, however obliquely, a degree of social stability, of political order, and of economic security. These might take the specific and direct form of patronage, or the general and indirect forms of aesthetic appreciation and intellectual stimulation. Underlying them all is a sense of achievement which serves as external referent: the shared experience of writer and reader, to be merely depicted, possibly affirmed, criticized or modified, but in any case acknowledged as the datum of literary expression. (1978: 138)

These conditions, as we shall have occasion to observe, seem to have been markedly absent during most of the Saljūq period; and, indeed, their absence is a cause of distress to a number of our authors.

Most early writers at least (despite their apparent praise of their warlike nature and natural qualities of leadership) seem to have regarded the Saljūqs as something of a necessary evil: strong (if somewhat crude) warriors for the faith who could be relied upon to support the caliphate and Sunnī Islam, protect the regions, guard the roads, and combat heresy and unbelief (see for example the views of Ibn Ḥassūl [1940] and of Ghazzālī [Hillenbrand 1988]). From the outset the Saljūqs (and, more importantly, their Sunnī administrators) cultivated the image of themselves as rescuers of the Sunnī caliphate from Shīʿī control, promoters of mainstream Sunnism (largely Ḥanafī and Shāfiʿī), implacable foes of heterodoxy (especially Ismāʿīlism, although their zeal was often exaggerated by later historians), and patrons of religious learning and the *ʿulamā*.[4] They have thus gained, retrospectively, the reputation of being sponsors of the so-called 'Sunnī revival' of the 5th/11th and 6th/12th centuries, not least through the institutionalisation of the *madrasa* system by the vizier Niẓām al-Mulk, whose Niẓāmiyya in Baghdad was opened in 459/1067; similar institutions were founded throughout the Saljūq domains, and it is thought that Niẓām al-Mulk intended in this way to produce a cadre of Sunnī administrators (see Klausner 1973: 22–3).[5] (Niẓām al-Mulk also attempted to organise the Saljūq administration according to the Persianate Ghaznavid model – a vision expressed in his *Siyar al-mulūk* – and to educate his prince Malikshāh in the traditions and values of Perso-Islamic kingship; in this, as his own work shows, he was largely unsuccessful.) Both Nīshāpūrī and Rāvandī, as we shall see, praise the Saljūq sultans for their religious patronage and their good works (the building of *madrasa*s, forts, *khānaqāh*s and so on), to which Rāvandī (seemingly alone) adds moral justification for their takeover (vengeance for Maḥmūd of Ghazna's unjust treatment of the ancestor of the house, Isrāʿīl ibn Saljūq).[6]

While under the Saljūqs Persian became the language of administration, many if not most of the Saljūq sultans (in contrast to their Ghaznavid counterparts) were illiterate and showed a 'lack of interest ... in written communication' (Luther 1977: 2; see also Luther 1971a: 27–32). Niẓām al-Mulk observes that, when holding court to supervise the redress of wrongs, the king should 'listen to the words of his subjects with his own ears, without any intermediary', although it is also 'fitting that some written petitions should also be submitted if they are comparatively important' (1978: 13). While Ghaznavid rulers supervised not only the content but the style of documents written by their secretaries, and often composed their own official communications (Bayhaqī provides numerous instances), the Saljūqs left this to their secretaries and officials. Few of the Saljūq sultans seem to have been great patrons of letters, other than works on religious or practical topics – astrology, medicine, and so on – and panegyric poetry, largely in Persian.[7] As a result of this lack of interest in literary production, Saljūq historiography enjoys a quite different relationship to the ruler than does Sāmānid or Ghaznavid; much of it was written by bureaucrats for other bureaucrats, in the figured rhetorical style which became the scribal ideal in the Saljūq and other eastern chanceries in the 6th/12th century (see further the Conclusion).

Cahen has argued that 'neither the beginning nor the end of Seljuq rule marks a true break in the development of Muslim historical literature' (1962: 60). This must be qualified. In Arabic, local histories continued to be written, as did the histories of such dynasties as the Fāṭimids, the Umayyads of Spain, and so on. Several important Persian histories were produced in the east (Bayhaqī, Gardīzī), but it was not until the early 6th/12th century that histories were written in the western Saljūq domains. If, 'at the moment when the Seljuqs appeared on the scene ... in the territories where they settled ... two languages, Arabic and Persian, were flourishing' (Cahen 1962: 60), in the next century a gap begins to appear between histories written in the two languages. The extent to which Arabic histories of the period may (or may not) have been used by Persian writers is unclear; they seem to have contributed little to the development of later Persian historiography. Ibn Funduq wrote, in Arabic, a continuation of 'Utbī, the *Mashārib al-tajārib*; Cahen supposes that the reason this work has not survived was perhaps because he 'had composed this work in Arabic in a country which was giving up this language and that, inversely, he probably lacked documentation on the Arab countries, which could have made certain of [its] preservation' in those regions (1962: 64–5. Cahen stated that it was impossible to tell whether this 'was a true general history or in fact a regional one'; it appears however to have covered the period from 410/1020 to 560/1165 (see *EIr*, art. 'Bayhaqī, Ẓahīr al-Dīn'), and was widely used by later Arabic historians such as Ibn al-Athīr, which may be the chief reason why the work itself did not survive. Cahen argued further that it seems 'out of the question that there was any important monument of Seljuq or eastern Iranian history between the end of Bayhaqī's History and the Mongol period', and that from the mid-6th/12th century 'there are two families of histories, each ignorant of the other, separated by a cleavage of language' (1962: 75).

In fact, with the exception of Ibn Funduq's history of Bayhaq the extant Persian histories written under the Saljūqs were produced in the west, notably in the regions of Fars and the Jibal (in or near Hamadan), that is, in the major administrative centres. An important early work was the so-called memoirs (actually a history of viziers and other officials) of the vizier Anūshīrvān ibn Khālid (d. 553/1158–9?), which 'Imād al-Dīn Iṣfahānī translated into Arabic and incorporated into his own history, the *Nuṣrat al-fatra*. Cahen assumed that 'Imād al-Dīn possessed his own unique, personal copy, which was no longer of interest once incorporated into his history, and that this work was not accessible to Persian historians (1962: 67); Luther (1969) however called attention to a hitherto unstudied source not mentioned by Cahen, the *Tārīkh al-vuzarā*, completed around 584/1188–9 in western Iran by an author (later identified as Najm al-Dīn Qummī; see Luther 1971a: 20) who was a friend of Jarbādhqānī, the translator of ʿUtbī's *Ta'rīkh al-Yamīnī*, which was intended as a supplement (*dhayl*) to Anūshīrvān ibn Khālid's memoirs.[8] Whether other such works will appear in the future is uncertain.

More popular than 'proper' history were the collections of anecdotes made by such writers as Niẓamī ʿArūẓī (d. 556/1161), 'who themselves declare that they drew on no historical work, contrarily to what they acknowledge of previous authors' (Cahen 1962: 75; no reference for this statement is cited, and the somewhat later ʿAwfī [d. after 628/1230–1], compiler of the *Javāmiʿ al-ḥikāyāt*, openly acknowledges his use of historical works). Such works do however contain historical materials, served up in the more entertaining form of anecdotes illustrative of general precepts. 'Mirrors for princes', which became popular during this period, also contain abundant historical materials. These, too, are largely anecdotal and generally brief; an exception, however, is seen in what is perhaps the earliest of these works composed in the Saljūq period, the *Siyar al-mulūk* of the vizier Niẓām al-Mulk.

NIẒĀM AL-MULK AND IRANIAN HISTORY

The genre of mirrors for princes had flourished under the early Abbasids, as Persian imperial ideals and administrative practices were introduced into Arabic-Islamic culture. But from the end of the 3rd/9th century until the late 6th/12th there was no major development in the genre until its resurgence in the early Saljūq period (for a survey see Lambton 1971). Such works intersect with history in that they draw upon the past (both Iranian and Islamic) for exemplary accounts of past rulers, and upon more recent history both for this purpose and for more pragmatic ends, as providing models of statecraft and administrative practice. Both purposes, but especially the second, are served by the historical materials in Niẓām al-Mulk's *Siyar al-Mulūk*, composed for Sultan Malikshāh.

Ḥasan ibn ʿAlī ibn Isḥāq Ṭūsī, who would later receive the title of Niẓām al-Mulk, was born in Ṭūs around 408/1018 or 410/1019–20 (the date given by Ibn Funduq), where his father, a native of Bayhaq, served as a tax collector under the Ghaznavids. When the Saljūqs took Khurasan ʿAlī ibn Isḥāq went to Ghazna, where his son Ḥasan probably worked in the Ghaznavid administration before returning, a few years later, to Khurasan, where he entered the service of its

Saljūq governor Chaghrī. When Chaghrī died (452/1060) he was succeeded by his son Alp Arslān, to whom Niẓām al-Mulk had for some time been advisor; and when Alp Arslān (455–65/1063–73) succeeded Ṭughril as Sultan of Iraq, Niẓām al-Mulk became the real power behind the Saljūq administration, and remained so for nearly thirty years (on his life and career see further Lambton 1988: 300–3). Alp Arslān's successor Malikshāh (465–85/1073–92) relied heavily upon him, especially in the first part of his reign, although in later years there was growing tension between the two as the Sultan sought to shake off the vizier's control. As H. Darke, the translator of the *Siyar al-mulūk*, observes, Niẓām al-Mulk's

> manner was not without arrogance; his habit of putting his friends and relations into the best posts began to arouse resentment, and his opponents were able to gain the ear of the sultan. As the sultan increased in maturity he asserted himself more vigorously, and there were times when he was on bad terms with his vazir. Perhaps it was at such a moment, when he was dissatisfied with the state of things in his kingdom and tempted to consider ways of replacing him, that he commanded Niẓām al-Mulk and several others to compose treatises on the art of government. (1978: x–xi)

Niẓām al-Mulk had a reputation for ruthlessness; it was he (according to Nīshāpūrī and Rāvandī) who brought about the fall from favour and murder of Ṭughril's former vizier ʿAmīd al-Mulk Kundurī (see further below). Although some scholars reject this imputation, there are numerous other examples of his instigating the destruction of rivals or of those he thought a danger to the state. He was a staunch Shāfiʿī and did much to promote the spread of Shāfiʿī Ashʿarism in Khurasan (see, on his activities in Nishapur, Bulliet 1972: 72–5). He was also a bitter opponent of the Shīʿīs (at least, as holders of administrative posts) and of heterodoxy, and particularly of the Bāṭinīs.

The *Siyar al-mulūk* was written in 484/1091 and revised in the following year, when eleven chapters were added to the original thirty-nine; according to one opinion, the work 'is in some sense a survey of what he [Niẓām al-Mulk] had failed to accomplish' (*EI*², art. 'Niẓām al-Mulk').[9] A note attached to the manuscript deposited in the royal library states that in 484/1092 Malikshāh commanded his nobles and learned men to reflect on his government, determine what unwise principles had been adopted, what had been concealed from him, what principles that had been observed by past rulers were neglected by himself, and which of these might be introduced into his empire. This order was given to several important officials, among them Niẓām al-Mulk and his bitter rival Tāj al-Mulk (of whom we will hear more). Each wrote what he felt appropriate on the subject and submitted it to the prince; none received greater approval than did Niẓām al-Mulk (1984: 36).[10]

The librarian's note informs us that Niẓām al-Mulk first composed the book 'ex tempore, in thirty-nine chapters' and delivered it to the Sultan. Later he revised his work, 'and because of the constant anxiety that was in his mind on account of the enemies of this dynasty he added another eleven chapters'. Before his fateful departure for Baghdad he gave the book to the librarian, who 'did not dare to publish [it] until the present time' (probably in the reign of Muḥammad ibn Malikshāh; 1978: 5–6, 246 n. 3). It was on that journey to Baghdad in 485/1092 with Sultan Malikshāh that Niẓām al-Mulk was murdered by an Assassin disguised as a Sufi petitioner.[11] Malikshāh himself did not live to see the *Siyar al-mulūk* in its final form. The revision reflects the accusations of nepotism and financial extravagance (particularly with regard to military expenditure) made against Niẓām al-Mulk by the ambitious Tāj al-Mulk Ibn Dārust, Keeper of the Robes for Malikshāh's wife Turkān (Terken) Khātūn, whose wish to promote her infant son Maḥmūd over Malikshāh's designated successor Barkyāruq Niẓām al-Mulk opposed. This caused Malikshāh to turn against him (though he did not in fact dismiss him). (Most historians consider that it was Tāj al-Mulk who plotted with Turkān Khātūn and others against the vizier and who instigated his murder.) The revision includes both a chapter advising against the interference of women in politics and a lengthy history of the Bāṭinī and related heresies; both are relevant to Niẓām al-Mulk's personal circumstances and to his political rivalries.

The *Siyar al-mulūk* (whose title, 'The Conduct [or Lives] of Kings', proclaims its affinity with history) contains a number of features seen in later works by Saljūq historians. The first is that of the transfer of rule, announced in the exordium: 'In every age and time God chooses one member of the human race and, having endowed him with goodly and kingly virtues, entrusts him with the interest of the world and the well-being of His servants' (1978: 9). This person is charged with removing corruption and restoring order, that the people may live secure under his rule. In times of 'disobedience or disregard of divine laws on the part of His servants, or ... failure in devotion and attention to [His] commands', God forsakes the people, 'kingship disappears', and warfare and bloodshed prevail until the wicked (along with many innocent victims) are cleared from the world.

> Then by divine decree one human being acquires some prosperity and power, and according to his deserts The Truth

> bestows good fortune upon him and gives him wit and wisdom, wherewith he may employ his subordinates every one according to his merits and confer upon each a dignity and a station proportionate to his powers.

He selects appropriate officials; and 'if his subjects tread the path of obedience and busy themselves with their tasks he will keep them untroubled by hardships.' He will remove corrupt or incompetent officials (but will also forgive them, after punishing them); he will cause the world to prosper through building and good works (including inns and schools built 'for those who seek knowledge'), 'for which things he will be renowned for ever; he will gather the fruit of his good works in the next world and blessings will be showered upon him' (1978: 9–10).

What is noteworthy here is the shift from the group or house to the individual, who may embody rule by a group (the Saljūqs) but stands both above it and apart from it.[12] (Compare Bayhaqī's statement that rule is transferred by divine decree from one group to another, even though the agent for that transfer is an individual chosen by God for this purpose – in this case, Sabuktigīn.) The reason for this may lie in the Saljūqs' manifest lack of connection with a royal house. Although Niẓām al-Mulk does refer to royal houses in what follows, his emphasis is, in the main, on the individual ruler.[13]

> Since the decree of God was such that this should be the era by which bygone ages are dated and the standard by which the deeds of former kings are judged, whereby He might bestow on His creatures a felicity granted to none before them, He caused The Master of the World, the mightiest king of kings, to come forth from two noble lines whose houses were cradles of royalty and nobility, and had been so from generation to generation as far back as the great Afrāsiyāb. (1978: 10)

The 'Master of the World' has been 'furnished ... with 'powers and merits such as had been lacking in the princes of the world before him, and endowed ... with all that is needed for a king' (a long list of kingly virtues follows); then he was given power and dominion, and the world subjected to his rule. This contrasts with the rule of 'some of the caliphs', when, 'if their empire became extended' (as has Malikshāh's), 'it was never free from unrest and the insurrections of rebels'; under Malikshāh's rule the world prospers and is at peace.

This idealised picture of the ruler will be repeated in later histories (for example in the *Mujmal*, the *Fārsnāma* and Nīshāpūrī's *Saljūq-nāma*, and in Rāvandī's encomia of the Saljūq ruler of Konya). It is seen also in Ghazzālī's *Naṣīḥat al-mulūk*, dedicated to either Muḥammad ibn Malikshāh or Sanjar (or perhaps both; see 1964: xvi–

xvii; Hillenbrand 1988: 91). The exceptionality of the 'new era' is underscored by Niẓām al-Mulk's designation of it as 'the era by which bygone ages are dated and the standard by which the deeds of former kings are judged' – a reference to the inauguration of the Jalālī calender in 466/1076. But despite this declaration that the past will be judged by the standard of the present age, in practice the situation is the opposite: the past is drawn upon to demonstrate the shortcomings of the present and to provide models in accordance with which the ruler might rectify these shortcomings.

The *Siyar al-mulūk* is, in a sense, history writ backward: instead of moving from an account of an event to the lesson it contains, Niẓām al-Mulk moves from precept to example from the past and (in most cases) back to the present. This scheme may be seen in Chapter 2 ('On recognizing the extent of God's grace towards kings'): kings must observe God's pleasure by acting beneficently towards His creatures, since they will be obliged to answer for their actions in the next world. Various examples follow (the death of Joseph; two Prophetic traditions; the death of ʿUmar ibn al-Khaṭṭāb); the chapter concludes: 'Of a certainty the Master of the World ... should know that on that great day [the Resurrection] he will be asked to answer for all those of God's creatures who are under his command'; therefore he must protect his subjects from tyranny and oppression, 'so that the blessings resulting from those actions may come about in the time of his rule and benedictions will be pronounced upon his age until the resurrection' (1978: 12–13).

The *Siyar al-mulūk* begins with general recommendations for the king's conduct and the proper treatment of subjects – recognising God's grace towards kings, holding court for the redress of wrongs, practising justice and virtue – but soon moves to more specific matters of statecraft and administration: keeping informed about the affairs of tax collectors and viziers so that they may not oppress the people; ensuring that officers given land grants do not mistreat the peasants from whom they take revenues; supporting judges, preachers and market inspectors, and obtaining information about all who hold positions of power and authority (Niẓām al-Mulk's admiration for the Ghaznavid intelligence system, the need to emulate which forms the subject of a separate chapter, permeates the book as a whole). The king must also 'enquire into religious matters ... be acquainted with the divine precepts and prohibitions and put them into practice, and ... obey the commands of God ... it is his duty to respect doctors of religion and pay their salaries out of the treasury, and he should honour pious and abstemious men.' He should take religious teaching from the scholars, and 'hear stories about just kings and tales of the prophets'. This will perfect his judgement and prevent heresy from spreading in his domains (1978: 59–60). The ruler is advised on the conduct of his household, over which he should appoint a reliable steward (an office which 'has fallen into disuse nowadays' [1978: 88]) and on a variety of other practical matters: the qualifications necessary for boon companions, the treatment of ambassadors, the advisability of keeping troops of various races (as did Maḥmūd) and of taking hostages, the training of pages (the example of the Sāmānid system is given) and so on, concluding with a chapter dealing with commanders of the guard, mace bearers, and instruments of punishment. These principles are illustrated by exemplary stories and historical anecdotes (some of which are quite lengthy); the general theme throughout is that many good customs of the past have fallen into desuetude.

The historical anecdotes are drawn from all periods of Iranian and Islamic history, but especially from the more recent past. The first lengthy anecdote, in Chapter 3 ('On holding court for the redress of wrongs'), tells of Ya'qūb ibn Layth's 'rebellion' in Sistan, his seizure of caliphal provinces in Khurasan and Iraq, and his march on Baghdad. Deceived by Ismā'īlī propagandists, he secretly swore allegiance to their cause, and 'hardened his heart against the caliph of Baghdad'. Then he gathered his armies 'and prepared to march to Baghdad to kill the caliph and overthrow the house of the 'Abbasids' (1978: 15). This long account emphasises Ya'qūb's heresy and the caliph's strategy, and ends with Ya'qūb's defeat, after which he fled to Khuzistan, where the caliph wrote to him offering a pardon and control of Iraq and Khurasan. But Ya'qūb's 'heart was in no way softened, nor did he repent of his actions'; he ordered a simple meal of leeks, onions and fish brought to him on a wooden tray, had the caliph's envoy brought in, and told him to deliver this message:

> 'Go and tell the caliph that I was born a coppersmith; I learnt that trade from my father, and my victual used to be barley-bread, fish, onions and leeks. The sovereignty, treasure and wealth which I enjoy, I have acquired by my own bold enterprise and daring; I neither have it as an inheritance from my father, nor did I get it from you. I shall not rest until I have sent your head to Mahdiyya and destroyed your family. Either I shall do as I say or I shall go back to eating barley-bread, fish and leeks. Behold I have opened the doors of my treasuries and summoned my troops; and I am coming in the tracks of the bearer of this message.' (1978: 18)[14]

Ya'qūb marched towards Baghdad, but died on the way; he was succeeded by his brother 'Amr, who is praised for his good rule. But though ʿAmr did not share his brother's beliefs, the caliph, still apprehensive, attempted to persuade the Sāmānid Ismāʿīl ibn Aḥmad to march against him (the rubric of this account is 'The story of the just king', and it begins with a description of Ismāʿīl as just, pious and generous to the poor; 1978: 16). Ismāʿīl defeated ʿAmr before Balkh; afterwards ʿAmr is said to have wandered through the camp searching for food and lamenting, 'I was an *amīr* in the morning; I became an *asīr* [prisoner] in the evening' (1978: 20). When ʿAmr was captured Ismāʿīl declared to his army and nobles, 'God granted me this success, and to no one am I indebted for this favour except to God.' He was inclined to ask the caliph to spare ʿAmr's life; but ʿAmr despaired of this, and sent him a message, saying, 'It was not you that defeated me, but it was your piety, faith and character, together with the displeasure of the Commander of the Faithful. God ... has ... taken away this realm from me and given it to you, and you are more worthy and deserving of this favour.' He produced the lists of his treasures and sent them to Ismāʿīl, who rejected them as having been 'taken from the people by extortion'.

> Such was his piety and fear of God that he did not accept the treasure-list but sent it back to ʿAmr. So he was not deluded by wordly goods. Is that like the amirs of these times who think nothing of making ten forbidden things lawful or nullifying ten just claims for the sake of one ill-gotten dinar? They have no regard for the consequences. (1978: 21)

One may regard the demonising of Yaʿqūb as expressing hostility towards the Ṣaffārids; but the implications are broader. Yaʿqūb's heresy is contrasted with Ismāʿīl ibn Aḥmad's piety (which, as the author of the *Tārīkh-i Sīstān* observed, was the reason for his victory over Yaʿqūb). Here, however, the emphasis is different: a good ruler is a pious ruler; a bad ruler is a heretic. At a time when accusations of heresy were commonly (and indiscriminately) wielded against rivals for power, the meaning is clear: those who challenge the ruler must, by implication, hold corrupt beliefs.

Some of Niẓām al-Mulk's historical anecdotes are drawn from the pre-Islamic Iranian past (for example, the long story about Bahrām Gūr and his evil vizier, which is not in the *Shāhnāma*; how Anūshīrvān the Just saved the property of an old woman from a rapacious governor, and so on). Others relate to the caliphate and to the Ṭāhirids, Sāmānids, Būyids and, in particular, the Ghaznavids. At one point a list of rulers exemplary for their just conduct is provided.

> When a king possesses divine grace and sovereignty, and knowledge withal is wedded to these, he finds happiness in both worlds, because everything he does is informed with knowledge

> and he does not allow himself to be ignorant. Consider how great is the fame of kings who were wise, and what great works they did; names such as these will be blessed until the resurrection – Afridun, Alexander, Ardashir, Nushirvan The Just, The Commander of the Faithful 'Umar [ibn al-Khaṭṭāb] ... 'Umar ibn 'Abd al-'Aziz ... Harun, al-Ma'mun, al-Mu'tasim, Isma'il ibn Ahmad the Samanid, and Sultan Mahmud (Allah's mercy be upon them all). The deeds and ways of them all are well known for they are recorded in histories and other books; men never cease reading about them and singing their praises and blessings. (1978: 61)

The length of some stories and the abundance of circumstantial detail they contain makes them closer to history than the usual brief anecdotes retailed by authors of mirrors for princes. The message is that rulers must learn from history; one who did not (it is implied) was Alp Arslān. In the chapter on the need for intelligence agents and reporters, after praising the efficiency of Maḥmūd of Ghazna's spy system, Niẓām al-Mulk observes,

> From ancient times onwards kings have preserved this system, except for the house of Saljuq who have shown no interest in the matter.
>
> Abu 'l-Fadl Sigzi once asked The Martyr Sultan Alp Arslan ... why he had no intelligence agents. He answered, 'Do you want me to cast my kingdom to the winds and alienate all my supporters? ... If I institute intelligence agents, my especial favourites ... will pay no attention to them nor offer them bribes; while my opponents and enemies will curry favour with them and give them money. Thus obviously the intelligence agents will always bring to our ears bad reports about our favourites and good reports about our enemies. Now, reports good and bad are like arrows: if you shoot enough of them, at least one will hit the target. In this way we shall become more displeased with our favourites every day and eventually banish them, while admitting our enemies further into our intimacy. In a short time you will find that all our favourites are estranged and their places taken by our enemies. By that time irreparable harm will have been done.'
>
> All the same it is better that there should be intelligencers, because having intelligencers is one of the rules of state-craft; and when they can be relied upon sufficiently to perform the function we have described, there is no anxiety. (1978: 71)

Another anecdote based on Niẓām al-Mulk's own experience while in Alp Arslān's service occurs in the chapter on ambassadors, among whose functions is to report on conditions in the domains and courts of those rulers to whom they are sent; such information enables them to take effective action on behalf of the rulers they serve. Alp Arslān, a devoted Ḥanafī,

> was so strict and exact in his religious observances that he was often heard to say, 'What a pity! if only my vazir were not of the Shafi'i persuasion.' He was exceedingly imperious and awe-inspiring and because he was so earnest and fanatical in his beliefs and disapproved of the Shafi'i rite I lived in constant fear of him.

Towards the end of his reign Alp Arslān determined on an expedition to Transoxania against the 'khan of Samarqand' (in 465/1072, the campaign on which he was murdered). He sent an envoy to the Khān; Niẓām al-Mulk also sent his own envoy, Dānishmand Ashtar, to report on what happened. The Khān duly sent back his own envoy, who ('as it is customary for ambassadors to have access to the vazir at any time') asked without warning to see Niẓām al-Mulk. The latter had been playing chess, and happened to be wearing a ring, taken as a forfeit, on the ring finger of his right hand. (This had been, since the time of Hārūn al-Rashīd, considered a Shī'ī practice.) As the ring was ill-fitting, he constantly twisted it, attracting the envoy's notice. The envoy said nothing; but when he returned home he informed his ruler of the details of the Sultan's court, whose only fault was that 'the sultan's vazir is a Rafidi [Shī'ī]', as evidenced by the ring. Dānishmand reported this to Niẓām al-Mulk, who went to a great deal of expense 'to prevent this report from reaching the sultan's ears' (1978: 96–7).

> Your humble servant has related this story because ambassadors are generally censorious and always on the look out to see what faults there are in kingdom and kingship, and what virtues ... With this in mind past kings, when they have been intelligent and alert, have always refined their manners, and adopted good customs, and employed worthy men of pure faith, lest anyone should find fault with them. (1978: 98)

The implication would seem to be that the Khān's ambassador jumped to conclusions; but the incident does not redound to Niẓām al-Mulk's credit either, as it suggests carelessness on his part. The Saljūq sultan's piety is emphasised, as is, again, the need for reliable informers. Perhaps not unintentionally, we are given a picture of the Saljūq court not only as relentlessly Sunnī (so that an accusation of corrupt belief, whether true or false, could bring down any official), but as rife with suspicion, factionalism and intrigue.

The thirty-seven chapters of Book 1 of the *Siyar al-mulūk* relate generally to various practical aspects of government. The eleven chapters of Book 2, which are closely interrelated, touch on themes of particular importance to Niẓām al-Mulk. As Darke observes, here 'all is different; the times are sick, the evil eye is at work; things are going seriously wrong and disaster is feared. In fact in the opening paragraph of chapter 40 all the ills are specified, but by a masterly piece of dissimulation the whole diagnosis is expressed as a hypothetical case' (1978: xx).

In fact it is not so hypothetical. Book 2 as a whole contains often explicit criticism of, and admonition concerning, current Saljūq policies. The exordium to Chapter 40 recapitulates the thematics of Chapter 2; but it does so in reverse order. (I have departed from Darke's translation in order to give a better sense of the immediacy of the original.)[15]

> At any time (it may happen that) a celestial accident occurs, and the kingdom is affected by the evil eye. Rule [*dawlat*] either changes, passing from one house to another, or is thrown into disorder because of seditions, riots, opposing swords, killing, burning, pillaging and wrongdoing. In such days of disturbance and slackness [*futūr*] noble men are crushed and the base become powerful; he who has strength does as he wishes. The affairs of the righteous falter and decline, and malefactors become rich. The least of persons rises to become an amīr, the basest a civil governor, and the noble (of birth) and learned are dispossessed. A worthless person does not fear to assume titles proper to the king and the vizier; Turks give themselves the titles of civil dignitaries [*khvājagān*], dignitaries adopt the titles of the Turks, and both Turks and Tāzīks [Persians] take the titles of scholars and religious leaders [*a'imma*]. The ruler's wives give orders; the Sharī'at is weakened; the populace are disobedient and the soldiers greedy; distinctions between men vanish, and no one remedies matters ... All the kingdom's affairs have fallen (and will fall) from their proper principle and order; and the ruler, with so many assaults, battles, and preoccupations, has no chance to attend to such matters or to think about the situation.
>
> Then, when through celestial good fortune the days of evil fortune pass away, and days of peace and security appear, God Most High brings forth a just and wise king of royal descent, gives him rule [*dawlat*] so that he vanquishes his enemies, and wisdom and learning so that he employs discernment in all affairs. He asks each person and investigates as to what have been the customs of kings in each affair, and reads books (on this subject), so that in a short time he is able to restore all the

> forms and customs of rule. He makes clear the proper degree of every person, places the worthy in their proper positions, restrains the unworthy and sends them about their proper tasks and trades. He removes the ungrateful from the (face of the) earth, is the friend of religion and the foe of oppression. He supports religion and removes schism, with God's permission and by His grace. (1978: 139–40)

This is no mere expression of generalities, but refers to specific abuses in the Saljūq polity of which Niẓām al-Mulk both disapproves and considers himself a victim. The current disorder of the realm carries with it the threat that the ruling house may fall and be replaced by another; the crushing of 'men of noble birth' in favour of the base-born may be exemplified by Niẓām al-Mulk's own case, as lesser men are preferred to him. The issue of titles will be taken up in detail later in the chapter; the interference of the king's wives is the subject of a separate chapter, and reflects Niẓām al-Mulk's conflicts with such powerful Saljūq women as Malikshāh's aunt Gawhar Khātūn (Alp Arslān's sister), for whose murder (early in Malikshāh's reign) he was responsible (see Lambton 1988: 42) and with Malikshāh's wife Turkān Khātūn.

Several stories follow which illustrate royal generosity to subjects, as well as instances of kindness and mercy towards animals, introduced, says Niẓām al-Mulk, 'so that The Master of the World ... may know what a good habit it is to be merciful ... If the king fears God and takes heed for the future, he is bound to be just in every case, and the just man is always merciful and kind' (1978: 147). Before moving to the subject of titles he observes:

> It has always been the custom of enlightened monarchs to have respect for old and experienced men, and to keep [in office] those who are skilled in affairs and tried in battle, giving each a position and rank; and whenever any matter important for the welfare and prosperity of the state required to be executed, such as promotion, dismissal, erecting lofty buildings, arranging an alliance, getting information about a [foreign] king, enquiring into religious affairs, and suchlike, they discussed it thoroughly with men of wisdom and worldly experience. On the other hand, whenever an enemy appeared or a battle threatened, they took counsel with men accomplished in warfare and skilled in such arts; with the result that the business was accomplished successfully. If war broke out they despatched to the front a man who had fought numerous battles ... and gained renown in the world for valour; but at the same time they always sent with him a man of ripe and wide experience so that nothing

> went amiss. But [nowadays] it happens that when a serious matter arises, they appoint inexperienced men and [even] boys and youths [to deal with it], and errors are committed. If due attention were given to these matters in future it would be better and less dangerous. (1978: 147–8)

These are strong words; and Niẓām al-Mulk clearly intends it to be understood that the current troubles are due to the ruler's failure to heed his experienced vizier.

Turning to titles, Niẓām al-Mulk complains that these have become abundant,

> and whatever becomes abundant loses value and dignity. Kings and caliphs have always been sparing in the application of titles; for it is one of the principles of government to see that titles are kept in relation to each man's rank and importance.

Distinctions between military and administrative titles are no longer observed. 'Turks give themselves the titles of Taziks, and Taziks take those of Turks, and think it no wrong. But titles always used to be dear' (1978: 148–9). The distinction between 'Turk' and 'Tāzīk' corresponds to that between the military and the bureaucracy – the men of the sword and of the pen – and reflects the prevailing opinion (among the Persian bureaucracy at least) that the two ethnic groups were best suited to specific functions: Turks to the military, Persians to administration, and that the distinction should be maintained.

A long story follows concerning how, after many victories, Maḥmūd of Ghazna requested more titles from the caliph, and was refused.[16] His request was motivated by the fact that his vassal, the Khāqān of Samarqand, had been given three titles to Maḥmūd's one. He was admonished by the caliph, who informed him that he had given the Khāqān ('an ignorant, outlandish Turk') three titles 'in order to swell his reputation and make up for his lack of wisdom', and that Maḥmūd should be content with his one meaningful title (1978: 150). Maḥmūd consulted 'a certain woman of Turkish birth' with whom he was closely acquainted; she initiated an elaborate ruse which eventually resulted in Maḥmūd receiving a second title from the caliph.[17]

'In these days the lowest official is angry and indignant if he is given less than seven or ten titles', Niẓām al-Mulk continues (1978: 156), noting the conservatism of the Sāmānids in this regard, discussing the titles appropriate to different functions, and so on. Observance of the proper decorum in this regard will ensure stability in the realm; when this happens, and the just and vigilant ruler pays close attention to affairs, enquires about the customs of his predecessors, and

> has a successful, knowledgeable and skilful vazir, then he will restore all matters to good order, he will reinstate the proper

> rules with regard to titles, and he will abolish all new-fangled customs through the exercise of his judgement, his authority and his sword. (1978: 157)

The next two chapters are more or less in the same vein. Chapter 51 warns against giving two posts to one man, or the same post to two, as this will result in neglect and inefficiency. Appointments should be given only to men of good religion and of noble origin. Nowadays,

> all distinction has vanished; and if a Jew administers the affairs of Turks, it is permitted; and it is the same for Zoroastrians, Rafidis, Kharijis and Qarmatis. Everywhere indifference is predominant; there is no zeal for religion, no concern for the revenue, no pity for the peasants. The dynasty has reached its perfection; your humble servant is afraid of the evil eye and knows not where this state of affairs will lead. (1978: 159)

Such would not have happened in the days of 'Mahmud, Mas'ud, Tughril and Alp Arslan', when 'no Zoroastrian or Christian or Rafidi would have dared to appear in a public place or to present himself before a Turk'; administrators were all professionals from Khurasan, orthodox Ḥanafīs or Shāfiʿīs, and heretics were never admitted into their employ. But now, the court and the administration are full of them, 'and their object is to prevent any Khurasanis from entering the service of this court and earning a living here' (1978: 159–60). Animadversions against the 'heretics of Iraq', who 'are of the same religion as the Dailamites and their supporters' – that is, not merely Shīʿīs, but Bāṭinīs – is followed by a selection of Prophetic traditions which mention (clearly anachronistically) the dangers posed by Rāfiḍīs, Bāṭinīs, and the like (1978: 159–61).

Niẓām al-Mulk now returns to his original topic.

> Whenever appointments are given to ignoble, unknown and untalented persons, while famous, learned and high-born men are left unemployed and wasted – when five posts are vested in a single man while another receives none at all, this is a sign of the ignorance and incompetence of the vazir; if the vazir is incompetent and ignorant it is indicated by the fact that he tries to cause the empire's decline and seeks to damage the king's interests. (1978: 165)

Such is the case at present with respect to 'just such a one who is seeking to ruin this country by recommending economies', and who is advising the ruler that, now that he has subdued the world and has no more enemies, he can reduce military expenditures. This is a false, and damaging, economy, 'for the more troops a king has, the wider his realm; the fewer troops he has, the smaller his dominion'. Troops whose names are erased from the rolls will look for another master, or will choose their own leader, and make trouble. 'If someone says to the king, "Take gold, and leave men," that person is in truth the king's enemy and is seeking to destroy the country.' This is the case too with ignoring the claims of 'deprived and destitute civil officials' who have performed great services to the empire but are now unemployed and destitute. Equally, learned men, noble men and men of valour are entitled to money from the treasury. If they are left unrewarded, they will become disaffected, and will eventually rebel, 'cause disturbances and rise against the king, throwing the country into confusion, just as they did in the time of Fakhr ad-Daula'. The ensuing story tells how a rebellion against that ruler was foiled by his wise and experienced vizier, the Ṣāḥib Ibn ʿAbbād (1978: 165–6).

Chapter 42 ('On the subject of those who wear the veil') begins:

> The king's underlings must not be allowed to assume power, for this causes the utmost harm and destroys the king's splendour and majesty. This particularly applies to women, for they are wearers of the veil and have not complete intelligence ... In all ages nothing but disgrace, infamy, discord and corruption have resulted when kings have been dominated by their wives. (1978: 179–80)

A number of exemplary stories (most quite brief), Prophetic traditions and wise sayings follow; the chapter as a whole has a somewhat aphoristic tone. Except for the story of Siyāvash and his stepmother Sūdāba (who attempted, unsuccessfully, to seduce him, and who is ultimately blamed for the wars between Iran and Tūrān/Turkistan), these stories are not 'historical' in the way that, for example, the story of Maḥmūd's titles, or others drawn from recent history, are (or, at least, purport to be). This points to an important generic and stylistic difference between mirrors and history; for in this chapter the *Siyar al-mulūk* becomes more like a mirror, with admonitions accompanied by exempla, and less like history, which furnishes lessons in statecraft through the examples of past kings. Narrative generated by precept gives way to a series of gnomic exempla, all geared to support the central topic.[18]

The chapters which follow (43–47) constitute a lengthy warning against heretics, and recount their activities both before and after Islam. This account, taken as a whole, forms a coherent narrative on its own, and is far from the generally fragmentary style typical of mirrors for princes and closer to that of heresiography. Darke considered that this account was motivated by Ḥasan-i Ṣabbāḥ's return from Egypt (which Darke dates to 483/1090), his occupation of the fortress of Alamut, and the general intensification of Bāṭinī activities in the Saljūq domains, especially in Isfahan (1978: xxi). Ismāʿīlī activity had been on the increase ever since the last years of Būyid rule; Ḥasan-i Ṣabbāh was active in Iraq in the late 460s/1070s, and after a brief stay in Egypt had returned there in 473/1081. Early in 485/1092 Malikshāh, probably on the advice of Niẓām al-Mulk, sent troops against the Ismāʿīlīs in Rūdbār (Alamut) and Quhistān. The Saljūqs were repulsed; Niẓām al-Mulk was murdered; and plans for a renewed attack were abandoned on Malikshāh's death (see Daftary 1990: 335–42).

Niẓām al–Mulk begins this section by inveighing against the iniquities of heretics, and specifically of the Bāṭinīs:

> Seceders [*khārijiyān*] have existed in all ages, and from the time of Adam ... until now in every country in the world they have risen up in revolt against kings and prophets. Never has there been a more sinister, more perverted or more iniquitous crowd than these people, who behind walls are plotting harm to the country and seeking to destroy the religion ... If in any way ... through some celestial accident any misfortune should befall this victorious empire (may Allah The Mighty strengthen it) these dogs will emerge from their hiding places, and will revolt against this empire ... The religion of Muhammad ... has no worse enemy than them, and the kingdom of The Master of the World has no more vile and more accursed opponent.[19]
>
> There are certain persons who on this very day hold privileged positions in this empire and who, having removed their heads from the collar of the Shiʿa, are members of this ... faction and secretly do its business, assist its policies and preach its doctrines. They try to persuade The Master of the World to overthrow the house of the 'Abbasids ... But – worse than that – as a result of their representations The Master of the World has become weary of his humble servant, and is not prepared to take any action in the matter, because of the economies which these people recommend, thereby making The Master of the World greedy for money ... One day The Master will realize their iniquity and treachery and criminal deeds – when I have disappeared. (1978: 188–9)

This comes close to being an indictment of Tāj al-Mulk and his party, without actually naming him; and one wonders if Niẓām al-Mulk really believed (or had evidence to that effect) that his rival had Bāṭinī sympathies. Isfahan (where Tāj al-Mulk served as *mustawfī* before his appointment as vizier after Niẓām al-Mulk's death) had long been a centre of Ismāʿīlī activity; and indeed, Niẓām al-Mulk states that 'whoever wishes to learn all the facts about them and all the disasters which they have caused to the kingdom and the religion of Muhammad ... should study the histories, especially the 'History of Isfahan'.

The first to introduce 'atheistic doctrines' (*mu'aṭṭala*) into the world was Mazdak, who was a chief *mawbad* in the reign of Qubād. An astrologer, 'he foretold that in that age a man was to appear who would introduce a religion to cancel the Zoroastrian, Jewish, Christian and idolatrous faiths', and that this new religion 'would last until the resurrection'. Imagining that he himself was this person, Mazdak 'began to ponder how he should convert the people and propagate a new cult' (1978: 190). An old priest from Fars at one point informed Qubād that the prophecy was true but that Mazdak was not the person indicated by it; it in fact predicted the appearance of an Arab prophet, who would bring a new scripture (1978: 196). By means of a false miracle Mazdak persuaded Qubād, as well as large numbers of the populace, to accept his religion. Qubād's son Anūshīrvān admonished the priests for failing to advise the ruler, and enjoined them to debate Mazdak and prove his falsehood; he also warned the nobles to beware of Mazdak's false teachings. After a long series of episodes, and despite Mazdak's being refuted in debate and Anūshīrvān's discovery of the secret of his 'miracle', Qubād remained unable to destroy Mazdak because of his many followers. Finally, by pretending to accept Mazdak's teachings Anūshīrvān obtained the names of his followers, and invited them to a feast, at which he arranged that they all be killed.

A brief account of the revolt of Sunbād at Rayy after the murder of Abū Muslim leads to a long (and largely inaccurate) narrative of the rise of the Qarmaṭīs during the Sāmānid period, and the success of the *dā'ī* Abū Ḥātim Rāzī in converting the Daylamid Asfār ibn Shīrūya by preaching that 'one should be an 'Alavi in religion, not in genealogy' and predicting the appearance of an Imām from among the Daylamis (1978: 211). 'The wretched Dailams and Gils "fled from the rain and resorted to the gutter": they sought the path of orthodoxy but they fell into the snare of heresy.' The Daylamis followed him until the time of the predicted Imām's appearance had come and gone; then they rejected him and forced him to flee, and he died in flight.

We have already noted Niẓām al-Mulk's accounts of Bāṭinī activities at the Sāmānid court (Chapter 1). The common thread in these accounts and those that follow is that it is the intent of the heretics to persuade rulers and important members of the court to accept their teaching; conversion of the populace provides a broader power base and makes it even more difficult to suppress such movements. The reason behind this is that they themselves seek rule

– or, at least, seek to be the real power behind the throne. Thus for example Sunbād preached that the time of Arab rule had come to an end; at Naṣr ibn Aḥmad's court Nasafī (Nakhshabī) 'became so influential that he could appoint or depose ministers, and the king did whatever he said' (1978: 213). Often, there is a wise advisor whose warnings are at first not heeded but are then accepted (if not by the ruler, then by someone in a position to influence him: Nūshīrvān the son of Qubād; the learned men and commanders who warned Nūḥ ibn Naṣr, who then persuaded his father to abdicate).

Niẓām al-Mulk notes the activities of the Bāṭinīs in Syria and the Maghreb (the *da'wa* which resulted in the establishment of the Fāṭimid caliphate; this account is highly fanciful in parts, as is the later account of the Qarmaṭīs of Bahrain). He asserts that Abū Bilāl, who appeared in the regions of Herat and Ghur in 295/907 in the reign of Ismā'īl ibn Aḥmad the Sāmānid, was a former boon companion of Ya'qūb ibn Layth and had 'succeeded him in the propagation of heresy' (1978: 220). While there are differences of doctrine between some of these groups, 'all have a common origin [and] the constant object of them all is to overthrow Islam'. This section ends with a further warning to the sultan to beware the activities of such persons in his own court, and to recall his servant's words of warning.

The final three chapters revert to more practical topics: the maintaining of treasuries, the dispensation of justice, and revenues. These are entirely consonant in tone with the chapters of Book 1; were they, perhaps, tacked on to draw attention away from the vivid accounts of heresies and the thinly veiled *ad hominem* references earlier in Book 2? The book ends with a final admonition: let the ruler 'be industrious and zealous in obeying the commands of The Truth and in performing his religious duties; then God Almighty will give him success in all his religious and secular affairs, and cause him to gain his ends in both worlds and attain all his desires' (1978: 244).

A. K. S. Lambton has observed that the *Siyar al-mulūk* is 'essentially an administrative handbook': 'It includes, in common with Mirrors for Princes, many anecdotes, but it is not a mirror. The purpose of these anecdotes ... is not to divert but to drive home the points which Niẓām al-Mulk wishes to make ... Niẓām al-Mulk is concerned, not with the theory of government or the justification of power, but with the practice of government by the sultan' (1984: 55–6). Significantly, however, Niẓām al-Mulk focuses not on those areas of administrative practice with which he is, presumably, content (that is, the governmental *dīvān*s under his own control), but with those which which he is obviously not. The historical anecdotes thus function to provide examples of how things should be done, and were done in the past. It is in this connection that we must interpret what Lambton terms his 'concern ... to preserve or revive the heritage of the past' (1984: 64).

If earlier writers stressed the repetitive nature of events (as does Niẓām al-Mulk in the section on heresy), what occupies him throughout is a sense of the changes – generally for the worse – that have accompanied the new *dawlat*. This may be seen in his references to 'celestial accidents' determining worldly events (this need not, I think, be taken literally, but as signalling the unprecedented nature of these events) and in his focus on the individual ruler, to whom (rather than to the group) he addresses himself. He might (in more ways than one) be seen as the Machiavelli of his time, caught between the vanished past and the uncertain, and unsatisfactory, present. Timothy Hampton has commented that Machiavelli's 'powerful demystification of historical repetition leaves action mired in the present, caught in an absolute contingency that kills the past and forestalls all possibility of resurrecting it'; yet despite this he still retains 'a residue of confidence in the voices of the past', a confidence that 'arises in response to the total desolation which Machiavelli sees as characteristic of his age', and still looks to 'the exemplary civilization of Rome' as an ideal model for contemporary emulation (1990: 76–7).

Much the same could be said of Niẓām al-Mulk, who, deeply disillusioned with the current state of government, where the good customs and practices of the past have fallen into desuetude, can still invoke that past – both the ancient and more recent pasts of Persia, and its exemplary rulers, in particular Maḥmūd – to illustrate the principles of government he seeks to teach his ruler. These principles are not merely matters of administrative practice; for behind practical measures lies an important moral dimension: the ethical bases upon which relationships between ruler and subjects, ruler and subordinates, are founded. Thus while not, strictly speaking, history, the *Siyar al-mulūk* demonstrates the uses of history, as well as the close connection between historical, ethical and political thought. In its enunciation of a changing thematics of the transfer of rule, focused on the individual rather than on the group, it anticipates the work of later historians. Thus it forms a bridge between two phases of Persian historiography, the Ghaznavid and the Saljūq.

THE *FĀRSNĀMA* OF IBN AL-BALKHĪ

This history of the province of Fars appears to be the earliest surviving Persian historical work from the Saljūq period. In 1912 G. Le Strange published a translation of the geographical section;[20] in his preliminary remarks, included in R. A. Nicholson's edition of the text (1962 [1921]), he described the work and discussed its historical and political background. Le Strange called the author 'Ibn al-Balkhī' because, as he himself states (1962: 3, 118), his grandfather originated from Balkh.[21] This grandfather had been sent to Fars in 492/1098 by Barkyāruq ibn Malikshāh (487–98/1094–1104) to serve as *mustawfī* under the Atabeg Rukn al-Dawla Khumārtigīn; the author accompanied him, and was educated in Fars. He was commissioned to write the work by Sultan Muḥammad (Tapar) ibn Malikshāh (498–511/1104–17) because of his knowledge both of 'the present condition of the people of Fárs' and of 'the events of their history, and ... the story of their kings and rulers, even from the days of Gayúmars down to this present time' (1962: xi, 3). The work must have been completed before the Sultan's death and that of Atabeg Chāvlī (d. 510/1116), Muḥammad's governor of Fars, who is mentioned frequently.

Le Strange provided a detailed summary of the contents of the *Fārsnāma*. The author begins with 'a summary description of the province', cites several traditions about Fars ascribed to the Prophet, then moves to 'the early Persian kings, whose history, much in epitome, closes with the last of the Sásánians and the rise of Islam'. He then briefly relates the history of the Arab conquest of Fars, ending with the caliphate of ʿAlī ibn Abī Ṭālib. This is followed by an account of the *qāḍī*s of Fars and by the geographical section. He returns to the history of Fars to provide 'an account of the Shabánkára tribes and the Kurds, and this narration of details of almost contemporary history is of importance, as it mentions facts and personages not noted, apparently, elsewhere'. Further new matter is the author's summary of the revenues of Fars down to his own time. He 'closes with a short note describing the days of the last Búyid rulers of Fárs, and the advent of the Seljúq Sultans' (1962: xi–xii).

Beginning with Barkyāruq, the Saljūq sultans customarily appointed their Atabegs to govern the provinces.[22] The first to be sent to Fars was Rukn al-Dawla Khumārtigīn; the next was Fakhr al-Dīn Chāvlī Saqāwa (Chāwulī; Jāwulī in the Arab sources), who succeeded, 'after much fighting ... in restoring order ... by curbing the power of the Shabánkára and subduing the various affiliated Kurdish tribes' (1962: xiii).[23] Le Strange provided an account of conditions in Fars under the Būyid Abū Kalījār Marzubān (Bākālījār; 415–40/1024–48) and his successors and of the situation at the time of the advent of the Saljūqs, when Fars was at the mercy of the Shabānkāra tribes, led by Faḍlūya (Faḍlawayh). The reigning Sultan Alp Arslān sent his brother Qāvurd to Fars to restore order. 'Faḍlúya, finding that matters were going against him', presented himself before Alp Arslān, and was reconfirmed as deputy governor of Fars. 'He, however, had not yet learnt wisdom, for once more seeking to be independent, he revolted.' Niẓām al-Mulk besieged and captured him in the fort of Diz Khurshah. From there,

> he was sent to the Castle of Iṣṭakhr, but managing in time to corrupt his guards, got the stronghold into his own hands. Sultan Alp Arslán on this lost patience, Faḍlúya was hunted down and caught, and to avoid further trouble, after being put to death, his skin was stuffed with straw as a manifest warning to his neighbours. (1962: xvi)[24]

After a detailed account of the lineage and history of the Shabānkāra tribes (he has little good to say either of them or of the Kurdish tribes settled in Fars by the Būyid 'Aḍud al-Dawla), Ibn al-Balkhī closes this section

> With a short discussion as to how the Persians, who are a refractory folk, may best be governed, whether by force or by clemency. In regard to the Shabánkára more especially, he remarks that you will certainly be respected by any one of these turbulent tribesmen if by force you take his turban and then restore it, and this much more than if in the first instance you had generously given him a new turban of your own as a present, for doing which indeed he would only despise you. (1962: xix)

We will return later to what Le Strange termed Ibn al-Balkhī's 'horror [of] the Shí'ite tendencies of the Búyids, whose heterodox beliefs (he further avers) had always when possible been combated by the Qáḍís of Shíráz' (1962: xix). According to Nicholson, Le Strange thought the book was 'merely a Persian version of Ḥamza Iṣfahání and contains, apparently, nothing new'. Nicholson disagreed, terming the work the 'oldest independent Persian prose history' of the pre-Islamic kings of Persia (Gardīzī presumably being unknown to him), predating the *Mujmal* (similarly dependent on Ḥamza) by about fifteen years (1962: xxii).

The *Fārsnāma* begins with the customary doxology, followed by a disquisition on kingship and praise of the Sultan.

> When God chooses one noble individual from amongst all His servants, places the reins of rule and kingship in his grasp, and gives him the task of ruling and protecting the world, the greatest favour that He commands with respect to that ruler in particular and to the inhabitants of the world in general is to make the aspiration of the ruler of the age incline towards learning and justice. For all virtues are contained within these two; and when the king's virtues are adorned by these two, this is a part of the parts of prophecy, for which noble state God most high has singled him out. People have found ease in the

> protection of his justice and compassion and the refuge of his beneficence and mercy; and he will obtain felicity in both worlds. (1962: 1)

The Sultan's noble nature and perfect reason have led him to be desirous of acquiring knowledge. This desire led him to commission the present book, in the wish that the situation of Fars,

> which is a great part of the royal domains ... and has always been the royal capital and seat of the Persian kings, be made clear, and that its nature and form, the conduct of the former kings, the customs of their army and subjects, the climate and fruits of each region, be made known; and the example of dealings according to the ancient law and to that law which is now honoured be made clear; so that the learning of the noblest of sultans – may his nobility be increased! – may encompass (all) that (knowledge). (1962: 2–3)

In obedience to this command the author undertook this task – for which he was particularly well suited both because he had been educated in Fars and because his grandfather had established the financial regulations now in force – and 'composed this collection [*majmū'a*] accordingly, by way of summary, and concisely' (1962: 3). He then praises the Sultan for his wisdom and eloquence.

The work proper begins with a brief description of Fars ('a most pleasant region because it has a bit of everything') and praise of its people, who

> have always been referred to as the 'nobles of Fars'.[25] The Prophet said, 'God has two most excellent (groups) in His creation: from the Arabs, Quraysh, and from the Persians, Fars.' The people of Fars are called *Quraysh al-'Ajam*; for their nobility amongst the Persians is as great as that of Quraysh among the Arabs. 'Alī ibn al-Ḥusayn, known as Zayn al-'Ābidīn, is called Ibn al-Khayratayn ['son of the two most excellent'], because his father was Ḥusayn ibn 'Alī and his mother was Shahrbānūya the daughter of Yazdigird the Persian. This is the reason for the superiority of the Ḥusaynids over the Ḥasanids ... The Persians' rule was founded on justice, and their conduct was ever justice and liberality. Every ruler of theirs who appointed his son heir-apparent would counsel him thus: 'There is no rule without the army, no army without money, no money without prosperity, and no prosperity without justice.' (1962: 4–5)

The Prophet, asked why all previous peoples – 'Ād, Thamūd, and their like – had 'soon perished, while the kingdom of the Persians lasted long, despite the fact that they were fireworshippers', replied, 'Because they made the country prosper and were just to (God's) servants.' In the Koran the Persians 'are mentioned twice and praised for their strength and manliness': they are termed 'mighty in war' (17: 6) and 'people of great valour' (48: 16). This second verse 'conveys the good tidings that the Muslims will conquer and fight a (mighty) people, and seize their lands, until they become Muslims' (1962: 5–7). This sets the book's prevailing tone: praise of Fars and its people generally, and more specifically for their role in Islam. The author concludes this section with a Prophetic tradition summing up this view (recalling those quoted by his predecessor, Abū Nuʿaym Iṣbahānī, in the exordium to his history of Isfahan; see Iṣbahānī 1931: 1–14): 'If this learning [*ʿilm*, religious knowledge] were suspended from the Pleiades, people from Fars would (still) attain it' (1962: 7).

After outlining the plan of his book (whose order 'will be maintained as no compiler of histories has (ever done) in so concise and succinct a fashion' [1962: 8]), and further praise of his royal patron, Ibn al-Balkhī begins with the chronologies and genealogies of the Persian kings (Pīshdādīs, Kayānids, Ashghāniyān, Sasanians; the Ashghāniyān, however, receive virtually no mention in the historical section proper). These are fairly cursory, except for occasional discussions of disputed genealogies, and refer briefly to accounts to be related in more detail in the historical section. Of Kisrā Aparvīz (Khusraw II Parvīz), whose famous deeds will be recounted later, he notes that this ruler's end is well known:

> Our Prophet received his inspiration during his rule, and summoned him (to Islam). He tore up the Prophet's letter; and the Prophet prayed for evil to befall him, (saying), 'As he tore up my letter, may You make his kingdom turn to nought'; and his prayer was answered. (1962: 24)

Yazdigird ibn Shahriyār

> was the last of the Persian kings. For twenty years his rule limped along. When he saw the victory of Islam he wanted to become a Muslim, but did not live to do so. He was killed by Māhūya the Marzbān of Marv, and the line of the Persian kings came to an end. (1962: 26)

Our author now turns to more detailed histories of the Persian kings, placing particular emphasis on the importance of Iṣṭakhr as the capital of Persia (Fars). According to the Pārsiyān, Gayūmarth's capital was Iṣṭakhr, although other historians say that it was originally Damavand and that he built Iṣṭakhr later (1962: 26; the *Mujmal* credits Hūshang with Iṣṭakhr's foundation [1939: 39]). Hūshang (the first of the Pīshdādīs) was invested at Iṣṭakhr; he was was called 'Pīshdād' because he was the first to institute good government and justice. He built places of worship and taught men to worship God, and established the institutions of kingship: sitting upon a throne and wearing a crown (1962: 27–8).

Hūshang's successor Tahmūras invented Persian writing and various kingly pursuits. He constructed two famous buildings in Isfahan which were renovated by Khumārtigīn. It was in his reign that idol worship began. The reason for this was that once, when Fars was afflicted by plague, 'every person who lost a dear one made an image in their likeness, at the sight of which they were consoled.' This became a tradition, and was retained by their successors, mainly in India, though its origin had been forgotten (1962: 29).

> Jamshīd ordered society into four classes. The first of these consisted of persons characterised by subtlety, wisdom and acuity. He ordered some to study religious learning, so that through them he might preserve the statutes of the faith, and some to study wisdom, so that people might have recourse to them concerning their worldly welfare ... For the interests of rule can be maintained by wisdom, just as those of religion are maintained by learning.
>
> The administrator of a kingdom must possess reason adorned by learning, and his learning must be made firm by reason. If a deficiency appears in either his administration will not be sound. There is much to be said on this; if discourse (concerning it) is requested from the eloquent [that is, the author], he can remedy this need. But that is not the purpose of this book; (therefore) we return to our original subject. (1962: 30–1)

Some members of this class were ordered to act as secretaries and accountants, so as to manage the realm's finances and transactions; 'for the best instrument of the preservation of order in the realm, both near and far, is an intelligent and prudent secretary [*dabīr*], so that gain and loss and the interests of the realm may not remain concealed from him.' It is he who at the slightest sign divines the ruler's wish and puts it into sweet and simple language, 'as if he were looking into the ruler's heart'. He should also possess a portion of every sort of knowledge. A secretary who combines these qualities should be appointed as a tutor, rather than as a (mere) *dabīr*; this was the custom of the Abbasid caliphs, who appointed such persons as Jāḥiẓ, Aṣmaʿī and their like as tutors, not as secretaries (1962: 31).

The remaining classes are: (2) warriors; (3) professions and agriculture; (4) menial and base occupations. Jamshīd was also the first person to order painting and image-making to be used in the decoration of palaces and other buildings. He made Iṣṭakhr the capital, and transformed it into a large city; in it he built a great granite palace and three fortresses. He commanded the kings of the surrounding regions to come to Iṣṭakhr to celebrate his accession, ordered a festival, watched for an auspicious portent, then ascended the throne, placed the crown on his head, and delivered an address to those assembled. This was the first Nawrūz. Then, after 316 years of prosperity, 'Jamshīd became ungrateful. The Devil tempted him; and his reversed fortune persuaded him to turn his intent away from God.' He ordered men and demons to worship him; and 'on that very day his *farr* and brillance vanished, and the angels who by God's command had protected him abandoned him. A clamour arose throughout the world: "Jamshīd claims to be God"' (1962: 33). The consequences we know: he was killed by Bīvārasf/Ẓaḥḥāk ('and it was he who established the Sabian religion'). 'May God most high destroy all the enemies of the (true) faith and of (this) conquering *dawlat*', our author concludes fervently (1962: 34), and praises the Saljūq ruler's piety and correct belief, which stand in contrast to Bīvārasf's corruption and impiety: a sorcerer and a parricide, he was not only evil and unjust, but was 'continually occupied with sin and corruption and wine-drinking in the company of women and minstrels'. (Ibn al-Balkhī refutes the story of the serpents on Bīvārasf's shoulders that fed on human brains: they were, he says, extra bits of flesh, which he could move 'as if they were snakes', and the brains were applied to ease the pain they caused [1962: 34–5]. Not for him – in contrast to the author of the *Mujmal*, as we shall see – the fanciful and the fantastic.) Ẓaḥḥāk was defeated by Kābī the smith (who came from Isfahan), who restored a legitimate successor, Afrīdūn; the latter established the festival of Mihragān to celebrate his imprisonment of Ẓaḥḥāk in Mount Damavand.

The treatment of the remaining Pīshdādīs is fairly summary. That of the Kayānids is more detailed, beginning with the reign of Kayqubād, who spent most of his time in Balkh, near the Oxus, fighting the Turks. (Our author makes considerably less of the ongoing conflict between Iran and Tūrān than do others, perhaps because it is of less relevance to Fars and of less interest to his Saljūq patrons.) Kaykāvūs spent much of his time in similar fashion. Our author denies the assertion that Kaykāvus built Tall ʿAqarqūf (near Baghdad; said by Ibn al-Faqīh to have been the burial place of the Kayānids [Yāqūt 1868, 1: 868]) in order to attempt a flight to the heavens: 'this is absurd; not even madmen devise such a plan, because no one in this world has the power to fly' (1962: 40–41). He states that before Siyāvash's son Kaykhusraw was brought to court, Kaykāvūs used to devote himself to pleasure and neglect affairs of state. This led to rebellions throughout his domains, so that he was constantly obliged to fight. He conducted a military adventure in Yemen, was defeated, imprisoned in a pit, and rescued by Rustam (this according to the Persian [Pārsiyān] historians; the Arab ones, we are told, have a different version). In return, Kaykāvūs rewarded Rustam with his freedom and the rule of Sistan and Zabulistan.

> The custom in the days of the Persian kings was that all commanders, generals and (various) ranks of the army were treated as if they were bought slaves. All wore the rings of slavery in their ears, old and young, lesser and great. When they went before the king it was the custom that each should gird a belt over his robe – they called this *kamar-bandagī* – and no one dared approach the king without his earring and his belt girded. It was absolutely not a custom that anyone should sit in the ruler's presence; all stood near the king, hands on belts. When Rustam performed this great service, Kaykāvūs freed him, removed the earring and the belt from his ear and waist, honoured him and treated him well. (1962: 43)

The text of the writ of emancipation (*āzādnāma*) follows. Among other things, it entitles Rustam to all the prerogatives of kingship – a gilded throne; a gold-threaded turban (*kulāh*) in place of the crown (*tāj*) – when in his own kingdom.

We are told that the Persians consider Kaykhusraw a prophet, and that this was the reason for his victory over the Turks. His successor, Luhrāsb, was the first to construct a royal military tent (*sarāy-parda*) and to establish the bureau in charge of military affairs (*dīvān-i ʿarḍ*). In old age he entrusted rule to his son Vishtāsf (Gushtāsb), who reorganised the administrative bureaux (*dīvān*s), placed a vizier in charge of all affairs, and reformed the style of chancery correspondence. Before this,

> the letters written by previous rulers had been brief; he commanded that they be written in a lengthy style, with explication and amplification. The head of the chancery ... was the wisest, most clever and most vigilant of all; because the *dabīr* is the ruler's tongue, and the interests of the realm are secured through his pen. (1962: 49)

Vishtāsf established *dīvān*s for revenues and expenditures, and placed a *dabīr* in charge of protocol so that everyone would know, and keep, their station. (Ibn al-Balkhī's emphasis on the antiquity of administrative practice contrasts both with Gardīzī's statement that Persian administrative practice was abrogated by the coming of Islam [1968: 92] and with Niẓām al-Mulk's preference for the Ghaznavid model.) The author notes Vishtāsf's acceptance of Zoroastrianism (the Persians had previously been Sabians).[26]

Zoroaster urged Vishtāsf to break the peace treaty between himself and Arjāsf, king of the Turks, and to summon Arjāsf to the Magian religion. Should he accept, the peace would continue; 'otherwise, make war on him.' In the ensuing war Vishtāsf's son Isfandiyār performed many great deeds, and defeated Arjāsf. Then 'slanderers' intimated to Vishtāsf that Isfandiyār sought to rule; Vishtāsf turned against him, and sent him here and there to fight fierce battles, which he always won. Finally Vishtāsf imprisoned him in the fortress of Iṣṭakhr, and he himself retired to occupy himself with reading Zoroastrian scripture and with pious worship. Isfandiyār was killed in battle by Rustam, 'as is well known'; no details are given.

A long section deals with the reign of Bahman ibn Isfandiyār (Artaxerxes Longimanus), whom Gardīzī stated would have been the best of kings, were it not for his ravaging of Sistan in revenge for Rustam's killing of his father. Bahman subjugated Rūm; and to punish the Jews for killing an envoy sent to them he ordered Bukht-Naṣṣar (Nebuchadnezzar) to sack Jerusalem, banish the Jews and destroy the Temple. 'Some historians said, that they found in a book' written by the Israelite prophet killed by the Jews in the reign of Luhrāsb, that

> God sent a revelation to Bahman, saying, 'I have chosen you and made you a messiah; you must circumcise yourself, uphold the law, treat the Israelites well and send them back to Jerusalem, and restore Jerusalem.' He did so, and found grace. (1964: 53)[27]

Bahman left two sons, Sāsān and Dārā, and three daughters, Khumānī (Humāy), Farang and Bahmandukht. 'Sāsān, though wise and manly, did not desire kingship; he chose the way of asceticism and disappeared into the mountains.' Humāy ruled in the name of her infant brother Dārā, who, some say, was her son by her father Bahman; but the 'correct account' is that Humāy never married, and remained a virgin till she died (1962: 54).

Dārā ibn Bahman established the *dīvān-i barīd* (intelligence service) and appointed spies everywhere. His son, Dārā ibn Dārā, harboured ill-will towards his father's vizier because the latter had poisoned a youth named Bīrī (or Pīrī), who had been raised with Dārā, after Bīrī had made an attempt on the vizier's life. (Compare the account in Ṭabarī 1987a: 87–8.) This vizier, who hated Dārā, encouraged Alexander to march against him; 'and the reason for Dārā's fall was the interference of that vizier.' Dārā earned universal loathing for his corrupt and oppressive rule, so that, when Alexander appeared, many of his nobles and commanders went over to him. Dārā's murder is laid at the door of 'two men from Hamadan, who conspired together, and in the midst of battle sank a lance in his back, then fled to Alexander's army' (1962: 55–6). (The 'two men from Hamadan' looks highly suspect. It was in Hamadan that Muḥammad Tapar had declared himself Sultan. Is this meant to suggest that the Hamadanis are innately opposed to tyranny, and will turn against unjust rulers?)

As Alexander's story is a long one, the author states that he will recount only what relates to the affairs of the Persians. His reasons for invading Persia were threefold: (1) Dārā's sending him a rude letter demanding Alexander pay taxes to him; (2) the interference of the former vizier; (3) Dārā's tyranny and that of his bad vizier. Alexander took many fortresses and cities by trickery; when he had conquered Persia he imprisoned its rulers and princes, then wrote to Aristotle saying that he feared they might rebel against him (as they were all brave, noble and manly), and that he wished to kill them all so that their seed would disappear forever. Aristotle advised against this ignoble act, arguing that in any case the soil of Persia (Fars) would again produce their like, and there would be enmity between Persia and Rūm forever.

After Alexander's death Ashk ibn Dārā, joined by the other petty kings, who acknowledged him (and his descendants) as their leader because of his descent from the Great Kings, rebelled and expelled the Greek governors set over them by Alexander. The petty kings (Ashgāniyān and Ardavāniyān) had no achievements worth relating. Ardashīr, who claimed descent from Sāsān ibn Bahman and who killed the last 'petty king', Ardāvān, and married his daughter, rebelled in Fars, took Iṣṭakhr, treated the army well, ascended the throne and crowned himself. The populace, who had suffered greatly under the petty kings, supported him. He established institutions of government 'which are so numerous that they constitute a separate book, and kings benefit from reading it, and their good fortune increases. He has covenants and testaments copies of which are still extant' (1962: 60).

I will return later to the detailed account of the appearance of Mānī in the reign of Shāpūr I and of his defeat and execution by Hurmuz ibn Shāpūr. The reign of Shāpūr II Dhū al-Aktāf is dominated by his campaigns against the Arabs, whose raids had provoked widespread complaints by his officials, and seems to bear a topical relevance, by analogy, to the later account of the disturbances caused by the Shabānkāra tribes and the author's advice as to how they should be dealt with. Shāpūr cleansed Fars and Khuzistan of Arabs, drove them from their islands in the gulf, and campaigned against them in Hajar and in Syria. Those Arabs who sought his protection he settled on the edges of the desert and on various islands. Shāpūr had built Madā'in and the Īwān Kisrā (*sic*) and moved the capital there while he dealt with the Arabs; on his return to Fars he resided in Iṣṭakhr. He is praised for his bravery in fighting in person (a marked contrast with Bayhaqī's criticism of Alexander for doing the same), and for his extensive use of spies, who provided him with truthful accounts of what went on in his domains. (Ibn al-Balkhī's repeated emphasis on the necessity for spies and informers recalls Niẓām al-Mulk's stress on the same topic.)

The high point of the account of the reign of Yazdigird al-Athīm, 'the Sinner' – so called because (among other things) he was 'hostile to the (religious) scholars' – is the story of how he was killed by a marvellous horse, said to have been an angel sent by God to punish him. It is particularly detailed and elaborated, and would have appealed to the horse-loving Saljūqs (horses were, moreover, one of their clan emblems, and clearly had earlier had a totemic significance). Yazdigird's hostility to learning contrasts with the avidity for it of his son, Bahrām V Gūr, whom his father sent to Hira to be taught horsemanship and other manly skills. At the age of six he demanded to be given tutors. Told by the Hiran ruler Mundhir ibn Nuʿmān that he was too young, he replied, 'You don't understand; I am a prince, and the king's adornment is learning and knowledge.' When Mundhir returned him to his father to show off his learning, Yazdigird paid him little attention, but demanded that he remain in service to him. Aware of his father's bad nature and conduct, Bahrām succeeded, through the intervention of the brother of the Qayṣar of Rūm (who had come to Yazdigird's court to sue for peace), in gaining permission to return to Mundhir. (Our author's account of Bahrām's reign differs in many details from other versions, and may reflect local traditions.)

A succession of unimportant rulers is followed by Qubād ibn Fīrūz, whose reign was 'orderly and brilliant' until, by divine decree, 'Mazdak the *zindīq* appeared.' I will reserve detailed discussion of this topic too until later. Briefly, Mazdak gathered many followers from among the poor, 'deceived Qubād and led him astray', and helped himself to Qubād's wealth and his women (1962: 84). Qubād was seized and imprisoned, and his brother Jāmāsp put in his place. After his sister had secured his freedom by means of a complicated ruse, Qubād married a daughter of one of his commanders, and told her that, should she bear him a son, she was to name him Anūshīrvān. Much later, Anūshīrvān and his mother were brought to Qubād, who, after an elaborate identity parade designed to see whether Anūshīrvān could recognise his father, accepted him and ordered celebrations. Anūshīrvān used his success to dissuade his father from following Mazdak; Qubād repented, and went off and defeated the Byzantines; on his return, he abdicated in favour of Anūshīrvān.

Kisrā Anūshīrvān, the Just, revived the covenants of Ardashīr and applied the counsels that they contained.

> Wherever there was a book on wisdom or government, he read it, and what he deemed suitable he chose and applied, and established principles of the protocols of kingship, military matters and justice in the world the like of which no Persian king had done (before). The details of his illustrious deeds are lengthy, and there is a famous book about them; but a few of the essentials will be discussed in this book. (1962: 88)

Anūshīrvān first dealt with Mazdak; he then turned to administrative reforms. He reorganised the army and the vizierate and appointed three deputies to report what his officials had written and whatever took place in their administration. (Nicholson comments that this was 'for the purpose of checking the dangerous power which had hitherto been concentrated in the hands of the Vizier (Buzurjmihr)' [1962: xxiv].)

> They say that one day Anūshīrvān said, 'The vizier is like a partner in rule; he judges and disposes in affairs of kingship, wealth and rule. These three persons are his hands and tongue. In this there is sound judgement; for they will not be ignorant of his doings, nor, because of this principle, will anyone be able to slander or lie about the vizier and make the ruler uneasy without cause.' (1962: 92)

Several times Anūshīrvān seized and imprisoned Buzurjmihr, for the vizier would sometimes become prideful or contemplate treachery (Anūshīrvān was also uneasy about him because he was descended from a line of kings); but those informants would usually set things right.

Anūshīrvān put the chief *mawbad* in charge of dispensing justice; he was the 'most noble, learned and pious man of his age' (the parallel with the pious chief *qāḍī* of Fars would not have gone unnoticed; see further below). His other officials were likewise noble and learned. Anūshīrvān is said to have observed,

> 'The *ḥājib* is the ruler's tongue with respect to those who are close, and the secretary is the ruler's tongue with regard to those who are far away or absent. These two must be more perfect, wiser and more perceptive than all others in the world.' (1962: 92–3)

He did not allow base-born persons, tradesmen or people of low state to hold official posts; he reorganised the tax system (details are given); the world prospered under him, and he was called 'the just ruler'. The birth of the Prophet, in the fortieth year of Anūshīrvān's reign, was marked by portents (one of the rare times that Ibn al-Balkhī incorporates *mirabilia*): the fires in the fire temples died out, twelve battlements of the Īwān Kisrā at Khusraw Parvīz's capital of Madā'in collapsed, the lake of Sava dried up, and so on. These marvels were explained to Anūshīrvān by the Arab soothsayer Saṭīḥ: the Prophet's community would extinguish the fire temples; twelve was 'the number of your successors before your [Persian] rule is terminated'. Thinking that, with so many successors, it would be a long time before that happened, Anūshīrvān gave Mundhir ibn Nuʿmān ibn Mundhir rule over the Arabs and instructed him to find out who it was that would become a prophet.

Kisrā Hurmuz ibn Anūshīrvān treated the populace well but disliked the nobles, whom he would kill and replace with base persons. This led to the weakening of his rule, challenged both by external enemies and by revolts by his fearful nobles. Hurmuz sent Bahrām Chūbīn against 'Khāqān Shāba', who had invaded Khurasan. After Bahrām had defeated him and had sent back rich spoils to Hurmuz, he then wanted to send him against the Turks. Bahrām did not think this a good idea; Hurmuz insulted him publicly, and when news of this reached Bahrām – 'who knew Hurmuz's disposition towards killing' – he was filled with loathing, and said to his nobles, 'This man will cut off everyone's seed; we must make our own plans.' They agreed that he should be king until Parvīz ibn Hurmuz, who had fled to Azerbaijan, should return. After Bahrām defeated an army sent by Hurmuz the nobles of Pars, 'who were fed up with Hurmuz, rose up and seized him. They did not think it licit to kill him, but they burnt out his eyes and imprisoned him' (1962: 99).

When (Khusraw) Parvīz learned what had happened, he hastened to Madā'in with his army, assumed the throne and placed the crown on his head. Then he went to his father and apologised, saying that he had fled not out of disobedience but from fear that 'slanderers would make (false) representations to you, and that you would commit a sin against your son' (1962: 99). Hurmuz instructed him to seek revenge, and to send him scholars and sages to be his companions. Realising that he could not defeat Bahrām, who was approaching with a large army, Parvīz put the women and children in a strong fortress and prepared to seek refuge and help in Rūm. His uncles Bindūya and Bisṭām, fearing that in his absence Hurmuz would put Bahrām on the throne, advised Parvīz to kill his father; when he did not answer, they took his silence for agreement, and strangled Hurmuz with a bowstring. 'The first king to agree to his father's death was Aparvīz; and consequently, in requital, he too was killed by his son Shīrūya' (1962: 100). The details of the ensuing accounts – how Parvīz obtained help (and a wife) from the Qayṣar of Rūm, defeated Bahrām and arranged his murder after he had fled to Turkistan, and married Bahrām's sister Gurdiya, who brought him Bahrām's soldiers and treasures – again differ notably from the Eastern versions.

Khusraw Parvīz was the most powerful and magnificent ruler of all the Persian kings; his conduct, however, was less than ideal. He sent an army against Nu'mān ibn Mundhir, who was seized in the desert and killed, his wealth plundered, and his children sold as slaves to the Arabs. This picture of Parvīz as an unjust ruler is linked to the appearance of the Prophet, who received his first revelation in the twenty-eighth year of his reign. 'After that, by the power of God most high, the *farr* and prosperity of Aparvīz and of the Persians became deficient and dwindled, and wherever they went they suffered some debility' (1962: 104). In the battle of Dhū Qār (2/624) the Persians suffered serious losses, and only a few survived, the rest being killed or captured. On the day of the victory the Prophet, in Mecca, is reported to have said, '"Today the Arabs have taken their just requital from the Persians." They wrote down the day', which later proved to be correct; this was one of the Prophet's miracles (1962: 106). Similarly miraculous was the Prophet's announcement, to envoys sent by Parvīz's governor of Yemen, Bādān, that he had been killed. When the envoys returned and reported this, and the Yemenis learned that it was true, they accepted Islam.

> Aparvīz was killed because he was constantly bad-natured, had no respect for the nobles, considered weighty matters trivial but punished the slightest fault heavily, and had no mercy. Just as at the beginning of his reign he had followed the path of justice, so at the end of it his conduct changed: he committed wrongs, extortions and illicit acts, and feared and loathed his retainers. He had no ambition but to amass wealth, both licit and illicit. (1962: 107)

His downfall came when he ordered his general Zādānfarrukh to kill all those held in prison (36,000 persons in all, nobles, great men, princes, soldiers, Arabs, officials and subjects). Zādānfarrukh considered this unjust; the army began to plot against Parvīz, while local rulers looked to their own affairs, and incited Shīrūya to rebel against his father. When he refused, they threatened to find someone who would; he finally agreed, and Parvīz was seized and strangled with a bowstring. 'And may such be the end of all the enemies and ill-wishers of Islam and of this conquering *dawlat*' (1962: 107).

> The last (period of) stability in matters of kingship in the *dawlat* of the Persians was the reign of Aparvīz. After that it fell into disturbance and civil strife, and never regained order. Every few months there was a (new) ruler; and after him [Parvīz]

> calamities occurred, like cholera, plague, famine and the like ... for six and a half years, until the reign of Yazdigird ibn Shahriyār, last of the kings of the Persians. (1962: 108)

Yazdigird had been saved by his nurse from Shīrūya's massacre of his male kin upon ascending the throne; he was taken to Iṣṭakhr and brought up by the nobles of Fars. When they learned of his predecessor Farrukhzād's bad rule the Persians (Pārsiyān) made Yazdigird, then fifteen years old, king. 'All the border regions of the realm had been seized by foreigners, and Islam had become strong. Yazdigird spent eight years at Madā'in, and ruled with ups and downs. He realized he could not remain there.' After sending his general Rustam ibn Farrukh-Hurmuz against the Muslims, Yazdigird took off the great crown of Anūshīrvān, which he sent to Turkistan for safe keeping; then he collected many ornaments and treasures and removed to Nihāvand. Following the Arab victory and the death of Rustam Farrukh-Hurmuz, the latter's brother Khūra-zād took Yazdigird to Khurasan, where he entrusted him to Māhūy, the governor of Marv, who wrote a document saying that he had received the king and his treasures. When the Hephtalites attacked Yazdigird, he discovered that Māhūy had helped himself to his wealth, and reviled him for his treachery; Māhūy killed Yazdigird and fled to the Hephtalites with his treasure. 'Yazdigird was killed in the eighth year of the irreligious and unrighteous tyranny and disobedience of ʿUthmān, the year 31 of the Hijra. The rule of the Persians fell, and Islam gained strength' (1962: 112).

After noting that this has merely been a summary of Persian history, and that he plans to write another, 'proper', history which will meet with the ruler's approval, Ibn al-Balkhī turns to the Muslim conquest of Fars. Most of Fars was taken by peace treaty (*ṣulḥan*), although revolts broke out when news of ʿUmar ibn al-Khaṭṭāb's murder arrived. Such was the case with Iṣṭakhr: taken peacefully, the city rebelled in 32/654; in the ensuing massacre of its inhabitants 40,000 people were killed. Another revolt took place in the caliphate of ʿAlī. But our author stresses that from the first appearance of Islam in Fars all its inhabitants 'were of the religion of the *sunna* and concensus, and no innovators could establish themselves there', nor do they incline towards Zoroastrianism. This was especially so after the ancestor of the present *qāḍī* of Shiraz came to Fars as *qāḍī al-quḍāt* in the caliphate of al-Rāḍī (322–29/934–40), 'upheld the order of the religion and the *sunna*, and established the matters of the Law upon a firm foundation' (1962: 117, and see also xix–xxi). There follows an account of the *qāḍī*s of Fars and their achievements, to which I shall return.

Next comes the geographical section. Administratively, Fars was formerly the capital and seat of power of the Persian kings, and 'Persia' extended from the Oxus to the Euphrates. With the coming of Islam Fars became part of Iraq, governed from Basra because it had been conquered by Basran troops. Its boundaries consist of four 'corners' (*arkān*) – Isfahan, Kirman, the coast on the Kirman frontier, and Khuzistan (Arrajan) – located at the four cardinal points. The province comprises five districts (*kūra*): Iṣṭakhr, Dārābjird, Ardashīr-khūra, Shāpūr-khūra, and Qubād-khūra; the names of the four latter derive from the founders of their major centres.

Iṣṭakhr (Persepolis) was founded by Gayūmars and expanded by Jamshīd. The author provides a detailed description of Persepolis, with its stone columns 'carved with the image of Burāq' (the winged steed which bore the Prophet heavenward on his Ascension); Jamshīd's portrait is also carved everywhere. Much of Iṣṭakhr was destroyed in the early Islamic revolts; the rest was demolished towards the end of Bākālījār's reign by the Saljūq Amīr Qutlumush, and now Iṣṭakhr is only a small village (1962: 126–7). Dārābjird was built by Dārā ibn Bahman in the form of a round city, with a fortress in the centre with four gates, surrounded by a moat filled with water; it is now in ruins. The citadel of Pasā (Fasā), destroyed by the Shabānkāra, has been restored by Atabeg Chāvlī. Jahram boasts a fortress built by an Arab in the time of Ḥajjāj; Faḍlawayh rebelled there, but was besieged by Niẓām al-Mulk and brought out; the town is now prosperous.

In the days of the Persian kings Shīrāz, the present centre of Ardashīr-khūra, was a district with only a few scattered forts. In the caliphate of ʿAbd al-Malik ibn Marwān its governor, Muḥammad ibn Yūsuf (the brother of Ḥajjāj), founded Shīrāz, which, some say, was as large as Isfahan or larger; but now it is in ruins, except for a few districts. Shīrāz was formerly unwalled; but Bākālījār, frightened of the Saljūqs, built a wall around it whose traces still remain. During the fighting between Qāvurd and Faḍlawayh it was plundered and destroyed; it was greatly restored by Khumārtigīn, and prospered, but suffered again during the disturbances after Malikshāh's death, when it was raided twice in one year by the Shabānkāra and by Turks and Turkmens, whose plundering and extortion drove the populace to destitution and despair. Now there is hope that, 'by the *farr* of the conquering *dawlat*', the city will once more become secure and prosperous. Its remaining inhabited districts are under the protection of the family of the *qāḍī* of Fars, whose good efforts on behalf of the poor and needy are lauded (1962: 132–4).

Throughout this section we hear of once-prosperous cities, towns and regions which were ravaged or destroyed both towards the end of

Būyid rule and during the more recent disturbances. One such place was the port of Sīrāf, a flourishing *entrepôt* until, in the last days of Būyid hegemony, its revenues were stopped when the Amīr Kaysh seized the offshore islands and cut off the sea route. Khumārtigīn contemplated redressing matters, but was ultimately bought off. Then Sīrāf was seized by a certain Khān of the island of Qays; sea trade was no longer possible, and the town fell to ruins. By contrast, we also hear repeatedly of the achievements of the present governor Chāvlī, who subjugated refractory regions, razed various dangerous forts and restored other sites. One such place was the centre of Shāpūr-khūra, Bēshāpūr (Arabic Shāpūr), destroyed during the revolt of the Shabānkāra Abū Sa'd Kāzarūnī, but now being restored.[28] The town of Kāzarūn itself, famous for its linen production, suffered a loss of revenues at this time, as merchants lost confidence in its goods, which because of widespread fraud were often found to be defective. Kāzarūn is now in ruins; but were things put right, much revenue would accrue from its cloth manufacture, land tax and customs duties.

Frequent comments of this sort accompany praise of Chāvlī's governance. The once large and pleasant town of Nawbanjān, in the district of Sha'b Bawwān, was raided, destroyed and burnt several times during the misrule of Abū Sa'd Kāzarūnī. 'For years it has been the refuge of lions, wolves and beasts of prey'; its inhabitants were scattered far and wide, and many died in exile. When Chāvlī removed Abū Sa'd, he began to restore the town, and it is hoped that, under the new regime, it will prosper once more. It is set in a pleasant, cool and fertile region, and would flourish if properly administered (1962: 146–7). Arrajān, the centre of the district of Qubād-khūra, was once a large town, but was destroyed during the recent period of troubles, when it was controlled by the heretics (*mulḥidān*, the Nizārī Assassins). The region is well watered and produces excellent fruits.

The author describes the rivers, seas, lakes and pasturelands of Fars, noting that Chāvlī has repaired the Band-i 'Aḍudī (an important irrigation dam built by 'Aḍud al-Dawla). The detailed description of the amenities of the pasturelands reflects the importance of such areas for the Saljūqs, with their numerous horses and herds. Next, the important forts of Fars are enumerated, with some comments of interest. Qal'a-i Khūrshah (near Jahram) was named after Khurshah, the local Arab tax governor under Muḥammad ibn Yūsuf, who amassed a great deal of wealth, built the fort and then rebelled.

> For this reason no governor has [since] been allowed to possess a fort. For wealth puts pride into men's heads, and (possessing) a fort is another (source of) pride; and when there are two (sorts of) pride in a man's head they bring about corruption. (1962: 157)

Qal'a-i Iṣṭahbānān belongs to the Shabānkāra Ḥasūyah; Chāvlī fought against him, and then made peace, but destroyed the fort, which has now been rebuilt. Ibn al-Balkhī notes that formerly there were more than seventy garrisoned forts in Fars; but Chāvlī seized and destroyed them, except for those mentioned previously. The descriptions of these forts, with details about their climate, water supply and fortifications, may be meant to provide information useful to the Saljūq governor, in addition to praising his achievements.

After a section on roads and itineraries, Ibn al-Balkhī moves to his account of the Shabānkāra and the Kurds of Fars, for both of whom he clearly feels disdain. In the ancient past the Shabānkāra tribes were occupied with shepherding, carrying wood and menial tasks. During the disturbed last days of Daylamid rule Faḍlawayh rose up, and the Shabānkāra became increasingly strong, so that with the passage of time 'they all became soldiers, bearing arms and living off land grants [*iqṭā*'s]' (1962: 164). The Ismā'īliyyān, the only noble tribe, trace their descent to Manūchihr; but they were military commanders, not kings. When the Muslims took Fars, they were defeated and dispersed, and took up shepherding. They rebelled in the time of Mas'ūd of Ghazna's governor of Isfahan, Tāsh Farrāsh (whose misgovernance is recorded in detail by Bayhaqī), who forced them to flee elsewhere. The Daylamids drove them out, and they wandered about 'from mountain to mountain', until at the end of Bākālījār's reign they seized Dārābjird. 'The *dawlat* of the Daylam had reached its end, and they could not defeat them' (1962: 165).

The genealogies of, and conflicts between, the Shabānkāra clans do not concern us here.[29] Their leaders were *condottieri* who rose to prominence under the Būyids and often acquired forts and land grants, as well as ideas above their station. (One leader of the Ismā'īlī clan, for example, had the temerity, during last days of Būyid rule, to have the fivefold royal fanfare [*panj nawbat*], reserved for sultans, struck for himself; Atabeg Chāvlī put an end to this.) Most of these leaders were put down by the redoubtable Chāvlī. As for the Kurds of Fars, Ibn al-Balkhī notes that whereas in ancient times the indigenous Kurds were the glory of the Persian armies, with the coming of Islam they were all killed in battle or dispersed, except for a sole survivor who converted and whose descendants still live. The present Kurds of Fars were settled there by 'Aḍud al-Dawla, who brought them from the region of Isfahan. They are a refractory lot, and need to be dealt with firmly.

> Now that which was inquired about – whether the people of Fars should be treated with contempt or with respect – has been made clear, the (royal) command has been obeyed, and the basis

> for kingship in the world has been established as justice, discipline, and righteousness. Each of these must be applied as appropriate: if, where discipline is needed, respect is applied, or vice versa, this will result in detriment. (1962: 168)

The soldiers of Fars, Shabānkāra and others, are contemptuous of those who treat them with gentleness, but will respect and obey a strong and firm commander or governor. 'But the remainder of the populace of this region are the servants of the conquering *dawlat*; they have suffered much in the past, and deserve mercy and observance of their rights' (1962: 169). A discussion of the revenues of Fars, and of their fluctuations under various rulers, leads to a final reference to the province's sufferings following the death of Bākālījār, since which time it has known only civil strife and hardship. Here the text ends, suggesting that the manuscripts used were incomplete, as one would expect a final reference to the author's hopes for renewed prosperity under the new regime.[30]

One of Ibn al-Balkhī's chief concerns was clearly to elevate the status of Fars and of its indigenous population: it was the seat of the ancient Persian kings; its inhabitants, the noblest of the noble, quickly converted to Islam, and remain to this day staunch Sunnī Muslims. The province suffered many hardships both after the death of Bākālījār and during the recent civil strife; but it is a wealthy province, and its prosperity could be restored. Absent, however, is any detailed reference to these recent disturbances, and in particular to the rivalry between the Saljūq princes over Malikshāh's succession, which was only finally resolved by Muḥammad's victory over his brother Barkyāruq in 498/1105. The *Fārsnāma* must have been written some time between Muḥammad's accession in 498/1105 and Chāvlī's death in 510/1116; I would incline towards a relatively early date in view of the Sultan's query about 'the current situation in Fars' and of Ibn al-Balkhī's constant reminders of the hardships it has suffered recently and his hopes for renewed prosperity under the 'conquering *dawlat*' of Sultan Muḥammad.

> There is no doubt that the population of areas under Saljuq control in this period suffered at the hands of the Saljuq princes and governors: under the year 495/1101–1102, Ibn al-Qalānisī, in distant Damascus, comments on the situation in the Saljuq territories of Khurāsān, Iraq and Syria, singling out 'the protracted discord, enmity, wars, corruption and mutual fear' experienced by the population, as a result of their governors being 'too preoccupied with dispute and fighting to pay attention to them and to keep an eye on their affairs'. As well as misrule, the period of Barkiyāruq's reign is characterized by

> decentralization, with the various Saljuq princes and Turkman *amīrs* often changing allegiances and jockeying for power, and by increasing fragmentation of the empire into semi-autonomous principalities on its peripheries. (Hillenbrand 1996: 206)

Not only does Ibn al-Balkhī not mention the succession struggle between Malikshāh's sons, he also omits any but passing references to contemporary Bāṭinī activities, although he does note, here and there, Chāvlī's efforts towards suppressing the heretics. Perhaps most remarkably, there is no mention whatsoever of Muḥammad Ṭapar's expulsion of the Bāṭinīs from Isfahan in 500/1107, which must have taken place before the work was written, as it was after this that the Sultan directed Chāvlī to set about the destruction of their forts in Arrajān.

As Carole Hillenbrand points out, it was between 488/1095 and 493/1100 that the Ismāʿīlīs 'achieved their greatest successes in Saljūq territory',

> at a moment of extreme disarray and weakness on the Saljūq side. As well as the seizure of citadels and the removal [by assassination] of prominent military and religious figures, there were rumours of the Ismaʿili 'contagion' infiltrating the Saljūq army and court circles.

Some sources – including Ibn al-Athīr – go so far as to suggest that Barkyāruq himself had Ismāʿīlī proclivities, particularly because he used Ismāʿīlī troops (1996: 206–8). Hillenbrand concludes that the sultans of the time used 'whatever troops were available to them, even if they were "Ismaʿili"'; all 'were accused at some time of using the Ismaʿilis to dispose of their enemies', but in reality none of them, 'including Muḥammad, considered the extirpation of "heretics" to be a major part of their military strategies' (1996: 207).

Le Strange noted Ibn al-Balkhī's deep antipathy towards heretics, whom he routinely curses whenever he mentions them. Three linked episodes take up this theme: those dealing with Mānī, Mazdak, and the Ismāʿīlī *dāʿī* who was run out of Fars by its Sunni *qāḍī*.

In his account of Mānī's appearance in the reign of Shāpūr I, Ibn al-Balkhī makes explicit connections between past and present.

> In his reign Mānī the *zindīq* appeared and introduced the way of *zandaqa*. The derivation of *zandaqa* is from the Zand, (the book) brought by Zoroaster; in Pahlavi *zandaqa* means the contradiction of the Zand, that is, opposition to it, in the same way that the heretics [*mulḥidān*] – may God destroy them! – contradict the Koran and distort its interpretation [*tafsīr*] and call this *ta'vīl* [allegorical exegesis] so as to deceive people. (1962: 62)

When Mānī appeared, 'discord [*fitna*] broke out throughout the world.' Shāpūr attempted to have him seized; he fled to Ṣīn (Turkistan), 'where he introduced the way of license [*ibāḥat*]' – a term clearly associated in this period with the Bāṭinīs.[31] Shāpūr's son Hurmuz (who ruled only two years) was unable to put down the *zindīq*s.

His brother Bahrām was more successful. Releasing some of Mānī's followers from prison, he treated them well, secretly told them that he had accepted Mānī's teachings, and urged them to persuade him to come to Bahrām, who would proclaim his religion openly. Mānī duly came,

> and Bahrām honoured him and listened to some of his preaching, so that he made him bold, and learned who his missionaries [*dā'iyān*] and followers were. Then he secretly assembled the scholars [*'ulamā*] and told them: 'I have caught that *zindīq* dog, Mānī! and I know who his followers are. I want to get rid of all of them, so that this *fitna* and corruption will subside; but it is not the custom of kings to kill someone without the necessary proof [*ḥujja*]. Now: tomorrow, at dawn, debate with him, and defeat him, so that I may punish him.' They agreed; Bahrām summoned Mānī and told him, 'Tomorrow the *'ulamā* will come; you must be ready to debate with them [*munāẓara*].' When Mānī left he secretly set someone to spy on him. The next day he sat him with the *'ulamā*; they debated, and Mānī was defeated and exposed, his trickery revealed, and he publicly disgraced – for when did the false [*bāṭil*] ever supplant the truth [*ḥaqq*]? Then (Bahrām) asked for a judgement [*fatwā*] concerning what he should do with him. They said, 'If he confesses that this religion he has brought is false, and repents, (the penalty of) death is lifted from him, but eternal imprisonment is his due, such that he shall not leave that place till he dies; but if he does not repent, he must be killed, as an admonition of which the people of the world will take note.' (1962: 64–5)

Mānī refused to repent, and chose death. Bahrām commanded that he be flayed and his skin stuffed with straw. This was, our author notes, the first instance of this punishment, 'and for this reason whoever is the chief of heretics [*mulḥidān*] and leader of *zindīq*s has his skin stuffed with straw.' (We may contemplate the fate of Faḍlawayh.) Then Bahrām assembled Mānī's followers. Those of their leaders and missionaries who repented were condemned to eternal imprisonment; those who did not were executed. Of those who did not know 'the inner secrets of the heresy' – soldiers and common people – he freed those who repented, and killed those who did not.

'And that matter was extirpated, except from the region of Ṣīn, where it still remains. And may God the Mighty and Exalted destroy all opponents of religion and state through His grace' (1962: 65).

What is striking about this passage is its use of Islamic terminology. While this is not unusual in itself, other chroniclers are more likely to employ, for example, terms like *mawbadān* (Zoroastrian priests) rather than the specifically Islamic *'ulamā*. Such terms as *dā'ī*, 'preacher', used for Ismā'īlī missionaries; *ḥujja*, a religio-legal proof; *bāṭil*, 'false, invalid', opposed to *ḥaqq*, 'truth', but also meaning 'God'; *mulḥid*, used generally for 'heretic', but specifically for apostates and especially for the Ismā'īlīs; *ibāḥa*; *fitna*, 'civil strife', but also 'schism', an attack on the very essence of the Muslim community; and the description of the *'ulamā* issuing a *fatwā* (a legal decision according to Islamic principles of jurisprudence), give this passage a decided, and no doubt deliberate, Islamic tone. Moreover, the distinction between 'leaders and missionaries' and the common people, uninitiated into the 'secrets' of the doctrine, leaves no doubt as to the intended parallel between Mānī's followers and the Bāṭinīs.

The same Islamic overtones characterise the description of Mazdak's appearance in the reign of Qubād ibn Fīrūz. He, too, introduced *ibāḥat*, calling it 'the religion of justice'.

> He removed the worship of God from the people, saying, 'Mankind are all from one father and one mother; the wealth of this world is their inheritance. But by virtue of power and tyranny one group takes it and deprives others of it. I have come to restore things as they should be.' He instituted this sort of heresy [*bid'at*], and made men's wives and children licit [*mubāḥ*] to one another. Because most people were poor and penniless, and indolent concerning worship, he gathered many followers. He deceived Qubād and led him astray; he then appropriated Qubād's power, took his wealth and possessions and gave them to the poor, and disgraced the women and delivered them to the rabble [*runūd*]. (1962: 84)

Again, the terms *ibāḥat* and *bid'at* (literally, 'innovation'; specifically, a 'new', heretical belief or practice) provide an Islamic context; while the reference to the 'rabble' suggests not only the credulity of the common people, but also that of uncultivated Turkish soldiery.

When Qubād was deposed in favour of his brother Jāmāsp Mazdak fled to Azerbaijan, where he gathered followers and grew so strong that no one dared attack him. We noted above how Qubād escaped, married, fathered Anūshīrvān, and ultimately accepted his son. Anūshīrvān had heard the story of Mazdak, and saw that his father had followed him because Qubād 'had the nature of soldiers, and was neither learned nor clever'. He waited for a suitable occasion, which came one day when he was speaking to Qubād of *'ulūm-i avā'il* (the 'learning of the elders', that is, the 'foreign', non-Islamic sciences, those of the Greeks and Persians). Qubād asked Anūshīrvān how he had recognised him; he replied, 'The king – may he live forever! – is the sun, and the sun does not remain concealed among the stars.' He then asked why he had been tested; Qubād answered that he had wished to make sure of his descent (*nasl*). Anūshīrvān said, 'In the religion of Mazdak lineage is not to be preserved; anyone can come from anyone.' This was effective ('the arrow hit the mark'). After some thought, Qubād said, 'This is what Mazdak says with respect to the common people.' Anūshīrvān pointed out that according to both the law (*shar'*, another Islamic term) and the beliefs of Mazdak, all are equal in religion. But Mazdak sought, not equality (as he preached), but rule, and had gathered followers for this purpose; and since Qubād had accepted his teaching, he would be helpless to prevent the plunder of his treasuries, the appropriation of his women and, in the end, the destruction of his kingship.

> '(He) has made people follow him because when there are a thousand poor there can be one who is wealthy. Thus when he says that all men are equal, and wealth should be equally distributed, if Mazdak plunders your treasuries you cannot prevent him, because you follow his belief. And if he comes into your private chambers and appropriates your women, again, you cannot prevent him, because you too are one of the children of Adam. This is not a small matter; it will take away (your) kingship, and take you away from God, if you do not remedy it.' (1962: 87)

Qubād repented, and ultimately abdicated in favour of Anūshīrvān, who set about his well-known reforms. Invoking the principle (attributed to Ardashīr) that 'rule (*dawlat*) is centered on religion, and until it has dealt with matters of religion it cannot consider anything else. The army must not be suspect in religion', he spoke with his officials about Mazdak, his father's negligence, and Bahrām ibn Shāpūr's killing of Mānī, asked their advice and told them his opinion: that because of his power and his many swordsmen, Mazdak could be dealt with only by deceit. Advising his council to keep the matter secret, he sent to Mazdak saying (as had Bahrām before him) that he, like his father, had accepted his teachings, and summoned him to 'come to us and make clear the right path'. Mazdak (who, unlike Anūshīrvān, was evidently impervious to the lessons of history) came, and was so well treated that 'he thought he had caught Anūshīrvān'. People began to talk (not knowing the inner truth of the matter), as Mazdak's missionaries and followers preached his religion openly.

'Anūshīrvān knew that that heretic dog had gained complete confidence (in him).' He told Mazdak that he had become tired of his soldiers and officials and wished to replace each of them with one of Mazdak's followers, and asked him to 'write a list of your nobles, soldiers, administrators and important men, so that I can appoint each to a post and occupation', as well as a list of his followers among the army and populace, so that he might treat them with fitting honour and respect. Mazdak wrote the list, which contained the names of more than 150,000 men (1962: 89–90). Anūshīrvān proposed to invite them all to the Mihragān feast and appoint them then; so Mazdak summoned them to Madā'in. In secret, Anūshīrvān arranged with his soldiers to hold a great feast on that day, and to seat Mazdak and his followers first. Then he himself would seize Mazdak and kill him; when he did so the soldiers should draw the swords previously concealed beneath their robes and kill all the others. He sent the names of Mazdak's followers to his provincial governors, ordering that they be seized and imprisoned on the same day. On the day of the feast, Anūshīrvān (who carried an axe, or a short spear – which he had invented for this purpose, as he could not appear at the feast with a sword) cut off Mazdak's head with a single blow, his soldiers killed all the other heretics, and those elsewhere were arrested and killed or imprisoned. He destroyed their forts and returned the property they had seized to its rightful owners, or gave it to the poor and the deserving and to (those who manned) the border forts.

These two accounts form the backdrop to the last and most recent episode, in the reign of Bākālījār, when 'the Sevener sect appeared' and all the Daylamis became Seveners – 'what they now call Bāṭinīs'. Their chief propagandist was a certain Abū Naṣr ibn 'Umrān, who 'was received among the Daylamis as if he were a prophet'.

> That man led Bākālījār astray, so that he converted to the Sevener belief. Then *qāḍī* 'Abd Allāh (the grandfather of the present *qāḍī* of Fars), out of zeal for the faith and the *sunna*, sought a strategy to get rid of that accursed one. He asked to see Bākālījār privately. Bākālījār, who held him in great respect, agreed. When he was closeted with him he said, 'You know that the business of kingship is delicate. This Abū Naṣr ibn 'Umrān has become powerful; all your troops follow him. If [he] wants to turn rule away from you, he can do it in a moment, for all your army will follow him.' Bākālījār became anxious at these words; he knew that [the *qāḍī*] had not spoken in jest. He asked *qāḍī* 'Abd Allāh, 'So what can be done?' He replied, 'He should

> be killed or got out of the country secretly, so that no one will know.' Bākālījār readied a hundred of his Persian horsemen, a hundred Turkish *ghulāms*, and a trusty representative of the *qāḍī*; they rudely set that propagandist on a riding mount, took him with them until they had crossed the Euphrates, and swore that if he returned his blood would be licit. The man went to Egypt. The purpose of this story is to make clear the way and belief of the people of this region, as was required. (1962: 119; on Bākālījār's conversion see Daftary 1992: 213.)

The depiction of the people of Fars as staunch Sunnīs is clearly meant to deflect imputations of heretical sympathies on their part. The facts, however, speak otherwise. The *dā'ī* in question was the famous al-Mu'ayyad fī al-Dīn Shīrāzī, who did indeed go to Egypt, where he became chief propagandist of the Ismā'īlī *da'wa* in Iraq and, eventually, vizier to the Fāṭimid caliph al-Mustanṣir; it was he who masterminded Basāsīrī's revolt. Nor did Bāṭinī activities in Iraq, the Jibal and Fars cease with his expulsion, but increased when the Nizārī–Musta'lī split in Egypt after al-Mustanṣir's death (487/1094) led to the arrival of large numbers of Nizārīs who, under the leadership of Ḥasan-i Ṣabbāḥ, seized numerous fortresses, including that of Alamut, and commenced their assassinations of important figures.

The head of the Ismā'īlī *da'wa* movement in central and western Persia was 'Abd al-Malik ibn 'Aṭṭāsh, based in Isfahan, who launched Ḥasan-i Ṣabbāḥ's career (Daftary 1992: 336). By 494/1100 'Abd al-Malik's son Aḥmad had converted the Shāhdiz garrison and taken possession of the fort. The Ismā'īlīs had been well entrenched in Isfahan for half a century, and 'had even been reaping the benefits of tax revenues from the outlying areas of Iṣfahān'. In 500/1107 Sultan Muḥammad with a large force besieged Shāhdiz. 'Here, it could be argued, he had no choice but to act. The Saljuq armoury and treasury were there, and the citadel at Shāhdiz held the key to domination of the city. Iṣfahān was the traditional centre of Saljuq rule and Muḥammad's own power and prestige were linked with posessing it' (Hillenbrand 1996: 209–10). Hillenbrand argues that 'it would be stretching historical credibility to attribute Muḥammad's prompt action against Shāhdiz to ideological fervour', and that in 'the only anti-Isma'ili initiative of his whole reign in which he participated personally, his motives were, in part anyway, more practical'. Nevertheless, he became 'the hero of the hour', and the process began 'whereby Muḥammad's activities are embellished by the Sunni chroniclers and result in the creation of his image as "the strong he-camel" of the Saljuqs' (1996: 209).

This process did not begin with Ibn al-Balkhī. Let us look more closely at the events in question.

> The siege and capture of Shāhdiz were delayed by a series of manoeuvres and tactics utilized by Aḥmad ibn ʿAṭṭāsh, and supported by friends and sympathizers of the Nizārīs within the Saljūq camp. Aḥmad managed to engage the Saljūqs in a series of negotiations, involving the Sunnī *ʿulamāʾ* of Iṣfahān in a long, drawn-out religious disputation. In a message to the sultan, Aḥmad argued that the Nizārīs were true Muslims, believing in God and the Prophet Muḥammad and accepting the prescriptions of the Sharīʿa. They differed from the Sunnīs only concerning the matter of the imāmate, and therefore maintained that the sultan had no legitimate ground for acting against them, especially since the Nizārīs were willing to recognize the sultan's suzerainty and pay him tribute. This message led to a religious debate. It seems that at first most of the sultan's advisers and the Sunnī jurists and scholars were inclined to accept the Nizārī argument; a few, notably Abū'l-Ḥasan ʿAlī b. ʿAbd al-Raḥmān al-Samanjānī, a leading Shāfiʿī divine, stood fast in refuting the Nizārīs, denouncing them as going outside the pale of Islam, and convincing the sultan to reject Aḥmad's request. The debate thus ended and the siege continued. (Daftary 1992: 361–2)

Further negotiations took place; but ultimately the defenders of the fortress were forced to surrender and sue for terms. It was agreed that some would be allowed to leave and go to Nizārī forts in Arrajān and Quhistān; the remainder, on hearing of their safe arrival, were to surrender, and would be permitted to go to Alamut. The first band left; but when news of their arrival came, Aḥmad and his remaining followers refused to come out, and fought until the final assault, in which most were killed. Aḥmad was captured, 'paraded through the streets of Iṣfahān and then skinned alive'. Subsequently the Nizārī fortresses around Arrajān were destroyed by Atabeg Chāvlī (Daftary 1992: 361–2; see also Ibn al-Athīr 1965, 10: 530–4).

Whatever Muḥammad's motives might have been, this victory met with great approval. It was, moreover, recent. Why then does Ibn al-Balkhī keep silent about it, even in his introductory praise of the Sultan? Was it because Ismāʿīlī influence was still strong at Muḥammad's court, among both the officials and the army? (Ibn al-Balkhī's recurrent stress on the necessity of correct belief among the soldiery seems to imply discreet criticism of the presence of heterodox elements in the army.) On the other hand, in view of Chāvlī's anti-Ismāʿīlī activities in Arrajān, it would be appropriate to make some reference to this event even in a work which deliberately confines itself to Fars.

In fact however there appears to be an implicit allusion to the event in the parallel episodes discussed above, one feature of which (except that concerning Bākālījār) is the occurrence of a debate between the religious scholars (*'ulamā*) and the heretic (Mānī, Mazdak), in which the latter is refuted and exposed, and he and his followers are dealt with summarily. In the debate between Ibn 'Aṭṭāsh and the Isfahani *'ulamā*, however, the latter wavered, with the exception of one staunch Shāfi'ī (who might well have delivered a *fatwā* condemning the heresy). Unlike the debates in the pre- (or proto-) Islamic past, this one was not an unqualified success. Hence, perhaps, another reason for not mentioning Muḥammad Ṭapar's greatest triumph. Isfahan is, in fact, not mentioned at all, even though it was Muḥammad Ṭapar's capital. Was Ibn al-Balkhī, suspicious of the heterodox Isfahani milieu, trying to present Fars (inhabited only by staunch Sunnīs) as an alternative power base?

The bulk of the *Fārsnāma* seems to be directed at the governor of Fars, Chāvlī, and intended to provide instructions towards the proper treatment of the province. It establishes Fars's importance in the past and suggests that this importance should be revived; it deals with matters of administration, clearly implying that the practices of the ancient kings, under whom Fars prospered, should be revived and emulated; it contains much specific information on resources, revenues past and present, and what we might call the potential for development of the region, were efforts made to administer it properly and to rectify the damage done during the recent civil war; it has the potential to provide the Sultan (who, as the historians concur, was fond of money) and his governor with much-needed income. There is also a certain strategic element present in the description of forts and of itineraries. Finally, in his one piece of open advice (directed, presumably, at Atabeg Chāvlī), Ibn al-Balkhī sums up the overall message of his work: treat the Pārsiyān well, and they will treat you well; but don't go easy with the Shabānkāra, or the Kurds, as they are potential rebels. The Sultan's questions with respect to Fars have now been answered.

THE *MUJMAL AL-TAVĀRĪKH VA-AL-QIṢAṢ*

The *Mujmal al-tavārīkh*, compiled around 520/1126, is a general history which also includes a brief account of the Saljūqs.[32] The author's identity is unknown; the editor of the text, M. T. Bahār, speculated that he was a native of Asadābād (south-west of Hamadan), that he had visited Isfahan and travelled to Ahvāz, and that he may have been a Saljūq secretary (1939: *dāl*. On Asadābād, see *EIr*, s.v. Hamadān passed to Saljūq control in 437/1045–6.). Cahen suggested that he was 'writing possibly at the court of the Kākūyid princes of Yazd in Fars' (1962: 64), but gives no reason for this opinion. There is no mention of a dedicatee or indication of the work's intended audience. It is however possible to elicit somewhat more information from the text, as will be discussed later. Bahār, who was chiefly interested in the work's philological aspects, described its style as 'fragmentary' (1939: *vāv*), as indeed it is, especially in the earlier sections.

Following the brief doxology in prose, the author states that since the world was created God sent mankind prophets to guide them out of unbelief, appointed over them kings worthy of His blessing so that the world might prosper, and bestowed learning and wisdom upon those kings so that, due to their experience and their long lives, they were able to attain all things and to accomplish wonders whose traces have passed down to us. In every age, sages and scholars have collected accounts of the past, in scattered form. Ṭabarī presented these accounts; but he did not say much about the Persian kings of the Fourth Clime, except for their chronologies.

> And though the accounts of the kings, Kisrās, rulers and nobles of the past outside [Ṭabarī's] History are manifest, and each has a complete and separate account; and though previous narrators have transmitted these from the books of the Persians, and left them (recorded) in verse and prose ... we (too) wished to compile the history of the kings of Persia, their genealogies, conduct and deeds ... in this book, in summary fashion, from what we have read in Firdawsī's *Shāhnāma*, which is the root, and in other works, which are its branches, and which other sages have versified. (1939: 2)

There follows a long list of works in Persian and Arabic which includes the *Shāhnāma* tradition and its offshoots in verse and prose, and the histories of Ṭabarī, Ibn al-Muqaffaʿ, and Ḥamza Iṣfahānī. 'Although these books ... do not agree with one another (for reasons which will be stated), everything that was confirmed and certain has been written down, so that when readers consider, the original intent will not be hidden.''Our goal', the author concludes, 'is to compile in these pages the accounts and histories from those books, and to explain some things expressed symbolically; and I have included few (examples of) verse, proverbs and wise sayings', except what is necessary or may prove of benefit (1939: 2–3).

After listing the book's chapters (twenty-five in all; the final chapter is missing), the author stresses the serious and cautious nature of his study of books of history. 'What is written (here) is nothing other than what I have read'; should readers come across any errors, he must be excused, as this is the fault of his predecessors. He has transmitted everything as he found it, except for ordering his materials and translating some from Arabic into Persian, 'which is the customary speech of this time'. He then describes his reason for writing the book.

> This idea occurred to me (once) when conversation turned to the kings of Persia and their chronology and deeds. A great lord [*mihtar*] from among the famous notables was present in Asadābād. He asked me about everything. Because he recognized (my interest), and saw my eagerness to read books and listen to oral reports, I told him what was in my mind; and spontaneously, over the wine, I wrote down a few words on the subject. Later I destroyed them, thinking that since this would remain (my) memorial, I should reflect upon it more, and take greater pains, so that benefit might be derived from it. Otherwise it should remain undone; for it is a lesser fault to say nothing. (1939: 8)

He concludes by stating that he began the work in 520/1126, and names the current rulers: the caliph al-Mustarshid; Sultan Sanjar ibn Malikshāh; and Sultan Maḥmūd (ibn Muḥammad) ibn Malikshāh.

Sultan Maḥmūd succeeded his father as ruler of Iraq in511/1117, at the age of thirteen. Sanjar, the senior member of the Saljūq house, ruled as supreme Sultan in Khurasan; under his reign, Rāvandī states that in this year (it was in fact in 513/1119) Sanjar invaded Iraq shortly after Maḥmūd occupied the throne. 'The amīrs of the court had persuaded him that he should make war on his uncle; he was defeated, and fled to Isfahan.' After Maḥmūd sent him apologies (via Abū al-Qāsim Ānisābādī Darguzīnī, the vizier, or *katkhudā*, of Maḥmūd's administrator ʿAlī Bār) Sanjar confirmed him as his deputy in Iraq (Rāvandī 1921: 169–70; compare Bundārī 1889: 120–1; see also Bosworth 1968c: 120; Bosworth 1970a: 88, 90; Makdisi 1963: 143–4). Rāvandī devotes approximately two pages to Maḥmūd's reign: amongst the Saljūq sultans he was 'the most serious and perceptive', but 'his life betrayed him, time did not aid him, and he could not escape the wiles of fate or the sting of hate.' He died in 525/1131. Rāvandī retells the story of Sanjar's defeat of Maḥmūd and his reinstatement of him in Iraq; Sanjar also gave him his daughter Mahmalak Khātūn as wife and when she died before reaching him, sent another daughter in her place. 'Maḥmūd's rule was secured, and he resided mainly in Isfahan and Baghdad. Once some unpleasantness occurred between him and the caliph al-Mustarshid; things came to the point where he besieged Baghdad, seized it, and (then) made peace with the caliph.' We are told that Maḥmūd liked to hunt, and spent much time in the women's quarters, but that he also paid close attention to state affairs (1921: 204–5).

The exordium makes clear that our author intends to focus on the history of Persia, pre-Islamic and post-Islamic, and more particularly on Iraq, that is, Fars and the Jibal. Some of his accounts range further afield; but there is a logic behind this, as we shall see. The first chapter deals chiefly with chronology. 'Know that in these chronologies there are many (different) traditions', our author warns; 'every group and religion has said something (different) on the subject ... and this difference can never be removed' (1939: 9). Establishing accurate chronologies is difficult because of the corruptions caused by the passage of time, by translation, and by the loss of older books of learning and history (Alexander's destruction of the Persian books is a case in point). Ardashīr revived Persian learning and established dating from the beginning of his reign. But even the 'soundest of chronologies', that of the Sasanians, presents discrepancies. Ḥamza Iṣfahānī (whom our author follows closely) spent much effort in attempting to rectify Sasanian chronology, but was unable to do so satisfactorily, as much had been forgotten and no books agreed on it (1939: 10–11).

Various opinions on the duration of the world, from the creation and/or the appearance of humankind to the Hijra, are now related, along with an excursus on solar versus lunar years and the need for periodic intercalation. This section concludes with a further comment on the age of the world.

> It is related that the Prophet said, 'From Adam's time till now is 7,000 years; this is the last millennium.' It is also related that someone said to the Prophet, 'Last night I dreamed of you, O Prophet of God, seated on a pulpit with seven steps; and you were on the last.' The Prophet replied, 'Yes; (the duration of) this world is 7,000 years, and I have come in the last thousand.' They also say that [Ibn] ʿAbbās used always to preach: 'This world is one of the Fridays of the Fridays of the Hereafter, and (will last) 7,000 years. 6,200 years have passed. In the last hundred years, there will be no one who will recognize God's Unicity and worship it.' In short, everyone agrees ... that the world's duration will be 7,000 years; but as to how much has passed and how much still remains, each one says something different. (1939: 12)

Chapters 2–7 consist of chronologies: of prophets; of 'some Persian rulers up to the year 520' (in fact, up to the Arab conquest); of the 'kings of Rūm, sages, and others'; of Arabian kings and of the

Prophet's ancestors; of the caliphate up to the present time (eight years into the reign of al-Mustarshid); and of kings and sultans up to the present Saljūq Sultan, Maḥmūd (eight years after his accession). With Chapter 8 begin accounts of the Persian kings, preceded by a discussion of the Zoroastrian cycle of twelve millennia and various creation legends, including the creation horoscope of the first Nawrūz (1 Farvardīn), in the time of Kayūmars, when the planets began their movement.[33] Chapter 9 consists chiefly of genealogies, with discussions of the meanings of names, discrepancies and conflicting identifications. The periodisation follows the quadripartite division: Pīshdādīs, Kayānids, Ashkāniyān, Sasanians. The section on the Sasanians includes descriptions of individual rulers taken from a *Kitāb Ṣūrat-i pādishāhān-i Sāsāniyān* (with variants of the title), in which each ruler was depicted, standing or seated on a throne, with robe(s), trousers, crown and other accoutrements (spear, shield, sword, and so on).[34] Thus for example Yazdigird III was depicted with a gown of red brocade, sky-blue trousers and red crown, 'a spear in his hand, and leaning on a sword; and all the Sasanian rulers [the author adds] had red boots'. Concluding, our author asserts that he has only recorded reliable genealogical traditions, and has not included others (for example, that Farīdūn, or Kāvūs, was Nimrod; that Siyāvash was Abraham, Jamshīd Solomon, and so on; that Rustam had an Arab lineage), 'because they are remote from the truth, and impossible, as is the Magians' habit; or there have been errors in transmission' over time (1939: 38).

The second section of this chapter records various achievements of the Persian kings, especially their buildings and the cities they founded, with a decided topographical slant towards Isfahan and other regions of Iraq, and with occasional narratives of varying length dealing with other events, some of which depart radically from traditional sources and may stem from local ones and from popular romances. For example, when at the end of his reign Jamshīd became ungrateful and rebelled against God. we are told that, faced by widespread rebellion, he repented, and 'knew himself once more'. When the Arab Ẕaḥḥāk rebelled Jamshīd fled, and 'wandered the world for ten years, alone and unrecognized'. He stayed a while in Zabulistan, and had a son by the daughter of its king; but after twenty years, when the secret of his identity was on the point of being disclosed, he fled to the interior of India, where he ruled as king for a hundred years and produced more children. 'Many an Indian maharajah made war against him, at Ẕaḥḥāk's command, until at last he was captured and taken before Ẕaḥḥāk. He was cut in half with a fishbone shaped like a saw, and then burned' (1939: 39–40). This bears all the hallmarks of popular romance; Jamshīd's wanderings provide the opportunity for many fabulous adventures. Here, as elsewhere, and despite his concern for the accuracies of genealogy and chronology and his disdain for the 'impossible tales' of the Magians, our author's propensity for the romantic and the marvellous leads to occasions when the storyteller replaces the scholar.

The account of Alexander's reign is, similarly, a mélange of historical and legendary materials. Our author's statement that the Iranians liked Alexander because he executed the murderers of Dārā (Darius) and married his daughter Rawshanak arouses Bahār's indignation: the Iranians, he asserts, 'never liked Alexander', who is called 'accursed' in all the old Persian books because of his wholesale destruction (1939: 56). A number of Alexander's marvellous adventures are related, among them his building of the famous wall against the peoples of Gog and Magog (on which more later). Our author follows Ḥamza in his account of Shāpūr I's founding of Jundishapur, where his observation that the city's plan was laid out like a chessboard leads him to comment briefly on other cities built in the shapes of various creatures: Shush in the form of an eagle; Shushtar in that of a horse; the fortress of Tabarak (in Rayy) in that of a scorpion (1939: 64; see Ḥamza n.d.: 39).

The reign of Yazdigird III receives only brief mention, as does the Sasanian defeat by the Muslim Arabs, when 'Persian sovereignty came to an end'. In the third and final section of Chapter 9 our author proceeds to correct Ḥamza's account of the Sasanians and to demonstrate the errors therein. Correct calculation of the total number of Persian rulers and the total length of their reigns demonstrates that Kayūmars and Adam were not the same person. Chapter 10 correlates the Persian kings with the prophets who lived during their reigns, and gives the names of *mawbad*s, generals and other famous men in the reign of each. Chapter 11 provides genealogies and historical accounts (*akhbār*) concerning the Turks, descended from Japheth; Chapter 12 lists the kings of India (descended from Ham, as are also the blacks [*zang*], the Berbers, the Copts and the Abyssinians). Our author states,

> I saw an ancient book of the Indians that Abū Ṣāliḥ ibn Shuʿayb ibn Jāmiʿ had translated from Hinduvānī into Arabic, and Abū al-Ḥasan ʿAlī ibn Muḥammad al-Jullatī, the librarian of Jurjan, translated into Persian in 417 [1026–7] for a Daylamī *sipahbud* ... in which according to Indian custom there was much speech of animals and birds in the style of *Kalīla wa-Dimna*; and I took (from it) the origins of the kings and brief stories about them, since these are found nowhere else. (1939: 107)

Then follow the kings of Greece and Rūm (Chapters 13, 14) and the chronology of the Copts and of the kings and scholars of the Jews (Chapters 15, 16). Finally (Chapter 17) our author moves to the history of the ancient Arabian kings, divided into five sections (there is no section 3 in the printed edition): the Arabs, descended from Shām (Shem) and Qaḥṭān; the kings of Ḥimyar, the Yemen and the Tubbaʿs; the Jafnids (Ghassānids) and the kings of Kinda.

This lengthy section comprises some thirty-five printed pages. Preceded by the chronologies and histories of those nations abrogated by the Arab Muslim conquests, it is followed by an account of the prophets, culminating with Muḥammad (Chapter 18), and thus leads directly to Islamic history. It also confronts the Persian historical world view with the Arab one: that the descendants of Shām's seven sons spread out over the earth and populated all its regions (see 1939: 149 for the details, in which the regions of the world are said to have been named for the various descendents of Shām). There is thus a direct link between the Arabs, Persians and Turks, a link that lends itself to legitimatory ends: if all the kings of the earth are descendants of Noah's offspring, they may be expected to produce both rulers (as did the Persians) and prophets (as did the Israelites and the Arabs).

This section includes many predictions of the coming of an Arab prophet, both in poetry and in prose accounts. Much of the poetry is attributed to Ḥimyarite and Yemeni kings or their poets; some is certainly apocryphal, but much is well known. This lengthy section builds up a direct line of the successive transfer of Arabian rule from the earliest kings of Ḥimyar and Yemen to Muḥammad. At every point along this line predictions multiply; thus for example Abraha, the Abyssinian ruler of Yemen, treats the tribe of Maʿadd (the ancestors of Quraysh) well 'because he knew that kingship would go to Quraysh' (1939: 167). In early Islamic times we hear of the conversion of Bādhān, Khusraw Parvīz's governor of Yemen: the Prophet informed his envoys of Khusraw Parvīz's death and sent them back to summon Bādhān to Islam; when they told him what the Prophet had said and he learned that it was true, he became a Muslim because of this Prophetic miracle (1939: 172).

Chapter 18, which relates the histories of the prophets, traces a similar direct line for the transfer of prophecy beginning with Adam and ending with Muḥammad. (Our author states that his source was Balʿamī's 'translation' of Ṭabarī [1939: 180].) The direct link between the Israelite prophets (who were also leaders of their people) is via Abraham's concubine Hagar and her son Ismāʿīl (Ishmael), whom Abraham abandoned at the site of Mecca, entrusting them to God's care. Later, when Ismāʿīl grew older, God commanded Abraham and him to build the shrine of the Kaʿba. 'According to the *Tāj al-tarājim'* ('Crown of Biographies': a Persian *tafsīr* by Shāhfūr Isfarā'īnī [d. 417/1078–9; see Mottahedeh 1976: 168–9 and notes] which our author cites frequently), Abraham spoke 'Syrian' (Syriac?) and Ismāʿīl spoke Arabic; 'each understood the other but answered in his own language.' Our author provides a representative snippet of their dialogue (1939: 191–2). Further prophetic legends follow, in which a recurrent theme is that of the Israelites falling away from God and the Torah, requiring God to send new prophets to them. Three persons combined kingship and prophecy: Joseph, David and Solomon; but other prophets are also seen as leaders of their people, if not as kings. Israelite and Arab prophets are followed by Christian ones: Jesus (in whose place another person was crucified; Jesus reappeared, sent Peter and Paul to Rome and other disciples elsewhere to preach, but Iblīs (Satan) and two devils spread the notion of the Trinity and deceived people [1939: 218–19]); John the Baptist; the Seven Sleepers of Ephesus and their dog; 'Samson the pious' (who was not a prophet but an ascetic) 'in the days of the petty kings' (1939: 223); and St George of Cappadocia.

The coming of the Prophet Muḥammad – the beginning of Islamic history proper (Chapter 19) – is preceded by a table of the dates of the Jāhiliyya and a note on the introduction of Hijrī dating (a solution to problems of chronology). Much is said concerning prophetic dreams in Persia at the time of the Prophet's birth; the celebrated collapse of the Īwān Kisrā in Madā'in was (according to a 'sounder' tradition) in fact a dream; various other dreams and miraculous events are mentioned. In connection with the story of the Prophet's conversion of Salmān the Persian and his brother, our author quotes Ḥamza's lost history of Isfahan to the effect that they received covenants from the Prophet written by ʿAlī ibn Abī Ṭālib (the Arabic text of which he reproduces), which are still in the hands of their descendants. He adds that he himself has heard, from 'a well-known and reliable source', that one such covenant was brought by one of Salmān's descendants from Shiraz to Isfahan, where it was shown to Sultan Muḥammad and copied for him (1939: 244–5).

At this point our author announces that he will now continue his history from the beginning of the Hijra up to the year 520. There follow accounts of the Prophet's battles, of the letters sent by him to various kings summoning them to Islam, and of the events which followed his death. The ensuing treatment of caliphal history consists in the main of anecdotal material, often of a quasi-legendary nature. We are told for example that Kaʿb al-Aḥbār foresaw the murder of ʿUmar ibn al-Khaṭṭāb, as he had read it prophesied in the

Torah, and that Lu'lu', the slave who murdered 'Umar, was a Zoroastrian.[35] In his accounts of the conquests there is a definite emphasis on Persian territories, and the names of the Persian generals who fought the Muslims are given.

Like the author of the *Tārīkh-i Sīstān*, our author too provides an admonition from the mouth of a Christian condemning the massacre of the 'Alids at Karbalā'.

> [After the battle] a group of the Banī Asad came from the village of 'Āḍariya and buried him [Ḥusayn] at Karbalā'; and 'Ubayd Allāh [ibn Ziyād] sent Ḥusayn's head, and the women and 'Alī Aṣghar, with Shimr Dhū al-Jawshan to Yazīd. Then there took place the story of that Byzantine envoy who told Yazīd, 'Out of respect for that donkey on which Jesus rode, we have covered thousands of donkeys' hooves in gold, placed them on our churches, and expended much wealth. But you kill the descendant of your Prophet! What kind of religion is this?' Yazīd grew angry and ordered him killed. He was a Christian. When it was about to happen he said, 'Last night's dream has come true. I saw Muḥammad, who treated me kindly.' He took Ḥusayn's head out of the golden basin, and continually kissed it and professed his faith [in Islam], until they killed him. (1939: 298)[36]

Our author's interest in the ethics of kingship surfaces in his discussion of the character of Sulaymān ibn 'Abd al-Malik, who enjoyed diverse types of foods and sweets.

> They say that during his caliphate people were only interested in eating, parties and lavish expenditure ... just as in the reign of his brother Walīd talk was (all) about building and making things prosperous, and constructing strange edifices in (various) shapes ... Similarly, later during the caliphate of 'Umar ibn 'Abd al-'Azīz everyone was occupied with reading the Koran and praying. Because of such experiences they have said, 'People follow the religion of their kings'; and now too, if you look around, it is the same. (1939: 306–7)

We also hear that Walīd ibn Yazīd held 'corrupt beliefs', that some say he was a *zindīq* and mocked Islam, and that he violated the mother(s) of his father's children.

Of the rise of the Abbasids our author notes briefly that 'there were disturbances in Khurasan' and that in 128/745 Abū Muslim was sent there to proclaim the *da'vat* openly 'for Abū al-'Abbās Saffāḥ' (1939: 315).[37] Following Ḥamza's history of Isfahan (which, he says, is more detailed than Ṭabarī) he states that Abū Muslim was a descendant of Shīdūs ibn Gūdarz ibn Kishvād (with some variants), and like him wore black in memory of the killing of Siyāvash (1939:

315). He also relates the story of Abū Muslim's choice of black as the emblematic colour of the Abbasids:

> Previously the Umayyad banners and robes had been green. Abū Muslim wanted to change this; so he sat alone in a room and ordered a slave to put on robes of yellow, white, red, dark blue, and every (other) colour and appear before him. When at last he appeared in a black robe, turban, cloak and gown, he found that (colour) to be magnificent and impressive; so he ordered black clothing, put it on, and unfurled the black banner that the Imam Ibrāhīm had given him, which he called *saḥāb* ['raincloud']. (1939: 317)

Meanwhile another ʿAlid, ʿAbd Allāh ibn Yaḥyā ibn Zayd, rebelled in the Yemen in the same year.

> He had no knowledge of Abū Muslim, and by chance adopted the same black garments, and called himself al-Nāṭiq bil-Ḥaqq. Then a certain Ḥamza rebelled in the Yemen in the ʿAlid cause; he took Mecca and Medina, and killed many Anṣār and Quraysh, so that loud outcries arose. He subdued Mecca and Medina, and the outcry reached Marwān: 'The black-robed ones have taken east and west ...' (1939: 317–18)[38]

Our author notes the various heresies that appeared in the late Umayyad–early Abbasid period. The reign of ʿAbd al-Malik ibn Marwān saw the Shīʿī rising in Kufa, the establishment of their *madhhab* and the commencement of missionary activities, as well as the beginnings of the Bāṭinī movement and various Khārijī revolts. A group of Bāṭinīs appeared in Khurasan in the reign of al-Manṣūr, who ordered that any who were found be killed. Later in al-Manṣūr's reign the Rāvandiyān (Rāwandiyya) appeared. They claimed that al-Manṣūr and his son al-Mahdī were divine, and wrote on (walls of) houses: *al-Mahdī rabbunā wa-rabb ābā'inā al-awwalīn* ('al-Mahdī is our Lord and the Lord of our forefathers'); when al-Manṣūr ordered them beaten and killed, they would cry, *anta! anta!* ('Thou! Thou!'), and would point at him. They grew so numerous that al-Manṣūr was only saved from death at their hands by the bravery of his general Maʿn ibn Ziyāda (1939: 329–30). (On these events see Ṭabarī 1995: 62–8, who does not mention al-Mahdī.) Muqannaʿ appeared in al-Mahdī's reign and 'preached what no one in Islam had ever done'. 'His name was Hāshim ibn al-Ḥakam [or: Ḥakīm]; he was a great sorcerer ... and claimed to be God.' The story of his end, related by the woman who survived the mass poisoning of his followers (1939: 335–6), is an elaborated version of that in Balʿamī.

Following his account of Abū Muslim's murder and the events which led up to it, our author observes: 'I have read that for as long as the world has existed (only) three persons have transferred rule and have caused rule to move from one place to another: Alexander the Greek, Ardashīr-i Bābakān, and Abū Muslim the Iṣfahānī (1939: 326).[39] The accounts of later caliphs will mark further turning points in the transfer of power to local dynasties, the first being the beginning of the Sāmānid *dawlat* in the caliphate of al-Muʿtaḍid, when Ismāʿīl ibn Aḥmad seized ʿAmr ibn Layth and sent him to Baghdad. (In the subsequent accounts of local dynasties the Ṣaffārids receive no mention.) Under the caliphate of al-Muktafī he briefly mentions the revolt of Zikrawayh the Qarmaṭī (a Fāṭimid propagandist in Iraq, who terrorised the region and disrupted the pilgrimage routes until he was defeated and killed in 294/907), which, he states, is not found in Ṭabarī, who 'died in Muktafī's reign, and did not relate Zikrawayh's affair because he did not live that long' (1939: 371).[40]

Our author follows Ḥamza in dating the beginning of the decline of the Abbasid *dawlat* to 308/920–1, in the reign of al-Muqtadir, 'when disturbances arose in every region, and their glory waned' (1939: 371). The incident that marked the onset of this decline was the raising of the price of bread by al-Muqtadir's vizier Ḥāmid ibn ʿAbbās (who had cornered the grain market); this provoked riots in Baghdad in which there was much destruction and many people were killed. (Miskawayh dates this event to 307/919–20; see 1920, 1: 72–5.) The next decade witnessed Qarmaṭī raids on the pilgrim caravans, violent protests against this outrage, an attack on Kufa by Zikrawayh's followers, the sack of Basra by the Zanj, and widespread abuses by al-Muqtadir's officials and commanders. In 315/927–8 rioting troops cursed al-Muqtadir publicly for failing to protect the pilgrims, and burned and looted his Thurayyā palace. The following year saw more riots, burning and looting. During these events 'they brought starving (war) elephants, wasted from hunger, before the gates of the palace; the people cried out, weeping and lamenting, and crying, "Alas! Muḥammad!"' (1939: 374).[41]

In 317/929 al-Muqtadir was briefly deposed in favour of Muḥammad ibn al-Muʿtaḍid, who was given the regnal title al-Qāhir ('the conqueror'), but was restored a few days later. The strife continued. There was more fighting in Baghdad; the Carmathians sacked Mecca and took away the Black Stone; the Daylamid Mardāvīj began his revolt. In 319/931 al-Muqtadir was dragged out of the caliphal palace and killed. (Miskawayh dates this to 320/932 [1920, 1: 233].) Under al-Qāhir the disorder continued; in early 322/934 he was deposed and blinded, and died shortly after. 'This (period) was the beginning of the Būyid *dawlat*, as will be told (later)' (1939: 377). In 334/945, in the caliphate of al-Mustakfī, Abū al-Ḥasan ibn Būya entered Baghdad; he and his brothers were granted titles by the caliph (his was Muʿizz al-Dawla), as well as patents, banners and robes of honour.

> After that the disturbances and civil strife subsided, and the populace became quiet. Muʿizz al-Dawla maintained an orderly rule; the affairs of the caliphate devolved upon him, and the caliph was content to obey. From then on the caliphs' acts were limited to sending banners and writs (of office), bestowing robes of honour, and responding to the rulers of (other) regions. (1939: 379)

From here on, caliphal reigns serve only to mark the rise and fall of independent dynasties. Under al-Qādir's reign our author observes:

> After Ṭāʿī all the caliphs withdrew (from public life) and secluded themselves, and were content to rule (only) their households. In this period the Sāmānid *dawlat* came to an end, and Sultan Maḥmūd ibn Sabuktigīn seized rule of the East; and the Būyid *dawlat* became associated with tyranny and improper actions, and introduced evil ways and corrupt beliefs, until Maḥmūd came to Rayy, seized the Shāhanshāh Rustam Majd al-Dawla, and put down the Qarmaṭīs and the Daylamīs. He was continually in correspondence with the Dār al-Khilāfa, and treated (the caliphs) with proper respect. (1939: 382)

The caliphate of al-Qā'im marks the beginning of the Saljūq *dawlat*, with Ṭughril's arrival in Iraq and his restoration of the caliphate following Basāsīrī's revolt. From al-Muqtadī's reign onwards it was 'the time of the Saljūqs', events concerning whom will be recounted in the section devoted to them (1939: 382). Our author concludes (in the reign of al-Mustarshid, when the caliph came out of retirement), 'The compiler of this book has mentioned the caliphs up to this point even as (their rule) has extended this far; should anyone wish to add more caliphs up to this time, (only) God knows best' (1939: 386).

Chapter 20 ('Kings and sultans in the reigns of the caliphs') begins with the Sāmānids. The Būyids receive more detailed treatment (our author names his source as the *Kitāb al-Tājī*); their genealogy is duly noted, and traced through Bahrām Gūr to Ardashīr, 'who was the first to be called Shāhanshāh; and it was for this reason that the sons of Ḥasani Būʾī were called Shāhanshāh' (1939: 391). There is a tendency to focus on events relating to Hamadan; thus our author states, in connection with the conflict between the Būyids and Mardāvīj (said to have been the son of the 'king of Gilan', whose line goes back to the time of Kaykhusraw [1939: 388]), who controlled Hamadan at the time:

> Mardāvīj was the one whom the people of Hamadan killed in revenge against the Daylamīs and (their) army. The people of the city had come out in a large group and killed many soldiers;

then Mardāvīj came and killed so many that fifty ass-loads of trouser-ties of the dead were taken from Hamadan to Rayy, and few remained in Hamadan. A group of the survivors went to the court at Baghdad to protest before Muqtadir, and Hamadan was emptied of men. The custom that the bride, or her father, gives [nothing] to the bridegroom dates from that time, because there were many women and few men. (1939: 389)

Such details, together with frequent attestations that the Būyids were favoured by fortune and the attention paid to details of Būyid relationships with the caliphate, the Sāmānids, the Ziyārids and the Ghaznavids (including, and especially, marriage alliances), give the Būyids, as seen from the perspective of Hamadan, a position of special importance in the *Mujmal*. Of particular interest are the accounts concerning Fakhr al-Dawla ibn Rukn al-Dawla, who governed Hamadan under ʿAḍud al-Dawla and was later installed by the Ṣāḥib Ibn ʿAbbād as ruler of Rayy. Fakhr al-Dawla married Sayyida Umm al-Mulūk (Shīrīn, daughter of the *sipahbud* of Sharvīn), whose ancestors were kings of Ṭabaristān and Daylamān. (Sayyida was in fact of Kurdish descent.) He later arranged a marriage between his son by Sayyida, Majd al-Dawla Abū Ṭālib Rustam, and the daughter of the Kurdish chieftain Badr (ibn) Ḥasanwayh in Hamadan.[42] The intermediary in this arrangement was Abū ʿĪsā Shādī ibn Muḥammad, a (Kurdish?) commander of Badr's, about whom we shall have more to say below. In 387/997 (the same year that Sabuktigīn and the Fāṭimid caliph al-ʿAzīz also died) Fakhr al-Dawla was poisoned by his brother Abū al-Ḥasan Khusraw Fīrūz while hunting; he was succeeded by Majd al-Dawla, who married a daughter of Maḥmūd of Ghazna. 'Sayyida Umm al-Mulūk controlled affairs of state'; Majd al-Dawla's brothers Shams al-Dawla Shāh Khusraw (his heir-apparent) and ʿAyn al-Dawla Abū al-Manṣūr were sent to govern Hamadan and Shiraz (1939: 397).[43]

The conflicts between Būyid princes, Kurds and others are recounted in some detail, and the Hamadani connection is clear throughout, as is the important role in affairs ascribed to Abū ʿĪsā Shādī, who was killed in 401/1010–11 by Badr's rebellious son Halīl (or Hilāl) and brought to Asadābād to be buried (1939: 399–400; see Ibn al-Athīr 1965, 9: 213–14, *sub anno* 400). Badr ibn Ḥasanwayh was killed in 405/1014–5; Shams al-Dawla died in 409/1017–8 at the age of twenty-eight, having recently entrusted his vizierate to Ibn Sīnā (Avicenna), and was succeeded by his son Samā' al-Dawla; in the same year the Kurdish prince Muḥammad ibn Dushmanziyār was given the title of ʿAla' al-Dawla, and also received titles, regalia and a standard from Baghdad. 'And this was the beginning of the Kākūyid *dawlat* in Isfahan, Hamadan and those regions' (1939: 402–03).[44]

> At this time the court at Rayy had been controlled by the Daylamīs for some time. They introduced bad customs and held corrupt beliefs; they pillaged both the surrounding areas and the city, burnt the bazaars, and plundered people's houses, so that no majesty or pomp remained to the ruler. Caravans were disrupted, so that they forced the pilgrims' (caravan) from Khurasan to change its route. Every week there was a new disturbance, on some absurd pretext, and the killing, pillaging and burning were worse than in Baghdad. Sayyida was ruler of Ṭabaristān; every so often she would come with an army and restore order, but then the strife would start up once again. There was no stability; for it was the end of the *dawlat*, and the rule is such that at the end of the *dawlat* customs are reversed. In the end, (the troops) rebelled against Sayyida and the Shāhanshāh and seized their property, and the bloodshed exceeded all bounds; they openly professed Rāfiḍī and Bāṭinī beliefs and philosophy, and had no more regard for Islam. (This went on) until God most High placed Maḥmūd ibn Sabuktigīn over them; he came to Rayy and, on Tuesday 9 Jumādā I 420 [26 May 1029], seized them all, and so much wealth of all sorts came to light as had no bounds ... (Maḥmūd) ordered many gibbets erected and hanged the Daylamī nobles from them; some of them he had sewn up in cowhides and sent to Ghazna; and he ordered that fifty assloads of the books of the Rāfiḍīs, Bāṭinīs and philosophers be taken from their houses and burnt under the gibbets on which they hung. I read in the copy of the *fatḥnāma* that Sultan Maḥmūd ordered written to the caliph in Arabic: 'There were fifty free women in the palace of their ruler, Rustam ibn 'Alī, and he had thirty children from these women. In Islam no more than four wives is permitted. Rustam ibn 'Alī Shāhanshāh Majd al-Dawla is expected to conform to this.' Sultan Maḥmūd dealt with them thus when he assembled all the *'ulamā* and *imām*s of the city, and their corrupt beliefs and conduct were proven and confessed to by their own tongues. He transferred the *dawlat* from the Būyids. Sayyida had fled somewhere, and had grown old and decrepit, and the Shāhanshāh had become witless. Some say he died in Rayy; others say they took him to Khurasan, and brought his corpse back from there; and this is a long story. More than this cannot be told here. (1939: 403–4)[45]

A brief section on the Ghaznavids precedes that on the Saljūqs. (Our author states that as of 525/1131 the Ghaznavids had reigned 136 years; the last ruler named is Bahrāmshāh, who had reigned two years. As Bahrāmshāh acceded in 511/1117, this must be a copyist's error. This suggests that our author was still writing in 525, the date of the death of Maḥmūd ibn Malikshāh.)[46] We are told that these accounts were based on the dictation of Amīr 'Imādī Maḥmūd ibn al-Imām al-Sanjarī al-Ghaznawī, which 'can be written down with confidence'. Other books – the histories of 'Utbī, Bayhaqī and 'other works written in (the time of) that *dawlat*' – tell of Maḥmūd's deeds and conquests, his campaigns, and so forth; but their relation 'is not appropriate to this summary; should we be granted success, we will tell them (elsewhere?)' (1939: 405). The account of Mas'ūd's death differs from those seen earlier (and from most other sources). Near the fort of Marikala,

> his *ghulāms* dug a deep pit and covered it with brush and wood, so that Mas'ūd fell into it. Then, since there were no stones there, they filled sacks with pebbles and threw them down on him. He caught them, piled them beneath his feet, and almost succeeded in climbing out. (The *ghulāms*), frightened, seized mortars and other heavy items from the kitchen (baggage) and threw them down on him, one after another, until he grew weak and was killed. This is more marvelous than (the story of) Rustam's pit, dug by Shaghād; for he [Mas'ūd] had enormous strength. (1939: 406; on the various accounts of Mas'ūd's death see Bosworth 1977: 20)

The Saljūqs' *dawlat* began with their appearance in Khurasan and their defeat of Mas'ūd at Dandānqān. The treatment of the early Saljūqs prior to Sanjar is concise (to say the least), and frequently notes events relating to Hamadan. The author briefly mentions the renewal of Bāṭinī activities in Isfahan during Malikshāh's reign, and the Bāṭinīs' seizure of many strong forts. He notes the occupation of Hamadan by Barkyāruq's uncle Tutush (in 488/1095), Sultan Muḥammad's struggle with Barkyāruq over the succession, his retaking of Dizkuh (Shāhdiz) in 501/1107 and his campaigns against the Bāṭinīs, his designation of Maḥmūd as his heir shortly before his death, and the disturbances which followed it (details of which are deferred until later). Sanjar receives encomiastic treatment. 'No other sultan achieved dominion over the house of Afrāsiyāb [the Qarakhānids] and the realm of Ghaznīn'; the poet Mu'izzī 'has versified his exploits and conquests, and, should God grant success, we will adorn the conclusion of the book with them and, since the *dawlat* of [both Sanjar and Maḥmūd] is at this time, join them together' (1939: 412).

Maḥmūd ibn Muḥammad ibn Malikshāh ascended the throne in Isfahan 'with the most auspicious of portents' in Dhū al-Ḥijja 511/1118, shortly before the accession of the caliph al-Mustarshid in

Baghdad. He sent his brothers Malik Mas'ūd to govern Mosul and Syria, Malik Ṭughril to Arran and Azerbaijan, and Malik Saljūqshāh to Fars. Various events in the early part of Maḥmūd's reign are recounted (mostly centering on Hamadan), including his defeat by Sanjar in 513/1119 (of which our author makes as little as possible); the rebellions of Mas'ūd (514/1120), whom Maḥmūd defeated at Asadābād, and of Dubays (516/1122), which forced the sultan to flee to Baghdad; and Maḥmūd's imprisonment of the Kākūyid 'Alā' al-Dawla Garshāsb in 512/1118 (the date as corrected by Bosworth [1970: 88]; the author gives 513). The manner in which these accounts are related assumes familiarity on the part of the audience with the events and their participants. After this brief summary (which further mentions the caliph's defence of Baghdad against Dubays in 517/1123, but not Maḥmūd's siege of Baghdad in 520/1126) our author states:

> I will write the details of these accounts of the Supreme Sultan (Sanjar) and the Great Sultan (Maḥmūd) during the reign of Mustarshid at the end, in their proper place ... for these three *dawlat*s are connected with one another. More than this, up to the year 520, I could not mention in this brief manner. But whatever occurs, and will occur, from the year 520 (onwards), I will relate in this same summary fashion at the end of this volume, so that the book will not become fragmented. (1939: 415–16)

I will return to the problems presented by this section later, after looking at the remainder of the *Mujmal*. Chapter 21 recapitulates, in tabular fashion, information provided earlier, beginning with the names and titles of Persian and other rulers (among them those of Turkish tribes, Soghdia, the Khazars, the Rūs, Rūm and the Maghrib, and the prophets, with, for the Ghaznavids and Saljūqs, their signatures and/or seals). Chapter 22 is devoted to the burial places of various prophets, kings, caliphs, and so on. A long section deals with the prophet Daniel (who is buried in Shush/Susa), Nebuchadnezzar (Bukht Naṣṣar) and the exile of the Jews, many of whom were sent to Isfahan (whose Madīnat al-Yahūdiyya was named for them). Daniel was among the captives taken to Susa, and it was there that he interpreted Nebuchadnezzar's two dreams. The first was of a figure with its head in the heavens and its feet rooted in the earth, its limbs made of different metals, with legs and feet of clay, which was shattered by a stone from heaven. This figure represents the Persians of all classes, and the stone which shattered it the coming, at the End of Days, of a prophet (named Muḥammad or Aḥmad) from the Tihāma, who will put an end to unbelief (1939: 440). The second dream was of a giant tree, rooted deep in the earth and stretching up to heaven, with many branches filled with birds of every kind. An angel descended from heaven and began to lop off its branches, until a voice cried, 'Leave a bit'; then he took an axe and cut down its trunk, but left its roots. The tree is Nebuchadnezzar's kingdom; the lopping off of its branches means that it will vanish. Daniel prophesied other details of God's punishment of Nebuchadnezzar and his ultimate fate, all of which came to pass as he predicted. When the Arab commander Abū Mūsā al-Ash'arī conquered Susa (17/638) he discovered Daniel's body. An Arab who bought a Hebrew book found with the body related:

> 'I asked Ka'b al-Aḥbār what was in it. He said, "This is the noblest and best of the spoils." "What is in it?" I asked; he replied, "The accounts of caliphs and (other) stories, and whatever will happen in this world until the Day of Resurrection."' (1939: 443–5; Bahār objects [1939: 444, n. 4] that Shī'īs do not consider Ka'b al-Aḥbār a reliable authority)

Daniel was reburied; our author states that he has visited his tomb.

Next the author turns to the sites of the tombs of Muslims: caliphs, members of the Prophet's family, his Companions and various Zaydīs. (The notices on later caliphs are clearly later additions, but that on al-Mustarshid may be genuine: 'He was seized by Sultan Mas'ūd's troops, after he had done battle with the sultan at Daymarj; they took him to Maragha, and the heretics burst through the door of his tent and killed him, and he was buried in Maragha' [1939: 453–4. Al-Mustarshid was killed in 529/1135, the year that Mas'ūd was acknowledged Sultan; see Bosworth 1968c: 127–8].) His treatment of the Shī'ī Imāms, and especially of the Zaydī Imāms of Ṭabaristān, is properly respectful, and I shall return to this section later. The author notes the burial sites of the Persian kings, most of which are located in Fars, and concludes with those of the Ghaznavids, Būyids and Saljūqs (the description of that of the last Great Saljūq sultan, Ṭughril II ibn Arslān, is clearly an addition).

Chapters 21–4 are geographical and topographical and include accounts (mostly legendary) of various famous sites. There is an interesting excursus on maps, of which several are included, among them one of the Seven Climes (Haft Kishvar) according to the old Iranian world view. The descriptions of Mecca, Medina and Jerusalem also include illustrations. (These may of course be later additions.) The accounts of ancient and legendary cities and buildings provides an excuse for what is essentially a collection of travellers' tales and *mirabilia* (Bahār considers this whole long section an interpolation [see 1939: 511, n. 2]). An account of some Islamic cities (Chapter 24) leads, finally, to the cities of the Jibal and Fars, beginning with

Asadābād, which, some say, was founded in the days of the Ṭāhirids by one Asad al-Dawla. 'But I have read in the *'Ajāyib al-'ulūm* that [it] was built by a man called Bāda Shīr, who was a brave and courageous man, in the reign of Yazdigird ibn Shahriyār, the last of the Persian kings' (1939: 519–20). This long account involves Bāda Shīr's killing of a pair of lions, in less than convenient circumstances, which earned him Yazdigird's admiration. Asadābād 'is a small town surrounded by mountains, seven farsangs from the city of Hamadan, with a little water; all its people are friendly to strangers' (1939: 520). Our author describes Hamadan in highly favourable terms, with several legendary accounts of its foundation; information on Karaj, Burūjird, Iṣfahān-i Yahūdiyya (described at some length), Shiraz, Rayy and Shādyākh (a suburb of Nishapur) concludes the book.[47] The colophon states that the copy was completed Monday 28 Jumādā I 813/11 September 1410.

A recurrent theme in the *Mujmal* is that of predictions of the Prophet's appearance. Shāpūr II's hostility towards the Arabs is explained as due to his having read in one of the prophecies of Jāmāsb that a prophet would appear among the Arabs who would overthrow Zoroastrianism. When, after killing many Arabs, Shāpūr went to Mecca and the Hijaz, the Prophet's grandfather Quṣayy ibn Kilāb came to him with a delegation of nobles. Shāpūr asked him if the prophecy were true; Quṣayy replied, 'That will not happen; it is a lie; but if it were to happen, and God has so decreed it, no one could change it.' Shāpūr said, 'You are right', rewarded him, and left the Arabs alone (1939: 66). Abd Allāh al-Sāmiṭ, sent by Abū Bakr on an embassy to the Ghassānid ruler and to Rūm, reported that the Byzantine ruler showed the envoys portraits of prophets said to have come from the treasures of Alexander, including one of Muḥammad ('the last prophet') painted on black silk (1939: 446). We have already noted that many prophecies of this sort occur in the section on the kings of Arabia.

It would seem to be our author's interest in the marvellous and in predictions, dreams and other portents that accounts for his attention to such prophecies, rather than a need to demonstrate local piety. Amongst the *mirabilia* he recounts is Alexander's building of the Wall against the tribes of Gog and Magog. He quotes the Arabic inscription said to have been written thereon, which predicts that the wall will remain until 860 years of the final millennium have passed. Then, as a result of the proliferation of sins and crimes, the severing of kinship bonds and the hardness of hearts, it will burst and countless numbers of these peoples will emerge. They will reach the place of the sun's setting, eat everything in sight and drink up all the waters; but in the end they will destroy one another (1939: 57).[48]

Our author's marked interest in the local monuments of the Jibal and Fars is also combined with his tendency towards the romantic and the marvellous. He cites Ḥamza's rejection in his history of Isfahan of Ṭabarī's statement that the Kayānid Kaykāvūs asked Solomon for the loan of his demons to build Persepolis (Kursī-yi Sulaymān), because its carvings include 'many images of pigs; and no animal is more hated by the Israelites than the pig'; further, its 'Pahlavi' inscriptions (interpreted at some point in the past by a *mawbad*) state that it was built by Jamshīd (1939: 47). He draws on local traditions when he states that the *sipahbud* Farhād created the (Achaemenid) rock carvings of Ṭāq-i Bisṭām near Hamadan, which are said to include portraits of Khusraw II Parviz, his beloved Shīrīn and her famous horse Shabdīz (1939: 79–80), and that the story of Vīs and Rāmīn (a famous pair of Persian lovers who form the subject of a well-known romance) took place in the reign of Shāpūr II (1939: 94). These and similar observations provide insights into the later interpretations of pre-Islamic Persian monuments, and into local traditions concerning those monuments, which were easily visible in the region where our author and his audience lived.

This brings us to the question of our author's identity and of his purpose in writing the *Mujmal*. That he was a native of Asadābād seems certain; and Cahen's suggestion that he was writing at the Kākūyid court of Yazd, in Fars, seems farfetched, especially in view of his clear concern to assert the primacy of the Jibal in both pre-Islamic and Islamic times, perhaps in response to Ibn al-Balkhī's promotion of Fars. There is however more that can be added to our author's profile than Bahār's speculation that he might have been a Saljūq secretary. At one point he mentions a book copied by his grandfather, Muhallab ibn Muḥammad ibn Shādī (1939: 344), which suggests that the latter might have been a scholar or a scribe. (I will return to this grandfather below.) He also states that he himself has written, or plans to write, other books on history (including one on the Barmakid family of viziers; 1939: 342–3), and his scholarly bent is obvious, not least from the sheer number of sources in both Arabic and Persian to which he refers.

Bahār claimed to detect 'prejudice against ʿAlī ibn Abī Ṭālib' in our author.[49] This is clearly Bahār's over-active Shīʿism at work (as, elsewhere, over-active Iranian nationalism colours his views); and it perhaps explains his failure to note, first, our author's esteem for the Zaydī Ḥasanids of Hamadan and, second, his own connections with them.

The section on the burial places of the ʿAlids contains a long notice on the descendants of Ḥasan ibn ʿAlī ibn Abi Ṭālib Amīr al-Mu'minīn (Caliph), many of whom were killed in various ʿAlid uprisings or died in prison. In 250/863–4 a group of Ḥasanids went to Ṭabaristān with the Zaydī Imām Ḥasan ibn ʿAlī ibn Zayd al-Dāʿī (read: Ḥasan ibn Zayd ibn Ḥasan; see Madelung 1975: 206), while many others settled in Rayy. Another group of Ḥasanids later accompanied Sayyid Abū al-Qāsim Buṭḥanī to Hamadan, took up residence there and bought property.[50] The Sharīf Abū ʿAbd Allāh al-Thānī built the fortress and other buildings. The Sayyid Abū al-Ḥusayn married a daughter of the Ṣāḥib Ibn ʿAbbād; their son Abū al-Faḍl married a daughter of Abū ʿĪsā Shādī ibn Muḥammad. Their son was the Amīr Sayyid Murtaḍā Abū Hāshim Zayd; and all the Sayyids of Hamadan are of this lineage. Sayyid Abū Hāshim and his sons held important offices under the Saljūq *dawlat*.[51] Some of the Amīr Sayyid Abū Hāshim's paternal uncles and brothers, among them ʿAlāʾ al-Dīn Sayyidī, have taken up residence in Isfahan. The tombs of the Sayyids are in Isfahan and Hamadan. The account includes a full genealogy of Sayyid Murtaḍā Abū Hāshīm; unfortunately, it is virtually illegible and part of it is missing (1939: 459–60).[52]

Our author's grandfather was Muhallab ibn Muḥammad ibn Shādī; it was Muḥammad ibn Shādī's daughter who married Sayyid Abū al-Faḍl, the son of Sayyid Abū al-Ḥusayn and the Ṣāḥib's daughter. Thus our author's paternal lineage goes back to Badr ibn Ḥasanwayh's commander Abū ʿĪsā Shādī, while he is connected through the collateral line with the Ḥasanid Sayyids as well as with the Ṣāḥib. It is clear that our author was well connected in both Hamadan/Asadābād and Isfahan. He was (to use Richard Bulliet's phrase) a member of the urban patrician class, and undoubtedly moved in court circles. The style of the *Mujmal* suggests that he was probably not (or not only) a secretary, but a scholar and, in all likelihood, a pedagogue, and that he may have written his book for a young Saljūq prince. His simple and direct (often telegraphic) style, his inclusion of marvels and local lore as well as handy sets of genealogical and chronological tables for easy reference, makes this seem a reasonable assumption. He states, moreover, that he was encouraged to write the book by a 'lord' in Asadābād who had asked him questions about history; the word by which he designates this personage, *mihtar*, is used elsewhere (for example, of the Būyid Majd al-Dawla) in the sense of 'ruler' or 'prince'.

As to who this prince might have been, we can only speculate; but an indication may be given by our author's treatment of Saljūq history. Cahen states that the *Mujmal* describes the reign of Maḥmūd ibn Muḥammad ibn Malikshāh 'with an exceptional abundance of detail' (1962: 68); this is difficult to accept in view of the rather summary (and decidedly circumspect) account of the first five years of his reign, which is far less detailed than is that of Maḥmūd's vizier Anūshīrvān ibn Khālid, who served him in 521/1117 and 522/1118, and who wrote in his memoirs: 'In Muḥammad's reign the kingdom was united and secure from all attacks; but when it passed to his son Maḥmūd, they split up that unity and destroyed its cohesion. They claimed a share with him in power, and left him only a bare subsistence' (Bundārī 1889: 134; translated by Bosworth 1968c: 119). Our author promised that in the final chapter of his book he would recount more fully the events of Maḥmūd's reign. This chapter is missing from the Paris manuscript, raising the question of whether it was in fact ever written; unless another manuscript should come to light, we may never know.

Maḥmūd's position was by no means as secure as our author suggests. Sanjar's invasion in 513/1119 was provoked by rumours that Maḥmūd was planning to attack him and was encouraging the Qarakhānids to do so as well. Maḥmūd's defeat resulted in his being forced to relinquish important territories, including Rayy, and to declare his absolute subservience to Sanjar. Maḥmūd's brothers rebelled against him regularly; and the caliphs, beginning with al-Mustarshid, took advantage of internal Saljūq dissension to strengthen their own position. In 520–1/1126 Maḥmūd marched on Baghdad, forced the caliph to make peace and exacted payment of the stipulated tribute; in the course of these events (unmentioned by our author) his troops sacked the caliphal palace (see Ibn al-Athīr 1965, 10: 635–8). Anūshīrvān ibn Khālid attributes this action (like other negative events in Maḥmūd's reign) to the machinations of the Sultan's then-vizier Darguzīnī:

> Among his repugnant deeds and his words that brought dishonour to the *dawla* was that he made it appear desirable to the sultan (who had arrived in Baghdad in 520) to advance with his army on the Dār al-Khilāfa. They said and did that which is not fit to mention, and sanctioned all that disgusts the hearing, and the sin of which is great. (Bundārī 1889: 151–2)

Our author mentions neither this event (which in the eyes of many must have seemed scandalous) nor Sanjar's second invasion in 525/1131, when he marched against the Sultan seeking the inheritance of his two daughters (who had been married to Maḥmūd), which the Sultan was unable to produce (see Bundārī 1889: 152–5). The most likely reason for this is that Maḥmūd was still alive while he was writing these sections; but then again, the promised laudatory account of Maḥmūd's deeds is also missing. Either the manuscript used by the later copyist was defective, or the project was broken off around the time of Maḥmūd's death.[53] Maḥmūd's young son Dā'ūd (whose tutor was Anūshīrvān ibn Khālid) was proclaimed Sultan in Hamadan by Darguzīnī; Mas'ūd proclaimed himself Sultan in Iraq, Saljūqshāh did the same in Fars, and Sanjar, to whom the dispute was referred, put forward his own protégé, Malik Ṭughril, whom he set on the throne in Hamadan. Dā'ūd fled to the protection of his Atabeg, Āq Sunqur Aḥmadīlī, in Azerbaijan (see Bosworth 1968c: 124–5). It is tempting to think that the *Mujmal* may have been written for that young prince and probable heir to Maḥmūd; but this must remain speculation.

THE *HISTORY OF BAYHAQ*

Ẓahīr al-Dīn 'Alī ibn Zayd al-Bayhaqī, known as Ibn Funduq (c. 490–565/c. 1097–1169), completed his history of Bayhaq in 563/1167.[54] Ibn Funduq (as I shall refer to him in order to avoid confusion with his earlier compatriot Abū al-Faḍl Bayhaqī) traced his family's descent to a Companion of the Prophet, Khuzayma ibn Thābit 'Dhū al-Shihādatayn'. He wrote some eighty books, in both Arabic and Persian, including his continuation of 'Utbī's *Ta'rīkh al-Yamīnī*, the *Mashārib al-tajārib wa-ghawārib al-gharā'ib*.[55] Few of his works survive; among them is his history of Bayhaq, written (says Qazvīnī) during the 'sultanate' of Ay Aba (d. 569/1174), 'one of the *ghulām*s of Sultan Sanjar, who took control of Khurasan immediately after Sanjar's death' (1965: *yā-jīm*), as seems confirmed by the prayer for the endurance of his rule (1965: 284; on Ay Aba, who governed Khurasan for the Saljūqs after Sanjar was taken prisoner by the Ghuzz [548/1153], see further below).

Despite occasional dryness, Ibn Funduq's style is generally lively and straightforward. Ornate rhyming prose is employed in the exordium and conclusion, and there is an extensive use of poetic and other quotations. There is no indication of a specific dedicatee or an intended audience (although Ibn Funduq speaks of a 'motive' or 'occasion' which encouraged him to revive neglected sciences and record the fame of Bayhaq's scholars); but the work's style, with its strong admixture of Arabic, suggests expectations of a high level of literary sophistication. Qazvīnī considered the work exemplary of the eloquent and flowing Persian prose of the period; he termed its style 'macaronic prose' (*nathrī mulamma'*) because of its mixture of Arabic and Persian (the dates are given in Arabic; the rubrification is in Arabic), but this is standard procedure in Persian prose works and is seen for example in Bayhaqī's history. More to the point is that Ibn Funduq often switches from Persian to Arabic in the course of a passage, or even a sentence, suggesting that he expected equal facility on the part of his audience. As a source of social and intellectual history

Ibn Funduq's work is of great value, as it provides a vivid picture of the life of one particular region over an extensive period of time.

Ibn Funduq begins with a doxology in rhyming prose, followed by his own genealogy, traced through Khuzayma to Imru' al-Qays to Qaḥṭān (and thus to the southern Arabs of Yemen and Ḥimyar), and ultimately to Noah, 'the second Adam' (1965: 2). He then launches into a complaint of the times and explains his motive for writing the book. In the past, he says, scholars (*ahl-i 'ilm*) were supported by sultans in their pursuit of knowledge.

> (But) in these unfortunate days and this treacherous age, a time of trying tests and civil unrest, when hopes and desires are about to expire, when the partisans of learning's freshness are obliterated and discriminated against, learning has become (as rare as) the Sīmurgh or red sulphur, and all have been rendered helpless by the hand of Time's oppression ... But suddenly a motive may present itself, so that one may choose to strive to the degree of his ability to revive the sciences, and be granted (the task of) renewing every art; 'and the efforts of the destitute are not negligible'. (1965: 3)

The sections which follow do much to enhance our understanding of Ibn Funduq's view of the sciences, and of his own task, as historian, in their revivification (*iḥyā*), a term certainly chosen for its echo of the title of his predecessor Ghazzālī's major work, the *Iḥyā' 'ulūm al-dīn* ('Revivification of the Religious Sciences'). He begins by listing the 'several types of precious science which, in these days, have been obliterated in Khurasan'. First is the study of Prophetic *ḥadīth*: nowadays, 'if someone writes down ten *isnād*s, five correct and five incorrect, few people can recognize' those which are sound, which *muḥaddith* transmitted from which master, which unique traditions he transmitted, who his pupils were, and which of them were accounted reliable or unreliable transmitters. 'This is a great cause for lamentation, and a dire affliction, that within (a radius of) more than a hundred farsangs there are not two scholars from the Prophet's faith who can evaluate *isnād*s and traditions' (1965: 3).

Also fallen into desuetude is the 'noble science' of genealogy. This science is specific to the Arabs: for as different peoples are noted for different arts – the Byzantines for medicine, the Greeks for wisdom, logic and the principles of medicine, the Indians for astronomy and mathematics, the Persians for ethics, the Turks for horsemanship and warfare, and so on – the Arabs, 'who are the noblest of peoples' because the Prophet came from among them, are famed for the sciences of genealogy and of proverbs, both of which are precious. No other people know the names of their ancestors as do the Arabs (1965: 4).

The third neglected science is history, 'for the age of the historians is extinct'. Now all pursue trivial, material pleasures and no longer enjoy the greater intellectual and scholarly pleasures, such as history (1965: 4). A passage in praise of learning is followed by the author's thanks to God that, although he – like all others in this troubled age – is afflicted by old age, weakness, an inhospitable time, penury and the need to care for his family, he has been given the gifts of learning and the ability to propagate it and compile it, and expresses his hope that at some future time learning will flourish once more.

A lengthy section enumerates the benefits of history. 'Histories are the treasure-houses of the secrets of affairs; they contain object lessons, admonitions and counsels.' History, whose coin was struck by the divine Decree, preserves people from the sharp blows of adversities; its witnesses are reliable and unimpeachable. 'The Prophet said, "Knowledge is twofold: the science of religions and the science of bodies"'; history combines the two (1965: 7). The science of religion deals with such matters as knowledge of the Creation, of the peoples of the past (prophets, caliphs, kings, and so on), of the different sects, of the history of the Prophet's time and his career; that of bodies involves the lessons of history, learned from its recurrent patterns.

> There is no event which can be thought of, good or evil, the like or near-like of which has not occurred in the past. Just as physicians base their treatments on sicknesses which have occurred in the past and (on) the great physicians who treated them, and emulate these and consider them their guide ... so (men) know the causes of events which have occurred, and the felicities which assisted (others) in the past, and avoid that which should be avoided as it was avoided in the past, and avert that which was averted. For there are few events the likes of which, or nearly, have not occurred before. (1965: 8)

Here Ibn Funduq echoes his compatriot Abū al-Faḍl Bayhaqī and the latter's predecessor Miskawayh, and reveals himself (as elsewhere) as following in their footsteps, even though his history is of a quite different sort. This becomes even more evident in the ensuing list of benefits to be derived from the study of history.

The first of these involves history's relation to the sources of human knowledge: reason, the senses (amongst which is hearing) and eyewitness. The conditions of the world cannot be known by reason (that is, they cannot be intellected); and since no human being can know through his own observations what the world's states have been as long as it has existed, the contemplation of history provides such knowledge 'and the benefits of this derive from hearing' (1965:

8). Another benefit is that the science of history is pleasant and agreeable, and is rarely tiresome or boring or too great to be taken in. It is not limited to the gains to be had from sensual perception alone.

> The state of the sense of hearing, in listening to accounts and stories, is like that of the eye in observing beautiful forms. For just as the eye (attains) perfection in contemplating beautiful forms, the ear attains perfection in listening to histories and accounts. And of man's external senses none are nobler than sight and hearing. (1965: 9)

Man has an instinctive desire for information and for seeking it out; witness his curiousity about great matters, even if he has no connection with them, and his difficulty in concealing information he has obtained (for which reason the keeping of secrets is considered praiseworthy). History is necessary to fulfil this love of information which, were it not inherent in mankind, would have meant that the accounts, customs, virtues and laws of the past would not have been transmitted to succeeding generations, and defects would have appeared in the world that it would be impossible to rectify. But for all its benefits, knowledge of history is easily accessible, since it is not merely acquired through pure memorisation (like other sciences), but is recollected when similar events occur; moreover, its memorisation is easier than that of other sciences. Through the study of history, one can in a short time acquire knowledge of the states of the world and of kings and kingdoms which it would take many lifetimes to acquire through observation, and will be able to imagine that he has witnessed these events himself. History increases the individual's experience and leads to greater maturity; moreover, he who is conversant with past events is like one who has consulted with all the wise men of the past (1965: 10–13).

This section is followed by another which begins, in tones reminiscent of Bayhaqī,

> No one is in more need of this science than kings and amīrs; for the welfare of the entire world depends on their opinion and judgement, and whatever happens in (their) kingdoms, good or evil, it is they who must command its promotion or rejection. They are in need of knowledge of events and battles for dominion, strategies of warfare and the policies of the kings of the past, just as the physicians of the present (need) the principles, remedies and books of their predecessors, and as cultured and eloquent men [require the same sort of knowledge of the past]. (1965: 15)

From reading or listening to histories, rulers can learn those virtues which assure the continuance of rule, as well as how to avoid that which will bring about its downfall. As for the reliability of historical accounts,

> Should anyone suspect that some histories are forgeries, falsehoods, or 'legends of the elders', which cannot be relied upon ... the solution is this: one should not regard that in which there is benefit with contempt and belittlement or lack of attentiveness. 'Whatever removes ignorance is praiseworthy.' The tales told by animals in the *Kalīla wa-Dimna* were written for benefit and experience, and are all useful and acceptable. (1965: 16)

Finally, kings, who are always preoccupied with affairs of state, can find relaxation in reading or listening to histories; for there is no more agreeable entertainment at times of rest than history.

It is rare to find such a detailed discussion of the purposes of history, which Ibn Funduq places on an equal footing with the more specifically religious science of Ḥadīth; the influence of Bayhaqī is clear. Lambton argued that Ibn Funduq 'understood history to be the collection of facts, not their interpretation' (1991: 236); but from the foregoing it is clear that the very act of writing history is an interpretive one, as history does not merely convey information but provides both edification and entertainment, and serves as a guide to wisdom and virtue.

The first sections of the history proper are general ones. A chapter on the famous provinces and regions of the inhabited world (fifty in all) is followed by one on well-known chronologies and another on the development of historical writing in Arabic and Persian, including mention of a variety of important authors and their works.[56] A brief description of the present work is followed by a section on the superiorities of Bayhaq, chief among them that a number of the Prophet's Companions either passed through or settled there in the early days of Islam. There is a short account of the conquest of Bayhaq by ʿAbd Allāh ibn ʿĀmir ibn Kurayz (the Bayhaqīs, like the Nishapuris, converted peacefully); two years previously, Yazdigird III, in flight, had camped outside Bayhaq. A discussion of Bayhaq's climate is accompanied by observations on different climatic and geographical conditions. There is a section on occupations associated with particular regions: sages with Greece, weavers with Yemen, papermakers with Samarqand, archers with the Turks, and so on; Bayhaq's claim to fame is its *udabā*. Diseases and other afflictions are also associated with certain regions. 'Mothers of regions' (their principal cities) are listed: Mecca in Arabia; first Basra and then Baghdad in Iraq, and next to it Isfahan; and Marv in Khurasan. Of the four elements, air, water and earth are the most important with respect to the characteristics of regions.

Ibn Funduq next discusses the derivation of the names of Bayhaq and its surrounding regions and towns. Bayhaq's most important city is Sabzavār (formerly called Bayhaq). Bahman ibn Isfandiyār founded the city of Bahmanābād; his son Sāsān settled at Sāsānābād (now Sabzavār) and built the city and its canal (*kārīz*), then went to Turkestan, where he founded another Sabzavār near Uzgand. Sāsān designed the overall plan of the region in the form of a mobilised army, with Jalīn its vanguard, Zamīj its left wing, Ṭabas its right wing, Sabzavār-Khusrawjird its centre, and Khusrawjird-Asadābād its rear (the author tells us he received this information in 555/1160 from pilgrims from the region of Uzgand [1965: 41]). People criticised Sāsān's faults and his low aspiration; moreover, his father had perceived that he was not fit for rule. Verses are quoted describing how Bahman sent Sāsān away, and he became a shepherd.[57] 'To this very day (people) call every base person with whom they find fault and whom they reproach "Sāsī", and call beggars "Sāsī" and "Sāsānī".' Sāsān was the progenitor of the Sasanians, whom other kings criticised for being 'descendants of Sāsān the shepherd'.

> And it is not surprising that, with such treatment, the image of Sāsān's *dawlat* became transformed, and the record of its good qualities erased. His father perished; his day turned to night; the Akāsira were all tyrants, except for Anūshīrvān, and during their reigns no subject dared cook fine and delicious food or sew a fine garment or teach his child knowledge and refinement or own a valuable riding animal. (1965: 42)

Local history continues with another account of the foundation of Sabzavār (and of Nishapur) by Sāsūya ibn Shāpūr. His son Yazad Khusraw founded yet more towns, and Nishapur was governed by his descendants 'in the old days'; the last of these died in 390/1000 at the age of ninety. We are told once more that with the coming of Islam the people of Sabzavār and Nishapur all became good Sunnī Muslims, and things remained this way until the arrival of the Khārijī Ḥamza ibn Āzarak and his army from Sijistan (Sistan) in 213/828–9. Ḥamza first came to Shashtamad (the author's birthplace), then fought a battle near Sabzavār, which he sacked, killing all its male inhabitants, both adults and children (the latter were, with their teachers, surrounded in the mosques, which were pulled down over their heads; more than 30,000 persons were killed).

Important events in Bayhaq involve chiefly the arrival in, or passing through, the region of various important personages. Yaḥyā ibn Zayd ibn 'Alī Zayn al-'Ābidīn fled to the *qaṣaba* (citadel) of Sabzavār in 126/743–4 after his father was killed in battle. Harūn al-Rashīd stopped at a nearby village on his way to Ṭūs. The caliph al-

Ma'mūn, on his way to Baghdad (at the time that his cousin Ibrāhīm ibn al-Mahdī had been put on the throne by the Abbasids) also stopped in Bayhaq, and lowered the region's taxes. Various accounts detail the history of the Friday mosque of the citadel: it was destroyed in the time of Ḥamza and rebuilt in that of Khujistānī (266/879–80) with an endowment provided by a wealthy and pious woman; Khujistānī's name and the date were inscribed on the *minbar*, made of ebony and walnut, which was seen by the author before its replacement by a new one in 556/1161. Further information on the mosque, on battles in Sabzavār, on the major earthquake of 444/1042–4 (the 'year of the earthquake', for which the horoscope is given), and on Sabzavār's own horoscope, leads to the statement that the *khuṭba* was pronounced in the name of Alp Arslān in 455/November 1063 in the mosque of Sabzavār, the first place in Khurasan where this was done (1965: 53).

Now begin the sections on the ancient and noble families of the region. First come the Sayyids of Bayhaq (Ibn Funduq excludes the Sharīfs because he has written a separate book on them), who trace their descent to the *ghāzī* Abū al-Ḥasan Muḥammad ibn Abī Manṣūr Ẓafar ibn Muḥammad ibn Aḥmad Zubāra (we shall have more to say on the Zubārids, the chief ʿAlid family in Khurasan, later). The longstanding philo-ʿAlidism of Khurasan is clear, both here and elsewhere, in the attention given and the respect paid to the Sayyids. Next, beginning a listing of the region's various rulers, 'as is the custom in the histories of regions' (1965: 65), Ibn Funduq notes that Bayhaq has produced no kings, only military commanders. The genealogies and chronologies of the Ṭāhirids, Ṣaffārids, Sāmānids, Ghaznavids and Saljūqs follow; the current sultan is named as Arslān ibn Ṭughril (1965: 73).

There follow sections (which also include more local history) on the major families of Bayhaq, beginning with that of perhaps its most famous son, the vizier Niẓām al-Mulk. Before his death Niẓām al-Mulk's grandfather Isḥāq, a *dihqān* from Ankū, entrusted the care of his family to his son Abū al-Ḥasan ʿAlī, who served as a customs official in the administration of Sūrī, the Ghaznavid governor of Khurasan, until the latter was made tax and customs official of Ṭūs. Abū al-Ḥasan accompanied him there, and Niẓām al-Mulk was born in Ṭūs. The author tells of Sūrī's fiscal abuses in Ṭūs towards the end of 'the Maḥmūdī *dawlat*', including his extortion of money, and written promises of yet more, from Abū al-Ḥasan. When the Saljūqs came Sūrī fled to Ghazna, while Abū al-Ḥasan came to Bayhaq with his son, the future vizier, described as intelligent and learned beyond his years. Ibn Funduq now relates a story told by his grandfather,

Shaykh al-Islām Amīrak, who resigned his position as *qāḍī* of Nishapur because of the disturbances there under the Saljūq occupation, and returned to Bayhaq. There he interceded for Abū al-Ḥasan ʿAlī with Bayhaq's *ra'īs*, who did not wish to receive Abū al-Ḥasan together with his son, in whom he saw signs of pride and arrogance. Finally Abū al-Ḥasan was admitted, unaccompanied, only to have the *ra'īs* bid him farewell as he was going to Masʿūd's vizier (Aḥmad ibn ʿAbd al-Ṣamad) in Ghazna, with whom he was on good terms. Shortly after, Abū al-Ḥasan also reached Ghazna safely; there he was seized by Sūrī and confined in the latter's house. He refused to break his fast at his table (it was ʿĪd al-Fiṭr), and rebuked Sūrī, who tore up the document Abū al-Ḥasan had signed promising him money. Abū al-Ḥasan presented himself to the vizier and complained about Sūrī. The vizier replied,

> Tomorrow, when the sun with its rays scatters beaten gold over the earth, and imprisons the demons of darkness in the prison of the earth, and Khvāja Sūrī comes to wait (upon me) so as to discharge his obligations, follow him in, so that you may be offered whatever is required by way of honour and favour. And thank Sūrī with abundance beyond expression and eloquence beyond human comprehension; for giving thanks to the orchard tree results in an increase of benificence. For today he is needed by the *dawlat*, whose time has reached its end; one cannot speak to him of punishment and chastisement. (1965: 82–3)

Abū al-Ḥasan did as he was told; and Sūrī returned the money he had taken from him.

The biographical sections which follow – on the important families of Bayhaq, its *ʿulamā* and religious leaders, its learned men, the syndics (*naqīb*s) of the ʿAlid Sayyids, and its Persian and bilingual poets, with, at the end, a brief account of important events in the region – contain a wealth of information concerning not only local history but the role played by Bayhaqīs in Khurasan as well as further afield. Because of the format of these sections and their arrangement by family, the broader picture is often obscure to modern readers, though it would have been clear enough to contemporaries acquainted with the families and individuals in question. A typical entry runs like this (I have chosen a short one):

> **Anmāṭiyān.** Their *nisba* goes back to Abū Isḥāq Ibrāhīm ibn Isḥāq ibn Yūsuf al-Anmāṭī. Abū Isḥāq al-Anmāṭī died in Nishapur in 303 [915–6]. He had many descendants in the *qaṣaba* (of Sabzavār) and the village of Shastamad, most of whom were pious men, cultivators and ascetics. It was from these Anmāṭīs that Abū al-Ḥusayn ʿAlī ibn al-Ḥusayn ibn Bishr al-Anmāṭī was

> descended; he used to be the *rāwī* [transmitter] of the poetry of the [Ṭāhirid] Amīr ʿUbayd Allāh ibn ʿAbd Allāh ibn Ṭāhir; he died in 535 [1140–1]. Their origin in the village of Shastamad was from Khvāja Abū Muḥammad ʿAbd Allāh ibn Muḥammad al-Anmāṭī; his son was the Muqrī [Koran reader] Abū ʿAlī Aḥmad ibn Abī Muḥammad ʿAbd Allāh ibn Muḥammad al-Anmāṭī; the sons of Abū al-Ḥasan ibn Abī Muḥammad were Muḥammad, ʿAlī, and Aḥmad al-Muqrī. (1965: 126)[58]

It may be of greater interest to look at this material in a more synthetic fashion.

The 'first family' of Bayhaq are the descendants of the Muhallabid governors of Khurasan, who are praised for their good governance, wisdom and generosity towards poets. Ibn Funduq quotes Muhallab ibn Abī Ṣufra's testament (*waṣiyya*) to his son Yazīd: 'Seek a wise *ḥājib*, and employ a refined secretary; for a man's *ḥājib* is his face, and his secretary is his tongue' (1965: 86; Ibn al-Balkhī attributed this statement to Anūshīrvān). Their local descendants included viziers, *faqīhs*, *ru'asā'* of Bayhaq (the *riyāsat* remained in their hands until Saljūq times, when the incumbent was killed early in Ṭughril's reign) and other important personages. As their Yemenite genealogy indicates, the Muhallabids are distantly related to Ibn Funduq's own family through Qaḥṭān; a more recent relationship is through the *ra'īs* Abū ʿAbd Allāh Muḥammad ibn Yaḥyā, the grandfather of our author's grandfather Abū al-Qāsim ʿAbd al-ʿAzīz ibn Yūsuf (about whom we will hear more); their writings (correspondence, *ikhwāniyyāt*) are still in Ibn Funduq's possession (1965: 91).

Ibn Funduq's paternal ancestors, the Ḥākimī and Funduqī families, originated from the region of Bust. Abū Sulaymān Funduq (d. 419/1028) was sent by Maḥmūd's vizier Maymandī to Nishapur as *qāḍī*, then served there as deputy of its chief *qāḍī* Abū al-ʿAlā' Ṣāʿid. (We will recall the *qāḍī* Abū al-ʿAlā''s conflict with the Karrāmi Ibn Maḥmashād as recounted by ʿUtbī.) When he resigned he bought property in Bayhaq and settled there. The author's grandfather, Shaykh al-Islām Abū Sulaymān Amīrak (420–501/1029–1107 or 8) was born in Nishapur; he was for a while its *khaṭīb*, as deputy of Ismāʿīl ibn ʿAbd al-Raḥmān Ṣābūnī, and preached admonitory sermons in the Old Mosque after Friday prayer by order of the caliphs and sultans. His father, Abū al-Qāsim Zayd ibn Muḥammad (447–517/1055 or 6–1123 or 4), lived for twenty years in Bukhara, where he had gone to study (a list of his teachers is given). Ibn Funduq's maternal ancestors were the Bayhaqīs. The mother of his maternal grandfather, Abū al-Qāsim ʿAlī ibn Abī al-Qāsim al-Ḥusayn al-Bayhaqī, was the daughter of Abū al-Faḍl ibn Abī Bakr Khwārazmī, who was the son of the historian Ṭabarī's sister; 'thus the compiler of this book has a hereditary inclination towards the compilation and writing of histories' (1965: 107; see Rowson's comment on this claim [1987: 658, n. 28]). The family were also related by marriage to the Mīkālīs of Nishapur and Bayhaq, an old and important family descended from Bahrām Gūr (1965: 117), from which the ill-fated vizier Ḥasanak stemmed.

Bayhaq's chief claim to fame is its production of scholars and littérateurs who played important roles in the intellectual life of centres such as Nishapur, Bukhara and Ghazna, as well as further afield. One such notable was the ʿAlid *naqīb* Sayyid Ajall Abū ʿAlī Zubāra. The Zubāra ʿAlids resided chiefly in Nishapur (as did Abū ʿAlī), and held the *niqāba* of the ʿAlids in a number of Khurasani cities and towns (on them see Rowson 1987: 657, n. 24 and the references cited); the family was related by marriage to the Ṭāhirids. Sayyid Abū ʿAlī was famous for the gatherings of scholars and men of letters in his home:

> Viziers, notables, religious leaders and judges would meet there. The debate between Abū Bakr Khwārazmī and Badīʿ Hamadānī [in 383/993], in the presence of the vizier Abū al-Qāsim, took place in his palace; all the important religious leaders were present, and Badīʿ Hamadānī composed a *qaṣīda* for him which begins, 'O travellers, on whose night-encampment Time has pitched his tents ...'. (1965: 56)[59]

Another famous son of Bayhaq associated with Abū Bakr Khwārazmī – who 'was at this time the most famous literary figure in the entire East' (Rowson 1987: 658), and was, moreover, a militant Shīʿī – was his teacher, the historian Abū ʿAlī al-Ḥusayn al-Sallāmī al-Bayhaqī, whose books are listed (1965: 154). Abū Naṣr Aḥmad ibn al-Ḥusayn ibn ʿAdl al-Bayhaqī debated with Khwārazmī (the subject is not noted). When Abū Naṣr experienced a reversal of fortune and appealed to Khwārazmī for assistance, he received a rude letter in reply, of which Ibn Funduq quotes an excerpt; it begins: 'Your letter arrived. I will not say that it troubled and saddened me; nay, I will say, it blinded and deafened me ...' (1965: 164). On the other hand, Khwārazmī dedicated a book (in quite laudatory terms) to Abū al-Ṭayyib Muḥammad ibn ʿAlī al-Kātib al-Bayhaqī, who was 'the boast not only of Bayhaq but of Khurasan' and was also praised by the poet Abū al-Fatḥ al-Bustī (1965: 171).

The renown of Bayhaq's *udabā* stretches far and wide. Abū Isḥāq Ibrāhīm ibn Muḥammad al-Bayhaqī al-Mughīthī (the grandfather of Imām Sadīd al-Dīn Ibrāhīm Mughīthī, 'the current *muftī* of Khurasan') came from the village of Mughīthiyya (which also produced the vizier of Kāshghar, al-Faḍl ibn Ḥamak, who built a *ribāṭ* there financed with the gold taken in holy war in Kāshghar). After studying in Bayhaq, Abū Isḥāq Ibrāhīm went to Baghdad, where he studied with the grammarians al-Mubarrad, Tha'lab, and Riyāshī (the teacher of Aṣma'ī). He was on good terms with the Ṭāhirid governor 'Ubayd Allāh ibn 'Abd Allāh ibn Ṭāhir; he also participated in a poetic competition with the Arabic poets Ibn al-Rūmī and Buḥturī (two lines of a response [*jawāb*] by Ibn al-Rūmī are quoted). He was noted for his love of jesting (*hazl*). Ibn Funduq recounts a practical joke that Ibrāhīm Mughīthī played on a friend, one Abū Sa'īd Ḍarīr, who was, apparently, blind (this is the only context in which the 'joke' makes sense). One day he took Abū Sa'īd's hand and led him to the entrance of the Ṭāhirid palace; he told Abū Sa'īd (whom he addressed as *Ustādh*, 'master') to mind his head as they passed through (the entrance was in fact so high 'that a mounted standard-bearer could pass through it without dipping his standard; for the Ṭāhirids took the dipping of a standard as a bad omen'). Abū Sa'īd duly bent double, which surprised the onlookers and they began to laugh. Reaching the edge of a stream, with still a short way to go, Ibrāhīm, 'realising that if Abū Sa'īd moved he would fall into the stream, said to him, "*Ustādh*, cross the stream by jumping over it." The unfortunate Abū Sa'īd gathered his robe around him, jumped, and fell into the stream.' Even so, Abū Isḥāq 'was not reproached for this; nor did he recall (the Arabic saying), "The believer is not bitten twice by a (viper from the same) nest; and he who tries the experienced will be visited by regret"' (1965: 152). As will be seen, Ibrāhīm did indeed have an occasion to regret his taste for jesting.

Abū 'Abd Allāh Muḥammad ibn 'Abd al-Razzāq al-Bayhaqī, from the *qaṣaba* of Sabzavār, was a poet whose collected poetry filled five volumes. He was related by marriage to the Daylamids, and dedicated his *Kitāb al-Dārāt*, 'in which there is much benefit', to Abū al-Ḥasan Sīmjūrī. When the Qayṣar of Rūm sent an Arabic *qaṣīda* to the caliph al-Muṭī' which was full of menaces, he was among the 'learned men of Islam' who composed answers to it, along with other prominent easterners (1965: 162–4). Aḥmad ibn Ibrāhīm al-As'arī al-Bayhaqī (the greatest of the notables of Khvār) served the Ṣāḥib Ibn 'Abbād and wrote panegyrics to him. A verse from one of these poems describing a camel is quoted; the Ṣāḥib criticised its uncommon and archaic Arabic vocabulary, saying, 'Were the weight and burden of the strange words with which you describe this camel to materialise, the camel would be unable to carry them' (1965: 161).

Religious scholars, as well as poets and *udabā* (although it is often difficult to make a precise distinction between the groups, as their accomplishments often overlapped), were similarly favoured both in

Khurasan and elsewhere. The great-grandson of the eponymous Funduq, Ja'far ibn Muḥammad, chief of the Ḥanafī *'ulamā* in Nishapur, was often received at the caliphal court in Baghdad. Qarātigīn (on whom see Treadwell 1991: 323–4; he was the father of Manṣūr ibn Qarātigīn, governor of Nishapur during Abū 'Alī Simjūr's revolt) built a *madrasa* next to the Raḥā mosque for Ja'far's son Yūsuf; and 'every Friday the Amīr of Khurasan, Nāṣir al-Dawla Abū al-Ḥasan Muḥammad ibn Ibrāhīm al-Sīmjūrī, would come to visit him and pay his respects.' The author still has letters sent to Yūsuf by the Amīrs of the time (1965: 104). Abū al-Ḥasan 'Alī ibn al-Ḥusayn ibn 'Alī al-Bayhaqī (from Khusrawjird), 'the Imām of his age', who taught in the Madrasa-i Kūy-i Sayyār in Nishapur, enjoyed the patronage of Maḥmūd of Ghazna's first vizier, Abū al-'Abbās Isfarā'īnī (whom Firdawsī praised) and was on familiar terms with him. Abū al-Ḥasan brought Abū Isḥāq Isfarā'īnī (the vizier's brother) and 'Abd al-Qāhir al-Baghdādī (the heresiographer) together in his *madrasa*, and asked the vizier to provide for their costs of living. (Abū Isḥāq Isfarā'īnī debated with the Karrāmī Ibrāhīm ibn Muhājir in the presence of Maḥmūd of Ghazna in 370/980; see Baghdādī 1935: 21 and n. 13.) Abū al-Ḥasan divided the time of those living in the *madrasa* into three parts: one for teaching, one for the dictation of *ḥadīth* and one for preaching admonitory sermons (1965: 172).

Many of the learned men of Bayhaq served in various administrations; others were, so to speak, coopted on occasion. Such seems to have been the case with Ibrāhīm Mughīthī. A protégé of the Ṭāhirids, 'when the sun of their *dawlat* was afflicted by its setting, and the turn of the house of Layth came', Ibrāhīm became secretary to Khalaf ibn Layth. One day Khalaf's *ḥājib*, Abū al-Ḥārith Sijzī, told him to write a letter 'instructing that half of the revenues of my villages be given in charity to the poor, in thanks for the fact that the kingdom of Khurasan has been delivered to Amīr Ya'qūb'. Bayhaqī wrote to the effect that all Abū al-Ḥārith's property was to be sold and its price distributed in charity. When the reply came that this had been done,

> Abū al-Ḥārith tore his robe and went to Ya'qūb ibn al-Layth, wailing and lamenting. Ya'qūb was a sour-faced, morose man; but when he heard this news he laughed so much, rolling about from one side of his throne to the other, that his courtiers were astonished. Then he told Abū al-Ḥārith: 'In exchange for these properties you will be given some of my own, and cash from the treasury, and your lands will be bought back; and you are free to take what requital you wish from Bayhaqī.' (1965: 152)

Bayhaqī fled, and remained in hiding for a year. One night, shortly before dawn, he went to get a book from his house to study during the day. In an alley he encountered Abū al-Ḥārith and his *ghulāms* coming out of the door of a bathhouse.

> He spotted Bayhaqī (Abū al-Ḥārith had many candles and torches with him) and Bayhaqī became so weak with fear that his limbs lost all power to move. Abū al-Ḥārith said to him, 'O enemy of God! Bayhaqī, what's your plan? The properties that I bought back, (and) that the Amīr gave me in exchange: will you not write another letter instructing that they be sold?' Bayhaqī answered, 'Truly, Ḥājib, you did not make a loss, and God gave you twice as much in exchange; so forgive me. "He who seeks forgiveness from his superior for his sin: let him forgive his inferior."' ... Abū al-Ḥārith told him, 'Go away; no one will molest you.' Bayhaqī replied, 'How can I go? I can't move!' Abū al-Ḥārith then told his *ghulāms*, 'Each of you give Bayhaqī a great slap to restore strength to his limbs, so that he may go in peace.' Bayhaqī relates: 'Slaps came at me repeatedly from left and right ... and I lost my strength; finally, through a clever trick, I threw myself in a canal, and escaped.' (1965: 153)

We may assume that the sole purpose of this story is not entertainment, nor even the fact of Ibrāhīm getting his comeuppance. His misadventure points to the crudeness and lack of culture of the early Ṣaffārids, as they were viewed by former members of the sophisticated Ṭāhirid court (and, indeed, by most historians); but it also suggests (as the other Bayhaqī pointed out) that subordinates should not antagonise their superiors.

Abū al-Ḥasan al-Mushaṭṭab al-Bayhaqī first served Rāfiʿ ibn Harthama, then ʿAmr ibn Layth, both of whom he lampooned in verse for their lack of generosity; his mocking verses on ʿAmr and his vizier cost him his life. Ibn Funduq digresses on the impropriety of insulting one's patrons in verse:

> It is a bad habit to criticise people, and to record such criticism in verse. For if someone bestows favour on someone, (that person) must, to the best of his ability, express gratitude for those favours; and if (the patron) withholds those favours, or cuts them off, he should be excused ... For God has allotted religious scholars money from the tax revenues; but poets have no right (to such) for reciting poetry. (1965: 148)

On occasion, however, poets had more serious motives for criticism or admonition. Abū al-Muẓaffar ʿAbd al-Jabbār ibn al-Ḥasan al-Jumaḥī al-Bayhaqī (from the *qaṣaba* of Sabzavār) enjoyed the favour of sultans and kings, and was praised by Thaʿālibi and Bākharzī. The latter states that Abū al-Muzaffar was head of the *barīd* of Khurasan in Masʿūd's reign, and wrote lampoons in Arabic and Persian against both the rapacious governor of Khurasan, Sūrī, and Mas'ūd himself. Examples are given; in one, he warns 'those who are prideful' to 'look at the works of Mas'ūd and of Sūrī; // Do not be dazzled with joy in this world; for death tumbles every wall [*sūrī*].' In another he states, 'Through Sūrī's tyranny and his (evil) deeds Mas'ūd's *dawlat* has been overturned'; in exploiting the people, he 'left not one stick upon another' in their houses. And in another he admonishes Mas'ūd:

> O Amīr, look towards Khurasan, for Sūrī ever brings money and wealth. If the hand of his wrongdoing remains outstretched, he will bring a long-lasting affair in your direction.
>
> Whatever realm you give to Sūrī, like a bad shepherd, he brings the brand to it.
>
> (1965: 178–9)

Service in the administration, and the preferment attached to it, were often passed down through members of the same families. Ibn Funduq's maternal great-great-grandfather Abū al-Ḥasan Bayhaqī (father of Abū al-Ḥusayn al-Shahīd, 'the martyr', the *ra'īs* killed in the reign of Ṭughril), served as an envoy between the Sāmānids and the caliphal court. His brother Abū Sa'd was deputy of the civil governor of Khurasan, Muḥammad ibn Manṣūr al-Nasawī, and in his service accompanied Alp Arslān on campaign against the Byzantines, from which he brought back many slaves. Abū Sa'd's descendants included Ismā'īl ibn Ibrāhīm ibn Ismā'īl al-Dīwānī; Ismā'īl al-Dīwānī served in the Ghaznavid administration and is mentioned in Bayhaqī's history (1965: 109; Bayhaqī states that he attended Ismā'īl Dīvānī's mourning ceremonies when he himself was fifteen, that is, in 400/1010 [1971: 458]). Ibn Funduq's grandfather, Abū al-Qāsim al-Bayhaqī, once admonished the vizier Kundurī, in an assembly where many notables were gathered, by pointing to him and reciting the Koranic verse (14: 45), '(You were a people who carried on the traditions) and dwelled in the houses of a wrongdoing people; and it has been made clear to you how We dealt with them, and made of them an example.' Those present fell to weeping, 'having grasped the meaning of this lesson'. Abū al-Qāsim refused a robe of honour in reward, saying, 'I wish only a public reward, which would be just, and not a personal reward. For in days of tyranny and inconstancy a personal reward has no benefit; but a public reward is the cause of the world's prosperity.' After further admonishing Kundurī, as the latter was about to leave Abū al-Qāsim warned him: 'Do not be heedless of the fire that blazes outside your tent, and do not kindle the flames of Hellfire with the rubbish of this world' (1965: 110–11). He similarly admonished Niẓām al-Mulk when he attained the vizierate after Kundurī's murder, and warned him against aspiration to high estate and influence, obeying his prejudices and following sensual desires. 'After that, Niẓām al-Mulk never drank wine or satisfied desires contrary to the Sharī'at' (1965: 112).

Among the 'Anbarī family were Khvāja Amīrak (Abū al-Ḥasan Aḥmad ibn Muḥammad al-Bayhaqī) and his brothers, Khvāja Abū Naṣr and Khvāja Abū al-Qāsim, all of whom served in the Ghaznavid administration. After the Ghaznavid defeat in Khurasan Amīrak Bayhaqī managed to hold the fortress of Tirmidh against the Saljūqs for fifteen years. But

> when the affairs of the Khurasanis became separated from those of the Maḥmūdīs, he delivered the fort of Tirmidh to Chaghrī. When Chaghrī offered to make him his vizier, he said: 'I will not serve one whom I knew in the past as obedient to my commands.'

He went to Ghazna, founded a *madrasa*, and served in the chancery under Mawdūd, 'Abd al-Rashīd and Farrukhzād, after which he retired. During Farrukhzād's reign he was insulted by an oppressive and influential eunuch (*khādim*), Abū al-Fatḥ al-Khāṣṣa, who called him a peasant; Amīrak ordered his *ghulāms* to shoot him down in a narrow alleyway, 'and no one investigated this because of the wrong-doing and bad conduct they had suffered from this eunuch' (1965: 120–1). As for his brothers: Abū Naṣr was secretary to Mas'ūd's governor of Rayy and to his vizier; Abū al-Qāsim was Abū Naṣr Mishkān's deputy, in charge of the correspondence to other rulers. Ibn Funduq quotes a letter written by Maḥmūd to Mas'ūd requesting that Abū al-Qāsim be freed from his duties and lent to Maḥmūd to accompany him on the campaign against Rayy.

Among Bayhaq's prominent and wealthy figures was al-Shaykh al-Ra'īs Abū al-Qāsim 'Alī ibn Muḥammad ibn al-Ḥusayn ibn 'Amr, who designated himself 'Mīkālī' (his lineage on his mother's side; which, says Ibn Funduq, is acceptable, because genealogists allow whichever lineage is nobler to prevail in designation). During Maḥmūd's reign he built four *madrasas* in the *qaṣaba*: one for the Ḥanafīs, in the name of Ibn Funduq's grandfather Abū al-Qāsim, which is still flourishing; one for the Shāfi'ī preacher Abū al-Ḥasan Ḥannānī, also flourishing; one for the Karrāmīs, of which nothing remains; and one for the 'Alids (the Sayyids and their followers), the Mu'tazilīs and the Zaydīs, which still remains.[60]

> The *ṣāḥib-barīd* informed Sultan Maḥmūd of this. The Sultan sent a *ghulām*, and he was brought to Ghazna, in Jumādā I 414 [July–August 1023]. When he reached the court the Sultan rebuked him, saying, 'Why did you not support that (legal) school in which you believe, and build a *madrasa* for its leaders? When someone builds and supports a *madrasa* for all groups, he acts

> in opposition to his own belief; and whoever acts in opposition to his own belief practises hypocrisy and seeks repute, not closeness to God.' Then the intercessors performed all the usages of intercession, and he was released. (1965: 194–5; see also Rowson 1987: 657, n. 24)

Another famous son of Bayhaq was the historian Abū al-Faḍl Bayhaqī. In his account of Bayhaqī's life Ibn Funduq quotes his advice concerning the conduct of officials. The sultan's servant should not amass wealth, as this is the prerogative of rulers; nor should he acquire immovable property, as this is the business of subjects. He who serves the sultan holds an intermediate degree, above the subjects but lower than the ruler; he should not seek to imitate either, but content himself with a stipend. He should own a house wherever the court moves about, so that it need not depend for lodging on the subjects; and if he possesses some sheep at such places, this is all to the good, as otherwise he could not provide suitable hospitality. Above all, he must be trustworthy regarding all that is written or spoken, so as to avoid punishment or dismissal (1965: 176–7).

When the Ghaznavids lost Khurasan, many of their former officials went into the service of the Saljūqs; one of these was Niẓām al-Mulk. Although the Saljūqs were reputed (at least retrospectively) to have been great patrons of religious learning, here we learn of their patronage of disciplines unrelated to the religious sciences. The Imām Muḥammad ibn Aḥmad al-Maʿmūrī al-Faylasūf ('the Philosopher'), who was 'unparalleled in wisdom' and an expert on conic sections, was in the service of Tāj al-Mulk in Isfahan, who became vizier after Niẓām al-Mulk's murder (Ibn Funduq says nothing about Tāj al-Mulk's possible complicity in this), during the period of civil strife when (in 485/1092) Malikshāh sent his troops against 'the people of the forts' (that is, the Ismāʿīlīs), who were 'severely tried by killing and burning'. Maʿmūrī cast his horoscope (which came out highly inauspicious), left Tāj al-Mulk's house, took refuge with a friend and, for safety, retired into a dark room. The mob were killing the 'people of the forts'; some women had gone up on the roof to watch, and were running back and forth. One of them looked through the window of the room, saw Maʿmūrī hiding there and shouted, '"One of the fort people is in this room!" – for at that time, fleeing and hiding was the custom of those people – and the mob rushed in and killed him.' When the news reached Tāj al-Mulk, he and the Imāms of Isfahan gathered and held mourning ceremonies and prayed over the corpse (talion, says Ibn Funduq, was not possible). The mob, he comments further, are the source of all evils and civil strife (1965: 233–4; Ibn Funduq's not unsympathetic attitude is worth noting).

Al-Imām al-Nādir Ẓahīr al-Din 'Alī ibn Shāhak al-Qiṣārī, although blind from youth, mastered an astonishing number of disciplines from the Arab and non-Arab sciences, including philosophy, mathematics and geometry; he was considered the best explicator to students of Euclid and the *Almagest*, and compiled, over a period of years, the astronomical tables for the region. Al-Ḥakīm Dā'ūd al-Ṭabīb (d. 480/1087–8) was born in Nishapur; of Jewish origin, he converted to Islam, and worked in the *qaṣaba* as an astrologer and physician. 'His treatments seemed dictated by divine inspiration'; his diagnostic skills were unequalled, and the book of his remedies, compiled by one of his pupils, was compared to the work of the famous physician Muḥammad ibn Zakariyyā' Rāzī (d. 313 or 23/925 or 35) (1965: 241–2). Al-Ḥakīm 'Alī ibn Muḥammad al-Ḥijāzī al-Qā'inī was born in Qā'in; when that town was destroyed he moved to Nishapur, where he disputed with the Imām 'Umar Khayyām and others on medicine and other topics.[61] Sent to Bayhaq, he treated patients and frequented the assemblies of kings. He left many books and epistles on medicine and other subjects, including the *Mafākhir-i Atrāk* ('Laudable Qualities of the Turks'), dedicated to Sanjar; he lived nearly one hundred solar years, dying in 546/1151–2. It seems clear from these biographies that the Saljūqs found themselves in need of the more practical sciences – medicine, astrology, geometry and mathematics – and, despite their conservative Sunnism, were not opposed to the patronage even of someone reputed as a philosopher. These reports may further reflect Ibn Funduq's own study of these subjects, particularly during his sojourn at Rayy (see further below).

The brief account which follows the biographical chapters, on the *nuqabā'* of the Sayyids (descendants of the Amīr of Medina Muḥammad Zubāra ibn 'Abd Allāh) provides further information on this family, and on 'Alid (particularly Zaydī) activities in Khurasan. A number of these Sayyids were acclaimed as caliph (Imām) in the time of the Ṭāhirids and the Sāmānids, among them Muḥammad ibn Yaḥyā Sayyid Āl-i Rasūl ('Head of the Prophet's Family') during the reign of Naṣr II ibn Aḥmad. He was taken to Bukhara, where he was held for a while, then released, honoured and given a stipend; 'he was the first 'Alid in Khurasan appointed a stipend (*arzāq*) from the sultan's *dīvān*, and was (therefore) called *Ṣāḥib al-arzāq*' (1965: 254–5; on subsequent developments concerning this family see further Rowson 1987: 656–7 and nn. 20, 22; see also Madelung 1975: 211–12).

The concluding account of important events in the region recapitulates much already included in the biographical entries and focuses chiefly on the hardships suffered during periods of political strife. Ibn Funduq comments on the famine which afflicted Khurasan during the latter days of Masʿūd's reign, when Sūbāshī, who had come with troops, cavalry and elephants to fight against the Saljūqs, could find no fodder or provisions. In the winter following Sūbāshī's defeat at Sarakhs (428/1037) Masʿūd sent a *ḥājib* to Bayhaq who allowed his troops to pillage the countryside. He also cut down all the pistachio trees (because the wood burned well), loaded the wood onto camels and sent it to Ghazna. For this reason he was called 'Ḥājib Clean-Sweep' (1965: 273). Ibn Funduq relates a story told him by his grandfather, Shaykh al-Islam Amīrak, concerning Sūbāshī.

> One day I went to see Sūbāshī, who was in the palace of Shādyākh in Nishapur, with a hundred thousand horsemen and two hundred elephants under his command. A scout entered and said, 'Ten thousand Turkmens have been seen in the region of Tukāb.' Sūbāshī ordered the drum beaten and the golden trumpet sounded, had his troops mount up, raised the amulets and Korans, and uttered prayers and blessings. He said to me, 'Khvāja Imām, don't withhold your prayers and supplications that I return safely without encountering them.' I answered, 'Amīr, so much caution and pessimism is not right. May you see nothing but good.' I went out, and told the people (who were there), 'The sun of this *dawlat* is setting.' (1965: 274)

The final part of this section concerns the battles around Bayhaq between the Saljūq and Khwārazmian forces in 561/1165–6 and 562/1166–7, during which part of the *qaṣaba* wall was destroyed when the troops of Mu'ayyid al-Dawla Ay Aba cast stones at it from mangonels in a battle in which many were killed. The fighting continued, off and on, and the region suffered much damage. In the end, the *khuṭba* for the Khwārazmshāh Īl Arslān ibn Atsiz was pronounced in Nishapur in 562/1167 (1965: 284).[62]

The lengthy *khātima*, in fairly simple rhyming prose, begins with an exhortation on the necessity for rulers to support scholars so that learning may flourish and the current disastrous state of the world be put right. Ibn Funduq states that he will not indulge in exaggerated praise, but will deliver admonition and advice. There follows what is basically a sermon: all men are equal before death; they should beware worldly temptations and false declarations of piety. The squabbling sects disagree on everything except that disobedience to God brings about loss and affliction. Several moral anecdotes about kings are related, and the 'ten faults of this world' are enumerated (1965: 286–92). Ibn Funduq concludes:

> This book, the History of Bayhaq, is finished, through the strength and power of God ... and its compiler has expended upon it that which is within the powers of human ability and

> his own skill. May God bestow His mercy and forgiveness on those who are gone ... and may he set those who survive firmly on the principle of the Sharī'at and the *sunnat*. (1965: 292; a note states that the copying of the book was completed on 4 Shawwāl 563/12 July 1168 in the village of Shastamad)

Despite obvious differences of genre, Ibn Funduq resembles in many ways his predecessor Abū al-Faḍl Bayhaqī. Like Bayhaqī, he shows a predilection both for drawing moral lessons from events and for digression, although in both cases he is somewhat more schematic, and the digressions sometimes hang on rather slender threads. Thus for example in the notice on Abū 'Imrān Muḥammad ibn Jibrīl al-Bayhaqī – of whom it is said only that he transmitted the following *ḥadīth*: 'If one of you is asked about something he does not know, let him say, "I do not know"; that is a third of learning' – Ibn Funduq states that, one night in Nishapur, he himself dreamed that the Prophet appeared to him and said, 'He who says concerning what he does not know, "I do not know," is the most learned of people.' This leads him to observe: 'This is a great mystery: that every error which casts its shadow in the world is because the ignorant person will not confess to his ignorance, and in ignorance speaks about religion.' He continues:

> There were a group of people, in appearance ascetics, but without learning. The common people, deceived by their asceticism, sought (religious) knowledge from them. That group of people felt it would be a disgrace and a fault to confess to their own ignorance, and were afraid that people would reject them. So in their ignorance they spoke (of religious matters); and because of their asceticism people accepted what they said in good faith, and heeded them, so that much error and innovation appeared in the world. The source of all errors in the religions of Moses, Jesus, and Muḥammad is due to the ignorant, seeming ascetic who has no learning. Since God created the world it has been a habit of the common people that, wherever there is an ignorant, unambitious ascetic, they become his sincere disciples, accept whatever he says, and quickly agree to it. It is difficult to remove this affliction. The scholars of every nation have been unable to declare invalid what the common people have accepted from sincere but ignorant ascetics, fearing that the populace would revolt and bring harm to the scholars; for whenever it was sought to invalidate them, the status of those unlearned ascetics has increased, and the populace have believed them even more. (1965: 143–4)

This anecdote must certainly relate to the Karrāmiyya (who receive occasional mention throughout); but it also has topical significance. In the *khātima* Ibn Funduq warns further against believing false declarations of piety; we may assume that, as a Ḥanafī, he had in mind both the Shāfiʿī-Ashʿarī pietists (against whom Rāvandī also inveighs) and, perhaps, the Sufis, as well as the Karrāmīs. His direct references to Sufism or to Sufis are, moreover, few and largely perfunctory: there is occasional mention of someone building a *ribāṭ* or *khānaqāh*; the notice on Abū Bakr Aḥmad ibn ʿAlī ibn al-Ḥasan al-Mu'addib al-Bayhaqī, known as al-Ustuwā'ī, states that he was a *murīd* of the famous Sufi Abū Sa'īd ibn Abī al-Khayr and tutored his children, and that he disputed with Abū al-Qāsim Qushayrī (1965: 201). There is also an almost total absence of references to the activities of heretics of any stripe (with the exception of the Khārijīs, whose violence in the region is described in detail). What Ibn Funduq rails against consistently is ignorance, especially ignorance that is disguised by false claims to learning and piety – claims that were all too likely to influence unsophisticated Turkish sultans and military leaders.

Ibn Funduq has left a fascinating record of the life of scholars and other individuals both within the Bayhaqī milieu and beyond it. This is social history, with many insights into matters that might appear too trivial, too individualised, to find a place in other types of history. Was Ibn Funduq, motivated by pride in his region, simply recording for posterity the achievements of the scholars of Bayhaq? He himself had had a rather peripatetic career, and had been associated with ruling circles. After studying literature and the sciences in Nishapur and Ḥanafī *fiqh* in Marv, in 521/1117 he returned to Nishapur and married the daughter of the Saljūq governor of Rayy, Shihāb al-Dīn Muḥammad ibn Masʿūd. For the next several years he was in the service of his father-in-law, who in 526/1132 secured for him the post of *qāḍī* of Bayhaq. Resigning after only a brief spell in this post, Ibn Funduq moved to Rayy, where he resided in Shihāb al-Dīn's home and studied mathematics and astrology. In 529/1135 he went to Sarakhs, then attempted (unsuccessfully) to establish himself in Bayhaq, and finally settled down in Nishapur, where he wrote his history. Several personal anecdotes attest to his connections with Sanjar's court, where he enjoyed the favour of the vizier Ṭāhir ibn Fakhr al-Mulk. In one, he mentions attending a *majlis* of Sanjar after the Sultan had returned from Iraq (no date is given, but this must have been Sanjar's second campaign against Sultan Maḥmūd in 525/1131). In his account of the poet Muḥammad ibn ʿAbd al-Razzāq's response to the poem sent by the Byzantine ruler to the caliph al-Muṭīʿ he relates how in 543/1148 Dmitri, the king of Abkhāz, sent an envoy to Sanjar with questions written in Arabic and Syriac (the subject is not stated, but they were presumably on religion); the Sultan instructed Ibn Funduq to answer them in both languages, and copies of these answers 'have travelled all over the world' (1965: 163).[63]

During the years which followed Sanjar's capture by the Ghuzz in 548/1153 Saljūq power in Khurasan rapidly disintegrated, despite Ay Aba's efforts, and the region was continually afflicted by marauding Ghuzz (see Bosworth 1968c: 150–7). Whatever prosperity Sanjar had brought to Khurasan quickly disappeared. Administratively, the region was in chaos, and it must have seemed highly uncertain upon whom rule would ultimately devolve; moreover, the depradations of the Ghuzz were accompanied by widespread civil strife in the towns. Ay Aba was however still in place (even though the *khuṭba* was read in the name of the Khwārazmshāh). The sermon contained in the *khātima* is explicitly stated as substituting for the more usual panegyrics; its style is, moreover, immediate and straightforward and virtually free from rhyming prose. We may recall that Bayhaqī's grandfather admonished both Kundurī and Niẓām al-Mulk; did he see himself in a similar role vis-à-vis some member of Ay Aba's court (or perhaps the ruler himself)? On the other hand, many features of the work (its abundant use of Arabic quotations, for example) suggests that the bulk of it was designed to appeal to a sophisticated audience drawn from the same class of learned men and administrators who figure in its biographical accounts – an audience which would certainly have appreciated his exhortations to revive the patronage of scholarship and letters. Whatever his specific purpose may have been, that it was not merely to record the superiorities of Bayhaq and its inhabitants seems clear.

LATE SALJŪQ HISTORIOGRAPHY: ẒAHĪR AL-DĪN NĪSHĀPŪRĪ

In the last decades of Saljūq rule two writers turned their attention to the history of that dynasty: Ẓahīr al-Dīn Nīshāpūrī (d. 582/1187) in his *Saljūqnāma* (571/1176) and Muḥammad ibn 'Alī Rāvandī in the *Rāḥat al-ṣudūr* (601/1204–5). They recorded the history of the Saljūqs from the time of their appearance in Khurasan up to their already visible decline and, in the case of Rāvandī, the collapse of the Great Saljūqs and the ensuing devastation of their Western domains. Both served at the Saljūq court in Hamadan; according to Rāvandī, they were also kinsmen (1921: 61). Rāvandī based a substantial portion of his work on Nīshāpūrī's, as he himself acknowledged (1921: 64); but he reworked his model substantially, as we shall see.

Nīshāpūrī's *Saljūqnāma* was long believed lost; but in 1953 the text was published by Ismā'īl Afshār.[64] The work's value lies chiefly in its unadorned accounts of events and as forming the basis for

Rāvandī's *Rāḥat al-ṣudūr*; therefore I shall treat it briefly here, returning to it later to point out comparisons between the two works with respect to both their content and their style.

In his brief preface in rhyming prose Nīshāpūrī states that in all of creation there are four classes of God's elect: the cherubim (the angels who enjoy proximity to God's throne), prophets, religious leaders and just rulers. Each group has a specific degree and rank; that of rulers is 'the shepherd of the people and the protector of the Sharī'at, the True Path and the Truth of creation from (all) types of affliction and peril'. Each group also boasts its own adornment: that of the angels is praise and glorification (of God), that of the prophets learning and worship, and that of kings justice and punishment. (The religious leaders do not appear here.) Nīshāpūrī states further: 'The just ruler who profits from the noble (religious) sciences is nobler, with respect to other kings, and closer to the rank of the prophets.' In addition to knowledge of the Sharī'at, of that which is required by piety and belief in God's unicity, and of the pillars of the faith, that knowledge which is particularly necessary for rulers pertains to

> the conduct of kings and the accounts and history of rulers. When (kings) become knowledgeable about these, and read about the conduct and customs of each (ruler), they will choose for their own gain that which is the essence of the moral virtues of past (rulers) and the cause of good repute in this world and reward and forgiveness in the next; they will make (these rulers) their models, and will reject that which reason condemns and the Law despises. (1953: 9–10)

Observing that many books, both compendious and brief, have been written on this subject, Nīshāpūrī continues:

> It is clear that in all the days and all the lives of the rulers of Iraq and Khurasan – Ṭāhirids, Ṣaffārids, Sāmānids, Gharchīs, Daylamids, Ghūrids and Saljūqs – none have been nobler, nor more compassionate towards their subjects, than the House of Saljūq. An abundance of good works have been made manifest and produced during the Saljūq *dawlat*: the revival of the signs of the true faith, the strengthening of the bases of Islam, (the construction of) buildings (such as) mosques, forts, and bridges, and (the provision of) stipends, sustenance and *waqf*s for religious scholars and leaders, ascetics and pious men, such as (was the case) in no (previous) age, the signs of which are evident throughout the lands of Islam; (as are) their efforts in commanding holy war against the infidel and the repulsion and suppression of mischief-makers ... Were the kings of this age to emulate their exemplary conduct, this would result in the

> strengthening of (both) religion and rule and the establishment of the realm on firm foundations. (1953: 10)

After briefly noting the Saljūqs' descent from the eponymous Saljūq ibn Luqmān and his five sons, their tribal affiliation, their noble lineage, their wealth and their well-organised armies, Nīshāpūrī gives a fairly succinct account of their rise to power in the reigns of Maḥmūd and Mas'ūd of Ghazna. Maḥmūd, who had allowed some groups of Turkmens to cross the Oxus to assist him in his fight against the Īlak, sought to enlist their support in the defence of Khurasan during his absences in India. He enquired how much assistance they might be able to provide; the eldest brother, Isrā'īl ibn Saljūq,

> took his bow from his weapons-bearer and, in the pride engendered by wine and the haughtiness of youth, replied, 'Should I send this bow to my people, thirty thousand fighting men will mount up at once.' The Sultan asked, 'And if more should be needed?' Isrā'īl threw down an arrow before Maḥmūd and said, 'Whenever I send this arrow as a sign to my horsemen, ten thousand more men will come.' (1953: 12)

Maḥmūd continued asking in this manner, and the numbers continued to mount. After some thought, he concluded that someone who could command such numbers should not be taken lightly. He entertained Isrā'īl and his party for three more days, and showered them with gifts and honours; then he commanded his amīrs to leave Isrā'īl, his son Qutlumush, and ten of his personal servants with him as his guests and to entertain the remainder of the party themselves. At night, after the wine had taken effect, Isrā'īl and his companions were seized, bound and imprisoned and sent to the fortress of Kalinjar in India. Then Maḥmūd sent robes and gifts to the other sons of Saljūq, along with the following message:

> 'When Isrā'īl came to our court we treated him with great honour. But because he had not seen a kingly court (before), and did not know its manners and protocol, while in a state of drunkenness he offended the honour [that is, the women] of the sultanate. He must be confined for a while, so that they may be free from anxiety about him, and will return to his (position of) honour as soon as possible.' (1953: 12–13)

This alarmed the brothers, who at first considered rebelling; but fearing the consequences, they sent the messenger back with declarations of obedience. Isrā'īl remained imprisoned for seven years, until he was rescued by some of his Turkmens and they set out for Khurasan. They lost their way, and Isrā'īl was recaptured. As his pursuers drew near Isrā'īl said to the Turkmens:

> 'Give up hopes of me. Convey my greetings to my brothers, and

> tell them to strive to gain rule over Khurasan, and to exert themselves; for this king is neither well-born nor honourable ... [lacuna] (and) his rule will not last. Strive to annihilate him, so that his kingdom will fall to you; because it was out of the tyranny and oppression engrained and fixed in his nature that he bound and imprisoned me, who committed no offence.' (1953: 13)

Isrā'īl died in prison, of poison; his son Qutlumush wandered unrecognised through Khurasan for several years, until, hearing of his father's death, with the help of his uncles in the region of Bukhara he sought his revenge. Later, Maḥmūd was persuaded to let the Saljūq Turks cross the Oxus and settle in various regions of Khurasan, where they harrassed the region until they successfully defeated Mas'ūd at Dandānqān.

The contrast between the noble Saljūqs and the unjust and treacherous Maḥmūd provides one justification of their rise to rule (which, as noble Turkmens and brave warriors, they richly deserved in any case). Divine sanction is also invoked. When the brothers Ṭughril and Dā'ūd, having occupied the fort of Dandānqān, were seeking an opportunity to sally forth on a night raid against Mas'ūd, they heard the following Koranic verse recited during the night-time devotions: 'O David [Dā'ūd], We have made you a vice-gerent in the earth' (38: 26). Dā'ūd asked for the verse to be explained, and rejoiced when he was told what it meant. He continued to listen until the reader recited: 'You elevate whom You will and humble whom You will; in Your hand is all good; verily You have power over all things' (3: 26). Again he asked what the verse meant; and when it was explained, both brothers took this as a good omen (1953: 16).

A further legitimating claim is made in the letter the Saljūqs are said to have sent to the caliph al-Qā'im following their victory over Mas'ūd, asking for caliphal recognition. In it they state,

> 'We, your slaves, the family of Saljūq ibn Luqmān, are a group who are obedient to, led by, and supporters of the Abbasid *dawlat*, and obedient to and supportive of Islam and its obligations. Most of the time we have exerted ourselves in making holy war against the enemies of the faith. We had an uncle, who was our leader and chief, named Isrā'īl; Yamīn al-Dawla seized him, although he had committed no crime or treachery or infraction, and sent him to the fort of Kalinjar ... where he was confined for seven years, until he died ... When Maḥmūd died and his son Mas'ūd (ascended) the throne, he did not protect the interests of the kingdom and the welfare of the people, but occupied himself with pleasure and entertainment and

> foolishness and enjoyment. The kingdom [lapsed; lacuna here] from justice, [and the bases of the faith?] were ignored and fell into desuetude; heretics found the opportunity to spread corruption. The notables and famous men of Khurasan asked us to look after them and defend them, and to rebel with their assistance and aid. Mas'ūd's commanders and troops attacked us several times ... Most of the time victory and triumph, which is (to) the benefit of the *dawlat* and a sign of good fortune, were ours. Finally, with [God's] support and His (granting of) victory ... and through the good fortune of the Prophet, we were victorious, triumphed over our enemies, and assumed rule. Thanks to that (divine) gift and blessing ... we have spread justice and equity amongst the people, and have avoided tyranny and injustice. We wish that this affair may proceed according to the principles of the faith and the law of Islam, by the caliph's command.' (1953: 17)

When Ṭughril occupied Nishapur in 429/1037, a caliphal envoy arrived with a letter warning him not to allow his troops to distress the populace or pillage the city. 'In short, that which the Saljūqs had hoped for was granted'; but carrying out the caliph's commands was another matter.

> On the day of the feast they began to attack and plunder Nishapur. Ṭughril Beg said, 'It is the day of the feast; the Muslims should not be distressed.' Chaghrī Beg looked dark, drew his knife (and said): 'If you do not let us plunder, I will stab myself with this knife and kill myself.' Ṭughril Beg expressed humility and benevolence, and satisfied him with the sum of 40,000 dinars. (1953: 18)

The Saljūqs continued to advance, taking various provinces, including Rayy, which Ṭughril made his capital. Having disposed of the last Būyid Amīr of Baghdad, they now became the 'protectors' of the caliphate, whom they restored to Baghdad from his exile in 'Āna following their expulsion of Basāsīrī from the city. The caliph was received into Baghdad by Ṭughril, who was then granted a formal audience. An arrangement was made for the caliph and his household to receive an allowance, and Ṭughril was installed as Sultan. '(And thus) the *dawlat* of the Abbasids was renewed' (1953: 21).

Nīshāpūrī's accounts of the early Saljūqs are brief and unadorned. From the time of Ṭughril's death in 455/1063 there were struggles over the succession to the Iraqi sultanate; the sultans themselves seem to have been incessantly occupied with military expeditions, and never remained long in one place. When Alp Arslān defeated his rival Qutlumush at Isfarā'īn, he sought to kill all the latter's followers, children and kin; but Niẓām al-Mulk advised against this on the grounds that 'killing kinsmen is a sin and unlucky', and suggested they be sent to the border regions to rule there and defend the Dār al-Islām (1953: 22). Thus the Saljūq amīrs and their troops spread through much of Syria and Azerbaijan.

The *Saljūqnāma* ends with the accession of Ṭughril (II) ibn Arslān – a minor 'transferred from the cradle to the throne' – in 571/1176 (1953: 83). Prior to this Nīshāpūrī notes a series of military clashes and the deaths of several important personages which preceded that of Arslān ibn Ṭughril (I), and which clearly signalled for him a decline in the dynasty's fortunes. The first death was that of the Sultan's mother, news of which reached the Sultan in Tabriz as he was returning from a campaign in Armenia (which was itself largely a disaster); Nīshāpūrī comments: 'You would say that the order of that kingdom and the stability of that rule depended on the survival of that noble lady.' A month later the Atabeg Shams al-Dīn Ildigiz died, and was buried in Hamadan. Shortly after, the Sultan himself fell ill, and died in Rajab 571/February 1176 (1953: 82).

Nīshāpūrī concludes with a brief passage on the state of affairs at Ṭughril's accession, the success of his Atabeg Muḥammad ibn Ildigiz Jahān Pahlavān in suppressing revolts by rebellious princes and amīrs, and Ṭughril's winning many over to his side through his generosity and good treatment, 'so that all ... are secure and safe, and pray to God for the continuance of his *dawlat* and the accumulation of blessings to him ... And the outpouring of this affection will require that in a short time all the regions of the world will be under the command of the sultan of Iran' (1953: 83).[65]

AFḌAL AL-DĪN KIRMĀNĪ'S *'IQD AL-ŪLĀ*

Before turning to Rāvandī's *Rāḥat al-ṣudūr*, I will briefly mention another work, written a little over a decade after Nīshāpūrī's and shortly before Rāvandī's was begun: the *Kitāb Iqd al-ūlā lil-mawqif al-a'lā* of Afḍal al-Dīn Aḥmad ibn Ḥāmid Kirmānī, composed in 584/1189 and dedicated to the Ghuzz conqueror of Kirman Malik Dīnār (582–91/1186–95).[66] Since this work is, strictly speaking, outside the geographical limits of this study, I will not deal with it at length; but as it provides an outstanding example of the ornate chancery style, seen also in the works of Rāvandī and Jarbādhqānī, it is of interest to consider it briefly.

Kirmānī was a boon companion of the Saljūq ruler of Kirman Malik Ṭughril Shāh (d. 558/1162) and his son Malik Arslān Shāh (killed 572/1176), and a *munshī* (scribe) of the Atabeg Muḥammad Buzqush (d. 592/1196). (The date of Malik Ṭughril's death is from

Kirmānī [1932: 8]; the *EI*² entry [art. 'Kirmān. History'] gives it as 565/1170.) Forced to leave Kirman due to the famine of 577/1181, Afḍal al-Dīn eventually ended up in Yazd, but returned to join Malik Dīnār's court, where he became secretary to the chamberlain (*vakīl-i dār*) Jamāl al-Dīn and to the vizier Qavām al-Dīn (see 1932: 16); they and the leader of the religious scholars, Malik al-ʿUlamā Nūr al-Dīn, encouraged him to write the *ʿIqd al-ūlā*. Kirmānī seems to have fallen out of favour after Malik Dīnār's death; he died around 615/1218 (see *EIr*, art. 'Afżīal al-Dīn Kirmānī').

Kirmānī provides us a detailed statement of why he wrote his book. In 'compiling these sections and ordering these principles' he envisioned several benefits: (1) to urge emulation of the noble virtues exemplified by the stories and accounts therein; (2) to furnish object lessons to the wise; (3) to express gratitude for Malik Dīnār's having brought an end to Kirman's period of trial and ushered in 'the season of ease'; (4) to record the achievements of the ruler who has transformed once-ruined Kirman into a Paradise, 'for to neglect and leave unrecorded the time of that *dawlat* would constitute sheer ingratitude and ignorance of the good and evil of Fate's happenings'; and (5) as a gift to Malik Dīnār on entering the service of his court.

> When I wished to prepare myself for service to Malik Dīnār, and to kiss the most noble carpet (of his court), I did not – as is the rule for servants who wait upon the courts of kings – have suitable gifts and agreeable rarities; for the affliction of exile and separation from my homeland, with (the exigencies of) a large family, and the changes in (my) circumstances, had left nothing remaining to me. So I followed the custom of Mutanabbī –
>
> You have no horses to give her, and no money:
> Then let speech aid you, if your circumstances do not –
>
> and thought: 'The gift of (religious) scholars is prayer, and that of poets is praise. No service to this *dawlat* is greater than that of composing a history of its royal sovereign's battles and his successive conquests, and to provide a record thereof so that the fame of this *dawlat* will survive the passage of time and its name be immortalised on the pages of Time's book; for the survival of (one's) name is a second life, and an elegant narrative a life recommenced. (1932: 3–5)

Concluding this section, he states that he has made 'the exordium [*tashbīb*] of these chapters, and the opening of the discourse, (the period) from the end of the Saljūq *dawlat*, the days of conquests, and the causes of the weakness of the kingdom of Kirman' (1932: 5).

Kirmānī now outlines the contents of his work: it will contain (1) an account of the last days of the Saljūqs and the ensuing period of disturbance (*fatrat*) in Kirman; (2) the arrival of the 'victorious royal banners' of Malik Dīnār, and a description of the ruler's virtues; (3) a section containing an exhortation to justice, a description of the ethics of kings, and information on the characteristics of Kirman and some of its history; (4) praise of the vizier Ṣāḥib Qavām al-Dīn, his virtues, his family and his forebears; and (5) a description of the author's circumstances and the reversals of fortune that have afflicted him (1932: 6). He observes that the calamities which were to afflict Kirman were signalled by the stars: the seventh conjunction of all the planets in Aries, in trine, occurred in 557/1161, and was followed by a total eclipse in 557/1162; the astrologers predicted that Kirman would be conquered by 'one who comes from the East' (1932: 7).

In Farvardīn 558/March 1162 Malik Ṭughril died in Jiruft; the 'signs of peace vanished and the signs of Judgement Day appeared' (1932: 8). The Turks sacked the city; the Atabeg Mu'ayyid al-Dīn Rayḥān restored order and set Ṭughril's third son, Bahrāmshāh, on the throne. Now began a long period of struggle between Ṭughril's three sons, a period of civil strife (*fitna*) that was to last for twenty years, marked by sieges and famines in which many perished. The author enumerates the 'bad principles, blameworthy practices and corrupt laws' from which Kirman suffered – cruel punishments and imprisonments, small slips punished by bloodshed, Muslims killed for the slightest crime, affairs in the hands of incompetent officials – and complains that control of the affairs of government was no longer in the hands of kings but in those of atabegs and Turks of low origins, with ideas above their station. Oaths and covenants were no longer respected, and everyone knew that the *dawlat* was in decline; but now (he adds), since those incompetents are gone, there is hope for recovery (1932: 13–16).

The astrologers agreed that when the seventh conjunction passed and the eighth took place, with the seven planets aligned in Libra, the world would be destroyed by a great windstorm, and Kirman would be in the worst state because its sign (*ṭāliʿ*) is Libra.[67] Afḍal al-Dīn corresponded with one Jalāl al-Dīn Kirmānī, a notable at Sanjar's court in Khurasan, who sent him a document written by Khvāja Farīd (al-Dīn) Nasawī (known as Kātib Khurāsānī) stating the falsehood of the prediction, and interpreting it figuratively: the 'tempest' referred to great changes in the world's circumstances and to the transfer (*intiqāl*) of kingdoms, and the prediction indicated that after the second conjunction there would be a new group in power. 'And that scholar's words were an eloquent omen and a true inspiration; and what other astrologers said – that Kirman would be the most ruined – turned out just the opposite. For the conjunction and coming together (of the planets) was the cause of Kirman's prosperity and the end of the weakness which had afflicted that kingdom' (1932: 17–18). This prosperity was the result of Malik Dīnār's takeover of Kirman, seen as no less than the result of divine providence.

We need not go into the details of Malik Dīnār's rule of Kirman, nor of the author's hyperbolic praises of him. Two features of Kirmānī's style, however, deserve consideration. First, it exemplifies the figured chancery style, employing rhyming prose, with frequent interpolations: Koranic verses, Prophetic traditions, wise sayings and, especially, poetry (including panegyrics on Malik Dīnār written by Kirmānī himself). In this, it anticipates Rāvandī's style, although it is even more ornamental. The second feature (not seen to any great extent in Rāvandī, and more reminiscent of ʿUtbī) is the use of descriptive passages written in the figured style. One example will suffice; it introduces an account of one of Malik Dīnār's many victories.

> When the cold weather, the intense cold of *zamharīr*, the season that makes the poor man fear, had passed, and the season of pleasant temperateness, (that of) spring, the world's ornament, arrived, spreading brocades of green on the dust-covered scene, and making verdant the earth's youthful cheeks, news reached the sublime court ... of a fort between Bam and Bardsīr, called Diz Āshūl. In that fort had gathered a group of thieves and ruffians, murderers and worthless ones, who were occupied with brigandry and the molestation of travellers. (1932: 45)

Such figured descriptive passages will scarcely be seen again until nearly a century later, with Juvaynī. Their effect is to deflect attention away from the exploits of Malik Dīnār (whom they ostensibly laud) to the language in which that praise is expressed. I shall have more to say on this point in the Conclusion; but I will note here that, did we not know better, we might think (following Luther [1990]) that such display was designed to obtain the author a position at court. In fact, he already had such a position, and the style is appropriate to the royal 'gift' he is presenting to the ruler as a demonstration of his gratitude; but one suspects that it is less the ruler's name that is meant to be remembered than the writer's, and that the disjunction between the ornate style and the often catastrophic events it records is further intended to drive home the ethical message of the *ʿIqd*: the exemplary tale of the vicissitudes of Time.

MUḤAMMAD IBN ʿALĪ RĀVANDĪ'S *RĀḤAT AL-ṢUDŪR*

The *Rāḥat al-ṣudūr wa-āyat al-surūr* ('Ease for Breasts and Marvel of Happiness') has often been harshly treated. As Saljūq history, it is judged to be derivative and unreliable; stylistically, it is considered excessively rhetorical and encumbered with irrelevant interpolations. This was the opinion of Muḥammad Iqbāl, who published the text in 1921.[68] And indeed, for a historical work the *Rāḥat al-ṣudūr* seems a very mixed bag, as it omits important events, adds episodes which sometimes defy credibility, is packed with quotations of all sorts, and contains a number of chapters on non-historical topics which form a sort of appendix to the history.

Was Rāvandī, as Ismā'īl Afshār suggests, a semi-literate, plagiarising hack who wrote his work to flatter a minor Saljūq sultan, the ruler of Konya Ghiyāth al-Dīn Kaykhusraw (Nīshāpūrī 1953: 6)? Did he (as Luther offered) write the work in order to display his rhetorical skills and obtain a post at that ruler's court (1990: 95)? Rāvandī himself provides an account of his life and of how he came to write the book. A native of Ravand (near Kashan), after his father's death he was raised by an uncle, Tāj al-Dīn Aḥmad, a scholar who was patronised by Ṭughril ibn Arslān's Atabeg Jamāl al-Dīn Ay Aba in Hamadan. (This Ay Aba – no relation to Mu'ayyid Ay Aba the governor of Khurasan – is the same atabeg whom Jarbādhqānī praises in his translation of 'Utbī; see further below.) Between 570/1174 and 580/1184 Rāvandī visited the major cities of Iraq and acquired the skills of calligraphy, gilding and bookbinding, by which he earned his livelihood, as well as studying other sciences. In 577/1181 Ṭughril appointed another of Rāvandī's uncles, Zayn al-Dīn Maḥmūd Kāshī, to teach him calligraphy; he then decided to produce a copy of the Koran in his own hand, and assembled illuminators and gilders to decorate it. Rāvandī was introduced into Ṭughril's court at Hamadan to assist in this project (1921: 39–44).

In 580/1184 Ṭughril expressed the desire for a collection of poetry. This was compiled by Zayn al-Dīn Maḥmūd and illustrated 'with portraits of each poet, followed by poetry and some humorous anecdotes'. Ṭughril was pleased with the work; and, inspired by this example, Rāvandī decided 'to choose some selections of poetry and prose and compile them into a collection so that (men) might learn from them.' He was forced to abandon his project by the disturbances in Iraq which followed Ṭughril's death in 590/1194, and forsook worldly pursuits to devote himself to study of the religious sciences. 'Then ... in 599 [1202] (I thought), that since eternal fame comes from compiling books, I too would make a compilation, and in accordance with my own ability arrange a book that time's long extent would not wear down and which would endure till Resurrection' (1921: 62).[69] In 585/1189 Rāvandī accompanied Zayn al-Dīn Maḥmūd on a diplomatic mission to the ruler of Mazandaran; there he fell ill, and was forced to remain for some time. Shortly after his return (in 586/

1190) to his home town of Ravand, he learned that Ṭughril had been seized and imprisoned by the Atabeg Qizil Arslān; although he was freed in 588/1192, the remainder of his reign was unstable, and he was killed in battle against the Khwārazmshāh outside Rayy in 590/1194. The book was finally completed around 601/1204–5 and dedicated to the Saljūq ruler of Konya, Kaykhusraw ibn Qilij Arslān.

The *Rāḥat al-ṣudūr* was originally intended as an edifying compilation, not, specifically, as a history. This accounts for many of the omissions or revisions of Nīshāpūrī's accounts; for this is, explicitly, history as edification. Rāvandī seems to have intended to write a separate historical work: describing the flourishing intellectual life at Ṭughril's court, he states, 'If the history of that house and the wonders of that realm were to be written, they would be more than ten *Shāhnāma*s and *Iskandarnāma*s,' and asserts that should he live he will 'write the history of Ṭughril's reign, and make of it a book in verse and prose. But in this compilation I have bound myself to follow several conditions, and were I to begin [to tell the details of Ṭughril's reign] (its) purpose would be lost' (1921: 44). Rāvandī's outline of the book illustrates the diversity of its contents. It will contain praise of God, His prophets, the *Ahl-i Bayt* and other religious figures, and the *'ulamā*; praise of Sultan Kaykhusraw; a brief history of the Saljūqs, including mention of the poets who recited in their courts, each reign ending with praise of Sultan Kaykhusraw; additional chapters on the etiquette of the *nadīm*, wine, chess and backgammon, horsemanship and hunting, court protocol, battle and feasting, calligraphy, and other useful subjects, and a final chapter containing anecdotes and jests, which was never written.

While the historical section of the *Rāḥat al-ṣudūr*, and in particular the history of the Saljūqs prior to Ṭughril II, is drawn, often verbatim, from Nīshāpūrī's *Saljūqnāma*, Rāvandī's elaborate rhetorical style signals a difference in purpose between his work and that of his predecessor. This is immediately apparent in the lengthy exordium, which begins with a doxology in verse of which these are the opening lines:

> Praise be to God Who made the world,
> Of Nīsān and of spring the Lord;
> Lord of Tammūz and of the fall;
> Lord of the world's creation all.
>
> (1921: 1)

It is not at all customary to introduce a history with verses; this opening resembles rather that of *masnavī*s such as Sanā'ī's *Ḥadīqat al-ḥaqīqa* or the verse romances of Rāvandī's contemporary Niẓāmī of Ganja. The verse passage goes on to introduce themes important to the work as a whole: that of the revolutions of time; and that of the concepts of reason and faith as twin tools for mankind's success in this world and salvation in the next.

The exordium continues with expressions of gratitude to God and praise of Him; praise of the prophets, especially Muḥammad; praise of the Prophet's Companions and Successors and of the 'leaders of the faith'. Of these, the caliph ʿUmar ibn al-Khaṭṭāb receives special mention: he

> bound the Persians to the Arabs and uprooted polytheism from the earth, crushed the palace of Kisrā, seized the palace of Caesar, and dispersed the Khān-i Khāqān and his kingdom. With swords that hewed and spears that flew and armies that no number knew he obliterated the kings of Persia ... and set up the *minbar* in place of the throne ... He shattered the law of the [Christian] bell, joined Khurasan to Iraq as well, and set up the *minbar*s of Islam in Rūm, Rūs, and Azerbaijan, throughout Iraq and Khurasan, to the borders of Turkistan ... (1921: 10)

Praise of ʿUmar and his successors, ʿUthmān and ʿAlī, is followed by that of the 'leaders of the faith', chief among them Abū Ḥanīfa. Here Rāvandī both criticises the disputes between Ḥanafīs and Shāfiʿīs and echoes (though with even greater vehemence) Ibn Funduq's castigations of ignorance in the garb of piety.

> There is no greater fraud than that, after a man has studied the Sharīʿat, the arts of language, Ḥadīth, history and the accounts of the precedessors, Arab and Persian, when he ascends the *minbar* the lowest ignorant foe or heedless old woman should tell him that he knows nothing; or that when a jurist has spent twenty years learning the sciences of disputation, and has reached the point where he can comment on a (legal) question in a gathering, someone who just entered the *madrasa* a month earlier can say that he has declared (on the question) wrongly. (1921: 13–14)

The final section of praise is devoted to the Saljūq Turks – devout Ḥanafīs who support the true faith with the sword – and to Sultan Kaykhusraw; it is followed by a lengthy list in Arabic of the titles of the Saljūq sultans, and concludes with more praise of the Sultan which combines panegyric verses by various poets into a lengthy encomium, ending with a *qaṣīda* by the author.

A lengthy quotation from the *Shāhnāma* forms the transition to the next section, which moves from praise of Kaykhusraw to that of the Saljūqs.[70] Kaykhusraw is hailed as 'the fruit of the tree of Saljūq', whose 'root is the strengthening and propagation of the faith and whose fruit' is good works. Because of the Saljūqs' love of learning and patronage of the *'ulamā*, throughout their domains scholars appeared who wrote many books on the religious sciences. Through their labours, 'the root of the faith became firmly implanted in (men's) hearts, so that the ambitions of those of corrupt belief were cut off, and, willy-nilly, the philosophers and adherents of abrogated faiths and believers in metempsychosis and materialists all bowed to the commands of the Sharī'at and the *muftī*s of Muḥammad's community' (1921: 29–30). Thus the kingdom prospered, amīrs and populace were at ease, the soldiers held correct beliefs, and none of the tyranny and oppression seen in these days was present then.

A verse introduces the next section, which contrasts the idealised past with the corrupt present, in which abuse of the populace and fiscal and administrative corruption have led to immorality and to the disgrace of the *'ulamā*:

> A king who robs the people of their wealth
> weakens the wall and makes the roof to fall.
> (1921: 30)

While Rāvandī's praise of the Saljūqs' good works is (loosely) based on Nīshāpūrī, this second section, which finds no parallel in the latter's work, details the causes of 'the ruination of the world' (1921: 30): unfounded and malicious accusations against religious leaders; envy and prejudice amongst them themselves; the malign influence of 'Rāfiḍīs and Ash'arīs' on the soldiery, who pretended to the sultans that their oppressive ways were in fact a means to surplus revenue; extortions and bloodshed committed by greedy officials and troops, who fostered wineshops, sodomy, fornication and other things forbidden by the Law. The passage, as it moves from past to present tense, describes not only past but present conditions. Rāvandī recounts how, in 598/1201–2, 'throughout Iraq books of learning and history and Korans were weighed in the scales and sold' cheaply; 'the pen of tyranny and extortion was drawn against the *'ulamā*, the mosques and the *madrasa*s, and just as they take the poll-tax from the Jews they demanded money from the *'ulamā* in the *madrasa*s. Consequently, the kingdom collapsed' (1921: 33). Now all the notables of Iraq are in exile and the populace reduced to misery; Rāvandī exhorts Sultan Kaykhusraw to 'revive the *dawlat* of the Saljūqs and uproot tyranny from the world' (1921: 38).

The following chapter includes the account of the author's life and circumstances; the next, on the book's composition, introduces the motifs of the writer's acquisition of fame and good repute through his works, of the necessity of fame for all, and of the fame of kings, acquired through pious works and through poetry composed in their praise. This is followed by the table of contents, more praise of Sultan

Kaykhusraw and, finally, a curse on anyone who might alter one word of the book:

> For this book has met with the favour and approval of the Pole of the World; and a hint to the noble is sufficient ... [I] have written ... these histories ... so that the victorious sultan Kaykhusraw (may God make his house endure!) may read them, and know that the adornment of the angels is praise and glorification (of God), that of the prophets learning and worship, and the adornment of kings justice and discipline. (1921: 64)

Here Rāvandī rejoins Nīshāpūrī; for while he does not repeat Nīshāpūrī's statement that kings who possess religious knowledge are nobler than others, he does include that on the value of history in providing models of kingly conduct, though he does not mention the corollary: that kings also learn from such examples what to avoid. He has written down these histories, he states,

> so that the victorious Sultan Ghiyāth al-Dīn may read them; that they may be viewed kindly and become honoured by his most noble regard and receive his praise and approval; and that he may contemplate how, from all those excellent endeavours, and from that wealth and pelf, treasure stores and buried hoards, precious gems, horses and weapons, nothing has remained except the good deeds [of those kings]. (1921: 67)

Now begins the historical section; but the history proper – that of the Saljūqs – is further delayed by a lengthy excursus on justice ('I begin with justice, for it is the custom of the just sovereign Ghiyāth al-Dīn' [1921: 68]). This section incorporates numerous quotations and anecdotes relating to justice and other kingly virtues, and concludes with a lengthy passage from Niẓāmi Ganjavī's *Khusraw u Shīrīn* ('Hurmizd's Punishment of Khusraw') which constitutes the final exemplary tale. Praise of Sultan Kaykhusraw, 'heir to the Saljūq *dawlat*' ('May God help him to revive these customs, to put down the enmity between Ḥanafīs and Shāfi'īs ... and to repair the endowments and *madrasa*s (built by) his ancestors, who attained rule because of their zeal for the faith and their patronage of the *'ulamā'* (1921: 84), is followed by a list of the Saljūq sultans, after which the historical section begins, where Nīshāpūrī's did, with the Saljūqs' lineage and their rise to power.

Rāvandī presents the Saljūqs as a noble band of warriors whose migration to Khurasan was motivated by their desire 'to avoid the Abode of Unbelief and to draw near the House of Islam, to make pilgrimage to the Ka'ba and frequent the leaders of religion' (1921: 86; other sources record correspondence between the Saljūqs and the caliph declaring such to be their intent [see Makdisi 1963: 80, 84, 85–6]).

This introduces a new element into Nīshāpūrī's account, whose broad outlines Rāvandī follows, while omitting some elements, adding others and embroidering upon others. For example: Isrā'īl ibn Saljūq, facing recapture, exhorts his followers not to lose hope and to continue fighting Maḥmūd, 'for this ruler is the offspring of a slave; he has no lineage, and is treacherous; he will not retain rule, and it will fall into your hands' (1921: 91). Rāvandī includes an account (as Nīshāpūrī did not) of Mas'ūd's campaign in Jurjan, which so weakened his soldiers that they could not withstand the Saljūqs. Ṭughril's piety and good works, which began from the commencement of his rule (dated to his occupation of Nishapur in 429/1037), are emphasised.

Here an account is inserted which is not in Nīshāpūrī, and which is clearly apocryphal. When Ṭughril came to Hamadan he encountered three Sufi *pīr*s, Bābā Ṭāhir, Bābā Ja'far and Shaykh Ḥamshā (Ḥamshād), who were standing at the city gates.

> Ṭughril saw them; he stopped the procession of his troops, dismounted, and, with his vizier Abū Naṣr al-Kundurī, went forward to them and kissed their hands. Bābā Ṭāhir appeared somewhat distraught; he said to him, 'Turk! How will you act towards God's creatures?' The Sultan replied, 'As you command.' Bābā (Ṭāhir) said: 'Do as God commands: "Verily God commands justice and benevolence [Koran 16: 96]".' The Sultan wept and said, 'I shall do so'; Bābā (Ṭāhir) took his hand and said, 'You have accepted (this) from me?' The Sultan replied, 'Yes.' Bābā (Ṭāhir) wore on his finger the top of a broken pitcher which he had used for his ablutions for years; he took it off, placed it on the Sultan's finger and said, 'Thus I have placed rule of the world in your hands; be just.' The Sultan always kept that (ring) among his amulets, and when a battle was near he would put it on his finger. Such was the purity of his belief. (1921: 99)

This virtual investiture by a pious *pīr* sets the ultimate seal on Saljūq legitimacy. Having, so to speak, topped Nīshāpūrī in respect to divine support for the Saljūqs, Rāvandī omits from his own account the episode involving Dā'ūd and Chaghrī in the fort of Dandānqān.[71] Investiture by a holy man, at the gates of what would become one of the principal centres of Saljūq rule, establishes the divine endorsement of their temporal rule.

Another significant addition comes in the account of how, after their victory at Dandānqān, the Saljūq brothers swore to end their internal dissension and rivalry and unite against their enemies. Nīshāpūrī's account is brief; Rāvandī, however, elaborates:

> I heard that Ṭughril Beg gave an arrow to his brother and said, 'Break it.' He heeded his words and broke it. (Then Ṭughril) gave him two together, and he did the same. He gave him three, and he broke them with difficulty. When they reached four, it was impossible to break them. Ṭughril Beg said, 'We are just like this: as long as we are separate, the least person will attempt to break us, but when united no one can conquer us. If there is dissension among us the world will not be conquered, the enemy will overpower us, and rule will pass from our hands.' (1921: 102)

This episode balances that of Isrā'īl's demonstration of the numbers he could call upon, which so disquieted Maḥmūd; thus the Saljūqs' rise and their success against the Ghaznavids are neatly framed. It also anticipates their decline and the fragmentation of their rule because of the disunity arising from conflicts and rivalries amongst different members of the house. Thus does Rāvandī introduce another of the recurrent themes of his history.

These early accounts, carefully structured and employing a rhetorically sophisticated style, constitute not merely a record of events in the past, but a multilayered evocation of that past both to explain the present and to provide admonition with respect to the future. This is clearly seen in the highly schematic treatment of Alp Arslān's reign, which establishes a structural pattern that Rāvandī will follow, and expand upon, in his accounts of later rulers. (For a detailed analysis see Meisami 1994: 193–5.) The rhetorical high point of this account, and the first event recorded, is the story of the murder of the vizier Abū Naṣr Kundurī. Rāvandī omits Nīshāpūrī's comment that it was because of the vizier's 'good judgement, sagacity, intelligence and perception' that Niẓām al-Mulk became his mortal enemy, and because of his own fear of his 'competence, knowledge, foresight and acuteness' that he instigated his murder (1953: 23). Kundurī's death scene, with its exemplary and allusive overtones, is virtually identical in both accounts, except for Rāvandī's interpolations.

After Ṭughril Beg's death, Alp Arslān arrested Kundurī and gave the vizierate to Niẓām al-Mulk. Somewhat later he ordered Kundurī killed, and

> Niẓām al-Mulk was complicit in this. 'When you seek counsel from the unwise, he will choose for you only lies.' … I heard that when the assassin came into his presence, (Kundurī) asked for a brief respite. He performed his ablutions, prayed two *rak'ats* of prayer, and then made (the assassin) swear, 'When you have carried out the king's command, take a message from me to the Sultan, and another to the vizier. Tell the Sultan: What an auspicious service was my service to you [the Saljūqs]:

> your uncle gave me this world, so that I governed it, and you have given me the next world, and provided me with martyrdom. Thus through serving you I have gained both this world and the next. And tell the vizier: You have introduced an evil innovation and a foul principle into this world by killing a vizier; I hope that you will see this custom once again with respect to yourself and your descendants.' Proverb: 'He who loves himself will avoid sins; and he who loves his son will be merciful to orphans.' (1921: 117–8)

Whereas Nīshāpūrī concludes his account of the murder succinctly – 'From that time onward no vizier died a natural death' (1953: 24) – Rāvandī ends with a long composite quotation from the *Shāhnāma* on the transience and trickery of this world, which both sums up the passage and marks its conclusion and the transition to the next episode: the battle of Malazgird.[72]

Here, again, Rāvandī omits both Nīshāpūrī's statement that the Muslims, greatly outnumbered, were in real danger of losing to the Byzantines, and his account of the Byzantines' capture of the Sultan (unrecognised by them), along with a hundred of his horsemen, while he was hunting; his safe return was engineered by the wily Niẓām al-Mulk (Nīshāpūrī 1953: 24–5). Other significant details in the remainder of this section vary considerably; and Alp Arslān's later conquests, recorded by Nīshāpūrī, are ignored by Rāvandī. Whereas Nīshāpūrī shows some concern for political motivation, Rāvandī's interest in the early Saljūqs is largely limited to how certain events in their reigns foreshadow the dynasty's ultimate decline. Thus for example the 'evil innovation' (*bid'at*) introduced by Niẓām al-Mulk would haunt the Saljūqs throughout their rule.

In imposing a coherent and meaningful structure upon Nīshāpūrī's narrative, and in his use of interpolations, Rāvandī follows the 'rhetoric of the secretaries' and the principles of *faṣl* and *waṣl*, dividing his account into seven carefully balanced segments (*fuṣūl*), for which quotations provide introductions, transitions and conclusions. Rāvandī's use of interpolations has been harshly judged: Iqbāl considered that 'the beauty of the book is to a great extent marred by a large amount of extraneous matter' (1921: xxi).[73] Afshār concurred: 'In the text of the history, without the most remote aptness or precedent or connection with the discourse, and mostly by violence, are packed [interpolated materials] which usually completely break the thread of the history and make the book's reader thoroughly fed up with the introduction of all this padding and excess material' (Nīshāpūrī 1953: 6). Luther disagreed, arguing that the 'extraneous matter' in the *Rāḥat al-ṣudūr* is not, in fact, extraneous,

> at least not from the author's point of view. It is all of a piece, a package of what he must have regarded as elegant and entertaining matter, a display of his eloquence and learning which was designed … to get him a position with … Ghiyās̱ al-Dīn Kay Khusraw. Doubtless, in his view, the elaborate exordium, which must have cost him so much effort, was worth far more than the skeletal history of the Saljūqs which he took mostly from [Nīshāpūrī]. (1990: 95)

Here, perhaps, Luther did not go far enough. Over and above Rāvandī's pragmatic purpose in writing the book (of which he himself leaves us in no doubt) there is another, ethical purpose; and the rhetorical style serves to make, and to mark, moral points.

In the accounts of other early rulers, which follow and expand upon the basic pattern, the nature of the interpolations gradually changes, as they take on topical as well as general significance. In the account of Barkyāruq's troubled reign, which follows Nīshāpūrī almost verbatim, the quotations emphasise the vicissitudes of fate and the treacherous nature of this world. 'Sultan Barkyāruq was a ruler of good disposition and handsome appearance, gentle and forgiving. "He who is magnanimous is forbearing; he who is noble is benevolent." … In his lifetime there were many calamities, and ups and downs without number' (1921: 139). These 'ups and downs' began when Malikshāh's widow Turkān Khātūn asked the caliph al-Muqtadī to appoint her son Maḥmūd sultan. The caliph declined, saying Maḥmūd was too young. A quotation from the *Shāhnāma* sets the scene for what will follow: dwelling on the transience of this world, its concluding lines also point to topical concerns:

> In times of joy, don't plant a tree
> that will bear poisoned fruit one day.
> There are such trees that, nurtured, give
> but baneful fruit and bitter leaves.
>
> (1921: 140)

Other proverbs and verses advert to what might be called the ethical thematics of this chapter. These include the enormous expenditures of wealth by Turkān Khātūn and her associates in securing Maḥmūd's accession ('He who holds money in disdain many hopes will entertain'; 'He who expends wealth gains much praise; he who squanders his dignity is deemed a slave' [1921: 141]), contrasted with that expended on Barkyāruq's coronation in Rayy ('The best wealth is that which satisfies needs and builds noble deeds'); the consequences of hasty action, seen for example in Barkyāruq's flight to Isfahan when threatened by the revolt of his uncle Tutush ('He who rides in haste will his efforts waste' [1921: 142]), and his surrender to Maḥmūd in Isfahan, after Turkān Khātūn's death in 487/1094, when he was seized and imprisoned ('A king highhanded in his policy and views is ruled by the swords of opponents and foes'). When Maḥmūd died of smallpox, Barkyāruq was released and placed on the throne; a quotation from the *Shāhnāma* dwells on the fickleness of this world. Barkyāruq too was afflicted by smallpox, but recovered, and in 488/1095 defeated Tutush outside Hamadan. (Neither Nīshāpūrī nor Rāvandī tells us this; see Ibn al-Athīr 1965, 10: 245; Bundārī 1889: 85.) In 489/1096 he set off for Khurasan to fight his maternal uncle Arslān Arghūn ('He who has recourse to judgement will rule; but he who merely endures things will fall'); but before he reached him Arslān Arghūn had been stabbed and killed by a page in Marv, 'his blood spilled without a sword' (1921: 143–4).

Rāvandī then takes up the account of Unur's (Öner) revolt, instigated by Barkyāruq's vizier Mu'ayyid al-Mulk 'Ubayd Allāh ibn Niẓām al-Mulk ('He who appoints an incompetent vizier endangers his rule, and he who trusts one who is untrustworthy assists in his own downfall').[74] When Unur was murdered by a Bāṭinī, Mu'ayyid al-Mulk fled to Muḥammad ibn Malikshāh in Ganja and urged him to claim the throne. A group of amīrs revolted against Barkyāruq, demanding the head of his *mustawfī* Majd al-Mulk Abū al-Faḍl Qummī (Balāsānī). Majd al-Mulk took refuge in Barkyāruq's tent, and the latter refused to give him up ('He who deviates from the wise man's advice will be consumed by his enemy's deceit'); but he was dragged out and torn limb from limb. Barkyāruq fled towards Rayy with a few personal slaves; Muḥammad proclaimed himself Sultan in Hamadan, with Mu'ayyid al-Mulk as vizier. In 494/1101 Barkyāruq defeated Muḥammad and captured Mu'ayyid al-Mulk, who persuaded him to restore him to office, where he committed numerous abuses ('Beware of slips of the tongue and you will be safe from the power of the sultan'); but one day the Sultan overheard criticism of him ('The blow of the tongue is more feared than that of the spear'), realised his error and executed the vizier. 'Barkyāruq and Muḥammad fought five battles' Rāvandī concludes; 'four times the victory went to Barkyāruq, but the last time Muḥammad captured Barkyāruq' (1921: 148).

In the chapter on Barkyāruq the tenor of the interpolations is both general (the vicissitudes of life, the fickleness of this world) and topical (the expenditure of wealth on base ends, the treachery of officials). By contrast, those in that on Muḥammad ibn Malikshāh are more brief and cover more varied topics: praise of piety, warnings against bad counsel and base companions, an exhortion to beware the guidance of the blind (1921: 156; this intervenes between a general account of the increase in the activities of the heretics [*malāḥida*] and the story of atrocities perpetrated by a blind Assassin in Isfahan), and so on. As we proceed to more recent rulers, there is a general decrease in interpolations, along with an increasing attention to their topicality; here too we find a greater occurence of quotations from Niẓāmi, and especially from *Khusraw u Shīrīn*, deployed in ways that differ from the use of other materials, as many are incorporated (with appropriate modification) into the narrative itself.[75] For example, in describing the caliph al-Qā'im's welcome of Ṭughril into Baghdad, Rāvandī inserts a passage from 'Khusraw's Arrival at the Court of Mahīn Bānū', substituting, in the opening line, 'the caliph' for Niẓāmi's 'Mahīn Bānū':

When the caliph of that arrival learned,
he sped in royal fashion to attend.
(1921: 106)

Where Mahīn Bānū set a seat for Khusraw 'beneath the throne', the caliph sets one for Ṭughril 'in the (caliphal) sanctuary'; where Khusraw asked after Mahīn Bānū's health, the caliph enquires after Ṭughril's; and where Khusraw apologised for any inconvenience to Mahīn Bānū, the caliph hopes that Ṭughril will find his reception to his liking. Like Mahīn Bānū with Khusraw, the caliph falls short of no service to the Saljūq prince.

Such interpolations become more frequent in the reigns of later rulers, and especially in those of Arslān ibn Ṭughril and Ṭughril ibn Arslān. The account of Arslān's defeat of the ruler of Abkhāz contains a passage from the lengthy section on 'Khusraw's Battle With Bahrām [Chūbīn]' (1921: 287–8), in which the Turks, who in Niẓāmi were Bahrām's supporters and thus on the losing side, become the Saljūq victors. That of Ṭughril's return to Hamadan in 583/1187 concludes with a lengthy passage (1921: 343; from 'Khusraw's Meeting With Shīrīn') completely incorporated into the narrative, as Ṭughril is greeted by officials and generals rendering him homage:

From every side new armies ever came,
and ranged themselves in lines around the king.
When they about the mountainside were massed,
the earth groaned to the Ox beneath their weight.

The people of Hamadan gave thanks from the depths of their hearts, and rejoiced. A heavy snow was falling; the Sultan turned towards the city, and Amīr Sayyid Fakhr al-Dīn 'Alā' al-Dawla [the *ra'īs*] paid him homage and offered him the palace of the *riyāsat* to alight in.

'O king, O lord,' to the sultan he said,
'I, and a thousand like me, are your slaves.'

A curious example comes towards the end of the lengthy description of the civil strife in Iraq following Ṭughril's death. The episode in question concerns the former *mamlūk* of Muḥammad Jahān Pahlavān, Nūr al-Dīn Kukja (Gökce), who, menaced by his opponents, seized control of Hamadan.

> Kukja knew that he would have to fight; he made a few raids, then came to Hamadan.
>
> He bade a crier proclaim throughout the land,
> 'Woe unto those who'd raise a violent hand
> 'Gainst others. Should a horse invade a field
> 'Or someone fruit from the fruit-grower steal;
> 'Or look upon the face of one forbidden;
> 'Install a Turkish slave for acts of sin:
> 'I will mete out that punishment that's fit.'
> He swore a mighty oath to this effect.
>
> He caught the people napping, and in this way acquired much wealth ... (1921: 392; on Kukja see further below)

In *Khusraw u Shīrīn* these lines precede the story of Hurmizd's punishment of Khusraw – the passage which concludes Rāvandī's excursus on justice. As such, they form an ironic cap to the fortunes of the Saljūqs, and complete the picture of decline and fall presented in the exordium. What might have been averted (for surely that is the message of the concluding part of the exordium) has come to pass.

Whereas Rāvandī's quotations from the *Shāhnāma* function primarily as examples of universal wisdom, those from *Khusraw u Shīrīn* seem to evoke living history. Is this an acknowledgement of the fact that *Khusraw u Shīrīn*, written in Rāvandī's own time and extolling both Ṭughril and Muḥammad Jahān Pahlavān, is intimately linked with both their history and his? This contrast parallels that between the style of the early and later parts of the historical section. The early reigns, highly schematised and highlighting selected significant events seen as both edifying and exemplary, form a backdrop for the accounts of later reigns. Of these, only the account of Ṭughril ibn Arslān is in any sense original. Between his (greatly expanded) account of events up to and immediately following Arslān's death and the beginning of Ṭughril's reign, Rāvandī inserts a number of panegyrics on Arslān and the Atabegs Muḥammad Jahān Pahlavān and Qizil Arslān. Ṭughril 'inherited a troubled reign, and donned an untried garment (of rule)', says Rāvandī (1921: 331), echoing Nīshāpūrī (1953: 83); the contrast between the 'tranquil' reign of Alp Arslān (not in Nīshāpūrī) and the troubled one of the last Great Saljūq sultan frames the history of the dynasty as a whole. Nīshāpūrī's brief notice on Ṭughril's accession ends with a prayer (voiced by his subjects) that his rule may prosper; Rāvandī, converting Nīshāpūrī's present tense to past, moves smoothly into his own account of Ṭughril's reign.

The sultanate prospered as long as it was under the firm control of the Atabeg Jahān Pahlavān; the Sultan was 'busy with feasting and pleasure, the Atabeg with battle and toil'. The Atabeg removed the rebellious amīrs and put his own *mamlūk*s in their place, 'in the hope that, since they were slaves, they would protect [his] offspring from foes'; but they ruined the kingdom for those offspring by dividing it up into land grants: 'every slave controlled a region, and from (other) regions the eyes of foreigners fell on the kingdom; and the results of this became apparent after the Atabeg's death' (1921: 335). The Atabeg allowed his slaves to exploit the province of Fars; 'and that was an evil action, as in it lay the ruin of the homes of Muslims in that region ... and those same slaves, on the pretext of (fighting) the Khwarazmians, did the same to Iraq, and destroyed their own lives, families and possessions with their own hands' (1921: 336).[76] Muḥammad Jahān Pahlavān died in 582/1187; the Atabegate was (after some delay) settled on his brother Qizil Arslān, ruler of Azerbaijan and Arran, who then went to Hamadan. The Sultan was completely under his control; but when two important amīrs rebelled, the Atabeg realised that he could not pursue them without the agreement of the amīrs and the Sultan, and paused to consider his situation. Meanwhile the Sultan had fled and joined the rebels. The Atabeg returned briefly to Hamadan; then (fearing the Sultan's arrival) he departed for Azerbaijan, and the Sultan re-entered Hamadan. The city was gripped by continual strife between amīrs and officials (as was also Isfahan); meanwhile the caliph had lent his support to Qizil Arslān, and a fierce battle took place outside of Hamadan between the latter, supported by caliphal troops, and the Sultan's army, in which the Sultan was eventually victorious.

Rāvandī's lengthy record of the troubles of Ṭughril's reign is largely confined to those events which he himself witnessed. In 585/1189 he and his uncle Zayn al-Dīn Maḥmūd, the Sultan's tutor, were sent to Mazandaran, where he fell ill and was obliged to remain for six months. Returning at last to his native Rāvand, continued ill health prevented him from rejoining the court, and he stayed there for a year and a half, suffering constantly. One day,

> suddenly, a friend knocked on the door ... and Felicity welcomed me and said, 'I have girded myself to attend to pleasing you, and with an auspicious omen have attached myself to you.' ... I heard the good tidings of the arrival of the Sultan ... Ṭughril ibn Arslān: 'He has come from Azerbaijan to the royal seat of Hamadan, and has seen many hardships and numberless

> vile tricks from unworthy foes and incompetent servants, and suffered many defeats and trials. He has bidden farewell to the sultan's throne and turned his face towards the world to come; he has cast aside the tools of rule and lost hope of servants and troops; he has sent his dear son to the Dār al-Khilāfa, and he himself has taken up residence near the tombs of his ancestors.' This news was disagreeable to me, and these words seemed unsuitable; that which I had thought a balm was a wound, and that which I had believed relief turned to grief. I said, 'Praise be to God, if the world does this to its guardian, what will it do to others? "What is this trial which has occurred suddenly?" Would that I had never existed, so that I would never have heard these words.' ... Now I said, 'Even a rule which is unstable is better (than that) the world be left without a guardian; the lamp of the Saljūq *dawlat* will not be blown out by the moth of the sphere; this kingdom will be settled on him who deserves it.' Again I said, 'Since rebellious servants have put the élite to flight and devastated their possessions, when was this brick placed in the mould? What trial is this which has occured, what calamity is this which has appeared?' (1921: 361)

Investigating, Rāvandī found the news to be all too true: the Sultan had been seized by Qizil Arslān's supporters and imprisoned. After briefly setting the young Sanjar ibn Sulaymān on the throne, Qizil Arslān, encouraged by the caliph, 'himself sat on the throne of the sultanate, and established a new usage; but his ingratitude and treachery brought him no good. And that was an evil deed which drew a line through Ṭughril's sultanate' (1921: 363).

Qizil Arslān was murdered by the amīrs who had conspired against Ṭughril; they quickly divided up the kingdom amongst themselves. The Sultan was freed and, briefly, restored. But the menace of the Khwarazmians was to prove fatal. 'The Khwārazmshāh's ingratitude towards his sovereign was his heritage from [his father] Atsiz, who had rebelled against Sultan Sanjar ... He took upon himself the title of Sultan, and, summoned by two or three (local) rulers, advanced on Iraq' (1921: 370). The final battle was fought outside Rayy.

> On the second charge (the Sultan) attacked in his own blessed person, and cast himself into the midst of the fray. 'When the appointed time comes, the camel runs round the well.' Suddenly the troops drew away from the Sultan; the Sultan and his parasol-bearer remained in their midst. He did not give in to them; they, too, meant to kill the Sultan, as they were filled with indignation against him and had suffered many trials. A single rider never fell as easily into the hands of his foes than

> such a king fell into their hands. They threw him down from his horse, cut off his head, and violated the honour of the sultanate ... In mourning for that prince, Jupiter is at war with Saturn, and from that mourning the face of Mars is (black) as pitch. Venus gathers the heart's blood from Mercury to write laments for that king on the face of the Moon; in the straits of separation from him Fortune wails like a lute-string, and the body of the *dawlat*, ruined by his absence, is lean and emaciated ... (1921: 371–2)

In the final chapter of the historical section Rāvandī describes the Khwārazmshāh's occupation of Iraq, which he divided amongst various Turkish amīrs, and the ensuing devastation of the region at the hands of rapacious Iraqi and Khwarazmian troops alike, compounded by attacks by Shīʿīs and heretics and by caliphal troops from Baghdad; when the latter sacked and looted Rayy, 'no one in all the lands of Islam was ever so merciless with respect to (shedding) the blood and (pillaging) the property of Muslims' (1921: 378).

> Through (the abuses of) religious leaders with corrupt beliefs and Turkish oppressors, Iraq reached the point where not only were the regulations regarding taxation not observed, but legal matters, such as judgeships, religious teaching, trusteeships and supervision of *waqf*s were parcelled out (in grant), and in every region such irreligious persons took control. (1921: 386)

Here Rāvandī digresses to observe that since the coming of Islam, four persons have been sought for and appointed to posts in order to ensure the stability of the realm: a just *qāḍī* who is not swayed by praise or blame in his decisions; an administrator who exacts justice for the oppressed from the oppressor and ensures equity for the weak against the strong; a wise vizier who administers the public treasury justly; and deputies and *ḥājib*s who report information correctly and honestly without departing from the truth (1921: 387).

These conflicts between rival amīrs, heretics and brigands, which brought devastation to Iraq the likes of which, says Rāvandī, had never before been witnessed, form a suitably apocalyptic climax to the history, and underline the necessity of action to remedy the situation. Prominent in these events were the sons of Muḥammad Jahān Pahlavān and a number of his former *mamlūk*s, who by no means formed a united front. Among the latter was Jarbādhqānī's patron, Ay Aba Ulugh Bārbak, who played an important role in affairs in Hamadan. On a visit to that city he paid his respects to Rāvandī's uncle Tāj al-Dīn Aḥmad in the *madrasa* he had built for that scholar; Rāvandī praises Ay Aba's respect for scholars and for learning. Kukja's depradations in the region are described at length. In 595/

1198–9 the Atabeg Abū Bakr (one of Jahān Pahlavān's sons, who after Qizil Arslān's death had taken his ring and regalia and departed for Azerbaijan) came to Isfahan and divided up Iraq, giving Hamadan to his brother Malik Uzbak (then ruler of Isfahan); Kukja was at the time in Rayy.

> In Isfahan the Atabeg, with his customary negligence, was occupied with drinking and pleasure, and paid no attention to affairs. Malik al-Umarā' Jamāl al-Dīn Ay Aba kept things in order for him, governing and ruling, while the Atabeg and all those associated with his rule were sitting in luxury. He ignored Kukja (who was his son-in-law); and no one could imagine what would come to pass ... Kukja's power increased, and the Atabeg had no troops ... People took note of this, and everyone sought to curry favour, putting it to Kukja that 'the Atabeg has no power to resist you; seize the kingdom ...' When the Atabeg left Isfahan most of the troops went over to Kukja. When he reached Hamadan Kukja could not rest, and planned to make a night raid (against the Atabeg). The Atabeg went towards Azerbaijan, and the army deserted him. And of that intelligence and ability, that judgement and learning, that giving of stipends and generosity, that military skill and prowess, the less I say the better! ... The harvest [of the past] has been consumed, and a tranquil kingdom left to the lowest of persons; and every Minglī and Yuvāsh and Chaghān and this one and that one have taken over the throne of the sultans. How can I describe the oppression of that bunch? To speak of them is a shame to nature; and the little good left in Iraq is due to Aytughmish, who protests, and applies himself, and who is marked by justice and magnificence. But with these Pharoahs Paradise itself would become disordered; and in the posts of viziers and positions of amīrs are those who – what shall I say of them, how can I even mention their names? ... They have acquired so much, and they still don't believe they are kings, or (know) what income is! Wet and dry are the same to them: wet, they graze on the plains; dry, they fall upon the poor and consume them. Once there was a Muslim army, who reproached the Sufis for license, for eating whatever they obtain. Now, in truth, the licentious are the Turks and soldiers in Iraq, who leave nothing remaining, and consume the property and lives of Muslims, and consider it licit, and leave the poor destitute. (1921: 401–3)[77]

Rāvandī now appeals to Sultan Kaykhusraw to

> restore this rule, and take his banners to this region – for Iraq is

> the memorial of Ṭughril and Arslān and Sanjar and Sulaymān and Malikshāh and Alp Arslān – so that by the *farr* of his youthful fortune he may bring forth the world's spring and remove the blight of autumn. (1921: 402–3)

The non-historical chapters of the *Rāḥat al-ṣudūr* are beyond the scope of this discussion. In the *khātima* Rāvandī explains that although he had intended to end the work with a chapter of humorous stories, 'some notables and friends' insisted that he not do so, as it would be 'impolite', but write a separate book on the subject, and conclude this one with 'a prayer for the good fortune of the Sultan of the world', Kaykhusraw. (One may imagine that the book, originally intended for Ṭughril, was destined to contain entertaining as well as edifying materials, but that after his death such a chapter would have been inappropriate.) Rāvandī entreats God to ensure the endurance of the Sultan's fortune 'until the coming of the Hour', and prays that he may 'become the inheritor of the kingdom, crown and throne of the Saljūq sultans' and that God may place in his hands '(all) the regions of the world, and the reins of binding and loosing men's affairs, and all the affairs of the world and the wellbeing of its inhabitants' (1921: 458). After quoting a panegyric in praise of Ṭughril ibn Arslān, he recounts the dream that inspired him to dedicate his work to the Sultan.

One restless night, as he lay lamenting the fall of the Saljūqs, he finally slept and dreamed he heard a heavenly voice announcing to him that a new sultan from the lineage of Isrā'īl ibn Saljūq had appeared. Just as Maḥmūd's treachery towards Isrā'īl had caused the Saljūqs to seek vengeance, and rule to pass to them, now that 'a group of rebellious servants have caused injury to that house, once again a sultan from Isrā'īl's line has appeared' (1921: 460–1). This inspired Rāvandī to complete his work quickly and go in search of this ruler, whom he at first identified with Kaykhusraw's younger brother Rukn al-Dīn Sulaymānshāh (597–601/1200 or 1–1204 or 5). But on learning that Rukn al-Dīn was a usurper, he continued his search, in vain, until the Khvāja Jamāl al-Dīn Abū Bakr ibn Abī al-ʿAlā' al-Rūmī arrived in Hamadan, where he spread word of the qualities, virtues and achievements of Sultan Kaykhusraw, who had recently conquered Antioch. 'The scholars in the *madrasa*s and the ascetics in their oratories made prayers for the *dawlat* of the ruler of Islam their litany.' Rāvandī revealed to the Khvāja the 'secret' of his book, and presented it to him; Jamāl al-Dīn approved, and undertook to take it to Konya, 'so that (all), small and great, young and old, may read it and know the greatness of their sultans' (1921: 461–2). Jamāl al-Dīn also advised Rāvandī not to be content with this book, but to write a general history for Sultan Kaykhusraw, 'so that he might peruse it and choose for himself that which is best and most noble' (1921: 463). Finally, Rāvandī prays that the book may reach the Sultan's court safely, and that he himself will be summoned to the Sultan's service.[78] The *khātima* looks forward to the revival not only of the author's fortunes but, more importantly, those of the Saljūq house under Sultan Kaykhusraw, who should now extend his triumphs against the Christians, and take back those territories in Iraq and elsewhere which are suffering such hardships.

The differences in style between Rāvandī and Nīshāpūrī provide clues as to their specific purposes and their intended audience(s). Nīshāpūrī's style is straightforward, concise and relatively unembellished; although his exordium is suitably rhetorical; and although he emphasises the importance of both religious and historical knowledge for rulers, he names no specific dedicatee. Rāvandī states that Nīshāpūrī was tutor to the Saljūq princes Arslān and Mas'ūd (1921: 64); Cahen observed that he was 'the sultan's preceptor' (1962: 73), that is, the teacher of Arslān ibn Ṭughril (I). Mas'ūd ibn Muḥammad ibn Malikshāh died in 547/1152, having ruled for seventeen years, at the age of forty-five; it seems unlikely that Nīshāpūrī (who died in 582/1187) could have tutored both him and Arslān (who died in 571/1176, having ruled fifteen years and seven months, at the age of forty-three), and perhaps some other Saljūq prince named Mas'ūd (who cannot be traced; a son of Arslān?) is intended. He may perhaps have taught Arslān; but as the work ends with the latter's death and the accession of his son Ṭughril, at the age of seven, it is probable that it was intended for Ṭughril himself. This is further suggested by the encomiastic reference to Ṭughril's accession and the prayer for his continued prosperity; that the work may have been presented to the young Sultan shortly after his accession is further implied by the celebration of Jahān Pahlavān's success in suppressing rebel amīrs, and the universal affection which Ṭughril had gained. His justice and compassion will inevitably lead to

> all the regions of the world soon becoming obedient to the commands of the sultan of Iran; especially since every day, (as) this ruler's ... manifestation of the traits of his predecessors and the characteristics of kingship and government are plainly witnessed, and the signs of kingship become clear upon his brow, the hopes of the slaves and amīrs of the *dawlat* will be placed in the continuance of the days of his sultanate. (1953: 83)

Rāvandī was introduced into Ṭughril's entourage in 577/1181, and seems to have been on familiar terms with him (see 1921: 344). He had originally intended to write a compilation for Ṭughril modelled on the anthology composed by his uncle Zayn al-Dīn Maḥmūd in 580/1184; to this he added Saljūq history, drawing on Nīshāpūrī for his basic framework. He had evidently been working on this compilation before the ill-fated trip to Mazandaran, and returned to it after Ṭughril's death (or perhaps earlier). We cannot know how much he had completed by that time; but it seems safe to assume that the early sections were more or less in place, and that the account of Ṭughril's reign was in progress when that reign itself was so rudely interrupted. The section on the subsequent devastation of Iraq has an immediacy to it which suggests it was written at the time (much of it is in the present tense, it breaks off around 595/1199, and it does not mention Kukja's murder in 600/1203). The exordium and the *khātima*, as well as the panegyrics to Kaykhusraw, were undoubtedly written last. (The other panegyrics included are chiefly to the Sultans Arslān and Ṭughril and to contemporary Atabegs, and were probably included in the earlier version.)

Thus the bulk of the work would have been composed for the young Sultan Ṭughril; it is no less appropriate, however, to its new dedicatee, Sultan Kaykhusraw, described as the 'spring of the House of Saljūq'. Luther's suggestion that the work was written solely, or even primarily, to gain Rāvandī a position at Kaykhusraw's court of Konya thus cannot be accepted: much of it was already written before that ruler's accession. The elaborate display of rhetoric, most conspicuous in the exordium, was however undoubtedly aimed (as Luther argued) at secretaries and officials, either at Ṭughril's court or at Kaykhusraw's; for in the system of court patronage preferment depended on influential backing. More to the point however is Rāvandī's constant exhortations to the new Sultan, descended from no less a person than the founder of the Saljūq house, Isrā'īl ibn Saljūq, to turn his attention to righting affairs in Iraq. Over and above personal ambition, it is this wish that seems to have motivated Rāvandī to place his hopes in the Sultan of Konya.

JARBĀDHQĀNĪ'S TRANSLATION OF THE *TA'RĪKH AL-YAMĪNĪ*

Abū al-Sharaf Nāṣiḥ ibn Ẓafar Munshī Jarbādhqānī (Jurbādhqānī, Jurfādhqānī; there are various spellings of the Arabised form of the *nisba* Gulpāyigānī, that is, from the town of Gulpāyigān in the province of Kashan) composed his translation of 'Utbī's history of the Ghaznavids in 603/1206–7.[79] Jarbādhqānī was a secretary in the administration of Jahān Pahlavān's former *mamlūk*, Jamāl al-Dīn Ay Aba Ulugh Bārbak, lord of the fortress of Farrazīn, who played a major role in the politics of the period which followed Ṭughril ibn Arslān's death.[80] The translation was commissioned by Ay Aba's vizier, Abū al-Qāsim ʿAlī ibn al-Ḥusayn ibn Muḥammad ibn Abī Ḥanīfa, who resided in Kashan (1966: 24). According to Najm al-Dīn Qummī, the author of the *Tārīkh al-vuzarā* (584/1188–9), who was a friend of Jarbādhqānī, the latter had recently been forced by his detractors to retire from his post as *munshī* in the *dīvān* of Sultan Ṭughril's vizier Qavām al-Dīn ibn Qāvam al-Dīn Darguzīnī (who replaced his brother Jalāl al-Dīn as vizier around 583/1187–8), and had returned to Jarbādhqān (see Luther 1969: 118–9; Klausner 1973: 110). He was evidently reinstated somewhat later, as he mentions having been at Ṭughril's court in Hamadan in 589/1193 (1966: 432). Little else is known about him, except from his own statements, but it is clear that he was skilled in both Arabic and Persian; he includes a number of his Arabic poems in the translation, and mentions his Arabic work the *Tuḥfat al-āfāq fī maḥāsin ahl al-ʿIrāq*, which was presumably a collection of biographies of notables, including poets and prose writers, of Iraq (see 1966: 25). Like ʿUtbī, Jarbādhqānī employed rhyming prose and a rhetorical style typical of that of the chancery; it must however be said that, generally speaking, his style is more flowing, and often more pleasant, than ʿUtbī's, and represents a high point in Persian rhetorical prose.

Jarbādhqānī begins his exordium with the doxology and praise of the Prophet, then moves to an extensive encomium of Jamāl al-Dīn Ay Aba Ulugh Bārbak, whom he lauds for his justice, his compassion towards the populace and his good works in Iraq: in a 'season of oppression and a time of tyranny the courts of his ardour and protection and the shelter of his favour and attention became a refuge for the weak, an asylum for the poor, a haven for the oppressed and a comforter for the wronged' (1966: 3–4). In 582/1186–7, 'when the Saljūq sultanate in Iraq came to an end, and the rule of the Great Atabeg Muḥammad [Jahān Pahlavān], who was the support of that realm ... was trapped in death's snare', civil strife erupted amongst the rebellious Turkish *mamlūks*; it has increased in intensity over the last twenty years. Ay Aba Ulugh Bārbak established himself in the fortress of Farrazīn, where he exerted himself to preserve the noble family of the Atabegs.

> For he knew that all (those rebels) would be bound to perdition and exhausted by chastisement, so that soon the courts of the *dawlat* would be emptied of their molestations: some, ensnared by greed, suffered ruin and loss, some became targets for the arrows of the prayers of the afflicted, and some fell captive to disappointment and destruction in the abyss of disobedience and ingratitude. (1966: 5)

The Khāqān-i Aʿẓam, 'King of kings of East and West' Aytughmish (who ruled Hamadan following Kujka's murder in 600/1203), married a daughter of Ay Aba Ulugh Bārbak. That alliance, and their mutual cooperation, strengthened Ay Aba's position, so that the two were able to maintain the Atabeg Abū Bakr ibn Jahān Pahlavān in place, and to fend off the armies of Syria, Armenia, Diyar Bakr and Khwarazm, whose covetous eyes were on Iraq.[81] Today, through their efforts, justice has been restored, and heresy and oppression obliterated. Jarbādhqānī goes on to state that since it is his good fortune, as a native of the region, to serve in the ruler's *dīvān*, 'in that place where the Solomon of kingship comes' it would be appropriate for him to write

> some volumes ... on the accounts and stories of kings and the histories of rulers, and bear it as a gift to the royal court, so that in times of leisure and moments of solitude (the ruler) might become accustomed to listening to them, and take admonition from (accounts of) the alterations of states and the replacement of noble men (one by another).

He was encouraged by the vizier Abū al-Qāsim 'Alī Ibn Abī Ḥanīfa, who suggested that he render 'Utbī's history into Persian, 'in wording that is easily understood, and that both Turk and Persian can grasp'; the vizier undertook to present the work to the Amīr (1966: 7–8).

'Utbī's history (said the vizier) contains two chief benefits for the ruler. One is that, by reading the accounts of the rulers of the past, who have all now vanished, leaving behind only their good name, he may be moved to emulate them; the other is that he may recognise the merits of scholars, and understand that whereas those past kings expended much wealth on the men of the sword and made them partners in government, it was the scribes (*dabīrs*) who, with their humble writing materials, 'inscribed their memory on the pages of the days, set their brand on the forehead of Time, and caused their name to be affirmed and immortalised' (1966: 8–9). For more than three hundred years men have told stories about the qualities of Maḥmūd and of the Būyids.

> But the memory of the Saljūqs ... will soon vanish, and their name be erased from the rolls of minds; for since men of learning did not prosper in their days, and paid no attention to recounting their deeds, their acts and their battles, no one will remember them, and there will remain no memorial of their efforts. (1966: 9; these comments, attributed to the vizier, undoubtedly express Jarbādhqānī's own views)

In obedience to the vizier's suggestion, Jarbādhqānī took this task upon himself. Should his own style be seen as falling short of 'Utbī's eloquence, he pleads two excuses: first, that he did not wish 'the book's purposes and meanings to become concealed by the veil of ambiguity through (the use of) artifice and excessive ornament', and second, that though his Persian style may be deficient, the superiority of his Arabic compositions cannot be doubted (in demonstration of which he mentions two of his Arabic prose works, as well as proposing to include in the translation a number of his own Arabic poems, beginning, here, with a long *qaṣīda* in praise of the vizier [1966: 10–11]). After more praise of the vizier and of his good works in Kashan he begins, where 'Utbī did, with the rise of Sabuktigīn.

Although Jarbādhqānī generally follows 'Utbī closely (though he often adds his own rhetorical flourishes), at times his departures from, or comments on, the text are noteworthy. Considerations of space preclude a full discussion of these; a few examples must suffice. One, which may be taken as representative, comes in the account of the Sāmānids' involvement with Khalaf ibn Aḥmad in Sistan, and the actions of Abū al-Ḥasan Simjūrī, who, we may recall, was criticised for his slowness to support Nūḥ ibn Manṣūr, dismissed from his post as governor of Khurasan and subsequently reinstated in Nūḥ's favour (see Chapter 2). 'Utbī writes:

> [Following this] he went to Quhistān, waiting (to see) how his affairs would recommence, and what plan of action would be decided for him [by the Sāmānid court]; until he was cast against Khalaf ibn Aḥmad [literally 'shot at (his) throat'], because the affliction caused by him seemed incurable, and the [Sāmānid] armies were permanently detained (attempting) to destroy him. So he set out for Sijistan. Between himself and Khalaf there (still) existed (relations of) friendship and firm bonds (despite the passage of time). He began by advising him [Khalaf] to allow al-Ḥusayn ibn Ṭāhir to occupy his fortress [the Arg] and to move to another of his strongholds, in order to make it possible for him [Abū al-Ḥasan] and for those generals of that *dawla* who had been there before (he came), besieging him [Khalaf], to depart, on the pretext of victory [in conquering the Arg] and (Ḥusayn's) apparent success. (Then) when he (Ḥusayn) was exposed to him (Khalaf) [that is, once the army had left], he (Khalaf) might return to take revenge upon him (Ḥusayn) and put an end to his control. (Khalaf) agreed, and left the Arg for the Ṭāq fortress. Abū al-Ḥasan ibn Sīmjūr entered (the Arg) and performed the Friday prayer therein, reviving the custom of the *khuṭba* in the name of al-Amīr al-Riḍā [Nūḥ ibn Manṣūr]. He informed (the Amīr) of the victory God had granted him, and facilitated (his extrication from) that difficult affair through his diligence and effort. He appointed al-Ḥusayn (ibn Ṭāhir) governor there, and put him in charge of the taxes,

> and left. (1869, 1: 104–5; the explanatory phrases are based on Manīnī's commentary)

Jarbādhqānī's version differs from 'Utbī's both in its stylistic elaboration and in matters of content.

> [Abū al-Ḥasan] left the plain of Khurasan and went to Quhistān, waiting to see what orders would come from the court. They commanded him to go to Sistan and, with cunning, boldness and skill, to bring success to this travail, which had become knotted as the Dragon's tail, and to that weighty matter, which was as complicated as an irrational root, and to free those troops from the straits of exile and the locks and bolts of affliction. Abū al-Ḥusayn [*sic*] Simjūrī went to Sistan. Between him and Khalaf there existed (relations of) affection, brotherly friendship, love and clientage from the past which were still strong and of firm foundation. When he arrived, he secretly sent someone to [Khalaf] and, by way of collusion (with him), intimated to him (as follows): 'Foreigners have remained in this country for a long time, (and) much damage has occurred throughout the kingdom. When that which is the subject of dispute, and to protect which head and life are exposed to danger, perishes and is buried in the earth, (all) efforts are wasted and (all) toil fruitless. The right path is this: that you should leave this place and go elsewhere, until I take this army out of this country on the pretext of having achieved the goal and acquired that which was desired. When the field is empty, choose and decide that which seems best.'
>
> Khalaf heeded this counsel and approved it, for he knew that these words were spoken in sincerity and frankness. He left the Arg fortress and went to the Ṭāq. Abū al-Ḥusayn and the [Sāmānid] generals entered the fortress and announced the good news. They sent a *fatḥnāma* to the court and the outlying regions, adorned the *khuṭba* and coinage with the auspicious titles of Nūḥ ibn Manṣūr, and set out for Khurasan. (1966: 46–7)

When we compare these passages two things stand out, beyond Jarbādhqānī's natural tendency towards amplification and occasional explanatory interpolations. First is the difference in style. 'Utbī is concise, with a minimum of rhetorical embellishment. Jarbādhqānī's style is, by contrast, complex; it features a high proportion of repetition, often accompanied by rhyme – for example, 'cunning [and] boldness' (*kiyāsat, shamātat*) rhyme with the verb 'to bring success' (*kifāyat kardan*); 'the straits of exile and the locks and bolts of affliction' (*mazāyiq-i ghurbat va-maghāliq-i kurbat*) are rhyming pairs – and a predominantly Arabic vocabulary. The description of the affair of Sistan as being 'knotted as the Dragon's tail' (an astrological metaphor) and 'complicated as an irrational root' (a metaphor drawn from mathematics) implies a high level of sophistication on the part of the intended audience. Though Jarbādhqānī was instructed to compose a work which could be understood 'by Turk and Persian alike', it is clear that his target audience was 'Persian' – that is, Persian bureaucrats and scribes, connoisseurs of the figured chancery style.

The second point involves both thematics and presentation. Whereas 'Utbī couched Abū al-Ḥasan Sīmjūrī's proposal to Khalaf in the briefest of terms (implying, moreover, that it was their ancient bonds of friendship which motivated the Sīmjūrid to employ this ruse), Jarbādhqānī presents this proposal in the form of a lengthy (and secret) communication to Khalaf, motivated, moreover, by complicity. Complicity in what? In the removal of foreign rule from Sistan – a motive which does not appear in 'Utbī (for whom the Sistanis were vassals of the Sāmānids) and which is closer to the perspective of the *Tārīkh-i Sīstān.* Since our Hamadani author cannot have had much interest in Sistani independence, it would seem that the interpolation is designed to allude to the contemporary situation: the interference in Iraq's affairs by the Khwārazmshāh (and, perhaps, by the Atabeg Abū Bakr, who resided in Azerbaijan, but who had divided Iraq's territories amongst the Pahlavānī *mamlūk*s).

Other examples could be cited; I will mention only a few. Following the split-up between Abū 'Alī Sīmjūrī and Fā'iq, the latter was summoned to court; a reconciliation took place, and he was sent to Samarqand to defend the border. Bughrākhān attacked him by surprise and defeated him; he fled to Bukhara, leaving the nobles of Samarqand exposed to the sword. Jarbādhqānī embellishes 'Utbī's final comment:

> No one doubted that his flight from Samarqand was in collusion (with Bughrākhān), and that it was his inner baseness and corrupt nature, and rebellion against his patron, *that made him bring disgrace to the realm and ruin upon that ancient house.* (1966: 95; emphasis added)

After Nūḥ returned to Bukhara, Abū 'Alī consulted his advisors as to how to extricate himself from a perilous situation. 'Utbī states:

> They advised him to work to restore himself to al-Riḍā's favour, and to begin treating him with politeness, and to employ every wile which would remove the impediment of estrangement, erase the signs of disobedience, and repair the breaches (made by) his shortcomings in respect to obedience. (1869, 1: 178)

Jarbādhqānī expands, playing on Nūḥ's name (Noah):

> They all said (to him): 'The clay [nature] of the House of Sāmān is mixed with the water of generosity and kindness, and their

> kings have ever been known for their forgiveness, and for overlooking the mistakes of their slaves and the slips of their servants. The way is this: you must seek this balm from them, and strive for pardon at their court. For in this whirlpool (your) life will not reach the shore in safety save in the ship of Nūḥ's favour, and this flood of tribulation will not subside save by the good fortune of Nūḥ's summons. You must go and seek (his) protection with sword and shroud, and knock upon the gates of his generosity and mercy ...' (1966: 99; 'sword and shroud' refers to the customary appearance of a penitent wearing a shroud, with a sword hanging from his neck, indicating his willingness to be killed in punishment)

Abū 'Alī prepared to do this (Jarbādhqānī continues) by amassing rich gifts to send to Nūḥ together with a fluent-tongued envoy who might sway him with his elegant words. 'Utbī makes no mention of the envoy, or of what follows.

> Then – in accordance with the proverb, 'Forethought is (equivalent to) distrust' – he thought otherwise, and said (to himself): 'Alas! It is too late! For, as they say, 'He who sows thorns will not harvest grapes.' In that place where I have sown the seeds of wrongdoing, how should I reap the harvest of loyalty? In that place where I have planted the sapling of rebellion, how should I expect the fruit of concord? To put a viper in one's sleeve and [not] expect to taste its venom is not among the deeds of the clever. Wise men have said: 'Kings, like crocodiles, have teeth in their bellies; they are like the sea which, even though it is the source of the water of life and the container of jewels and of benefits, sometimes a wave will with a single blow destroy and bring down an entire world.' (1966: 99–100)

Not only is this last passage not in 'Utbī (Abū 'Alī's change of heart came after Fā'iq fled to him seeking refuge; see 1869, I: 179), but it is clearly also oriented towards Jarbādhqānī's own contemporary concerns. For both writers, the issue of loyalty is an important one; but for Jarbādhqānī, disloyalty includes not merely the violation of personal bonds, but also collusion with foreigners against the legitimate ruler. The passage above, which in its style and use of proverbs approaches Rāvandī at his most exemplary, points up a lesson concerning the evils of civil strife (one made earlier, and repeated later, in connection with Jarbādhqānī's own time): that disloyalty and rebellion will eventually rebound upon their practitioners.

These and other similar examples show that Jarbādhqānī saw in 'Utbī's history a work both admirably suited to the presentation of an idealised view of the past – the reign of that exemplary sovereign

Maḥmūd (who played a similar role in the *Siyar al-mulūk*) – and containing materials relevant to contemporary issues. We noted earlier, in the section on ʿUtbī, Jarbādhqānī's observation (absent in ʿUtbī) concerning the youth and inexperience of Nūḥ ibn Manṣūr; did he perhaps see a parallel with the unfortunate Sultan Ṭughril? His version of ʿUtbī's accounts of the fate of Tāhartī and the abuses of Abū Bakr Maḥmashād shows both a heightened animosity towards the Bāṭinī heretics and an indifference to the Karrāmiyya (Abū Bakr is merely called 'the shaykh of the Sunnīs'), who were of no relevance to the situation in Iraq. This, combined with the elaborate rhetorical style and the frequent use of interpolations (far more than is the case with ʿUtbī), places Jarbādhqānī's translation on the same level as Rāvandī's exemplary history of the Saljūqs themselves.

There is another parallel with Rāvandī: for just as he followed the accounts of rulers up to the accession of Ṭughril, based on those of his model Nīshāpūrī, with his own eyewitness account of Ṭughril's reign and its aftermath, which owes nothing to Nīshāpūrī and is quite different in tone from the earlier sections, so Jarbādhqānī follows his translation of ʿUtbī with his own account of the decline and fall of the Saljūqs following the death of Jahān Pahlavān in 582/1186.

> Since the translation is finished, a concise and brief account will follow concerning some of the circumstances of this age, of the various discords and disturbances during the time of the *futūr*, of strange happenings, of the nobles who participated (in events), of the ruin of the region of Iraq and the situation of Jarbādhqān. (1966: 419)

In 582 there occurred a Great Conjunction of all seven planets in the Balance (Libra). The astrologers predicted that at that time a great windstorm would appear which would destroy everything and usher in the End of Days. 'This (idea) dominated men's minds, so that a great dread settled in their hearts.'

> A notable of Khurasan related (this) Tradition ('and his is the responsibility for what he relates'): 'The Prophet was asked, "When will be the Day [*al-Qiyāma*]?" He replied: "*al-Qiyāma*" [that is, "Whenever it comes"]. They returned several times; (each time) he gave the same answer.' Intelligent persons pondered this word, and submitted it to calculations; its letters added up to 582.[82] These numbers corresponded to the astrologer's judgements and to the Hijrī year; thus these fancies became strengthened, and many distinguished, affluent and wealthy people decided to take up residence and refuge in caves. Some made strong rooms, and built fortified places in the drains and underground channels.

> In Rajab [582], the date of the conjunction, by God's decree it so happened that for a month not a leaf moved on a tree, and the crops remained in the fields, because the wind gave no assistance with their gleaning. It became clear to people that the astrologers' statements and their lies were all so much wind, and that they were all deficient in knowledge, and ignorant of the truths and fine points of their own craft, and do not know that when God brings a people's affair into decline and sends calamity upon them, the world of forms has no part in this. And that which God says in his Holy writ [41: 42] ... and which is mentioned in several places with respect to ʿĀd and Thamūd and other peoples ... is figurative. (1966: 419–21)

The true meaning of such figurative expressions is that, in accordance with the divine custom (*sunnat*), in every age a group appear who, aided by divine support, take control of one of the regions of the world, and are entrusted with its rule and the governance of its inhabitants. God's wisdom in this is that through them the world may remain prosperous and that they may protect the populace according to the way of justice and bar the path to aggression and tyranny. As long as they continue to do so divine support for them will increase, and God will protect them against their enemies and ensure the people's obedience to and love for them.

> But when divine favour towards them begins to wane, and the time of their betrayal and ruin arrives, then from among the progeny and servants of those kings and lords comes the turn of a group who expose themselves to God's anger and wrath. Compassion departs from their hearts, and tyranny dominates their natures; and because of them the subjects, who are God's trust to them, encounter trials and tribulations. People's hearts become heavy towards them, and they aspire to the ruin of their kingship and government, and utter prayers for evil (to befall them) at the end of their (public) prayers and in private. Then the cold and tempestuous wind of civil strife stirs, and the consequences of 'We placed over them their inferiors' [Koran 15: 74] become manifest and the miracle of 'And We cast among them enmity and anger' [Koran 4: 66] ... is realised. (1966: 421–2)

This is what 'we have witnessed in our own age, and seen in our own lifetimes, during the twenty years of this conjunction'. The Saljūq armies were once united 'in raising the standard of rule and preserving the throne of the sultanate, which was firmly established in the center of Iraq, which is the navel of the earth and the cream of this world'; fear of them enabled the Saljūqs to impose their rule from East to West and caused the world's rulers and commanders to submit to their rule.

> Each, in that region where he was, found prosperity in obeying and following them, and all firmly believed that this rule would not decline till Resurrection, and that the star of their might and greatness would be liable to no setting or decline. (1966: 422)

But with the death of the Atabeg Muḥammad Jahān Pahlavān 'the order of their necklace, the foundation of their affair ... was loosed, and the kingdom remained like a lifeless form.' Friends drew swords against each other; lords ignored the rights of their servants, and servants forgot their obligations towards their lords; friends and relatives made war on one another.

> Were [all that happened in those days] to be described, it would not be exhausted in (many) volumes; but one marvel will be written down and stated: that every one of those chiefs, generals and nobles of this community, wherever he fled and in whatever region he sought refuge, from that (same) place came the cause of his destruction; like the moth, he cast himself into the flame, and it was as the Arabic proverb says: 'Like one who runs after his death with his own feet'. (1966: 421–3)

The reason for this state of affairs was that Sultan Ṭughril ibn Arslān, 'who was the ruler and commander of all', called on the Khwārazmshāh for assistance in his conflict with the Atabeg's army. But when the Khwārazmshāh came to Iraq, the Sultan's opponents took refuge under his protection. 'An army as numerous as ants and locusts came to the gates of Rayy'; Ṭughril, with only a small force, engaged them, and fought against them personally until he was surrounded and killed. His headless corpse was exposed on a gibbet in the bazaar of Rayy (a detail Rāvandī omits), 'and people saw with their own eyes what they had not dared to imagine' (1966: 423–4).

After quoting an elegy on Ṭughril, in Arabic, of his own composition, Jarbādhqānī takes up the events which preceded the Sultan's defeat. After his brother Jahān Pahlavān's death Qizil Arslān came to Iraq, where he was encouraged to claim the sultanate. (Jarbādhqānī does not mention his imprisonment of Sultan Ṭughril.) His marriage to his brother's wife, Inānch Khātūn, strengthened his position; but shortly after, he was murdered by an Assassin (1966: 426).[83] In the ensuing period of revolts and shifting allegiances (in the account of which Sultan Ṭughril is presented in a less favourable light than he is by Rāvandī), Qutlugh Inānch (one of Inānch Khātūn's rebellious sons) summoned the Khwarazmians to assist him against Ṭughril; when the Khwārazmshāh arrived, however, he had Qutlugh Inānch killed.

The accounts of these revolts of former servants of the Saljūqs and their Atabegs serve primarily to illustrate the principle enunciated earlier: that each met his destruction in the same quarter wherein he sought support and refuge. Such was the case with Nūr al-Dīn Kukja, 'who towards the end (of this period) found the field of Iraq empty and took control of it ... (but) because he had no weapon but the sword, and was ignorant of the customs of kingship, he elevated some persons, but in the end was killed by them'.[84]

Jarbādhqānī continues,

> I have recounted these stories to show that in the face of God's decree men's plans are in vain; and that he upon whom the decisive decree descends, and whose known Hour arrives, must willy-nilly go to meet his death and keep his appointment with annihilation. (1966: 428)

After a lengthy Koranic quotation (3: 154), he concludes:

> And no one knows that, should he choose a place of flight or plan a site of refuge, he must do so at the Holy capital and the Court of divine might, and must seek refuge with Him and safety from Him ... and must cling to lofty aspiration, right belief and praiseworthy conduct.

This is what was done by the 'just ruler' Ay Aba Ulugh Bārbak, 'a sample of whose calamities has been described', who has, along with his sons, enjoyed God's protection 'from afflictions and from the tempest of this bloodthirsty conjunction and this treacherous age' because of his justice and charitable works (1966: 430).

Jarbādhqānī provides an example of God's grace towards this ruler, who was imprisoned by Ṭughril after the latter had himself been released from prison by a group of amīrs, and was deprived of food, so that all despaired of his survival. The Sultan had also killed Ay Aba's son-in-law Alp Arghūn and displayed his head to his prisoner. When Ṭughril captured the fort of Farrazīn he sent Ay Aba there. Jarbādhqānī was at court when these events took place (in 589/1193), and he observed the compassionate attitude of the vizier Abū al-Qāsim towards Ay Aba, as well as his pious behaviour. Things went on in this way until 'God caused one of the commoners of Kashan, in the bazaar of Hamadan', to remark that Jahān Pahlavān had bought Jalāl al-Dīn Ay Aba for two or three hundred dinars, and to exclaim: 'Would that the Sultan would sell him to us for a hundred thousand!' For the people had seen much good from him, and would gladly have ransomed him. A passing courtier heard this and informed the Sultan, whom God inspired, in a dream, to a change of heart: thinking that it would earn him a bad name to harm someone of such good repute, he set Ay Aba free. This should be taken as an object lesson (1966: 431–2;

for a somewhat different version of these events see Rāvandī 1921: 365–6).

During these troubled times the state of the populace of Iraq was beyond description. All the old families perished; their houses were pillaged and their belongings sold off cheaply. The roads were unsafe because of the wild beasts that had made their homes in the fields and in the abandoned houses of the peasants. There were frequent famines in which many perished, especially the poor.

> The custom of officialdom [*khvājagī*] and of wearing the turban vanished, and the sons of officials turned to disobedience and idle ways, changed their garments from those of their fathers and forefathers, and abandoned their pens and inkwells for knives and swords. Mischief-makers and corrupt people triumphed, affairs fell out of order, and wise men wished for death. (1966: 432)

Jarbādhqān shared in these afflictions, in particular because it was located between two capitals and near several fortresses, and because each year it was given over in grant (*iqṭā'*) to 'two or three oppressive grantees ... who left nothing of the Muslims' lives or their property'. In the end, most of its inhabitants decided to abandon the town and go abroad. But God heeded the cries of the poor, and (by His intervention) the administration of the region fell to Ay Aba and his vizier. They took pity on its distressed inhabitants, displayed their piety and restored justice and order. Praise of the general 'Umar ibn Abī Bakr ibn Muḥammad, whom they appointed *ra'īs* of the city, and of Ay Aba, the vizier, and the *mustawfī* 'Alī ibn Muḥammad ibn Abī al-Ghayth, 'with the support of whose resolve this book has reached completion' (along with a panegyric in his honour) follow.

Jarbādhqānī concludes this account, and the book, with a passage in elaborate Arabic rhyming prose, in which he complains of living 'in a time when the free man is a stranger amongst his own people, and the noble man is feared by his own group', and in two states of exile, both calamitous: those of learning, and of remoteness from homeland and family. This august assembly is filled with servants of the court; yet 'it would no longer coo should the dove of its learning meet with ruin, nor produce an echo should the cymbals of its talent sound.' However,

> should it wish to add a heavy (one) to its light weights, or a discerning person to its state, I would frequent it day and night, and serve it as bodies serve souls; for in this would be greatest honour and most enormous felicity. (1966: 440–1).

To whom is this addressed? It is clearly a plea for preferment (and, again, the resemblance to Rāvandī is palpable). Jarbādhqānī was currently in the service of Ay Aba Ulugh Bārbak's vizier Abū al-Qāsim; what further preferment might he have been seeking?

Jarbādhqānī's elegant figured style is clearly meant to impress members of his own class: sophisticated, educated administrators and bureaucrats, connoisseurs of both Arabic and Persian style.[85] His own style is, in general, more flowing and immediate, and less encumbered with interpolations (though there is no lack of these), than is Rāvandī's. Moreover, he adds explanatory, as well as moral, comments, and often clarifies points which might be obscure to a contemporary reader. It is possible that, in addition to seeking to impress his peers, he also sought a position as tutor. We know from Rāvandī (1921: 393) that in 594/1197–8 a son was born to Malik Uzbak (whose wife was a daughter of Sultan Ṭughril), and was named Ṭughril. Ay Aba had been made Uzbak's Atabeg the year before; Uzbak became ruler of Hamadan a year later (see Rāvandī 1921: 389, 400). In 603/1206–7 the young prince Ṭughril would have been eleven – just the age to embark on a serious education, including the study of history. But this is only conjecture; we know nothing of the fate of this prince. Or did he have a more ambitious aim: to write the history of the Saljūqs themselves? This we cannot know either.

We do know, however, from a slightly later source that Jarbādhqānī's hopes, whatever they might have been, remained unrealised. Sa'd al-Dīn Varāvīnī, the author of the *Marzubānnāma*, provides in his introduction to that work a lengthy list of books he has studied as models of rhetorical eloquence. Among them is the *Tarjuma-i Yamīnī*, of which he says:

> If they swear with solemn oaths that its translator possessed great eloquence, this is no false swearing. And if, because of having suffered a loss in the bargain, like Firdawsī he expressed repentance for what he had written, and wished to dissociate himself from it, and, having sown his seed in salt ground and planted his sapling in base earth, he obtained no harvest, and said,
>
> My fortune has harmed me, and my right hand has withered:
> I have wasted my efforts in translating the *Yamīnī*,[86]
>
> yet Time still recites 'His fingers have not withered, nor has his tongue grown weary' over those elegant pages. (1909: 4)

Bahār wrote that under the Saljūqs 'Iraq reached the summit of advancement with respect to learning and letters, because the Saljūq rulers and viziers were all lovers of learning', although in the disturbed period towards the end of the 6th/12th centuries many of its learned men fled elsewhere – to the caliphal court at Baghdad, to the court of the Saljūqs of Rūm at Konya, to Khwarazm, and even as far as India, to the court of the kings of Delhi – while others remained at home and bemoaned the current situation (1932, 2: 387). There is no compelling evidence to indicate that the sultans (with a few possible exceptions) or their Atabegs were great 'lovers of learning'; and while their officials (those who were not, as Anūshīrvān ibn Khālid complained, ignorant and semi-literate) may have patronised works of religious learning (chiefly in Arabic), and poetry (chiefly in praise of themselves), the period as a whole cannot be seen in the glorious light in which Bahār was inclined to depict it. The handful of historical works that survive, and their authors' repeated lamentations of the decline of learning, tell a quite different story.

NOTES

1. Makdisi doubts that religious beliefs were of real importance in the eyes of Turkish, and Arab bedouin, amīrs, and that their 'decision ... to ally themselves with one or the other of the rival caliphs depended only on the particular circumstances of the moment' (1963: 91). For a different view of Basāsīrī's motives see the entry in *EI²*, s.v. (M. Canard). See also Hoffmann 1992, who notes the rapidly changing allegiances of the amīrs but does not discount the possibility of Shī'ī leanings on the part of some of them, including Basāsīrī.
2. 'Politically the Saljuq empire was a loose confederation of semi-independent kingdoms over which the Great Saljuqs exercised nominal sovereignty. Only during the last five years of Malik-Shāh's reign was any degree of unity achieved. Generally speaking, the central government did not have the power to maintain permanent control over the different parts of the empire, and the local Saljuq rulers' – of Rūm, Syria, and Kirman – 'broke away at an early date' (Lambton 1988: 111). A further factor contributing to instability and fragmentation of rule was the conflict of interest between the caliphs and the Saljūq sultans, and the caliphal policy of supporting rival candidates. For a detailed discussion see Makdisi 1963, Chapter 2; Makdisi 1969.
3. The supposed genealogical claim to descent from Afrāsiyāb, cited by Kafešoglu on the basis of 'Alā' al-Dīn Muḥammad ibn 'Alī ibn Ḥassūl's (d. 450/1058) *Tafḍil al-Atrāk* (1988: 22–3), seems based on a misreading; the claim does not appear in Ibn Ḥassūl's text (1940: 49 [Arabic text]), which was composed as a refutation of Ṣābi''s *Tājī* and dedicated to the vizier Kundurī. The 'House of Afrāsiyāb' refers to the Qarakhānid rulers of Transoxania. The claim is absent from the *Māliknāma*, the earliest known work on the origins of the Saljūqs, who are presented as tribal warlords (on this work see Cahen 1949). Niẓām al-Mulk's vague reference in the *Siyar al-mulūk* to Malikshāh's lineage encompassing 'two royal houses' that stretch back to Afrāsiyāb (1978: 10) presumably reflects the fact that Malikshāh's chief wife Turkān (Terken) Khātūn was a Qarakhānid princess.
4. This image seems, by and large, to have been cultivated by administrators like Niẓām al-Mulk, and by later historians, including

Arabic historians outside the Saljūq domains, presumably to encourage their (mainly Ayyūbid) patrons to similar enterprise against both the Ismā'īlīs and the Crusaders. On Ghazzālī's justification of the rule of the Turks – the possessors of real power – as supporters of the caliphate and of Sunnī Islam (and, in the process, his legitimation of the caliph al-Mustaẓhir, 487–512/1094–1118) see Hillenbrand 1988. Ghazzālī 'praises the Turks, emphasizing their zeal as warriors for the faith, and deflects attention away from the reality, namely that they have usurped power. To depict them as insubordinate, wayward creatures whose fundamental loyalty to Islam is nevertheless unswerving constitutes a plea for some kind of accommodation with this alien implant into the Islamic body politic; but it cannot of course possibly reflect a true picture of how turbulent must have been the daily contact between the Persian-Arab bureaucracy and religious elite on the one hand and the Turkish military leadership and their nomadic followers on the other.' Hillenbrand points out that only the educated élite would have understood either the argument or the ornamental style of this panegyric; thus it 'is directed at those who have to deal at ceremonial, legal and bureaucratic level with this alien power group' (1988: 86). Lambton observes that, under the later Saljūq sultans, when the Būyids had been defeated and the Fāṭimids were no longer a threat, the 'strict orthodoxy followed by the first two sultans' was modified (see 1988: 236–7).

5. Makdisi (1973) takes issue with this traditional view, arguing that Maḥmūd of Ghazna was already 'pursuing a traditionalist Sunnī policy under the caliph al-Qādir' (156) and that it was the caliph's promulgation of what has been called the 'Qādirī creed' early in the 5th/11th century that made this creed 'the law of the land in the realm of the Eastern caliphate' (168). Klausner's argument that the Saljūq sultans consciously attempted 'to link central government with the religious institution through state support for the *madrasa* system' (1973: 22) must be revised; it was Niẓām al-Mulk who developed both the *madrasa* system and, apparently, the Saljūq claim to legitimacy as upholders of the *sunna*.
6. In anticipation of this theme of the Saljūqs' building activities, which looms large in Nīshāpūrī and Rāvandī, we may note that there is little in the archaeological record to substantiate these claims (or, indeed, in textual records either). Most *madrasa*s, for example, were private constructions; there appears to be no Friday mosque built entirely in the Saljūq period (although there were additions to existing ones); there are no remains of Saljūq palaces. For a discussion of the architecture of the period, see Sourdel-Thomine 1973.
7. See for example the works on such subjects mentioned by Ibn Funduq (below). The first Persian work on opthalmology was written for Malikshāh in 480/1087–8; while its author invokes the topos of *translatio studii* as the accompaniment to *translatio imperii* (stating moreover that now most people speak Persian, as does the current ruler), it is doubtful to what extent Malikshāh himself might have been appreciative of the implications (see Richter-Bernburg 1974: 57).
8. Luther also identified the correct title of Anūshīrvān's work as *Nafthat al-maṣdūr fī ṣudūr zamān al-futūr wa-futūr zamān al-*

ṣudūr (1969: 120 and n. 2). I have not been able to consult the edition of the *Tārīkh al-vuzarā* published in Tehran (1984).

9. Scholars often speak of 'Saljūq' policies as if the Saljūq rulers themselves were the initiators of these policies (see for example Klausner 1973: 4–8; Marlow 1997: 132, on the Saljūqs' 'attempt to create a centralised government'). R. S. Humphreys states that from their appearance in Khurasan until the death of Malikshāh the Saljūqs 'presided over a major ideological effort to restate the principles of Iranian kingship in Islamic terms' (1991: 154). Such efforts were rather the work of their (Persian) administrators, most prominently Niẓām al-Mulk, and reflect earlier Ghaznavid 'ideology'. Anūshīrvān ibn Khālid's memoirs make clear the extent to which Saljūq policies, especially after the deaths of Niẓām al-Mulk and Malikshāh, were dictated by the self-interest of their officials.
10. The passage giving the date of, and the names of those who received, Malikshāh's instruction does not appear in either Darke's edition (1968) or his translation (1978); it does appear, however, in the translation published by Schefer in 1893, republished in 1984 with notes by Jean-Paul Roux. Darke speculated that the first part was written between 479/1086 and 484/1091, the date of its revision in its final form (1978: xiv).
11. The purpose of Malikshāh's last visit to Baghdad was to expel the caliph al-Muqtadī and rebuild 'Ṭughril City' (the residence that Sultan had constructed), with a view to installing the son recently born to his daughter, the caliph's wife, as caliph; he had given the caliph a ten-day ultimatum to leave the city. See Makdisi 1969: 262.
12. Mottahedeh argues that this was also the case in earlier periods (see 1980: 175–90); but in view of the emphasis placed by Ghaznavid historians on the ruler's obligations of loyalty towards his subordinates this cannot have been entirely the case. This theme is however virtually absent (if on occasion implied through anecdote or example) from Saljūq historiography.
13. Marlow asserts that 'the Turks ... had their own royal traditions, and were no strangers to stratification and hierarchy' (1997: 132); the contemporary sources indicate that this was manifestly not the case, and it is Niẓām al-Mulk's purpose to instruct his ruler in such traditions.
14. The anachronistic reference to Mahdiyya (the Fāṭimid capital in North Africa, founded in 308/921) functions to confirm, to contemporary readers, Ya'qūb's Ismā'īlī loyalties. The episode is not found in the *Tārīkh-i Sistān*. For the story in other sources see Bosworth 1994: 197, who does not note Niẓām al-Mulk's version.
15. The general present tense is used in this passage to refer to the future – 'when such and such occurs this will happen'; but the effect of the cumulative present-tense verbs is to suggest that this is the situation now, in the present.
16. The account is anachronistic, as it mentions Maḥmūd's conquests of Rayy, Isfahan and Hamadan – the latter two occurred after his death – as well as his destruction of Somnat, after which the caliph did indeed bestow upon him a new title. On his accession Maḥmūd had been given the titles Yamīn al-Dawla ('Right hand of the state') and Amīn al-Milla ('Trustee of the community'); Niẓām al-Mulk – who clearly knew better – makes this the second, final title awarded by the caliph.

17. This woman 'often used to come to Mahmud's palace; she was educated, well-spoken and knew several languages; she would talk, joke and play with Mahmud, sometimes reading him Persian books and stories; in fact she was on most familiar terms with him' (1978: 150). The ruse which resulted in the somewhat grudging bestowal of a second title is recounted at length, and makes for highly entertaining reading.
18. Much has been made of Niẓām al-Mulk's 'misogyny'. His animadversions against women interfering in rule undoubtedly reflect his hostility to Turkān Khātūn (see Lambton 1988: 269). This is moreover a common topos in mirrors for princes (as opposed to history, which is generally more neutral); Bayhaqī, for example, invokes it in the context of his advice to Sultan Ibrāhīm concerning the need for a strong ruler (1971: 485). But as we have seen, he also praises Ḥasanak's mother for her fortitude, and clearly approves of the intervention in politics on Mas'ūd's behalf by his paternal aunt Ḥurra-i Khuttalī after Maḥmūd's death (see 1971: 13–14).
19. Once again the general present is used, and we may take the passage as referring to events in the present – 'these dogs emerge and revolt' – rather than to the future.
20. Le Strange also began work on an edition of the text; this was completed by R. A. Nicholson and published in 1921 (I have used the 1962 reprint).
21. He is also so called by Ḥamd Allāh Mustawfī Qazvīnī and by Ḥajjī Khalīfa, who stated that he was *mustawfī* in Fars in the reign of the Saljūq sultan Muḥammad ibn Malikshāh (see 1962: x, n. 3). The *mustawfī* was head of the *dīvān-i istīfā*, the bureau in charge of finances and the keeping of accounts. Each tax district 'was responsible for remitting revenue in accordance with the tax statement drawn up by' this bureau (Klausner 1973: 16).
22. The atabegs were Turkish amīrs charged with the protection and education of young Saljūq princes; they frequently married the mothers of their charges. They were often appointed provincial governors. Their power increased to the point where they established their own independent dynasties. See further Lambton 1988: 228–33.
23. Ibn al-Athir reports Chāvlī in Fars as early as 493/1099; he refers to Khumārtigīn as Najm (not Rukn) al-Dawla (Ibn al-Balkhī 1962: xiii, n. 1).
24. Ibn al-Athīr states that this happened in 464/1071, and that Fars was then put under control of Khumārtigīn (Ibn al-Balkhī 1962: xv, n. 1). See also *EI*[2], s.v. 'Faḍlawayh, Banū'.
25. The words used are (Arabic) *aḥrār* and (Persian) *āzādagān*, that is, 'freeborn', hence not clients or freedmen of the Arabs.
26. The Sabians, whose religion Ibn al-Balkhī states was founded by Zaḥḥāk, are mentioned several times in the Koran among the 'Peoples of the Book'. What sect this term originally referred to has been much debated. It was appropriated by the pagans of Ḥarrān in the reign of al-Ma'mūn, who had ordered them to explain their religion, so that they could claim the same status as other 'protected' religions. See *EI*[2], art. 'Ṣābi'a'.
27. Earlier (1962: 5–6) Ibn al-Balkhī refers to Bukht-Naṣṣar's sack of Jerusalem and exile of the Israelites in punishment for their killing

their king, whom he also terms a prophet. Vishtāsf/Gushtāsb is said to have rebuilt Jerusalem; Bahman is also credited with both its destruction and its later restoration. See Ṭabarī 1987a: 42–50.

28. Abū Sa'd Kāzarūnī, of the Karzūbiyān clan of the Shabānkāra, became a soldier in the service of the Būyid ʿAmīd al-Dawla. During the last days of Būyid rule he seized Kāzarūn and pillaged the surrounding areas, until Chāvlī removed him, leaving his son Faḍlawayh (named for the famous rebel) the only remaining Karzūbī of note. Under his leadership his clan prospered, but during Malikshāh's reign they were suppressed by Chāvlī; now only a few of their notables remain (1962: 167).

29. Bosworth identifies (on the basis of V. F. Büchner's article 'Shabānkāra', in *EI*[1]) the Shābānkāra (or their forerunners) with the (infidel) 'Kurds' in the army of the Ṭāhirid official ʿAlī ibn Ḥusayn in Kirman, 'since the Shabānkāra only appear in recorded history during the Būyid period' (1994: 145 and n. 421).

30. What follows in one of the mss. is illegible; the other has simply a scribal colophon, dated 1273/1856, suggesting that the manuscript copied from was defective. See 1962: 172, and, on the mss. used, xxiv–xxvi.

31. *Ibāḥa*, 'libertinism' or 'licence', refers to the teachings of various antinomian groups concerning aspects of religious praxis and scriptural interpretation. Ibn al-Balkhī's contemporary Ghazzālī composed a refutation of the *Ibaḥiyya*. See *EI*[2], art. 'Ibāḥa (II)'; Hillenbrand 1988.

32. The text was published by M. T. Bahār in 1939; his edition was based on a photocopy of the unique manuscript in the Bibliothèque Nationale (dated 813/1410) owned by M. M. Qazvīnī. The poor state of the manuscript and the difficulties of editing from a photocopy, coupled with Bahār's reliance in his apparatus criticus only on books and manuscripts available to him, resulted in an edition which is neither scientific nor critical; these editorial problems are further compounded by the abysmal quality of the printed text.

33. Our author states that Ḥamza got this account 'from another Persian book in a strange language' (1939: 23); Ḥamza states that his source was 'a book translated from the Avesta' (n.d.: 50).

34. This is quite possibly the same book which Mas'ūdī, in his *Kitāb al-Tanbīh wa-al-ishrāf*, claims to have seen in Iṣṭakhr, in the home of 'one of the noble Persian families', which contained portraits of the Sasanian rulers; he states that it was compiled on the basis of documents found in the 'treasure of the Persian kings', was completed in 113/731, and was 'translated from Persian to Arabic' for Hishām ibn ʿAbd al-Malik ibn Marwān (1896: 150–1). Ḥamza also mentions a *Kitāb Ṣuwar mulūk Banī Sāsān* and describes the portraits therein. The emblematic colours of garments and crown may have had astrological significance.

35. According to Ṭabarī, he was a Christian (see 1939: 280, n. 9). Bahār comments: 'It is amazing that ... Ṭabarī too recounts this forged and baseless story; for if it were so, then Ka'b would have been an accomplice of Lu'lu' and aware of the plot' (1939: 280, n. 4).

36. Bahār comments, 'This account is not in (any of) the sound histories' (1939: 298 n. 2). The story of the 'donkeys' hooves'

covered in gold may be a reminiscence of the Byzantine shell design used in the decoration of churches.

37. Bahār is surely right to consider the last phrase an interpolation (1939: 315 n. 1), as our author makes it clear that Abū Muslim was the agent of the Imām Ibrāhīm.
38. Among those who raised the black, anti-Umayyad banners was Ḥārith ibn Surayj in Khurasan, who was killed in 128/745 (see Ṭabarī 1985a: 28–30 and n. 72). 'Ḥamza' is Abū Ḥamza the Khārijī, who in 129/747 led the pilgrimage on behalf of the Zaydī rebel ʿAbd Allāh ibn Yaḥyā Ṭālib al-Ḥaqq, who had revolted against the Umayyad caliph Marwān, and raised the black standards in Mecca; shortly after, he occupied Medina, and many of its inhabitants perished in the fighting. Both ʿAbd Allāh ibn Yaḥyā and Abū Ḥamza were killed in the same year (see Ṭabarī 1985a: 90–92, 112-20).
39. 'Those who are ignorant of history', he states further, call Abū Muslim 'Marghazī' (Marvazī) 'because he rebelled in Marv', just as they call Salmān 'Fārisī' (the Persian) 'because the Arabs called all the land of Persia "Fārs"', whereas he too was from Isfahan ('although some think that he was from Fārs') (1939: 326). This seems further to indicate a rivalry between the Jibal and Fars which was observable in Ibn al-Balkhī.
40. While Ṭabarī's first recension of his History ends with the year 302/915, 'recensions containing additions beyond the year 302 may also have circulated'; there may also have been others which ended before 302, and many subsequent historians cease to quote him from around 295/908. On this problem see Rosenthal's introduction to Ṭabarī 1985c: xiii–xix; see also the index, s.v. 'Zikrawayh b. Mihrawayh'; on Zikrawayh see also Halm 1996: 66–70, 183–90.
41. Bahār (1939: 374, n. 7) states that this account is found only in Ḥamza; see Ḥamza n.d.: 158, where a slightly different version is dated to 316/928. (Our author's dates are generally a year off in relation to Ḥamza.)
42. On the Ḥasanwayh Kurds see *EI*[2], s.v. 'Ḥasanwayh, Banū'; Badr's territories in the Jibal included Asadābād.
43. The statement that ʿAyn al-Dawla was the father of Muḥammad ibn Dushmanziyār ʿAlā' al-Dawla ibn Kākū (1939: 398) must be a copyist's error; ʿAlā' al-Dawla's father was Sayyida's maternal uncle Rustam Dushmanziyār. As Bahār notes (n. 3) this portion of the text is somewhat incoherent. I have so far found no other references to ʿAyn al-Dawla.
44. According to Madelung (1975: 294), the sources state that ʿAlā' al-Dawla was appointed governor of Isfahan shortly after 398/1007. See also Bosworth 1970a: 74.
45. The author states that he has taken this account from the compilation of Abū Saʿid Ābī (d. 314/1030), Majd al-Dawla's vizier, and from other sources. This is perhaps Ābī's (lost) history of Rayy (see Meisami and Starkey 1998, s.v.). Sayyida died in 419/1028.
46. Nāẓim considered our author 'dismissive of the Ghaznavids' (1971: 8). Cahen states that Bahār's edition 'does not contain the chapter on the Ghaznawids, particular to the Paris MS.' (1962: 64, n. 23). If however this ms. (which I have not been able to consult) is unique, what would explain this? Moreover, the relation of folio numbers to printed lines (approximately thirteen) is consistent throughout.

47. The entries on Tamīsha (in Ṭabaristan) and Shādyākh (1939: 526–7) are clearly interpolations (and far from our author's concern with local topography): the former gives the date of the town's rebuilding, by Ardashīr ibn Ḥasan, in 589/1193; Shādyākh was destroyed after Sanjar's death when Nishapur was sacked by the Ghuzz (no date is given).
48. Bahār comments that 'the historians and geographers of the early Islamic centuries thought so little of this inscription of Alexander's and his prophecy that not one of them mentioned it, even though all wrote down tales, both true and false, about Alexander's Wall' (1939: 57, n. 2).
49. For example, when he states that the dying Prophet was carried to 'Ā'isha's house by Faḍl ibn 'Abbās, he omits mention of 'Alī 'out of extreme prejudice' (1939: 257, n. 2; see also, for example, 259, nn. 2, 4).
50. The text has Baṭḥā'ī; I owe the correction to Professor Wilferd Madelung. On Ḥasan ibn Zayd and his successors see Madelung 1969: 28–33. The Buṭḥānīs were associated with the circle of the Ṣāḥib Ibn 'Abbād in Rayy; see Madelung 1975: 219–21.
51. Anūshīrvān Ibn Khālid relates that in 500/1106–7, when he was appointed Sultan Muḥammad's treasurer, the Sultan's attitude towards Sayyid Abū Hāshim, the long-serving *ra'īs* of Hamadan, altered because of intrigues against him by 'some of the notables of the *dawla*' in Hamadan, who supported a rival, and who alleged that a large sum of money was due from him. The Sayyid was confined in his house along with his sons; he managed to raise the sum 'without borrowing or requesting money from anyone'. Anūshīrvān was sent to Hamadan to collect the money, which he deposited in the Sultan's treasury in Isfahan. There, he interceded with the Sultan on Abū Hāshim's behalf, and the latter was reinstated (Bundārī 1889: 97–8). When Sayyid Abū Hāshim died in 502/1108–9 the Sultan appointed one of his sons, whom he particularly favoured, as his successor (Bundārī 1889: 102). For a different version of this story see Nīshāpūrī 1953: 42–3, who presents it as an illustration of Sultan Muḥammad's 'inclination to amass money'; Rāvandī 1921: 162–5; and see also Lambton 1988: 317–8.
52. The genealogy, going back to Zayd ibn al-Ḥasan ibn 'Alī ibn Abī Ṭālib, can be reconstructed on the basis of Ibn 'Inaba's *'Umdat al-ṭālib*, on 'Alid genealogies (1961). It appears to be as follows: (12) Abū Hāshim Zayd ibn (11) al-Amīr Abū al-Faḍl al-Ḥusayn (married Abū 'Īsā Shādī's daughter) ibn (10) Abū al-Ḥasan 'Alī (married the Ṣāḥib's daughter) ibn (9) Abū 'Abd Allāh al-Ḥusayn (al-Thānī?) ibn (8) Abū al-Ḥasan 'Alī (*ra'īs* of Hamadan) ibn (7) Abū 'Abd Allāh al-Ḥusayn ibn (6) al-Ḥasan al-Baṣrī ibn (5) Abū Muḥammad al-Qāsim ibn (4) Muḥammad al-Buṭḥānī ibn (3) Abū Muḥammad al-Qāsim ibn (2) al-Ḥasan ibn (1) Zayd ibn al-Ḥasan ibn 'Alī ibn Abī Ṭālib.
53. Our author says nothing about the negative aspects of Maḥmūd's reign or of his character (Rāvandī states that as a result of excessive sexual intercourse the young sultan was subject to a variety of chronic ailments) or about the influence over him of corrupt and intriguing officials. Anūshīrvān ibn Khālid introduces his account of Maḥmūd's reign with a list of the 'ten major causes of corruption' which characterised it, among them the intrigues of his (often incompetent) officials, Maḥmūd's extravagance and greed,

and his predilection for beautiful slave boys and women; see Bundārī 1889: 119–24.

54. The text was edited by Aḥmad Bahmanyār and published with an introduction by M. M. Qazvīnī in 1938–9 (I have used the second printing, c. 1965). The edition was based on photocopies of 3 mss.: one from the British Museum (the earliest, copied in 735/1334–5, considered the best and most complete), one from the Staatsbibliothek in Berlin (late), and one from Tashkent (also late). On mss. of this work see further Husaini 1959: 196–202; on Bayhaq, an important district of Khurasan near Nishapur, see *EIr*, s.v.
55. See *EIr*, art. 'Bayhaqī, Ẓahīr al-Dīn'. For an attempt at reconstructing Ibn Funduq's life and career see Husaini 1954; on the *Tārīkh-i Bayhaq* see Husaini 1959; on Ibn Funduq's other works see Husaini 1960; and see also Yāqūt 1923, 5: 208–18.
56. This list includes, among others, Ibn Isḥāq, Wahb ibn Munabbih, Ṭabarī, Miskawayh, Abū Isḥāq Ṣābi''s *Tājī*, 'Utbī, the *Mazīd al-ta'rīkh* 'compiled by Abū al-Ḥasan Muḥammad ibn Sulaymān in the reign of Maḥmūd', Ibn Ṭabāṭabā's *al-Tadhkira wa-al-tabṣira* on chronologies and genealogies, and Bayhaqī's history of the Ghaznavids. There follows a brief list of histories of regions and cities, mostly in Arabic but including some in Persian, among them an earlier (uncompleted) Arabic history of Bayhaq.
57. According to the *Shāhnāma*, Bahman, dying, declared that any offspring born to his daughter Humāy (who was six months' pregnant by him) was to be his heir; Sāsān, distraught, went off to Nishapur, where he married a noble woman; it was his son, also named Sāsān, who became a shepherd in order to make his living.
58. *Anmāṭī* is a term for a maker or seller of woven coverings, which was presumably the occupation of the eponymous ancestor.
59. According to Rowson, it was Abū 'Alī's brother Abū al-Ḥusayn who eventually hosted this meeting, which had been proposed by Abū 'Alī, but which Khwārazmī was reluctant to attend. See 1987: 660–1, and, on Khwārazmī and the 'great debate' held at the house of the vizier Abū al-Qāsim (whose identity is unclear), 658–68. Ibn Funduq appears to conflate the two meetings. Hamadhānī's poem is translated by Rowson, 662–3.
60. Bosworth speculates that the Karrāmī *madrasa* in Bayhaq was probably destroyed during the civil strife in Nishapur in 489/1096 between the Ḥanafīs and Shāfi'īs, on the one hand, and the Karrāmiyya on the other, when the fighting spread to that region (1960: 13).
61. Qā'in, in Quhistaan, was a center of Nizārī Ismā'īlī activity from around 485/1092; the 'destruction' may refer to the seizure of its fort by the Nizārīs. See Daftary 1992: 341.
62. The transfer of rule in Khurasan from the Saljūq sultanate in Iraq to the Khwārazmshāh Īl Arslān is discussed in Luther 1976. Unable to defend Khurasan against the Khwārazmshāh, Ay Aba offered him the *khuṭba* and coinage in his name. Ay Aba was killed by the Khwārazmshāh Takish in 659/1174 (see Juvaynī 1958, 1: 289–91; see also Bosworth 1968c: 185–6). Arslān ibn Ṭughril, named as the reigning sultan, acceded in 556/1161.
63. See *EIr*, art. 'Bayhaqī, Ẓahīr al-Dīn'. Yāqūt quotes a panegyric by Ibn Funduq to Sanjar's secretary Mukhliṣ al-Dīn Abū al-Faḍl

Muḥammad ibn ʿĀṣim, a nephew of the poet and vizier Ṭughrāʾī (d. 514/1120–1) (1923, 5: 213–14). Husaini's claim (1954: 310) that Ibn Funduq was himself governor of Rayy seems based on a misreading of a passage in Yāqūt's account (1923, 5: 214; the 'catastrophe' [*nakba*] referred to is not Sanjar's seizure by the Ghuzz, in 548/1153, but the execution of ʿImād al-Dīn Iṣfahānī's uncle al-ʿAzīz, an important official of Sultan Muḥammad ibn Malikshāh, in 527/1131 [see Bundārī 1889: 166–88]; the account is related by ʿImād al-Dīn's father). That he may have been a candidate for Sanjar's vizierate, as Yāqūt asserts, is somewhat more plausible.

64. Afshār's edition was based on the text of the *Saljūqnāma* incorporated in the 8th/14th-century historian Qāshānī's collection of chronicles, the *Zubdat al-tawārīkh* (see Cahen 1962: 73). The edition is by no means critical; its many clear errors and frequent unintelligibility due to the poor quality of the printed text have necessitated a certain freedom in translation. On the *Saljūqnāma* see further Luther 1971b.
65. The *Saljūqnāma* is followed by a continuation (*dhayl*) by Abū Ḥāmid Muḥammad ibn Ibrāhīm, written in 599/1202–3, which contains a brief and summary account of events up to the death of Sultan Ṭughril, written in a straightforward style which is even less adorned than that of Nīshāpūrī. As it is a fairly perfunctory account I will not discuss it here.
66. The text of the *ʿIqd al-ūlā* was published by ʿAlī Muḥammad ʿĀmirī Nāʾīnī in 1932. Afḍal al-Dīn authored two other works on the history of Kirman, the *Badāyiʿ al-azmān* and a continuation (*al-Muḍāf*), which are beyond the scope of this discussion; see *EIr*, art. 'Afżal al-Dīn Kirmānī'.
67. This prediction was made by, among others, the poet Anvarī, then at Sanjar's court, who fell into disgrace when the prophecy was falsified (see Browne 1928, 2: 367–8; the Khvāja Farīd mentioned by Kirmāni composed a lampoon on Anvarī on this occasion). Kirmānī gives the date of Anvarī's prediction as 581/1185; Jarbādhqānī (who also notes its falsification and provides a 'figurative' interpretation) gives 582/1186 (see further below). Ibn al-Athīr, *sub anno* 582 (1965, 11: 528) speaks of a conjunction of five planets predicted for this year.
68. See Rāvandī 1921: xxii–xiii; see also Afshār's introduction to Nīshāpūrī 1953: 5–8. All references to the *Rāḥat al-ṣudūr* are to Iqbāl's edition (I have been unable to consult the later edition by Mujtabā Mīnuvī, Tehran 1954). For more detailed discussions of some of the stylistic issues treated here see Meisami 1994, 1995b.
69. It is not really clear when the original decision was made, but it does seem clear that Rāvandī began his work during Ṭughril's reign. Later, mentioning a pupil whom he tutored around 593–4/1197–8, one Shihāb al-Dīn Aḥmad al-Qāsānī, Rāvandī states: 'At that time this composition was in my mind; and I agreed to include his noble name in the book ... and leave a memorial to him on this earth and express my gratitude for his patronage' (1921: 49). Rāvandī's tutelage of Shihāb al-Dīn Aḥmad was preceded by that of the ʿAlaviyyān brothers, which lasted about six years, and presumably began after his return from Mazandaran (see 1921: 45–6; see also xvii–xviii). See further the conclusion to this section.

70. These verses, taken from different sections of the *Shāhnāma*, are structured into a coherent whole placed in strategic relation to the larger context within which they are included. Rāvandī shows no interest in the narrative or historical content of the *Shāhnāma*. Iqbāl speculated that he 'probably had in hand a selection of moral verses from that book and quotes them at random' (1921: xxii). An anthology of selections from the *Shāhnāma* (the *Ikhtiyārāt-i Shāhnāma* or *Kitāb-i intikhāb-i Shāhnāma*), which contained 'extracts from Firdausī's poem under various headings' and in which 'the narrative content of the *Shāh-nāmah* plays no role', had been compiled for Malikshāh by one ʿAlī ibn Aḥmad in 474/1081–2 (de Blois 1992: 152); Rāvandī may well have utilised this work. That the arrangement of lines is the work of Rāvandī rather than the anthologist is conjectural, as I have not been able to consult a manuscript of the *Ikhtiyārāt*; however, it is consistent with the style and organisation of the prose passages.
71. This episode receives yet another permutation in Jūzjānī, where the first verse, heard by Dā'ūd as he was advancing on Marv, inspired him to put to the sword all of Masʿūd's troops in that city, and the second occurs in an exchange between Masʿūd's envoy and Dā'ūd outside Marv. Dā'ūd had the verse written down and given to the envoy; when Masʿūd received it, and was told of Dā'ūd's simple military style of life, he realised that Ghaznavid rule of Khurasan had come to an end (1970, 1: 126–7; the account does not occur in contemporary sources).
72. On Kundurī's career in the service of Ṭughril and Alp Arslān, and the circumstances surrounding his murder, see Lambton 1988: 299–300; Makdisi 1963: 106–8, 124–7, who provides details from other sources absent in Nīshāpūrī and Rāvandī.
73. In enumerating the various types of interpolation (Koranic verses, Prophetic *ḥadīth*, Arabic proverbs, poetry – including Rāvandī's own – and anecdotes (1921: xxii), Iqbāl made no distinction between their type or function.
74. Anūshīrvān ibn Khālid considers Mu'ayyid al-Mulk to have been the most capable member of Niẓām al-Mulk's family, and praises him abundantly, stating that it was he who defeated and killed Tutush and restored order and stability to Barkyāruq's rule. He makes no mention of Unur or of his taking refuge with Muḥammad ibn Malikshāh. Mu'ayyid al-Mulk was finally killed by Barkyāruq. See Bundārī 1889: 85–9. Ibn al-Athīr gives a substantially different account of Unur's revolt; see 1965, 10: 289–91. See also Lambton 1988: 244–5.
75. It might be argued that Rāvandī's use of quotations from Niẓāmī, whose works were well known, is in many cases ironic. This issue is beyond the scope of the present study, but I hope to treat it elsewhere. That Rāvandī does not quote from Niẓāmī's *Haft Paykar*, completed in 593/1197 and dedicated to the Aḥmadīlī Atabeg of Maragha, suggests that either he did not know the work, or that its emphasis on ideal kingship was inappropriate to his purpose.
76. On these events see Luther 1971a; Lambton 1988: 106–7. It is difficult to see Jahān Pahlavān's action as constituting a major 'administrative reform', as Luther did, or to agree with his

conclusion that the 'trio of concepts which in theory brought them loyalty from Muslims of varying classes and backgrounds' upon which they had originally relied – 'the concept of the Sultan, deputy of the Caliph wielding power in his name; the idea of the Persian king ... and the image of the Turkish Khan' – were at this time 'giving way to a slave system in which the only really enduring institutional tie was that between slave and master' (1971a: 403). The 'concepts' in question were certainly never more than theoretical; and the slave system based on loyalty, which the Saljūqs seem to have adopted early on (after having been themselves slaves, as so many writers are pleased to point out), had been in place for centuries.

77. Minglī was a *mamlūk* of Malik Uzbak; the others are unidentified. Kukja was ruler of Persian Iraq from 595/1198–9 until his murder in 600/1203. See Luther 1971a: 401.
78. Iqbāl argued that the first edition of the book was dedicated to Rukn al-Din, but that after Kaykhusraw's restoration Rāvandī was obliged to change his dedication; he also revised the book and made the alterations appropriate for presentation to the new Sultan. This, in his opinion, 'was not very carefully done, for we find many traces of the former dedication' (1921: xix–xx).
79. The text was edited and published in 1966 by J. Shi'ār (for details of the manuscripts used see 1966: 29–39), who was not always sensitive to the alterations to the original. Although in his notes he often refers to 'Utbī, his consultation of that work seems to have been cursory at best. Mistakes in the mss. are left uncorrected (e.g., Abū al-Ḥusayn for Abū al-Ḥasan Sīmjūrī, Ibn Gharīr for the vizier Ibn 'Uzayr), and the editor often attributes statements or opinions to Jarbādhqānī which in fact derive from 'Utbī. Thus for example he states that Jarbādhqānī implies that Maḥmūd of Ghazna 'called himself Yamīn al-Dawla wa-Amīn al-Milla' on the evidence of 'the inscription on the wall of Yanāltigīn's tomb' (1966 (introd.): 18–19); the tomb was in fact that of the Khwārazmshāh Ma'mūn ('Utbī 1869, 2: 258; see Chapter 2). He also asserts that Jarbādhqānī was a 'fanatic Sunnī' on the basis of 'Utbī's description, at the beginning of the account of Tāhartī, of Maḥmūd's devotion to religious learning (1966: 28).
80. Farrazīn, located halfway between Hamadan and Isfahan near the town of Karaj-i Abū Dulaf, was a strong fort to which the Saljūq sultans sent their prisoners and their treasures. Ay Aba established himself there after Sultan Ṭughril's death and repaired the fort.
81. According to Ibn al-Athīr, Aytughmish (Aydughmish) set up Uzbak ibn Jahān Pahlavān as king, while he himself ruled. Ibn al-Athīr calls him astute, courageous but tyrannical, in contrast to the just Kukja (1965, 12: 195; compare Rāvandī 1921: 388–92). Aytughmish ruled until 608/1211–12, when the Pahlavani *mamlūk*s went over to Uzbak's *mamlūk* Minglī; see Luther 1971a: 401.
82. The calculations were based on *ḥisāb al-jumal*, that is, on the numerical value of the letters of the Arabic alphabet.
83. Bosworth (1968c: 180–2) states that according to most sources this was done by, or at the instigation of, Inānch Khātūn, whom Ṭughril later executed, and that it was her son Qutlugh Inānch who summoned the Khwarazmian army to Rayy, which Ṭughril

initially defeated but with whom he refused to negotiate a truce; he also refused to wait for reinforcements before engaging them again.

84. Jarbādhqānī seems to share Rāvandī's negative opinion of Kukja; and indeed, his brief account of these events seems like a condensation of Rāvandī's. As Rāvandī's account ends five years before Kukja's murder, it is possible that Jarbādhqānī might have had access to an early version of it.

85. Whether it would have been appreciated by Ay Aba himself is another matter. As Luther notes of the amīrs (1971a: 402), 'They are generally characterized as rapacious ... but some of them, notably Jamāl al-Dīn Āy Abah Ulugh Bār-bak were of good repute and even pious ... Some of the members of this class apparently had at least the elements of a literary education, but, again, there is too little to allow one to generalize. One can only say that they had the opportunities for education which money, power, and high position allowed.'

86. The verse puns on the meanings of *yamīn*: '(my) fortune', '(my) right hand', and *Yamīnī*, the title of 'Utbī's work.

Conclusion

THE THEMES OF HISTORY

The two and a half centuries covered by our survey witnessed many changes. The Sāmānids, original sponsors of the Persian cultural and literary revival, fell. Their Ghaznavid successors, defeated by the Saljūqs after some forty years of rule in Khurasan, retreated to their eastern territories, where they survived for a little over a century more. The Saljūqs, who also ended Būyid hegemony in the west, were divided and destabilised for most of their last century of rule. The earliest histories in our survey were written at a time of political and cultural expansion; the authors of the latest saw their own time as one of political upheaval and intellectual decline. These changing circumstances could not but affect the course of historical writing. For all that, throughout these two and a half centuries writers of history shared a number of fundamental concerns, which they expressed in terms relating to the basic themes of historical writing.

First and foremost, and central to both Arabic and Persian histories, is the term *dawla*, whose literal meaning of 'alternation', 'revolution' (of time) and 'turn', is extended to mean '(term of) fortune', 'success', '(period of) rule' (of an individual ruler and/or a larger group) and 'dynasty'. In this last sense it takes on increasing significance in later histories, as writers sought reasons for the rise, and more especially the fall, of the *dawla* with which they were associated. For early historians like ʿUtbī, Gardīzī and Bayhaqī the replacement of the Sāmānids by the far greater *dawla* of the Ghaznavids, headed by rulers of the stature of Sabuktigīn and Maḥmūd, represented progress, particularly as it resulted in the restoration of order; and though Gardīzī and Bayhaqī were writing in troubled times, this note of optimism may still be seen. For Saljūq historians the situation is more problematical: the *dawlat* is most often that of the current sultan; the concept of a collective Saljūq *dawlat* appears relatively late, as a largely retrospective construct.

Opposed to *dawla*, prosperous rule, are *fitna*, 'civil strife', and *fatra*, 'slackening', the weakening of authority which leads to discord, violence and injustice. Wansbrough observes that *fitna* 'comprehends a fairly extensive semantic field generally reducible to the notion of communal fragmentation/disintegration/dissolution', and that (at least in early Islamic history) 'the issue was one of political authority, not religious doctrine' (1978: 119). But it was always easy to brand a rebel a heretic; and for Saljūq authors in particular (Niẓām al-Mulk, Ibn al-Balkhī) *fitna* is spread by heretics like Mazdak, Mānī or the Bāṭinīs, whose preaching challenges the established order. *Fatra*, on the other hand, results from political weakness, the inability to maintain order, administrative incompetence and official corruption: financial extortion, abuse of the populace, incitement of the mob to violence. *Fatra* also means 'period' and 'interval'; in this sense it refers to periods of disorder and civil strife which accompany the transfer of rule.

Increasingly our authors seek to identify the signs which attend, and perhaps predict, the conditions of this transfer. For Bal'amī the decline of Abbasid authority was anticipated almost from the outset by the caliphs' mistreatment of their Persian supporters and advisors; for 'Utbī, the fall of the Sāmānids was triggered by their military adventures in Sistan, and finally brought about by the disloyalty and treachery of their commanders; for Bayhaqī, the Ghaznavids' loss of Khurasan was due both to flaws in Mas'ūd's character and to the machinations of his inexperienced and self-interested favourites. For Rāvandī the fall of the Saljūqs was caused by their failure to maintain respect for religious scholars and learning, and by their appointment of corrupt and irreligious officials who were allowed to abuse the populace with impunity; for Jarbādhqānī it was the division of Saljūq territories amongst ambitious and self-serving Pahlavānī *mamlūk*s that led to the ruin both of those territories and of the *mamlūk*s themselves.

Legitimacy of rule is thus not a matter of power but of morality. Politically, it is further linked to the issue of authority. In Islamic political thought the highest authority is that of the caliph, the leader of the Islamic community as a whole, through whose sanction rule must be legitimated. Makdisi cites Jacques Maritain's distinction between authority and power: '*Power* is the force by means of which you can oblige others to obey you. *Authority* is the *right* to direct and command, to be listened to or obeyed by others' (1963: 70; author's emphases). Thus for example the Ṣaffārids, Būyids and Saljūqs endeavoured to gain caliphal endorsement, even though they were often in a position of greater power; thus, too, the caliphs used their authority to exploit internal dissensions within those houses, or between them and their rivals. But Abbasid authority itself was challenged, especially by such Shī'ī groups as the Zaydīs, Qarmaṭīs, and Fāṭimids; the latter in particular, with a fully established caliphate in Cairo, provided alternative sources of authority to those in search of power or of independence from Abbasid hegemony (see Bosworth 1962; Makdisi 1963). Others might support counter-claimants to the Abbasid caliphate; thus the Sāmānids refused to recognise the Būyid-appointed caliph al-Qādir and favoured the deposed al-Ṭā'ī.[1]

In moral terms the legitimate ruler is the just ruler. But justice is not simply a matter of maintaining equity amongst subjects (this is, so to speak, its minimum requirement), but also of practising virtue. That the study of history can aid in the acquisition of virtue is stressed by many of our authors, perhaps most conspicuously by Bayhaqī, but also by Ibn Funduq, Nīshāpūrī, Rāvandī and Jarbādhqānī. The closely related virtues of justice and loyalty provide important themes, especially for those historians writing recent or contemporary history: both involve the recognition of rights and the discharge of obligations. Subordinates owe loyalty to their superiors – *mamlūk*s to their masters, scribes to their administrative heads, soldiers to their commanders, military and administrative officials to their rulers; but the just ruler must also observe the rights of subordinates, and especially of loyal servants.

History teaches practical as well as moral lessons, particularly with respect to governance and administration. This is a crucial issue for Saljūq writers especially: Niẓām al-Mulk holds up the Ghaznavid administration as a model; Ibn al-Balkhī dwells on the antiquity of the administrative practices of Fars. Again, the political and the moral are interconnected: improper administrative practice (abandoning the spy system; awarding inappropriate titles; appointing Turks, Shī'īs and heretics to official positions) leads to injustice, corruption and civil strife. The examples of the past provide guides to present and future conduct.

THE PATTERNS OF HISTORY

History imparts its lessons through presenting recurrent patterns of events and of human conduct. Thucydides wrote that his work was intended to benefit those who wished 'to understand clearly what has happened and what will happen, when, in accordance with human nature (or things), events like this and of this kind will occur again' (quoted by Trompf 1979: 110). Miskawayh wrote his 'Experiences of the Nations' because, as he stated, the study of the past provides both models and warnings with respect to present and future action: whatever is likely to happen in the future has a likeness in the events of the past.

Many of what Noth and Conrad (1994) designate, with respect to early Islamic histories, as 'topoi' and 'schemata' express this underlying concept. A topos, defined as a narrative motif which functions to specify content and which 'is normally bound to description of a specific situation, definition of a brief moment, or characterization of a person', may have 'a basis in fact'; but when topoi 'move from the domain of life to that of literature ... they become transferable', and may provide 'powerful means to promote certain distinct tendencies and biases'. A schema is a narrative motif concerned chiefly with form, 'with connecting, relating, and organizing matters of content'; schemata tend to be paradigmatic, and 'any relation at all to historical fact ... is purely a matter of coincidence' (1994: 109–10). The assumption that once such topoi and schemata (particularly the latter) have been identified they may be ignored (see for example 1994: 201) raises questions that cannot be fully addressed here; but regardless of whether such topoi and schemata bear any relation to 'historical fact' (and I would argue that they do, and that both reflect a broader hermeneutic effort to endow historical data with meaning, as well as lending themselves to polemic), their use points to a belief in history's recurrent patterns.[2]

Scholars who have related the notion of recurrence to concepts of time as represented by human history have sometimes posited two opposing concepts of historical time: one cyclical, repetitive and influenced by astronomical movements (as in Greek views of time as cyclical or circular, 'returning perpetually on itself'), the other linear, proceeding from a finite beginning to an eschatological end (as in the Christian view of time).[3] Cyclical theories however deal primarily with cosmic history; human history, inscribed therein, is fundamentally linear. As de Romilly writes:

> The cyclic pattern has been grossly overestimated. If it is true that the Greeks have always been deeply impressed by the order of the cosmos – with the regular evolutions of the sun and moon or of the stars, and with the regular succession, for men, of nights and days or summers and winters – and if it is true that they have often used this cyclic order as a starting point for their cosmologic or cosmogonic representations or even as a metaphor for their view of human life, there is not one single instance of a Greek author having developed a cyclic view of history. (1991: 9–10)[4]

The Christian view of time as linear led Augustine, for one, to ponder two questions. First, since the world is not eternal and 'human history has a limit', how old is the human race? (His calculations produced 'a figure of less than six thousand years between Adam and Augustine's present'.) Second, if 'at least one radical, irreversible change, the Incarnation, has taken place within history', have there been other such changes? (Augustine, studying the Old Testament's record of 'abrupt changes in God's dealings with mankind', arrived at a total of six dispensations, each of which 'has lasted about a thousand years ... Thus there are six millennia of human history corresponding to the six days of creation, and to the six ages of man' [Kemp 1991: 19–20]). Muslim historians also conceived of successive dispensations, culminating in that of Muḥammad, and in this way integrated Islam into the overall framework of world history (see Wansbrough 1978: 88–9). While some philosophers, and esotericists like the Ismāʿīlīs, developed cyclical or circular notions of time, historians presented human history as proceeding from a finite beginning – the Creation – to a preordained end.[5] For them, recurrence was not a matter of the same event repeating itself, but of certain types of event recurring throughout the course of history.

Astrological history associated specific conjunctions with particular types of event: the appearance of a prophet, a period of calamities, the transfer of rule. Niẓām al-Mulk spoke of 'celestial events' which produced disorder and civil strife, followed by the restoration of order and justice by a divinely chosen ruler; and we may recall the metaphorical interpretation of one such event (the conjunction of 582/1186–7) as presaging the transfer of rule. Alternation in human affairs is often compared to the alternation of the seasons: as the heavenly sphere turns bad times follow good, as autumn follows spring. Firdawsī often adverts to the theme that Time, or Fortune, is now friendly, now inimical, that it elevates one only to bring him down and set another in his place (although, in the end, all are equal in death). Other writers quote the Koranic verse (3: 26), 'O Lord of sovereignty, You give rule to whom You will and take rule away from whom You will; You elevate whom You will and humble whom You will; in Your hand is good, and verily You are powerful over all things', to affirm the workings of the divine plan.

But it is human agency that brings about the fall of states. Greek writers explained the 'degeneration of governments' in terms of ethical change: rulers characterised by 'arrogance, impiety, or greed ... turned an order of lawfulness and political responsibility into a regime of injustice, lawlessness, and depravity' (Trompf 1979: 106–7).[6] Such thinking was further linked to 'notions of the successive emergence and dissipation of empires' (Trompf 1979: 186). The ethical interpretation of historical events leads to exemplary history, which depicts recurrent event-types as embodied in the deeds of great men of the past.

These great men function as exemplars. Their words and deeds may be presented briefly, in sententiae or anecdotes, or more extensively, in the form of historical narrative. Timothy Hampton argues that in the latter case, if the exemplar's 'ideological function of inspiring the reader is to be effective [he] must demonstrate consistently admirable action', but that the narrative form itself 'undermines the persuasive power of the exemplar', as it may consist of actions connoting both virtue and vice. Thus 'the persuasive function of the name may be undermined by the ambiguity of certain of the hero's acts' (1990: 26–7). Names do indeed carry the power to evoke specific qualities; but this is perhaps the least complex level of exemplarity, that of name/quality in fixed association, seen in panegyric clichés and in the schematic, gnomic anecdotes of mirrors for princes (where 'Umar ibn al-Khaṭṭāb, for example, typically figures the pious ruler, or Anūshīrvān the just king). Such automatic associations may be called into question, as in divergent treatments of Alexander (rapacious destroyer versus ideal ruler), Anūshīrvān (whose injustice towards the pious Buzurgmihr earns him a place in Hell), or more recent figures such as Alp Arslān (whose reign, described by Rāvandī as 'tranquil', begins with the murder of Kundurī). Exemplarity functions not merely to provide generalised ethical models, but to serve political, and polemical, ends.

Similarly, exemplary event types or situations are not devoid of ambiguity, and may be presented with varying degrees of complexity. Expanding upon Noth and Conrad's terminology, we can distinguish two chief methods of presentation: schematic, where parallel events of particular significance recur throughout a narrative (Ibn al-Balkhī's three heresy episodes), and topical (for example, Bayhaqī's digressions, usually introduced by some such phrase as 'these events remind me of ...' or 'such things have happened in the past', and deal with such topics as the bravery of women, punishment excessive to the offence, politically incriminating letters, and so on). The two types often overlap. Schematic representations, while they present generalised object lessons (the dangers of heresy, the murder of a vizier), are also of clear relevance to present concerns.

HISTORY AND AUTHORITY

For history of any sort to be persuasive, it must be authoritative. Bayhaqī asserted (as had Ibn Farīghūn a century before) that the sources of historical information are twofold: eyewitness accounts, based on autopsy or on the testimony of reliable informants, and books. Other writers point out that since one cannot experience all the events that take place even in one's own time, books are indispensable guides to both past and contemporary history.

Kemp argues that for medieval historians, 'every history must have an authoritative, ancient source, and every medieval historian who is not chronicling events within living memory begins by naming his *auctours*.' Authors of romances similarly claim for their works a past source, or sources, in order 'to redeem [them] from the sin of invention. The medieval mind would not tolerate the new, the original; every work of literature or art must be a recapitulation of the universal atemporal unity of what is already known' (1991: 51–2). But although our authors term themselves 'compilers' of the deeds and words of men of the past, and some provide detailed mention of their sources, each reworks his materials, and each 'imposes his own interpretive voice' upon them (Hampton 1990: 35). None recapitulates past history (even that of the ancient past) in a uniform fashion. This is not only because writers drew upon different, sometimes conflicting, accounts; for once they had chosen one version over another, invention played its part in elaborating the raw materials. Educated audiences would have been aware of different versions and, confronted by an unexpected treatment, would have asked, 'Why this particular version?'

Lambton asserts that writers of both general and local histories 'rarely weighed the reliability of their sources [and] seldom made a distinction between ascertained fact and tradition' (1991: 235). In fact they did; we have only to recall Bal'amī's corrections of Ṭabari, the author of the *Mujmal*'s insistence that he has written down only what was in his sources, or Ibn Funduq's affirmation of the reliability of history. While we may question the inclusion in some works of obviously legendary materials, or of *mirabilia*, prophecies, omens and the like, for our authors these were part of history and served its purposes of edification and entertainment.[7] But claims to reliance on authoritative sources serve a variety of purposes other than the seemingly obvious one. They establish that the work undertaken is both serious and scholarly. They may be designed to stress the historian's impartiality, or to distance him from controversial material. They may be meant to dispel incredulity or doubts as to the author's own reliability. They serve to demonstrate the author's erudition, and in that sense also his credentials (as historian and/or as candidate for a post at court). Appeals to authority should not always be taken at face value.

The appeal to authority is also linked to the appropriation of prior authoritative narratives. Notker (c. 885), writing during the 'Carolingian renaissance', articulated the notion of *translatio studii*, averring that 'knowledge [had] passed *per successum* from Paradise through the great custodians of culture – the Hebrews, the Egyptians, the Athenians, and the Romans – finally coming to rest at Paris' (Trompf 1979: 247). For Muslim historians the trajectory of the transfer of knowledge was a different one; but for Arabic writers of the 3rd/9th and 4th/10th centuries the learning of the past had definitely come to rest at Baghdad. Balʿamī's Ṭabarī brings the Persian learning appropriated by the Arab conquerors home to Bukhara, completing a circle at the beginning of which (according to the translators of the *Tafsīr*) the knowledge 'from Paradise' had been imparted to Adam in the original prophetic language, Persian. *Translatio studii* accompanies, and symbolises, *translatio imperii*; and for early authors Persian history has passed from its Arab expropriators to its rightful owners and is expressed in its rightful language.

The earliest initiatives to encourage Persian historical writing, taken at the highest levels by rulers, viziers or local princes, produced translations which reappropriated Persian learning and the Persian past. The final history in our survey is also a translation; but whereas Balʿamī's Ṭabari led logically to the Sāmānids as rulers of the East (as, for Gardīzī, all Eastern history led to the Ghaznavids), for Jarbādhqānī Ghaznavid history does not lead to the Saljūqs, whose deeds, unrecorded by historians, will soon fade from memory. Jarbādhqānī's decision to write in the language in which he was least competent, Persian, might be compared to that of the sixteenth-century Latin stylist Guillaume Budé to write his *Institution du prince* (dedicated to François I) in 'the language in which I am least practiced', French. Budé observed that 'the illustrious deeds of French kings have remained uncelebrated by the world at large because the French have neglected to cultivate great orators and writers'; to 'translate' ancient history into French would both 'vindicate the Gallic tradition and encourage the great deeds of Francis'. This new narrative, linking past and present, would '[bring] the light of history to elucidate the deeds of the French Pompey' (Hampton 1990: 41–2).

Jarbādhqānī celebrates no Saljūq Turkish Maḥmūd; nor is there any evidence of a sense of connection between past and present. Quite the opposite: there is a great 'black hole' between the end of ʿUtbī's history in 412/1021 and the year 582/1186, that of the death of Muḥammad Jahān Pahlavān. Jarbādhqānī does not propose to memorialise the Saljūqs; still less does he see their succession to the Ghaznavids as part of an unbroken line of transfer of rule (although he does state that one of the benefits of ʿUtbī's history is to encourage emulation of the great deeds of past rulers [1966: 9]). His complaints of lack of Saljūq patronage parallel Budé's with respect to the French, and the historical gap already noted is also, as for Budé, a literary one, which Jarbādhqānī proposes to fill with his translation, accessible to both 'Turk and Persian'. But the link between present and past is, for him, a weak and fragile one. *Translatio studii* is no longer a necessary, and symbolic, accompaniment to *translatio imperii*; and Jarbādhqānī does not so much appropriate ʿUtbī's history as use it to point to the break in the chain of succession of which Balʿamī and Gardīzī were so conscious.[8]

The writing of recent or contemporary history presents different problems of authority. The method its authors employ is to collect eyewitness reports (oral or written) and other contemporary materials (letters, documents, poetry) and to organise these into a continuous history which will fix events into a narrative before they fade from memory. (Bayhaqī states that his purpose in writing his history of Masʿūd is to record the achievements and qualities both of that ruler and of those notables who served him, lest they be forgotten.) The ultimate authority for this narrative becomes the historian himself: it is he who determines what will be included, what omitted, what emphasised and what passed over with only brief mention. Because of his position as eyewitness to, and participant in, many of the events he records, he also acquires the right to write history *in propria persona*.[9]

LANGUAGE, STYLE AND HISTORY

All our historians either served courts – often at a high level – or were closely associated with courts; and all, despite differences in style, wrote rhetorical history, that is, history designed to be persuasive rather than simply to convey facts. To persuade, a narrative must be convincing, that is, it must appear to be true; this is especially crucial in the case of contemporary history, whose events are still present in living memory and have not yet been reduced to the schematic narratives of the more remote past.

Beginning his account of Masʿūd's seizure of the Turkish commander Ghāzī, Bayhaqī observes: 'It would be absurd to write something that might seem incredible ... But in truth it must be known that Sultan Masʿūd was not inclined to bring down Ghāzī' (1971: 298). The account which follows attributes Ghāzī's fall both to the enmity of the Maḥmūdī party, who turned the Sultan against him, and to his own youth and disrespect for his elders; it includes details for which no eyewitness testimony is cited, and concludes with an exhortation to beware the treachery of this world, followed by a brief digression of similar purport explicitly designated as an admonition. While it might indeed seem incredible that Masʿūd would, against his own inclination, bring down a loyal servant and that Ghāzī's detractors would stop at nothing until their victim was destroyed, the circumstantial detail provided leaves the reader in no doubt as to the truth of these events; that they also relate to a recurrent pattern of behaviour seen throughout the history, as well as to a more general truth about human affairs, further reinforces their credibility.

The historian's task is to elicit meaning from the raw materials of history, whether these are derived from books, from eyewitnesses, or from documentary sources.[10] He begins with the facts at hand, which he develops through the introduction and elaboration of corroborative testimony, employing his rhetorical skills in 'the imaginative creation of verisimilar materials which build up the *données* into a winning larger structure' (Ray 1986: 68). The resulting account, and the materials which serve as its rhetorical proofs, should not be viewed as 'fictions', although the strategies employed resemble those associated with the writing of fiction.[11] These strategies are essential to the composition of a convincing narrative; for as the author of the *Ad Herennium* stated, 'there is no use in telling the truth if the audience will not believe it. Even the truth must meet the standard of verisimilitude, for the facts themselves may be incredible' (Ray 1986: 71–2).

The effect of verisimilitude is heightened by the incorporation into the narrative of materials such as documents – letters, reports, decrees, oaths, and so on; inscriptions, like that which Maḥmūd of Ghazna had placed on the tomb of the Khwārazmshāh Ma'mūn – of poetry, and of formal and informal speeches and dialogues, contemporary with or relevant to the events related (on the use of such materials see Rosenthal 1968: 118–28). While scholars like Noth and Conrad view such 'insertions' with suspicion, it seems more sensible to accept Wansbrough's view that they

> are not aesthetically or logically intrusive ... The narrative unit might as easily contain/be a document or poem as a report or anecdote. Thus to speak of "insertion" may be misleading, there being in that term some connotation of superfluity or dispensability. (1978: 36)

The function of such materials is 'testimonial, that is, witness to action as cause and effect' (1978: 36, and see 32–9).

The secretary-historian writing past or contemporary history had access not only to books but to official documents. Lambton argued that 'Persian historians had no archives to draw upon', although 'service to rulers gave them access to some records' (1991: 234); Bayhaqī's accounts show that chanceries made copies of the documents which passed through them and retained them in their archives.[12] Some probably kept diaries of current events, as did Bayhaqī, who also possessed personal copies of many documents. Although some of these were destroyed, he still retained many which he used in his history.

Documents are often considered neutral sources of information;

but medieval chancery documents were carefully composed and designed for persuasive effect. Their use in histories is calculated to contribute to the historian's overall concerns. (This is true even of Ibn al-Balkhī's apparently dry record of fluctuations in the tax revenues of Fars, which serve his purpose of promoting a revival of Fars's economy.) Many of the letters Bayhaqī includes in his history are at odds with his own accounts of the events to which they relate; for example, a letter written on Mas'ūd's behalf by Bayhaqī himself to the Qarakhānid Arslān Khān after the defeat at Dandānqān, which was designed to persuade the Khān to commit troops, under his own leadership, to come to Mas'ūd's assistance, puts the whole disastrous sequence of events in the best possible light, suppressing the less flattering details of the campaign which are seen in Bayhaqī's own account of these events. (The Khān, it seems, was not impressed, and did not respond to this appeal.)

Poetic insertions, especially those of the type termed 'historico-documentary' (Rubinacci 1964: 268), also serve testimonial purposes.[13] For dynastic historians such as 'Utbī, panegyric (as well as satirical and elegiac) poetry served not as mere embellishment, but as documentary material. The official function of panegyric was to spread the ruler's fame, and it was widely disseminated (see Niẓāmi 'Arūẓī [1899: 42–9] on rulers' need for poets to memorialise them). 'Utbī never misses an opportunity to incorporate panegyrics to Maḥmūd (and others) in his history; Rāvandī and Jarbādhqānī quote lengthy panegyrics (many of their own composition) to contemporary figures. It is all the more surprising therefore to find that Bayhaqī includes no contemporary panegyrics to Mas'ūd, an omission which constitutes a deliberate break with customary practice.

On several occasions Bayhaqī explains this omission, stating for example that such poems are all recorded in *dīvān*s, that to include them would make the work too long and that 'it is well known what sort of (poetry) is recited at feasts' (1971: 697, and see also 360; he also notes that Mas'ūd desired such poetry and paid handsomely for it). Since Bayhaqī had included panegyrics on Maḥmūd in his account of that ruler, and since elsewhere he has few reservations about the length of his work, this seems disingenuous.[14] The omission of contemporary panegyrics to Mas'ūd is made all the more conspicuous by the inclusion of two long poems in praise of the Ghaznavids composed twenty years later, at his own request, by Bū Ḥanīfa Iskāfī, who had never served them.[15] Several of Bū Ḥanīfa's panegyrics to Sultan Ibrāhīm are also quoted; Bayhaqī observes that this is the type of poetry which should be written for kings, 'sound and strong and (full of) advice' (1971: 494). The sole quotation from a poet contemporary with Masʿūd consists of several verses by his court poet Masʿūd Rāzī, in which the poet warns the prince that if his enemies were once ants, they have now grown into serpents, and should not be ignored lest they become dragons.[16] The inclusion of these critical verses, together with the deliberate omission of poems in praise of Masʿūd, suggests that Bayhaqī had no intention of allowing the panegyrists' image of that ruler to compete with his own.

Perhaps the most problematic category of insertions is that of reported speech. Formal orations do not figure importantly in Persian histories, as they do in Arabic; their place is largely taken by panegyrics.[17] Such exchanges as that between the caliph al-Manṣūr and Abū Muslim quoted by Balʿamī and Gardīzī ultimately derive from the Arabic sources, and have become set pieces employed for dramatic effect. Of greater interest is the use of reported speech by contemporary historians such as Bayhaqī. Some are based on written sources – for example, conversations included in ʿAbd al-Ghaffār's account of Masʿūd's youth, which Bayhaqī received both orally and in writing, or those contained in letters reporting events which took place away from court. Others, such as conversations between Bayhaqī and his master Bū Naṣr Mishkān, or between Bū Naṣr and other officials, were most probably recorded in their broad outlines, and clearly express the views of the parties concerned. Despite Bayhaqī's obvious stylistic embellishment of such materials, we are not at liberty to conclude that they were made up out of whole cloth. More problematic are such utterances as Kundurī's final words to his assassin, which reiterate a topos seen earlier in Bayhaqī (where it is voiced by Ḥasanak's mother), and which clearly serve both admonitory and argumentative ends.

Such inserted materials are disposed within the overall narrative framework of the history so as to contribute to its persuasive impact.[18] In general our historians employ a chronological framework; but the selection and presentation of events is dictated, first and foremost, by thematics, which means that some materials are grouped together in relation to themes rather than in strict chronological order.[19] The resulting apparent disregard for chronology is sometimes seen as demonstrating an affinity between histories and *adab* anthologies, in which discrete accounts are grouped together under thematic rubrics (see for example Khalidi 1994: 83–130). But this affinity relates more to the common edificatory and exemplary purposes of both history and *adab* than to formal organisation. Thematic concerns dictate both the omission of information that does not further the major themes and the elaboration of materials that are thematically significant. There are of course differences in approach. Bayhaqī's grouping of thematically related materials (digressions, accounts of prominent individuals and families, flash-backs to earlier Ghaznavid history) at appropriate points regardless of chronology, and his abundant use of circumstantial detail, which gives the impression that everything thematically relevant has been included, contrasts with Rāvandī's more schematic approach, where everything is omitted that does not contribute to his overall thematic concerns.

Cicero enjoined Latin writers to 'become "elaborators" (*exornates rerum*), not simply "purveyors of the details" (*narratores*)'.[20] By this he meant something other than ornament in its technical sense, although this too is of course a marked feature of much rhetorical history, especially when written in the figured chancery style.[21] The Arabic chancery style had adopted many 'poetic' devices – metaphor, figures of speech and thought, and balanced phrasing, either un-rhymed or accompanied by rhyme (*saj*ʿ, rhyming prose) – as well as a refined use of quotations. Such devices became part and parcel of the Persian chancery style as it developed; but in both languages the figured style came to be used in a wide variety of genres unrelated to official purposes. (For overviews of Arabic and Persian artistic prose see Heinrichs 1997; Meisami 1997; see also Kanazi 1989: 137–43; Luther 1977; Niẓāmī ʿArūẓi 1899: 22–42.) Questions relating to the development and the specific features of the Persian chancery style cannot be discussed here;[22] what seems clear however is that the differences between the relatively unadorned styles of Balʿamī, Bayhaqī or Nīshāpūrī and the figured style employed by Kirmānī, Rāvandī or Jarbādhqānī cannot be attributed solely to the delayed penetration of the Arabic chancery style into Persian, as Arabic historians of the 4th/10th century exhibit similar differences (Miska-wayh's style for example is far less ornamental than is ʿUtbī's).

Luther used Bayhaqī as his standard for comparison between the styles of writers trained in the Ghaznavid and in the Saljūq chan-ceries. But Bayhaqī is quite capable of employing, where appropriate, the figured style which Luther associated with the later Saljūq period.[23] The choice of style has much to do with matters of decorum, of what is appropriate to specific contexts. The Arabic critic Abū Hilāl al-ʿAskarī (d. after 400/1010), discussing the principles of *kitāba* (chancery prose), asserted that 'the cardinal rule of composition is an awareness of the social status and linguistic ability of the addressee' (Kanazi 1989: 140–1). He further recommended that whereas corres-pondence directed from the capital to the provinces should be straightforward and unequivocal, secretaries in regional areas writing to their superiors should employ indirection (especially metonymy and wordplay) in conveying sensitive matters, and should demonstrate their rhetorical ability in such awkward situations as, for example, writing an apology for a defeat (Kanazi 1989: 141–2). These two points – the need to take into account the addressee's social status and linguistic ability, and the recognition that direct and indirect styles are appropriate to different situations – make it useful to think in terms of a continuum between the 'transparent' or 'plain' style and what Richard Lanham (1973) terms the 'opaque' style, and to see both as rhetorical stances which may moreover coexist in the same work.

Lanham argues that the opaque style has the danger of calling attention to itself, that it transfers attention from what is being said to how it is being said and thus invites 'ironical scrutiny' (1973: 169). Our authors wrote in a courtly milieu in which indirection and oblique expression were as much a feature of ordinary verbal communication as of written style and where to voice open criticism was to invite reprisal. Especially in the writing of contemporary history, much tact was required to avoid offending patrons or provoking enemies. The invitation to interpret ironically passages marked by high-flown rhetoric may often be deliberate: one thinks of 'Utbī's extravagant praise of Abū Bakr Maḥmashād's piety, which (as Mānīnī noted) underlines his hypocrisy. Style is not merely 'a function of genre' (Fornara 1983: 19); it has also to do with questions of addressee and of audience, which will be further addressed in the next section.[24]

RHETORIC AND POLITICS

In the Introduction we noted that comparisons have sometimes been made between the 'Renaissance of Islam' and the Italian Renaissance. Joel Kraemer, in particular, has drawn parallels between the rise of 'Islamic humanism' and that of Italian humanist scholarship (see 1986a: 5–12). Both looked to the learning and the examples of the past. Professionally, the principle representatives of both were drawn from the administrative classes. Kraemer also sees a common feature in what Burckhardt termed the 'discovery of the individual', citing for writers of the Būyid period the growing importance of personal experience, the emphasis by historians such as Miskawayh on the superiority of eyewitness accounts to written ones, and the rise of letter-writing as an important literary genre.

This comparison should not be overdrawn; but it might profitably be extended to include other political and social factors. The rise of Italian humanism coincided with that of the city state, 'where social structure required an educated elite able to read and write good administrative Latin'. The stylistic models for such education were

Roman (see Hampton 1990: 14–15). Along with this return to past ideals however came a new interest in writing contemporary history which was 'guided ... by the exigencies of political propaganda'; the rulers of city states patronised the writing of histories that were typically 'organized around a single personage who was to be glorified through the recitation of his deeds' (Ianziti 1988: 5–6). The authors of these histories were humanist secretaries who served in the chanceries of these princes and were deeply involved in their policies and in their legitimatory projects. They were, in short, 'participants in power ... the architects and exponents of policy, the wielders of authority. It was their daily business to support and promote the regime upon which their livelihood and fortunes directly depended.' In many cases their writing of history 'grew out of their daily routine as a natural extension of their normal administrative duties' (Ianziti 1988: 90).

Italian humanist history was linked both to increasing urbanisation and to the rise to power of city states ruled, often as not, by *condottieri* who had achieved rule by force. Islamicate society was, by contrast, already highly urbanised. But while under the early Abbasids political and cultural life had been centred on Baghdad, with the weakening of caliphal authority and the rise of semi-autonomous local rulers urban centres proliferated, and competed in the political and cultural spheres with one another and with Baghdad. The writing of history was one arena in which this competition was played out; and if histories written by court officials were not necessarily focused on a single individual, the emphasis on individual rulers – the Būyid ʿAḍud al-Dawla, Maḥmūd of Ghazna – is palpable.

The writing of history was in many instances an 'extension of the duties' of our secretary-historians, if not always a 'natural' one. Balʿamī was commissioned to translate Ṭabarī; Ṣābi' was coerced into writing his *Tājī*. But it appears that by Bayhaqī's time the dynamic which had motivated such earlier projects was beginning to flag. At the end of the section on virtue which precedes the account of Masʿūd's reign he observes that, as he writes, he knows that

> there are (other) great men in this noble court who, were they to occupy themselves with writing the history of this ruler [Masʿūd], would hit the mark, and would show men that they are the riders and I on foot ... and that they should write and I learn, and when they speak I listen. (1971: 128)

But these men are occupied with the important business of the *dawlat*, and in making sure 'that no breach may occur that would make any enemy, envier or slanderer happy and satisfied', and are unable to devote themselves to the task of writing history.

> Therefore I have undertaken this task, as their deputy; for if I delayed, waiting for them to take up this charge, they might not do so, and with the passage of time these accounts would grow far from men's eyes and minds. (Then) someone else might appear (to do) this work who could not ride this mount as I can; and the great traces of this famous house would be effaced. I have seen histories written before me about past kings by their servants, in which they have made additions and omissions, intending thereby adornment. The situation of the kings of this house ... is different, since – praise be to God! – their grandeur is resplendant as the sun. (1971: 128–9)

Like many of Bayhaqī's statements, this need not be taken at face value. If it is the duty of courtiers to write the history of their rulers, Bayhaqī implies that it is not simply that those who ought to be writing Ghaznavid history are too busy to do so, but also that they are either disinclined to or that there is no patronage for such a project. As a veteran servant of the Ghaznavids, at a time when the *dawlat* is under threat, he has taken it upon himself to record and publicise their achievements; but unlike previous 'servants' who have written the histories of past kings (one thinks of Ṣābi'), and who amplified some matters and omitted others, he will tell the whole truth about this house, whose grandeur is, in any case, 'resplendant as the sun'. If those earlier histories are to be rejected as mere propaganda, Bayhaqī's own propagandistic motive is clear both in his determination to memorialise (and publish) the Ghaznavids' achievements, and in his apparent need (provoked by what circumstances we cannot know) to justify his undertaking.

The comparison of history to propaganda may seem invidious; but all of our historians share propagandistic motives, in that their work is closely bound up with the legitimation (either contemporary or retrospective) of their rulers or with the promotion of the special status of their region and its inhabitants. But the audiences who were to be persuaded by their arguments vary. Here we may return to Abū Hilāl's principle of the stylistic decorum to be observed with respect to both the social status and the linguistic ability of one's addressee – and, more broadly put, of one's audience. For it will have become evident that there is often a considerable difference, both in status and in linguistic ability, between a work's official addressee and its actual intended audience, and that as time passes the relation between status and linguistic competence is reversed from that which obtained in the period when the first Persian histories appeared, due to what Luther identified as changed circumstances of communication which produced an increasing gap between the official and the actual addressees both of chancery correspondance and of other prose writing.

Luther argued that Saljūq scribes 'were acutely conscious that their work was always subject to the most critical scrutiny by other scribes, including superiors, envious peers and sworn enemies', and that it 'was always on display'. Their 'discovery' of the figured style enabled them to compose official letters or documents which constituted display texts testifying to 'elegance and fine workmanship'. Such documents

> were tokens in a system of exchange among members of the ruling elite. The most important ones were read aloud in solemn assembly and were expected to be among the most perfect examples of the craft. The rhetorical figures must have seemed a welcome addition to the repertoire of stylistic devices by scribes who were called upon to produce displays of skill. It gave the craft a new dimension and [allowed] the practitioners to develope an ornate, artful Persian prose which came to be regarded as the only appropriate style for this type of interchange among members of the ruling class. (1990: 94)[25]

The essential features of this picture have not changed from Ghaznavid (or even Sāmānid and Būyid) times: the constant scrutiny of the scribes' work, the rivalries, the production of display texts (primarily in Arabic correspondence addressed to the caliphal court or to Būyid administrators with a taste for rhetorical eloquence). What has changed is that, while the members of the ruling class may have exchanged such documents, in the case of the Saljūq sultans few if any could have read them.

The communication gap between rulers and administrators that characterised the Saljūq period meant, on the one hand, that the latter became the guardians not only of style but of literacy itself; and it is not unlikely that one reason for the development of the rhetorical style was the wish to preserve that literacy at a high level.[26] But, on the other hand, this disjunction opens up possibilities for communication between administrators over the heads, as it were, of their rulers. It is the administrators who are the intended audiences for the rhetorical histories; it is they who will peruse the work and convey its message to its royal dedicatee; and it is they whom our more rhetorical authors wish both to impress and to persuade.[27] It is they who may exert their influence not only to obtain the author a post (for which they would have been the arbiters), but to persuade the ruler addressed to take the political action advocated in his work. This may account for the use of more straightforward language in describing contemporary political circumstances in need of redress:

such language would have been more accessible, and more persuasive, to the work's official addressee.

Many questions with respect to the overall picture of early Persian historiography still remain open. What has been attempted here is to survey the texts which have survived, within certain geographical and chronological limits, and to place them in a larger perspective with respect both to Islamicate and to other pre-modern historical writing, in the hope that this will encourage more detailed studies which will further advance our understanding of this as yet largely unexplored field.

NOTES

1. Compare, on the need for rulers who have established themselves by force to gain endorsement from higher authorities, Ianziti's illuminating study of Sforza Milan (1988). In Islamic political theory there could be only one leader (caliph) of the polity; the proliferation of counter-claimants at various periods, like the *mamlūks*' installation of a token Abbasid caliph in Cairo after the Mongol sack of Baghdad, testifies to the persistence of the need for a higher source of legitimation.
2. A recurrent topos is that of the ruler who spends his time drinking and pursuing pleasure rather than attending to affairs of state; this usually signals the impending end of his rule or the collapse of the dynasty. We may recall the fate of the young Ṣaffārid Ṭāhir (who also spent much time in the company of pigeons and mules). Bayhaqī describes Mas'ūd's heavy drinking, which increased towards the end of his reign, in psychological terms as the behaviour of a ruler seriously depressed by a deteriorating situation. In such cases there is little reason to doubt the 'facts' of the matter. By contrast, Rāvandī's description of Mas'ūd as a drunkard who neglected affairs of state so that rule passed to the Saljūqs is a deliberately polemical evocation of this topos.
3. The Zoroastrian view of cosmic history, with its twelve successive millennia culminating in the final victory of Ahura Mazda over Ahriman, has also been taken as representing the cyclical category, and has been contrasted with Islamic 'linear' time (see for example Bausani 1975: 46–8); however, this concept also posits a beginning and an end both to cosmic history and to human history within the millennial cycles.
4. True cyclical theories, such as Greek catastrophe theory, 'postulate great periodic upheavals interrupting the life of the whole cosmos, including ... the human race'. Such theories assume the eternity of the world, and some go so far as to posit periodic returns 'of the same world and the same people'; more often there is a belief that the paradigmatic course of human history begins anew after each catastrophe. The 'cycle of movement through various types of government' posited by Polybius in his *Anacyclōsis* 'operates strictly within historical bounds' (Trompf 1979: 7, 9, 13). For Muslims, as for Christians, belief in the eternity of the world was unacceptable, even heretical (although it was held by some philosophers).

5. Ismā'īlī hiero-history was based on 'a circular conception of time divided into eras ... a correspondence between the macrocosm and the microcosm such that all events are both actual and symbolic and a view of history which contrasted vividly with contemporaneous Islamic conceptions of the past'. Time is broadly divided into 'two principle eras, the Era of Concealment [of the Imām] ... and the Era of Disclosure'; the seven cycles of prophecy are linked with the movements of the seven planets (Khalidi 1994: 160, 162, and see further 158–62). On cyclical notions of time in Zoroastrianism and Ismā'īlism see Corbin 1982; Halm 1996: 16–22.
6. The Greek term *stasis*, referring to political deterioraton, civil strife and factionalism (see Trompf 1979: 107), but which means literally a sluggishness of the blood, closely resembles *fatra*, used in the same political senses as well as in that of 'transitional period', whose root (*f-t-r*) means 'to flag', 'to grow languid, sluggish'. The breakdown of social order which results from the ruler's moral decline is seen as a disorder of the body (politic), an unnatural and harmful condition. Islamic historians do not develop the 'body-state analogy' characteristic of Roman historiography (see Trompf 1979: 188–92); ethical philosophers did however compare a well-ordered and well-functioning society to a healthy body (see for example Fārābī's analogy between the human body and the polity quoted in Marlow 1997: 52–3).
7. Some writers exclude such materials. Miskawayh states that he has not given accounts of Prophetic miracles 'because the people of our own days will find no experiences therein from which they can profit as they strive to solve their problems' (1909, 1: 5; translated by Khalidi 1994: 174). Both he and Bayhaqī believed that 'fantastic' tales were not true history; this did not prevent Bayhaqī from including accounts of dreams and prophecies of future greatness experienced by Mas'ūd and by his grandfather Sabuktigīn.
8. The apparent failure of the Saljūqs to exploit the legitimatory uses of history may be contrasted with later dynasties – Mongols, Timūrids, Ottomans – who sponsored both historical writing and extensive programmes of copying and translation. This may have something to do with the Saljūqs' peripatetic lifestyle and lack of centralised rule, which inhibited the growth of stable centres of patronage and of literary/scholarly production. On this issue see especially Schnyder 1973.
9. Compare Fornara's discussion of Greek *historia* (the word itself means 'inquiry', 'research', 'investigation'), the method of which 'consisted basically of the interrogation of witnesses and other informed parties and of the redaction of the answers into a continuous narrative'. History 'became an act of synthesis and validation quite as much as of presentation'; and the resultant narrative, pieced out from the information obtained, 'attested the diligence of the seeker' (1983: 47). *Auctoritas* becomes the authority of officials, 'the authority of offices held, of armies commanded' (1983: 54).
10. In classical and medieval rhetoric this process of eliciting meaning is termed invention (*inventio*), that is, the elaboration by rhetorical means of the materials at hand. Arabic and Persian rhetoric lacks a corresponding term; however, there was a similar understanding of the relationship between the writer and his materials. I discuss this

issue in a forthcoming study of medieval Arabic and Persian poetics (to be published by Curzon). Western studies of *inventio* are numerous; see for example Ray 1986; Vickers 1990, index, s.v.; Kelly 1978.

11. See for example Wansbrough 1978: 118–19; Waldman 1980: 19; Robinson 1997: 227. Since medieval writers did not share the modern distinction between 'scientific' and 'fictive' writing, to put the problem in these terms is perhaps misleading. The techniques employed are rhetorical rather than 'literary', and are utilised for a wide variety of types of writing, including history.
12. The archiving of documents seems to have been practised from early Islamic times; see Wansbrough 1978: 37. Documents – especially those granting patents and titles, announcing conquests, and so on – were copied and widely disseminated to publicise a ruler's achievements. Compare Ianziti's discussion of Quattrocento chanceries and the use of archival documents in histories (1988, especially 55–6, 152–9).
13. Rubinacci classified ʿUtbī's poetic quotations under three headings: (1) 'artistic-literary', or more generally moralising; (2) 'anthological' (verses by contemporary poets or courtiers); and (3) 'historico-documentary', composed in connection with contemporary events (1964: 266–8). Bosworth (1980), discussing the poetic quotations in Bayhaqī, argued that the increase in the first, 'moralising' category over earlier works represented 'a borrowing from the Arabic style of the 4th/10th century as used in Iraq and at the Būyid courts of Western Persia' (1980: 43). Bosworth found it surprising that Bayhaqī does not quote from Firdawsī's *Shāhnāma*, whose 'heroic motifs ... would have provided him with trenchant and apposite quotations when he was describing Sultan Masʿūd's campaigns' (1980: 51). In view of Bayhaqī's antipathy to the pre-Islamic Persian past, this omission is to be expected.
14. For example, after an account of the Tabbānī family he states that, should a reader ask why he has gone on at such length, 'the answer is, that I am recording the history of fifty years, which takes up thousands of pages, in which there are the names of many great men and notables of all classes', and is discharging his obligations to his compatriots by publicising the merits of this noble family (1971: 250).
15. Bayhaqī met Bū Ḥanīfa around 451/1059, and asked him to compose a poem, to be included in the history, which would deal with Maḥmūd's death, Muḥammad's accession and Masʿūd's arrival from Isfahan to claim the throne – this although the poet had 'not [lived] in the time of the past sultans' (1971: 360). A second poem by Iskāfī was not 'written ... to enspirit Sultan Masʿūd after his defeat ... by the Seljuqs' (Bosworth 1980: 46), but is also retrospective. When, after Masʿūd's defeat at Dandānqān, Bayhaqī composed the letter to Arslān Khān mentioned earlier, he sought to find someone to 'compose a few lines of verse, so that it would be both verse and prose', but could find none of the poets who had served that *dawlat* to do so, until, in 451/1059, he asked Bū Ḥanīfa to compose such a poem (1971: 853).
16. This poem too was not written after the defeat at Dandānqān (Bosworth 1980: 52), but was recited at the feast of Mihragān 430/

1039. Mas'ūd, angered by it, exiled the poet to India. Bayhaqī comments: 'It was good advice, even though impudent; but poets should not act thus with kings' (1971: 789–90; see also 812–13, and see Meisami 1990: 41, 44 n. 61).

17. Noth and Conrad assert that the speeches which appear in early Arabic histories 'must [be viewed] as fictions from beginning to end' (1994: 87, and see 87–96). In view of the importance of the spoken word and of oratorical eloquence in pre- and early Islamic society, and despite the likelihood of later embellishment, I see no reason to reject the speeches out of hand. By the 4th/10th century Arabic political oratory was in decline (see Kanazi 1989: 139); and we may assume that it was never a prominent feature in Persian-speaking society. Most Arabic orations quoted by Persian writers (for example, those in Bal'amī's Ṭabarī) relate to events in the distant past. Addressing the debate over the authenticity of speeches in Greek and Roman histories, Fornara argues that 'we are not entitled to proceed on the assumption that the historians considered themselves at liberty to write up speeches out of their own heads' (1983: 154, and see 142–68; on wholly invented speeches which nevertheless 'are not arbitrary creations but a functional element in the story', 166; on the rhetorical recasting of speeches from earlier sources, 167–8).

18. The rhetorical principle of disposition (*dispositio*) relates to the ordering of materials, applicable to short, self-contained texts (orations, letters), to sections within a longer text and to the organisation of longer works. For structural analyses of several Persian *inshā'* texts of the 6th/12th and 7th/13th centuries, including one by the historian Juvaynī, see Luther 1977.

19. On Bayhaqī, see Bertotti 1991: 41–2; compare Ianziti on Lodrisio Crivelli's history of Francesco Sforza, which abandoned strict chronological sequence in favour of a 'meaning sequence' in which events are 'arranged according to their connection with an overall theme or themes' (1988: 112–14); see also Fornara 1983: 70–1, on Cornelius Sisenna.

20. Fornara argues that *ornare* means not merely 'to decorate, embellish', but 'to take a fact and from it to set a scene, developing its latent possibilities' (1983: 136). Bayhaqī states that he introduces anecdotes, digressions, verses, and so on so that the history might be 'adorned' thereby (1971: 39). The Persian verb *ārāstan* means 'to adorn, embellish', but also 'to arrange, set in order'; we might perhaps compare it to the Latin *ornare*.

21. Rhetorical ornament (*elocutio*) includes tropes and figures (or schemes) of thought and of speech; the first category 'involves a change or transference of meaning, and works on the conceptual level', and the second has to do with 'the placing or disposition of words into a structure which is natural yet goes beyond the normal or minimum needs of communication' (Vickers 1990: 315–16).

22. It is greatly to be regretted that Allin Luther was unable to complete his study of this topic, and to publish more of his findings, before his untimely death. One hopes that his work will provide the basis for more extended studies by other scholars.

23. See for example the section encompassing the announcement of Farrukhzād's death, Ibrāhīm's accession and the subsequent

excursus on kingship (1971: 480–6). The opening passage, 'On the Meaning of This World', is set off from the preceding historical narrative by the use of rhyming prose, also seen in the eulogy of Farrukhzād, which follows a series of poetic quotations on the transience of this world. The excursus on kingship which comes after the hyperbolic encomium of Ibrāhīm is studded with Prophetic traditions and other wise sayings.

24. Questions of genre present difficulties in view of the partial state in which many texts have come down to us. It is problematic whether some of these texts were actually 'published' in complete form or were presented piecemeal, in a partially finished state, while in progress, as were Ṣābī''s *Tājī* and (for different reasons) Firdawsī's *Shāhnāma* (compare Fornara 1983: 59–60; Ianziti 1988: 103–4). There is also the question of whether some projects (Gardīzī's history, the *Mujmal*, the *Tārīkh-i Sīstān*) constitute completed histories or compilations intended to provide raw materials for further elaboration.

25. Luther stressed the importance of 'following the rules' enjoined by manuals for secretaries, and viewed such rules as constraints which forced the writer (especially the secretary-historian) to write in a particular way. 'A capable scribe would have been able to reduce the effect this formalizing influence would have on what he had to say, but it would still restrict him, constrain him to subordinate a statement of facts to the formal, esthetic requirements of *inshā'* in this regard' (1977: 5). This does not account for the continued use of the 'transparent' style by some Saljūq writers, nor for the use of both figured and plain styles by Rāvandī and Jarbādhqānī. Nor does Luther's argument that the rhetorical histories were written primarily to obtain their authors a position at court sufficiently explain their choice of style; as noted earlier, this argument breaks down in the case of Kirmānī, whose *'Iqd al-ūlā* was intended as a 'gift' in return for royal patronage. Rāvandī's history may have been intended as a similar gift (before the fact, as it were), as may also have been Jarbādhqānī's translation of 'Utbī.

26. This seems even more the case for post-Mongol writers, whose rulers can scarcely have appreciated, in an aesthetic sense, the rhetorical pyrotechnics of a Juvaynī or a Vaṣṣāf. Nor can it be pure coincidence that many Arabic histories written for the Ayyūbids or the *mamlūk*s also employ the figured chancery style. The subject calls for a detailed comparative study.

27. The pattern is already seen in Ibn Ḥassūl's epistle on the virtues of the Turks, a model of Arabic chancery style, which was addressed to the vizier Kundurī (praised for his learning, administrative competence and eloquence), who was to convey it to Sultan Ṭughril.

Appendix

The Major Iranian Dynasties, 204–590/819–1194

(Excluding the Ṣaffārids and the Būyids)

The Sāmānids, 204–389/819–997

204–50/819–64	Aḥmad I ibn Asad ibn Sāmān (governor of Farghana)
250–79/864–92	Naṣr I ibn Aḥmad
279–95/892–907	Ismā'īl I ibn Aḥmad
295–301/907–14	Aḥmad II ibn Ismā'īl
301–31/914–43	Naṣr II ibn Aḥmad
331–43/943–54	Nūḥ I ibn Aḥmad
343–50/954–61	'Abd al-Malik I ibn Nūḥ
350–65/961–76	Manṣūr I ibn Nūḥ
365–87/976–97	Nūḥ II ibn Manṣūr
387–9/997–9	Manṣūr II ibn Nūḥ
389/997	'Abd al-Malik II ibn Nūḥ
390–5/1000–5	Ismā'īl II al- Muntaṣir

The Ghaznavids, 387–582/997–1186.

(366–87/977–97	Sabuktigīn)
387–8/997–8	Ismā'īl ibn Sabuktigīn
388–421/998–1030	Maḥmūd ibn Sabuktigīn
421/1030	Muḥammad ibn Maḥmūd
421–32/1030–41	Mas'ūd I ibn Maḥmūd
432/1041	Muḥammad ibn Maḥmūd
432–40?/1041–8?	Mawdūd ibn Mas'ūd
440?/1048–9?	Mas'ūd II ibn Mawdūd
440?/1048–9?	'Alī ibn Mas'ūd
440?–3?/1049?–52?	'Abd al-Rashīd ibn Maḥmūd
443–51/1052–9	Farrukhzād ibn Mas'ūd I
451–92/1059–99	Ibrāhīm ibn Mas'ūd I
492–508/1099–1115	Mas'ūd III ibn Ibrāhīm
508–9/1115–16	Shīrzād ibn Mas'ūd III
509–11/1116–17	Malik Arslān ibn Mas'ūd III
511–52?/1117–57?	Bahrāmshāh ibn Mas'ūd III
552?–5/1157?–60	Khusrawshāh ibn Bahrāmshāh
555–82/1160–86	Khusraw Malik ibn Khusrawshāh

The Great Saljūqs, 429–590/1038–1194

429–55/1038–63	Ṭughril Beg
455–65/1063–72	Alp–Arslān
465–85/1072–92	Malikshāh I
485–7/1092–4	Maḥmūd I
487–98/1094–1105	Barkyāruq
498/1105	Malikshāh II
498–511/1105–18	Muḥammad I
511–52/1118–57	Sanjar (ruler in eastern Iran from 490/1097)
511–25/1118–31	Maḥmūd II
525–6/1131–2	Dā'ūd
526–9/1132–4	Ṭughril I
529–47/1134–52	Mas'ūd
547–8/1152–3	Malikshāh II
548–55/1153–60	Muḥammad II
555–6/1160–1	Sulaymānshāh
556–71/1161–76	Arslān
571–90/1176–94	Ṭughril II

The Ildigizid Atabegs, 531–622/1137–1225

531–70/1137–75	Shams al Dīn Ildigiz
570–81/1175–86	Nuṣrat al–Dīn Muḥammad Jahān Pahlavān
581–7/1186–91	Muẓaffar al-Dīn Qizil Arslān 'thmān
587–91/1191–5	Qutlugh Inanj
591–607/1195–1210	Nuṣrat al–Dīn Abū Bakr
607–22/1210–25	Malik Uzbak

Bibliography

LIST OF ABBREVIATIONS

BSOAS	*Bulletin of the School of Oriental and African Studies.*
EI[1]	*Encyclopaedia of Islam* (First Edition).
EI[2]	*Encyclopaedia of Islam* (New Edition).
EIr	*Encyclopaedia Iranica.*
JAOS	*Journal of the American Oriental Society.*
JNES	*Journal of Near Eastern Studies.*
JRAS	*Journal of the Royal Asiatic Society.*
JSS	*Journal of Semitic Studies.*

Ahmad, M. Hilmy M. 1962. 'Some Notes on Arabic Historiography During the Zengid and Ayyubid periods (521/1127–648/1250).' In *Historians of the Middle East*, ed. Bernard Lewis and P. M. Holt, 79–97. London: Oxford University Press.

Al-Azmeh, Aziz. 1990 [1982]. *Ibn Khaldūn*. London: Routledge.

Altheim, Franz. 1958. 'The Most Ancient Romance of Chivalry.' *East and West* 9:129–44.

Arkoun, Mohammed. 1967. 'Éthique et histoire d'après les *Tajarib al-Umam*.' In *Atti del terzo Congresso di Studi Arabici e Islamici, Ravello 1966*, 83–112. Naples: Istituto Universitario Orientale.

Baghdādī, 'Abd al-Qāhir. 1920. *Moslem Schisms and Sects (Al-Farḳ Bain al-Firaḳ); Being the History of the Various Philosophic Systems Developed in Islam. Part I.* Trans. Kate Chambers Seelye. Columbia University Oriental Studies, vol. 15. New York: Columbia University Press.

——. 1935. *Moslem Schisms and Sects (Al-Farḳ Bain al-Firaḳ). Part 2.* Trans. Abraham S. Halkin. Tel Aviv: Palestine Publishing Co., Ltd.

Bahār, Muḥammad Taqī. 1932. *Sabk-shināsī, yā tārīkh-i taṭavvur-i nasr-i Fārsī*. Tehran: N.p.

Bal'amī, Abū 'Alī. 1974. *Tarīkh-i Bal'ami*. Ed. Muḥammad Taqī Bahār. Rev. Muḥammad Parvīn Gunābādī. 2nd edn. Tehran: Zavvār.

——. 1984. *Les prophètes et les rois de la création à David*. Trans. H. Zotenberg. Paris: Sindbad.

——. 1994. *Tārīkhnāma-i Ṭabarī, bakhsh-i chāp-nāshuda*. Ed. Muḥammad Rawshan. 3rd edn. Tehran: Nashr-i Alburz.

Bausani, Alessandro. 1975. 'Muhammad or Darius? The Elements and Basis of Iranian Culture.' In *Islam and Cultural Change in the Middle Ages*, ed. Speros Vryonis, Jr., 43–57. Wiesbaden: Otto Harrassowitz.

Bayhaqī, Abū al-Faḍl. 1971. *Tārīkh-i Bayhaqī*. Ed. 'Alī Akbar Fayyāẓ. Mashhad: Dānishgāh-i Mashhad.

Bertotti, Filippo. 1991. *L'opera dello storico persiano Bayhaqī*. Istituto Universitario Orientale, Seminario di Studi Asiatici, Series Minor, no. 38. Naples: Istituto Universitario Orientale.

Biesterfeldt, Hans Hinrich. n.d. *Die Zwiege des Wissens: Theorie und*

Klassifikation der Wissenschaften im mittelalterlichen Islam in der Darstellung des Ibn Farīgūn. Habilitationsschrift. Bochum: N.p.
Bīrūnī, Abu Rayḥān. 1879. *The Chronology of Ancient Nations*. Trans. C. E. Sachau. London: W. H. Allen.
——. 1973. *Al-Biruni's Book on Pharmacy and Materia Medica*. Ed. Sami K. Hamarna. Karachi: Hamdard National Foundation.
Bosworth, C. E. 1960. 'The Rise of the Karāmiyyah in Khurasan.' T*he Muslim World* 50:6–14.
——. 1962. 'The Titulature of the Early Ghaznavids.' *Oriens* 15:210–33.
——. 1963. 'Early Sources for the History of the First four Ghaznavid Sultans (997–1041).' *Islamic Culture* 7:3–22.
——. 1968a. 'The Armies of the Ṣaffārids.' *BSOAS* 31:534–54.
——. 1968b. 'The Development of Persian Culture Under the Early Ghaznavids.' *Iran* 6:33–44.
——. 1968c. 'The Political and Dynastic History of the Iranian World (A.D. 1000–1217).' In *The Cambridge History of Iran*, vol. 4: *The Mongol and Saljuq Periods*, ed. J. A. Boyle, 1–202. Cambridge: Cambridge University Press.
——. 1969a. 'The Tahirids and Arabic Culture.' *JSS* 14:45–79.
——. 1969b. 'The Tahirids and Persian Literature.' *Iran* 7:103–06.
——. 1970a. 'Dailamīs in Central Iran: The Kākūyids of Jibāl and Yazd.' *Iran* 8:73–95.
——. 1970b. 'An Early Arabic Mirror for Princes: Ṭāhir Dhū l-Yamīnain's Epistle to his Son ʿAbdallāh (206/821).' *JNES* 29:25–41.
——. 1973a [1963]. *The Ghaznavids: Their Empire in Afghanistan and Eastern Iran, 994:1040*. 2nd edn. Beirut: Librairie du Liban.
——. 1973b. 'The Heritage of Rulership in Early Islamic Iran and the Search for Dynastic Connections with the Past.' *Iran* 9:51–62.
——. 1977. *The Later Ghaznavids: Splendour and Decay; the Dynasty in Afghanistan and Northern India, 1040–1186*. New York: Columbia University Press.
——. 1980. 'The Poetical Citations in Baihaqī's *Ta'rīkh-i Masʿūdī*.' *Zeitschrift des Deutschen Morgenländische Gesellschaft. Supplement IV: XX Deutscher Orientalistentag in Erlangen*:41–56. Wiesbaden: Franz Steiner.
——. 1981. 'The Rulers of Chaghāniyān in Early Islamic Times.' *Iran* 19:1–20.
——. 1994. *The History of the Saffarids of Sistan and the Maliks of Nimruz (247/861 to 949/1542–3)*. Columbia Lectures on Iranian Studies, no. 8. Costa Mesa and New York: Mazda Publishers.
Browne, Edward G. 1928. *A Literary History of Persia*. Cambridge: University Press.
Bulliet, Richard W. 1972. *The Patricians of Nishapur: A Study in Medieval Islamic Social History*. Harvard Middle Eastern Studies, no. 16. Cambridge: Harvard University Press.
Bundārī. 1889. *Histoire des Seldjoucides de l'Irâq ... d'après Imâd ad-dîn al-Kâtib al-Isfahânî*. Ed. M. Th. Houtsma. Recueil de texts relatifs à l'histoire des Seldjoucides, vol. 1. Leiden: E. J. Brill.
Cahen, Claude. 1949. 'Le Malik-Nameh et l'histoire des origines Seljukides.' *Oriens* 2:31–65.
——. 1962. 'The Historiography of the Seljuqid Period.' In *Historians of the Middle East*, ed. Bernard Lewis and P. M. Holt, 59–78. London: Oxford University Press.
Chabbi, Jacqueline. 1977. 'Remarques sur le développement historique des mouvements ascétiques et mystiques au Khurasan, IIIe/IXe siecle – IVe/Xe siecle.' *Studia Islamica* 46:5–72.

Corbin, Henry. 1982. *Temps cyclique et gnose ismaélienne*. Paris: Berg International.

Czeglédy, K. 1958. 'Bahrām Čōbīn and the Persian Apocalyptic Literature.' *Acta Orientalia Hungaria* 8: 21–43.

Daftary, Farhad. 1992 [1990]. *The Ismā'īlīs: Their History and Doctrines*. Cambridge: Cambridge University Press.

Daniel, Elton L. 1990. 'Manuscripts and Editions of Bal'amī's *Tarjamah-i tārīkh-i Ṭabarī*.' *JRAS*:282–321.

——. 1995. 'The Samanid "Translations" of Ṭabarī.' Paper presented at the International Conference on 'The Life and Works of Muḥammad ibn Jarīr al-Ṭabari', University of St Andrews, 30 August–2 September 1995. Typescript.

de Blois, Francois. 1992. *Persian Literature: A Bio-Bibliographical Survey*. Vol. 5, part 1. *Poetry to ca. A.D. 1100*. London: The Royal Asiatic Society.

de Bruijn, J. T. P. 1983. *Of Piety and Poetry: The Interaction of Religion and Literature in the Life and Works of Ḥakīm Sanā'ī of Ghazna*. Publications of the 'de Goeje Fund', no. 25. Leiden: E. J. Brill.

de Fouchécour, C.-H. 1976. 'Une lecture du Livre des Rois de Ferdowsi.' *Studia Iranica* 5:171–202.

de Romilly, Jacqueline. 1991. *The Rise and Fall of States According to Greek Authors*. Thomas Spencer Jerome Lectures, no. 11. Ann Arbor: The University of Michigan Press.

Farrukhī Sīstānī. 1932. *Dīvān*. Ed. 'Alī 'Abd al-Rasūlī. Tehran: Maṭba'a-i Majlis.

Firdawsī, Abū al-Qāsim. 1962–71. *Shāhnāma*. Ed. E. Bertel's. Moscow: Akademia Nauk SSSR.

Fornara, Charles William. 1983. *The Nature of History in Ancient Greece and Rome*. Eidos: Studies in Classical Kinds. Berkeley: University of California Press.

Frye, Richard N. 1965. *Bukhara: The Medieval Achievement*. Norman: University of Oklahoma Press.

Gardīzī, 'Abd al-Ḥayy. 1968. *Zayn al-akhbār*. Ed. 'Abd al-Ḥayy Ḥabībī. Intishārāt-i Bunyād-i Farhang-i Īrān, 37; Manābi'-i Tārīkh va-Jughrāfiyā-yi Īrān, 11. Tehran: Bunyād-i Farhang-i Īrān.

Ghazzālī. 1964. *Ghazālī's Book of Counsel for Kings (Naṣīḥat al-Mulūk)*. Trans. F. R. C. Bagley. London: Oxford University Press.

Gibb, H. A. R. 1982 [1962]. 'Tarikh.' In *Studies on the Civilization of Islam*, ed. Stanford J. Shaw and William R. Polk, 108–37. Princeton: Princeton University Press.

Halm, Heinz. 1996. *The Empire of the Mahdi: The Rise of the Fatimids*. Trans. Michael Bonner. Handbuch der Orientalistik. Abt. 1: Der nahe und mittlere Osten, vol. 26. Leiden: E. J. Brill.

——. 1997 [1991]. *Shiism*. Islamic Surveys, vol. 18. Edinburgh: Edinburgh University Press.

Hampton, Timothy. 1990. *Writing from History: The Rhetoric of Exemplarity in Renaissance Literature*. Ithaca and London: Cornell University Press.

Ḥamza Iṣfahānī. n.d. *Ta'rīkh sanī mulūk al-arḍ wa-al-anbiyā'*. Beirut: Dār Maktabat al-Ḥayāt.

Hanaway, William L. 1978. 'The Iranian Epics.' In *Heroic Epic and Saga*, ed. Felix J. Oinas, 76–98. Bloomington and London: Indiana University Press.

Heinrichs, Wolfhart. 1997. 'Prosimetrical Genres in Classical Arabic Literature.' In *Prosimetrum: Cross-Cultural Perspectives on Narrative in Prose and Verse*, ed. Joseph Harris and Karl Reichl, 249–75. Cambridge: D. S. Brewer.

Hillenbrand, Carole. 1988. 'Islamic Orthodoxy or Realpolitik? al-Ghazālī's Views on Government.' *Iran* 26:81–94.

——. 1996. 'The Power Struggle Between the Saljuqs and the Isma'ilis of Alamūt, 487–518/1095–1124: the Saljuq Perspective.' In *Medieval Isma'ili History and Thought*, ed. Farhad Daftary, 205–20. Cambridge: Cambridge University Press.

Hoffmann, Gerhard. 1992. 'An Isma'īlī/Fatimid Stronghold in Iraq? the Case of al-Basāsīrī.' In *Shī'a Islam, Sects and Sufisms: Historical Dimensions, Religious Practice and Methodological Considerations*, ed. Frederick de Jong, 26–34. Publications of the M.Th. Houtsma Stichting. Utrecht: N.p.

Humphreys, R. Stephen. 1991. *Islamic History: A Framework for Inquiry*. Revised Edition. Princeton: Princeton University Press.

Husaini, Qari Syed Kalimulla. 1954. 'Life and Works of Zahiru'd-Din al-Bayhaqi, the Author of the Tārīkh-i-Bayhaq.' *Islamic Culture* 28:296–318.

——. 1959. 'The Tārīkh-i-Bayhaq of Zahiru'd-Din Hasan 'Ali b. Abil Qasim Zayd al-Bayhaqi.' *Islamic Culture* 33:188–202.

——. 1960. 'Contribution of Zahiru'd-Din al-Bayhaqi to Arabic and Persian Literature.' *Islamic Culture* 34:49–59, 77–89.

Ḥusaynī, Abū al-Ḥasan 'Alī ibn Nāṣir. 1933. *Akhbār al-dawla al-Saljūqiyya*. Ed. Muḥammad Iqbāl. Lahore: University of the Panjab.

Ianziti, Gary. 1988. *Humanistic Historiography under the Sforzas: Politics and Propaganda in Fifteenth-century Milan*. Oxford: Clarendon Press.

Ibn al-Athīr, 'Izz al-Dīn. 1965–7 [1851–76]. *al-Kāmil fī al-ta'rīkh*. Ed. C. J. Tornberg. Beirut: Dār Ṣādir.

Ibn al-Balkhī. 1962 [1921]. *The Fársnáma of Ibnu'l-Balkhí*. Ed. G. Le Strange and R. A. Nicholson. E. J. W. Gibb Memorial Series. New Series, vol. 1. London: Luzac & Co.

Ibn Funduq, 'Alī ibn Zayd al-Bayhaqī. 1965 [1938–9]. *Tārīkh-i Bayhaq*. Ed. Aḥmad Bahmanyār. 2nd edn. Tehran: Furūghī.

Ibn Ḥassūl. 1940. *Tafḍīl al-Atrāk (Ibni Hassul'ün Türkler hakkında bir eseri)*. Ed. 'Abbās 'Azzāwī. Trans. Şerefettin Yaltkaya. *Belleten* 4:235–66 (Arabic text: 1–51).

Ibn 'Inaba. 1961. *'Umdat al-ṭālib fī ansāb Āl Abī Ṭālib*. Ed. Muḥammad Ḥasan Āl al-Ṭāliqānī. 2nd ed. Najaf: al-Maṭba'a al-Ḥaydariyya.

Iṣbahānī, Abū Nu'aym. 1931. *Geschichte Iṣbahāns*. Ed. Sven Dedering. Leiden: E. J. Brill.

Iṣṭakhrī. 1870. *Kitāb Masālik al-mamālik*. Ed. M. J. de Goeje. Bibliotheca Geographorum Arabicorum, vol. 1. Leiden: E. J. Brill.

Jarbādhqānī, Abū Sharaf Nāṣiḥ ibn Ẓafar. 1966. *Tarjuma-i Tārīkh-i Yamīnī*. Ed. Ja'far Shi'ār. Majmū'a-i mutūn-i Fārsī, no. 30. Tehran: Bungāh-i Tarjuma va-Nashr-i Kitāb.

Jūzjānī, Minhāj al-Dīn. 1970. *Tabaḳāt-i-Nāṣirī, a General History of the Muḥammadan Dynasties of Asia*. Trans. H. G. Raverty. New Delhi: Oriental Books Reprint Corporation.

Juvaynī, 'Aṭā Malik. 1958. *The History of the World-Conqueror*. Trans. John Andrew Boyle. Manchester: Manchester University Press.

Kafešoglu, İbrahim. 1988. *A History of the Seljuks: İbrahim Kafešoglu's Interpretation and the Resulting Controversy*. Trans. and ed. Gary Leiser. Carbondale: Southern Illinois University Press.

Kanazi, George J. 1989. *Studies in the Kitāb aṣ-Ṣinā'atayn of Abū Hilāl al-'Askarī*. Leiden: E. J. Brill.

Kelly, Douglas. 1978. 'Topical Invention in Medieval French Literature.' In *Medieval Eloquence: Studies in the Theory and Practice of Medieval Rhetoric*, ed. James J. Murphy, 231–51. Berkeley: University of California Press.

Kemp, Anthony. 1991. *The Estrangement of the Past: A Study in the Origins of Modern Historical Consciousness.* New York and Oxford: Oxford University Press.

Khalidi, Tarif. 1994. *Arabic Historical Thought in the Classical Period.* Cambridge: Cambridge University Press.

Kirmānī, Afḍal al-Dīn. 1932. *Kitāb ʿIqd al-ūlā lil-mawqif al-aʿlā.* Ed. ʿAlī Muḥammad ʿAmirī Nāʾīnī. Tehran: N.p.

Klausner, Carla L. 1973. *The Seljuk Vizierate: A Study of Civil Administration, 1055–1194.* Cambridge, MA: Harvard University Press.

Kraemer, Joel L. 1983. 'Apostates, Rebels and Brigands.' In *Religion and Government in the World of Islam,* ed. Joel L. Kraemer and Ilai Alon. Israel Oriental Studies, vol. 10. Tel Aviv: Tel Aviv University.

——. 1986a. *Humanism in the Renaissance of Islam: The Cultural Revival During the Buyid Age.* The Dayan Center for Middle Eastern and African Studies, Studies in Islamic Culture and History Series, vol. 7. Leiden: E. J. Brill.

——. 1986b. *Philosophy in the Renaissance of Islam: Abū Sulaymān al-Sijistānī and His Circle.* The Dayan Center for Middle Eastern and African Studies, Studies in Islamic Culture and History Series, vol. 7. Leiden: E. J. Brill.

Krasnawolska, Anna. 1978. 'Rostam Farroxzad's Prophecy in Šah-name and the Zoroastrian Apocalyptic Texts.' *Folia Orientalia* 19:173–84.

Lambton, A. K. S. 1971. 'Islamic Mirrors for Princes.' *Quaderno dell'Accademia Nazionale dei Lincei* 160:419–42.

——. 1984. 'The Dilemma of Government in Islamic Persia: The Siyāsat-nāma of Niẓām al-Mulk.' *Iran* 22:55–66.

——. 1988. *Continuity and Change in Medieval Persia.* London: I. B. Tauris.

——. 1991. 'Persian Local Histories: The Tradition Behind Them and the Assumptions of Their Authors.' In *Yād-nāma in memoria di Alessandro Bausani,* vol. 1: *Islamistica,* ed. Biancamaria Scarcia Amoretti and Lucia Rostagno, 227–38. Università di Roma 'La Sapienza', Pubblicati dal Dipartimento di Studi Orientali, vol. 10. Rome: Bardi Editore.

Lanham, Richard A. 1973. 'Opaque Style and its Uses in *Troilus and Criseyde.*' *Studies in Medieval Culture* 4:169–76.

Lassner, Jacob. 1986. *Islamic Revolution and Historical Memory: An Inquiry into the Art of ʿAbbāsid Apologetics.* Americal Oriental Series, vol. 66. New Haven: American Oriental Society.

Lazard, Gilbert. 1975. 'The Rise of the New Persian Language.' In *The Cambridge History of Iran,* vol. 4. *From the Arab Invasion to the Saljuqs,* ed. Richard N. Frye, 595–632. Cambridge: Cambridge University Press.

Lewis, Bernard. 1973. 'Islamic Concepts of Revolution.' In *Islam in History,* 253–63. London: Alcove Press.

Luther, K. Allin. 1969. 'A New Source for the History of the Iraq Seljuqs: The *Tārīkh al-Vuzarā*'. *Der Islam* 45:117–28.

——. 1971a. 'Bayhaqi and the Later Seljuq Historians: Some Comparative Remarks.' In *Yādnāma-i Abū al-Faḍl Bayhaqī,* 14–33. Mashhad: Dānishgāh-i Mashhad.

——. 1971b. 'Rāvandī's Report on the Administrative Changes of Muḥammad Jahān Pahlavān.' In *Iran and Islam,* ed. C. E. Bosworth, 393–406. Edinburgh: Edinburgh University Press.

——. 1976. 'The End of Saljūq Dominion in Khurasan.' In *Michigan Oriental Studies in Honor of George C. Cameron,* ed. Louis L. Orlin, 219–25. Ann Arbor: The University of Michigan, Department of Near Eastern Studies.

——. 1977. 'Chancery Writing as a Source of Constraints on History Writing in the Sixth and Seventh Centuries of the Hijra.' Unpublished Paper. University of Michigan.
——. 1990. 'Islamic Rhetoric and the Persian Historians, 1000–1300 A.D.' In *Studies in Near Eastern Culture and History in Memory of Ernest T. Abdel-Massih*, 90–98. Ann Arbor: University of Michigan, Center for Near Eastern and North African Studies.
Madelung, Wilferd. 1967. 'Abū Isḥāq al-Ṣābī on the Alids of Ṭabaristān and Gīlān.' *JNES* 26:17–56.
——. 1969. 'The Assumption of the Title of Shahanshah by the Buyids and "The reign of the Daylam (Dawlat al-Daylam)".' *JNES* 28:84–108, 168–80.
——. 1971. 'The Spread of Māturīdism and the Turks.' In *Actas IV Congresso de Estudos Árabes e Islâmicos, Coimbra-Lisboa 1968*, 109–68. Leiden: E. J. Brill.
——. 1975. 'The Minor Dynasties of Northern Iran.' In *The Cambridge History of Iran*, vol. 4. *From the Arab Invasion to the Saljuqs*, ed. R. N. Frye, 198–249. Cambridge: Cambridge University Press.
Makdisi, George. 1963. *Ibn 'Aqīl et la résurgence de l'Islam traditionaliste au XIe siècle (Ve siècle de l'Hégire)*. Damascus: Institut Français de Damas.
——. 1969. 'The Marriage of Ṭughril Beg.' *IJMES* 1:259–75.
——. 1973. 'The Sunnī Revival.' In *Islamic Civilisation, 950–1150*, ed. D. S. Richards, 155–68. Papers on Islamic History, no. 3. Oxford: Cassirer.
Marlow, Louise. 1997. *Hierarchy and Egalitarianism in Islamic Thought*. Cambridge Studies in Islamic Civilization. Cambridge: Cambridege University Press.
Mas'ūdī. 1896. *Le livre de l'avertissement et de la revision*. Trans. R. Carra de Vaux. Paris: Imprimerie Nationale.
Meisami, Julie Scott. 1989. 'Mas'ūdī on Love and the Fall of the Barmakids.' *JRAS*:252–77.
——. 1990. 'Ghaznavid Panegyrics: Some Political Implications.' *Iran* 28: 31–44.
——. 1993. 'The Past in Service of the Present: Two Views of History in Medieval Persia.' *Poetics Today* 14:247–75.
——. 1994. 'Rāvandī's *Rāḥat al-ṣudūr*: History or Hybrid?' *Edebiyat* n.s. 5:181–215.
——. 1995a. 'Exemplary Lives, Exemplary Deaths: The Execution of Ḥasanak.' In *Actas XVI Congreso UEAI*, 357–64. Salamanca.
——. 1995b. 'The *Šâh-nâme* as Mirror for Princes: A Study in Reception.' In *Pand-o Sokhan: Mélanges offerts à Charles-Henri de Fouchécour*, ed. Christophe Balaÿ, Claire Kappler, and Živa Vesel, 265–73. Bibliothèque iranienne, no. 44. Tehran: Institut Français de Recherche en Iran.
——. 1997. 'Mixed Prose and Verse in Medieval Persian Literature.' In *Prosimetrum: Cross-Cultural Perspectives on Narrative in Prose and Verse*, ed. Joseph Harris and Karl Reichl, 295–319. Cambridge: D. S. Brewer.
Meisami, Julie Scott, and Paul Starkey, eds. 1998. *Encyclopedia of Arabic Literature*. London: Routledge.
Mélikoff, Irène. 1962. *Abū Muslim le 'porte-hache' du Khorassan dans la tradition épique turco-iranienne*. Paris: Adrien Maisonneuve.
Minorsky, Vladimir. 1956. 'The Older Preface to the *Shāh-nāma*.' In *Studi orientalistici in onore de Giorgio Levi della Vida*, vol. 2, 159–79. Pubblicazioni dell'Istituto per l'Oriente, no. 52. Rome: Istituto per l'Oriente.

——. 1962. 'Ibn Farīghūn and the *Ḥudūd al-'ālam*.' In *A Locust's Leg: Studies in Honour of S. H. Taqizadeh*, 189–96. London: Percy Lund, Humphries & Co.

Miskawayh. 1909. *The Tajarib al-umam*. Vol. 1. To *A. H. 37*. Ed. Leone Caetani. Leiden: E. J. Brill; London: Luzac.

——. 1920–21. *The Eclipse of the 'Abbasid Caliphate: Original Chronicles of the Fourth Islamic Century*. Ed. and trans. H. F. Amedroz and D. S. Margoliouth. Oxford: Basil Blackwell.

——. 1968. *The Refinement of Character*. Trans. Constantine K. Zurayk. Beirut: American University of Beirut.

Mohl, Jules. 1966. *Dībācha-i Shāhnāma*. Trans. Jahāngīr Afkārī. Tehran: Kitābhā-yi Jībī.

Mottahedeh, Roy P. 1976. 'The Shu'ûbîyah Controversy and the Social History of Early Islamic Iran.' *IJMES* 7:168–82.

——. 1980. *Loyalty and Leadership in an Early Islamic Society*. Princeton: Princeton University Press.

Mujmal al-tavārīkh va-al-qiṣaṣ. 1939. Ed. Muḥammad Taqī Bahār. Tehran: Khāvar.

Muqaddasī. 1906 [1877]. *Aḥsan al-taqāsīm fī ma'rifat al-aqālīm*. Ed. M. J. de Goeje. 2nd edn. Bibliotheca Geographorum Arabicorum, vol. 3. Leiden: E. J. Brill.

Nāẓim, Muḥammad. 1971 [1931]. *The Life and Times of Sultān Maḥmūd of Ghazna*. 2nd edn. New Delhi: Munshiram Manoharlal.

Nīshāpūrī, Ẓahīr al-Dīn. 1953. *Saljūqnāma*. Ed. Ismā'īl Afshār. Tehran: Gulāla Khāvar.

Niẓām al-Mulk. 1968 [1962]. *Siyar al-mulūk (Siyāsatnāma)*. Ed. Hubert Darke. 2nd edn. Majmū'a-i mutūn-i Fārsī, no. 8. Tehran: Bungāh-i Tarjuma va-Nashr-i Kitāb.

——. 1978 [1960]. *The Book of Government or Rules for Kings*. Trans. Hubert Darke. London: Routledge & Kegan Paul.

——. 1984 [1893]. *Traité de gouvernement, Siyaset-Name*. Trans. Charles Schefer. Intro. by Jean-Paul Roux. Paris: Sindbad.

Niẓāmī 'Arūẓī. 1899. *The Chahár Maqála ('Four Discourses')*. Trans. E. G. Browne. Hertford: N.p.

Nöldeke, Theodor. 1979 [1930]. *The Iranian National Epic, or the Shahnamah*. Trans. Leonid Th. Bogdanov. Philadelphia: Porcupine Press.

Noth, Albrecht. 1994. *The Early Arabic Historical Tradition: A Source-Critical Study*. In Collaboration with Lawrence I. Conrad. Trans. Michael Bonner. 2nd edn. Studies in Late Antiquity and Early Islam, no. 3. Princeton: The Darwin Press.

Partner, Nancy F. 1985. 'The New Cornuficius: Medieval History and the Artifice of Words.' In *Classical Rhetoric and Medieval Historiography*, ed. Ernst Breisach, 5–59. Studies in Medieval Culture, vol. 19. Kalamazoo: Western Michigan University.

Rāvandī, Muḥammad ibn 'Alī. 1921. The *Ráḥat uṣ-ṣudúr wa áyat as-surúr*. Ed. Muḥammad Iqbal. E. J. W. Gibb Memorial Series. New Series, vol. 2. Leiden: E. J. Brill; London: Luzac.

Ray, Roger. 1986. 'The Triumph of Greco-Roman Rhetorical Assumptions in pre-Carolingian Historiography.' In *The Inheritance of Historiography, 350–900*, ed. Christopher Holdsworth and T. P. Wiseman, 67–84. Exeter Studies in History. Exeter: University of Exeter.

Richter-Bernburg, Lutz. 1974. 'Linguistic Shu'ūbīya and Early Neo-Persian Prose.' *JAOS* 94:55–64.

Robinson, Chase F. 1997. 'The Study of Islamic Historiography: A Progress Report.' *JRAS*:199–227.

Rosenthal, Franz. 1968 [1952]. *A History of Muslim Historiography*. 2nd revised edn. Leiden: E. J. Brill.

Rowson, Everett K. 1987. 'Religion and Politics in the Career of Badīʿ al-Zamān al-Hamadhānī.' *JAOS* 107:653–73.

Rubinacci, Roberto. 1964. 'Le citazione poetiche nell'al-Ta'rīḫ al-Yamīnī di Abū Naṣr al-'Utbī. In *A Francesco Gabrieli; studi orientalistici offerti nel sessantesimo compleanno dai suoi colleghi e discepoli*, 263–78. Università di Roma. Studi orientali pubblicati a cura della Scuola Orientale, vol. 5. Rome: Dott. Giovanni Bardi.

——. 1982. 'Upon the "al-Ta'rīkh al-Yamīnī'" of Abū Naṣr al-'Utbī.' In *Studia Turcologica memoriae Alexii Bombaci Dicata*, 463–7. Seminario di Studi Asiatici. Series Minor, vol. 19. Naples: Istituto Universitario Orientale.

Rypka, Jan. 1968. *History of Iranian Literature*. Dordrecht: D. Reidel.

Schnyder, Rudolph. 1973. 'Political Centres and Artistic Powers in Saljūq Ḳrān.' In *Islamic Civilisation 950–1150*, ed. D. S. Richards, 201–9. Papers on Islamic History, no. 3. Oxford: Cassirer.

Shafíʿ, Mohammed. 1933. 'The Sons of Mikal.' Reprinted from the Proceedings of the *Idára-i-Ma'árif-i-Islámia*, First Session. Lahore.

Shahbazi, A. Shahpur. 1990. 'On the *Xʷadāy-Nāmag*.' In *Iranica Varia: Papers in Honor of Professor Ehsan Yarshater*, 208–29. Acta Iranica, vol. 30. Leiden: E. J. Brill.

Sourdel-Thomine, Janine. 1973. 'Renouvellement et tradition dans l'architecture saljūqide.' In *Islamic Civilisation 950–1150*, ed. D. S. Richards, 251–63. Papers on Islamic History, no. 3. Oxford: Cassirer.

Spuler, Bertold. 1962. 'The Evolution of Persian Historiography.' In *Historians of the Middle East*, ed. Bernard Lewis and P. M. Holt, 126–32. London: Oxford University Press.

Stern, S. M. 1971. 'Yaʿqūb the Coppersmith and Persian National Sentiment.' In *Iran and Islam; in Memory of the Late Vladimir Minorsky*, ed. C. E. Bosworth, 535–55. Edinburgh: Edinburgh University Press.

——. 1983. *Studies in Early Ismāʿīlism*. The Max Schloessinger Memorial Series. Monographs, no. 1. Jerusalem: The Hebrew University.

The Tārīkh-e Sistān. 1976. Trans. Milton Gold. Literary and Historical Texts from Iran, vol. 2. Rome: Istituto Italiano per il Medio ed Estremo Oriente.

Tārīkh-i Sistān. 1935. Ed. Muḥammad Taqī Bahār. Tehran: Zavvār.

Tarjuma-yi Tafsīr-i Ṭabarī. 1988. Ed. Ḥabīb Yaghmā'ī. 3rd edn. Tehran: Intishārāt-i Tūs.

Ṭabarī. 1985a. *The History of al-Ṭabarī*. Vol. 27. *The 'Abbāsid Revolution*. Trans. John Alden Williams. Albany: State University of New York Press.

——. 1985b. *The History of al-Ṭabarī*. Vol. 35. *The Crisis of the 'Abbāsid Caliphate*. Trans. George Saliba. Albany: State University of New York Press.

——. 1985c. *The History of al-Ṭabarī*. Vol. 38. *The Return of the Caliphate to Baghdad*. Trans. Franz Rosenthal. Albany: State University of New York Press.

——. 1987a. *The History of al-Ṭabarī*. Vol. 4. *The Ancient Kingdoms*. Trans. Moshe Perlmann. Albany: State University of New York Press.

——. 1987b. *The History of al-Ṭabarī*. Vol. 22. *The Reunification of the 'Abbāsid Caliphate*. Trans. C. E. Bosworth. Albany: State University of New York Press.

——. 1992a. *The History of al-Ṭabarī*. Vol. 36. *The Revolt of the Zanj*. Trans. David Waines. Albany: State University of New York Press.

——. 1992b. *The History of al-Ṭabarī*. Vol. 31. *The War Between Brothers*. Trans. Michael Fishbein. Albany: State University of New York Press.
——. 1995. *The History of al-Ṭabarī*. Vol. 28. *'Abbāsid Authority Affirmed: The Early Years of al-Manṣūr, A.D. 753–763/A.H. 136–145*, trans. Jane Dammen McAuliffe. Albany: State University of New York Press.
Treadwell, W. L. 1991. *The Political History of the Sāmānid State*. PhD Diss. University of Oxford.
Trompf, G. W. 1979. *The Idea of Historical Recurrence in Western Thought from Antiquity to the Reformation*. Berkeley: University of California Press.
'Utbī, Abū Naṣr. 1869. *Al-Ta'rīkh al-Yamīnī*, with the commentary of Shaykh Aḥmad Manīnī. 2 vols. Cairo: N.p.
Varāvīnī, Sa'd al-Dīn. 1909. *The Marzubán-náma*. Ed. M. M. Qazwini. E. J. W. Gibb Memorial Series, vol. 8. Leiden: E. J. Brill; London: Luzac.
Vickers, Brian. 1990 [1988]. *In Defence of Rhetoric*. Oxford: Clarendon Press.
von Grunebaum, G. E. 1955. 'Firdausi's Concept of History.' In *Islam: The Making of a Cultural Tradition*. London: University of Chicago Press.
——. 1962. *Medieval Islam*. 2nd edn. Chicago: Phoenix Books.
Waldman, Marilyn Robinson. 1980. *Toward a Theory of Historical Narrative: A Case Study in Perso-Islamicate Historiography*. Columbus: Ohio State University Press.
Walzer, Richard. 1956. 'Some Aspects of Miskawaih's Tahdhīb al-akhlāq.' In *Studi orientalistici in onore di Giorgio Levi della Vida*, vol. 2, 603–21. Pubblicazioni dell'Istituto per l'Oriente, no. 52. Rome: Istituto per l'Oriente.
Wansbrough, John. 1978. *The Sectarian Milieu: Content and Composition of Islamic Salvation History*. London Oriental Series, vol. 34. Oxford: Oxford University Press.
Ward, John O. 1985. 'Some Principles of Rhetorical Historiography in the Twelfth Century.' In *Classical Rhetoric and Medieval Historiography*, ed. Ernest Breisach, 103–65. Studies in Medieval Culture, vol. 19. Kalamazoo: Western Michigan University.
Yāqūt. 1868. *Jacut's geographisches Wörterbuch*. Ed. F. Wüstenfeld. Leipzig: N.p.
——. 1923–31. *The Irshád al-aríb ilá ma'rifat al-adīb, or Dictionary of Learned Men*. Ed. D. S. Margoliouth. London: Luzac.
Yarshater, Ehsan. 1983. 'Iranian National History.' In *The Cambridge History of Iran*, vol. 3 (1). *The Seleucid, Parthian and Sasanian Periods*, ed. Ehsan Yarshater, 359–477. Cambridge: Cambridge University Press.

Index